LINUX
IN A NUTSHELL

A Desktop Quick Reference

LINUX
IN A NUTSHELL

A Desktop Quick Reference

Second Edition

Ellen Siever
and the Staff of O'Reilly & Associates, Inc.

O'REILLY®

Beijing · *Cambridge* · *Köln* · *Paris* · *Sebastopol* · *Taipei* · *Tokyo*

Linux in a Nutshell, Second Edition

by Ellen Siever and the Staff of O'Reilly & Associates, Inc.

Copyright © 1999, 1997 O'Reilly & Associates, Inc. All rights reserved.
Printed in the United States of America.

Published by O'Reilly & Associates, Inc., 101 Morris Street, Sebastopol, CA 95472.

Editor: Andy Oram

Production Editor: Nicole Gipson Arigo

Printing History:

January 1997:	First Edition.
November 1997:	Minor corrections.
February 1999:	Second Edition.

This book is printed on acid-free paper with 85% recycled content, 15% post-consumer waste. O'Reilly & Associates is committed to using paper with the highest recycled content available consistent with high quality.

ISBN: 1-56592-585-8

Table of Contents

Preface

This is a book about Linux, a freely available clone of the Unix operating system for personal computers. Linux was first developed by Linus Torvalds, who built the first Linux kernel and continues to centrally coordinate improvements. The operating system continues to grow under the dedicated cultivation of a host of other programmers and hackers all over the world, all connected through the Internet. Beyond the kernel code, Linux includes utilities and commands from the Free Software Foundation's GNU project, Berkeley Unix (BSD), and a complete port of the X Window System (XFree86) from the X Consortium, in addition to many features written specifically for Linux.

This book is a quick reference for the basic commands and features of the Linux operating system. As with other books in O'Reilly's "In a Nutshell" series, this book is geared toward users who know what they want to do and have some idea how to do it, but just can't remember the correct command or option. We hope this guide will become an invaluable desktop reference for the Linux user.

Other Resources

This book will not tell you how to install and maintain a Linux system. For that, you will need *Running Linux*, by Matt Welsh and Lar Kaufman. For networking information, check out *Linux Network Administrator's Guide* by Olaf Kirch. In addition to O'Reilly's Linux titles, our wide range of Unix, X, Perl, and Java titles may also be of interest to the Linux user.

The Internet is also full of information about Linux. One of the best resources is the Linux Documentation Project at *http://metalab.unc.edu/LDP/*. For online information about the GNU utilities covered in this book, FTP to *prep.ai.mit.edu* in the *pub/gnu* directory (or one of the dozens of mirror sites around the world), or look on the Web at *http://www.gnu.ai.mit.edu/*. The Free Software Foundation, which is in charge of GNU, publishes its documentation in a number of hard-copy books about various tools.

Conventions

The desktop quick reference follows certain typographic conventions, outlined below:

Bold
> is used for commands, programs, and options. All terms shown in bold are typed literally.

Italic
> is used to show arguments, options, and variables that should be replaced with user-supplied values. Italic is also used to indicate filenames and directories, and to highlight comments in examples.

`Constant Width`
> is used to show the contents of files or the output from commands.

`Constant Bold`
> is used in examples and tables to show commands or other text that should be typed literally by the user.

`Constant Italic`
> is used in examples and tables to show text that should be replaced with user-supplied values.

%, $
> are used in some examples as the *tcsh* shell prompt (%) and as the Bourne shell prompt ($).

[ ]
> surround optional elements in a description of syntax. (The brackets themselves should never be typed.) Note that many commands show the argument [*files*]. If a filename is omitted, standard input (e.g., the keyboard) is assumed. End with an end-of-file character.

EOF
> indicates the end-of-file character (normally **CTRL-D**).

|
> is used in syntax descriptions to separate items for which only one alternative may be chosen at a time.

→
> is used at the bottom of a right-hand page to show that the current entry continues on the next page. The continuation is marked by a ←.

The owl icon designates a note, which is an important aside to its nearby text. For example . . .

 When you see the owl icon, you know the text beside it is
a note, like this.

Contact O'Reilly & Associates

A final word about syntax. In many cases, the space between an option and its argument can be omitted. In other cases, the spacing (or lack of spacing) must be followed strictly. For example, −w*n* (no intervening space) might be interpreted differently from −w *n*. It's important to notice the spacing used in option syntax. We have tested and verified all of the information in this book to the best of our ability, but you may find that features have changed (or even that we have made mistakes!). Please let us know about any errors you find, as well as your suggestions for future editions, by writing:

> O'Reilly & Associates, Inc.
> 101 Morris Street
> Sebastopol, CA 95472
> 1-800-998-9938 (in the US or Canada)
> 1-707-829-0515 (international/local)
> 1-707-829-0104 (FAX)

You can also send us messages electronically. To be put on the mailing list or request a catalog, send email to:

> *info@oreilly.com*

To ask technical questions or comment on the book, send email to:

> *Ibookquestions@oreilly.com*

Acknowledgments for the Second Edition

This second edition of "Linux in a Nutshell" is the result of the cooperative efforts of many people. Thanks to Andy Oram for his editorial skills, to Val Quercia for her project management skills, and to both of them for pitching in to check existing chapters, updating and writing new material as needed.

Special thanks again to Stephen Figgins in O'Reilly technical support for providing much material for both editions, particularly in the system and network administration chapters; to Stephen Spainhour for writing about RCS, CVS, and many other end-user commands; and to Johan Vromans for the Perl quick-reference.

For technical review, thanks go to Matt Welsh of *Running Linux* and *Installation and Getting Started Guide* fame, Michael K. Johnson of Red Hat Software, Robert J. Chassell, Phil Hughes of the "Linux Journal," Julian T. J. Midgley, and Terry Dawson.

Many thanks also to O'Reilly production editors Nicole Gipson Arigo, who worked on a tight deadline in the middle of the holiday season, and Jane Ellin, who helped her; to Lenny Muellner for answering my many questions and for all his tools work; to Seth Maislin for the index; and to Claire Cloutier LeBlanc and Sheryl Avruch for quality control.

Acknowledgments from the First Edition

I'd like to thank all my friends at O'Reilly for helping with this book—my editors, Andy Oram and Robert Denn; the production editor, Jane Ellin; Stephen Spainhour, who finished it when my RSI wouldn't let me do the work myself; Seth Maislin, who provided (as always) an excellent index; David Futato, who did the early production work; Madeleine Newell and Kismet McDonough-Chan, who also helped with production; Clairemarie Fisher O'Leary and Sheryl Avruch for quality control; everybody in the tools group (especially Lenny Muellner, who did most of the tools work for this book, but also Erik Ray and Ellen Siever); and Edie Freedman, who created the cover. Norm Walsh and Tanya Herlick, my various managers, were gracious enough to provide me with time to work on this project (even when I was supposed to be working for Norm full time). Special thanks go to Stephen Figgins in O'Reilly technical support for testing large numbers of commands, and even rewriting many to fit the facts. Thanks also to Greg Hankins of the Linux Documentation Project for his technical review. Finally, this book owes a great debt to all the O'Reilly books which I consulted extensively (that's a polite phrase for copied). It was built on a solid foundation.

The actual months I spent writing Linux Nut are fading into very hazy memories, but I well remember those people who got me through that summer: Dave Vernal, JD Paul, Paul Berger, Elizabeth Haynes, Kevin Lyda, Neil Laughlin, my mother, and my brother. Adam, I hadn't met you yet, but I like to pretend that you have retrospective influence. And, of course, much love to my cat, who shed on the monitor and let me know when I'd been working too long.

CHAPTER 1

Introduction

In just four years, Linux has grown from a student/hacker playground to an upstart challenger in the server market to a well-respected system taking its rightful place in educational and corporate networks. A freely redistributable clone of the Unix operating system, Linux is turning up everywhere. People use it for Web servers, file servers, and workstations instead of—or alongside—systems from traditional Unix vendors as well as Windows NT. In addition to its role in large networks (because it's a friendly fellow that fits in very nicely with other operating systems), Linux is popular among Windows users who just want to try something that gives them more speed, more power, and more control.

If you haven't obtained Linux yet, or have it but don't know exactly how to get started using it, buy the O'Reilly & Associates book *Running Linux*, by Matt Welsh and Lar Kaufman. This will give you everything you need in order to install your Linux system, configure it, and start becoming productive. The book you're looking at now will then prove useful.

The Excitement of Linux

Linux is first of all free software: anyone can download the source from the Internet or buy it on a low-cost CD-ROM. But Linux is becoming well-known because it's more than free software—it's unusually good software. You can get more from your hardware with Linux (particularly on Intel systems, where it was originally developed) and be assured of fewer crashes; even its security is better than many commercial alternatives.

As free software, Linux revives the grand creativity and the community of sharing that Unix was long known for. The unprecedented flexibility and openness of Unix—which newcomers usually found confusing and frustrating, but which they eventually found they couldn't live without—continually inspired extensions, new tools like Perl, and experiments in computer science that sometimes ended up in mainstream commercial computer systems.

Many fondly remember the days when AT&T provided universities with Unix source code at no charge, and the University of Berkeley started distributing its version in any manner that allowed people to get it. For these older hackers, Linux can bring back the spirit of working together—all the more so because the Internet is now widespread. And for the many who are too young to remember the first round of open systems (such as the hordes of students attracted to Linux) or whose prior experience has been woefully constricted by proprietary operating systems, now is the time to discover the wonders of freely distributable source code and infinitely adaptable interfaces.

The Linux kernel itself was originally designed by Linus Torvalds at the University of Helsinki in Finland, and later developed through collaboration with many volunteers worldwide. By "kernel" we mean the core of the operating system itself—not the applications (such as the compiler, shells, and so forth) that run on it. Today, the term "Linux" is often used to mean the kernel as well as the applications and complete system environment.

Most Linux systems cannot be technically referred to as a "version of Unix," as they have not been submitted to the required tests and licensed properly.* However, at least one Linux distribution has in fact been branded as POSIX.1. Linux offers all the common programming interfaces as standard Unix systems, and as you can see from this book, all the common Unix utilities have been ported to Linux. It is a powerful, robust, fully usable system for those who like Unix.

The economic power behind Linux's popularity is its support for an enormous range of hardware used with IBM-compatible personal computers. People who are accustomed to MS-DOS and Microsoft Windows are often amazed at how much faster their hardware appears to work with Linux—it makes efficient use of its resources.

For the first several years, users were attracted to Linux for a variety of financial and political reasons, but soon they discovered an unexpected benefit: it works better than many commercial systems. With the Samba file and print server, for instance, Linux serves a large number of end-user PCs without crashing. With the Apache Web server, it provides more of the useful features Web administrators want than competing products.

Distribution and Support

While it is convenient to download one or two new programs over the Internet, and fairly feasible to download something as large as the Linux kernel, getting a whole working system over phone lines is an absurd proposition. Over the years, therefore, commercial and non-commercial packages called *distributions* have emerged. The first consisted of approximately 50 diskettes, at least one of which was usually bad and had to be replaced. When CD-ROM drives and disks became widespread, Linux really took off.

After getting Linux, the average user is concerned next with support. While Usenet newsgroups offer very quick response and meet the needs of many intrepid users,

---

* Before an operating system can be called "Unix," it must be branded by X/Open.

you can also buy support from the vendors of the major distributions and a number of independent experts. Linux is definitely supported at least as well as commercial software.

Intel is still by far the most common hardware running Linux, but Linux is also now commercially available on a number of other hardware systems, notably the Alpha (created by Digital Equipment Corporation, now Compaq), the Sparc, and the m68k. Other ports are on the way.

Commands on Linux

Linux commands are not the same as standard Unix ones. They're better! This is because most of them are provided by the GNU project run by the Free Software Foundation (FSF). GNU means "GNU's not Unix"—the first word of the phrase doesn't stand for anything.

Benefitting from years of experience with standard Unix utilities and advances in computer science, programmers on the GNU project have managed to create versions of standard tools that have more features, run faster and more efficiently, and lack the bugs or inconsistencies that persist in the original standard versions.

While GNU provided the programming utilities and standard commands like *grep*, most of the system and network administration tools on Linux came from the Berkeley Software Distribution (BSD). In addition, some people wrote tools specifically for Linux to deal with special issues such as filesystems that only Linux supports. This book documents all the standard Unix commands that are commonly available on most Linux distributions.

The third type of software most commonly run on Linux is the X Window System, ported by the XFree86 project to standard Intel chips. This book does not discuss the X Window System; O'Reilly offers other books for that.

What This Book Offers

Based originally on the classic O'Reilly & Associates quick reference, *Unix in a Nutshell*, this book has been expanded to include much information that is specific to Linux. The current edition includes a chapter on booting for Intel systems. It also contains our popular Perl pocket reference and a number of commands that are specific to Linux.

Linux in a Nutshell doesn't teach you Linux—it is, after all, a quick reference— but novices as well as highly experienced users will find it of great value. When you have some idea what command you want but aren't sure just how it works or what combinations of options give you the exact output required, this book is the place to turn. It is also an eye-opener: it can make you aware of options that you never knew about before.

Like computer systems from the age in which Unix was born (the early 1970s), Linux is mostly a command-driven system. Most versions of Linux provide a few graphical tools, and several commercial products are available, but none of these graphical utilities are central to Linux. That is why this book, like the traditional

Unix in a Nutshell reference, focuses on the shell and on commands you run from the shell.

Of course, Linux offers a windowing system—a very rich and flexible one, as befits a rich and flexible operating system. But a lot of the time you'll just open a simulated VT100 terminal (the *xterm* program) and enter commands into that. You'll find yourself moving back and forth between graphical programs and the commands listed in this book.

So the first thing you've got to do, once you're over the hurdle of installing Linux, is to get used to the most common commands. These are described in Chapter 2, *Linux User Commands*. If you know absolutely nothing about Unix, we recommend you read a basic guide (there's an introductory chapter in *Running Linux* that can get you started). But if you know a few commands already and have an idea where to look, Chapter 2 will provide a wealth of information.

All commands are interpreted by the shell. The shell is simply a program that accepts commands from the user and executes them. Different shells sometimes use slightly different syntax to mean the same thing. Under Linux, two popular shells are **bash** and **tcsh**, and they differ in subtle ways (one of the nice things about Linux, and other Unix systems, is that you have a variety of shells to choose from, each with strengths and weaknesses). We offer several chapters on shells. You may decide to read these after you've used Linux for a while, because they mostly cover powerful, advanced features that you'll want when you're a steady user.

Before then, you'll have to learn some big, comprehensive utilities, so you can get real work done: an editor, a compiler or scripting tool, and so on. Two major editors are used on Linux: **vi** and Emacs. Both have chapters in this book. O'Reilly also has a separate book about each one (as we do about each of the major utilities in this book) which you may want, because neither is completely intuitive upon first use. (Emacs does have an excellent built-in tutorial, though; to invoke it, press **CTRL-h** followed by **t** for "tutorial.")

Programming utilities are covered in Chapter 12, *Programming Overview and Commands*. The Unix programming environment has become something of a model for other systems, and it rewards a little study with great support for building programs, debugging, and so forth.

RCS (Revision Control System) and CVS (Concurrent Versions System) manage files so you can retrieve old versions and maintain different versions simultaneously. Originally used by programmers who have complicated requirements for building and maintaining applications, these tools have turned out to be valuable for anyone who maintains files of any type, particularly when coordinating a team of people. CVS is a layer on top of RCS that makes it easier for multiple people to edit a file simultaneously. Chapter 13, *RCS and CVS*, presents RCS and CVS commands.

System and network administration are major topics that are covered in Chapter 15, *System and Network Administration Overview*, and Chapter 16, *System and Network Administration Commands*. Your Linux distribution probably provides graphical interfaces for some functions. But commands are necessary for many functions, and these commands are all in this book. A few additional books you may find useful, in order to get the background necessary to understand these complicated tasks, are *Essential System Administration*, Second Edition, by Æleen Frisch, *Linux Network Administrator's Guide*, by Olaf Kirch, and *TCP/IP Network Administration*, by Craig Hunt.

Most users do not want to completely abandon other operating systems (whether a Microsoft Windows system, OS/2, or some Unix flavor). Linux often resides on the same computer as other systems. The user can boot the system he or she needs for a particular job. Chapter 17, *Boot Methods*, lists the commonly used booting options on Intel systems, including LILO (Linux Loader) and Loadlin.

Every distribution of Linux is slightly different, but you'll find that the commands we document are what you use most of the time, and that they work the same on all distributions. Basic commands, programming utilities, system administration, and network administration are all covered here. But some areas were so big that we had to leave them out. The many applications that depend on the X Window System didn't make the cut. Nor did TₑX (a text-processing tool used extensively in academia and by Linux users in general), or Tcl/Tk (the Tool Command Language and its graphical toolkit). These subjects would stretch the book out of its binding.

Our goal in producing this book is to provide convenience, and that means keeping it small. It certainly doesn't have everything the manual pages have. But you'll find that it has what you need 95% of the time.

Sources and Licenses

When you get Linux, you also get the source code. The same goes for all the utilities on Linux (unless your vendor offered a commercial application or library as a special enhancement). You may never bother looking at the source code, but it's key to Linux's strength. The source code has to be provided by the vendor, under the Linux license, and it permits those who are competent at such things to fix bugs, provide advice about the system's functioning, and submit improvements that benefit all of us. The license is the well-known General Public License, also known as the GPL or "copyleft," invented and popularized by the Free Software Foundation (FSF).

The FSF, founded by Richard Stallman, is a phenomenon that many people would believe to be impossible if it did not exist. (The same goes for Linux too, in fact—seven years ago, who would have imagined a robust operating system developed by collaborators over the Internet and made freely redistributable?) One of the most popular editors on Unix, GNU Emacs, comes from the FSF. So do *gcc* and *g++* (C and C++ compilers), which for a while used to set the standard for optimization and fast code.

Dedicated to the sharing of software, the FSF provides all its code and documentation on the Internet and allows anyone with a whim for enhancements to alter the source code. One of its projects is the Debian distribution of Linux.

In order to prevent hoarding, the FSF requires that the source code for all enhancements be distributed under the same GPL that it uses. This encourages individuals or companies to make improvements and share them with others. The only thing someone cannot do is add enhancements and then try to sell the product as commercial software—that is, to withhold the source code. That would be taking advantage of the FSF and the users. You can find the GPL in any software covered by that license, and online at *http://www.gnu.ai.mit.edu/copyleft/gpl.html.*

As we said earlier, many tools on Linux come from BSD instead of GNU. BSD is also free software. The license is significantly different, but that doesn't have to concern you as a user. The effect of the difference is that the people who created BSD keep control over further development.

CHAPTER 2

Linux
User Commands

This section presents the user-level Linux commands (as opposed to the program-ming-level or system-administration–level commands). Each entry is labeled with the command name on the outer edge of the page. The syntax line is followed by a brief description and a list of all available options. Many commands come with examples at the end of the entry. If you need only a quick reminder or suggestion about a command, you can skip directly to the examples.

Typographic conventions for describing command syntax are listed in the Preface. For additional help in locating commands, see the index at the back of this book.

If you can't find a command in this section, it may be listed as a programming-level or administration-level command. See the alphabetical listings in those sec-tions. Applications using the X Window System are not covered in this book.

---

apropos *string* ... Search the short manual page descriptions in the **whatis** database for occurrences of each *string* and display the result on the standard output. Like **whatis**, except that it searches for strings instead of words. Equivalent to **man −k**.	apropos
arch Print machine architecture type to standard output. Equivalent to **uname −m**.	arch
at [*options*] *time* Execute commands at a specified *time* and optional *date*. The commands are read from standard input or from a file. (See also **batch**.) End input with *EOF*. *time* can be formed either as a	**at**

→

numeric hour (with optional minutes and modifiers) or as a keyword. It can contain an optional *date*, formed as a month and date, a day of the week, or a special keyword (*today* or *tomorrow*). An increment can also be specified. Details are given in the following entries.

Options

-c job [job...]

Cat the specified jobs to standard output. This option does not take a time specification.

-d   Same as **atrm**.

-f *file*   Read job from *file*, not standard input.

-l [*job_id*] Report all jobs that are scheduled for the invoking user, or, if *job_id* is specified, report only for those. Same as **atq**.

-m   Mail user when job has completed, regardless of whether output was created.

-q *letter*   Place job in queue denoted by *letter*, where *letter* is any single letter from a–z or A–Z. Default queue is a. (The batch queue defaults to b.) Higher-lettered queues run at a lower priority.

-V   Display the version number.

-v   Display the time a job will be executed.

Time

bb:mm [*modifiers*]

Hours can have one digit or two (a 24-hour clock is assumed by default); optional minutes can be given as one or two digits; the colon can be omitted if the format is *b*, *bb*, or *bbmm*; e.g., valid times are 5, 5:30, 0530, 19:45. If modifier **am** or **pm** is added, *time* is based on a 12-hour clock. If the keyword **zulu** is added, times correspond to Greenwich Mean Time.

midnight | **noon** | **teatime** | **now**

Use any one of these keywords in place of a numeric time. **teatime** translates to 4 p.m.; **now** must be followed by an *increment*.

Date

month num[, *year*]

month is one of the 12 months, spelled out or abbreviated to its first three letters; *num* is the calendar date of the month; *year* is the four-

digit year. If the given *month* occurs before the
current month, **at** schedules that month next
year.

day　　　　One of the seven days of the week, spelled out
or abbreviated to its first three letters.

today | tomorrow
Indicate the current day or the next day. If
date is omitted, **at** schedules **today** when the
specified *time* occurs later than the current
time; otherwise, **at** schedules **tomorrow**.

Increment

Supply a numeric increment if you want to specify an execution
time or day *relative* to the current time. The number should precede any of the keywords **minute**, **hour**, **day**, **week**, **month**, or
year (or their plural forms). The keyword **next** can be used as a
synonym of **+ 1**.

Examples

Note that the first two commands are equivalent:

```
at 1945 pm December 9
at 7:45pm Dec 9
at 3 am Saturday
at now + 5 hours
at noon next day
```

---

atq [*options*] [*job–id*]　　　　　　　　　　　　　　　**atq**

List the user's pending jobs, unless the user is a privileged user;
in that case, everybody's jobs are listed. If *job-id* is specified,
report on only those jobs. Same as **at-l**.

Options

−q *queue*　　Query only the specified queue and ignore all
other queues.

−v　　　　　Show jobs that have completed, but not yet
been deleted.

−V　　　　　Print the version number to standard error.

---

atrm *job* [*job...*]　　　　　　　　　　　　　　　　　**atrm**

Delete a job that has been queued for future execution. Same as
at −d.

banner	**banner** [*option*] [*characters*]

Print *characters* as a poster on the standard output. If no *characters* are supplied, **banner** prompts for them and reads an input line from standard input.

Option

    −w *width*   Set width to *width* characters. Note that if your banner is in all lowercase, it will be narrower than *width* characters. If *−w* is not specified, the default width is 132. If *−w* is specified but *width* is not provided, the default is 80. |
| **basename** | **basename** *name* [*suffix*]
basename *option*

Removes leading directory components from a path. If *suffix* is given, removes that also. The result is printed to standard output.

Options

    −−help   Print help message.

    −−version   Print the version of the **basename** command.

Examples

```
% basename /usr/lib/libm.a
libm.a

% basename /usr/lib/libm.a .a
libm
``` |
| **batch** | **batch** [*options*] [*time*]

Executes commands entered on standard input. If time is omitted, executes them when the system load permits (when the load average falls below 0.5). Very similar to **at**, but does not insist that the execution time be entered on the command line. See **at** for details.

Options

    −f *file*   Read job from *file*, not standard input.

    −m   Mail user when job has completed, regardless of whether output was created.

    −q *letter*   Place job in queue denoted by *letter*, where *letter* is any single letter from a–z or A–Z. Default queue is a. (The batch queue defaults to b.) Higher-lettered queues run at a lower priority. |

–V	Print the version number to standard error.	batch
–v	Display the time a job will be executed.	

bash [*options*] [*file* [*arguments*]]
sh [*options*] [*file* [*arguments*]]

batch

bash

Standard Linux shell, a command interpreter into which all other commands are entered. For more information, see Chapter 4, *bash: The Bourne Again Shell.*

bc [*options*] [*files*]

bc

bc is a language (and compiler) whose syntax resembles that of C, but with unlimited-precision arithmetic. **bc** consists of identifiers, keywords, and symbols, which are briefly described in the following entries. Examples are given at the end.

Interactively perform arbitrary-precision arithmetic or convert numbers from one base to another. Input can be taken from *files* or read from the standard input. To exit, type **quit** or **EOF**.

Options

–l, ––mathlib
> Make functions from the math library available.

–s, ––standard
> Ignore all extensions, and process exactly as in POSIX.

–w, ––warn
> When extensions to POSIX **bc** are used, print a warning.

–q, ––quiet
> Do not display welcome message.

–v, ––version
> Print version number for this function.

Identifiers

An identifier is a series of one or more characters. It must begin with a lowercase letter, but may also contain digits and underscores. No uppercase letters are allowed. Identifiers are used as names for variables, arrays, and functions. Variables normally store arbitrary-precision numbers. Within the same program you may name a variable, an array, and a function using the same letter. The following identifiers would not conflict:

→

Alphabetical Summary of Commands — bc   11

x	Variable *x*.
x[*i*]	Element *i* of array *x*. *i* can range from 0 to 2047 and can also be an expression.
x(*y*,*z*)	Call function *x* with parameters *y* and *z*.

Input-output keywords

ibase, **obase**, **scale**, and **last** store a value. Typing them on a line by themselves displays their current value. You can also change their values through assignment. The letters A–F are treated as digits whose values are 10–15.

ibase = *n*   Numbers that are input (e.g., typed) are read as base *n* (default is 10).

obase = *n*   Numbers that are displayed are in base *n* (default is 10). Note: Once **ibase** has been changed from 10, use the digit A to restore **ibase** or **obase** to decimal.

scale = *n*   Display computations using *n* decimal places (default is 0, meaning that results are truncated to integers). **scale** is normally used only for base-10 computations.

last   Value of last printed number.

Statement keywords

A semicolon or a newline separates one statement from another. Curly braces are needed when grouping multiple statements.

if (*rel-expr*) {*statements*} [**else** {*statements*}]

Do one or more *statements* if relational expression *rel-expr* is true. Otherwise, do nothing, or, if *else* (an extension) is specified, do alternative *statements*. For example:

```
if(x==y) {i = i + 1} else {i = i - 1}
```

while (*rel-expr*) {*statements*}

Repeat one or more *statements* while *rel-expr* is true; for example:

```
while(i>0) {p = p*n; q = a/b; i = i-1}
```

for (*expr1*; *rel-expr*; *expr2*) {*statements*}

Similar to **while**; for example, to print the first 10 multiples of 5, you could type:

```
for(i=1; i<=10; i++) i*5
```

GNU bc does not require three arguments to **for**. A missing argument 1 or 3 means that those expressions will never be evaluated. A missing argument 2 evaluates to the value 1.

break	Terminate a **while** or **for** statement.
print *list*	GNU extension; it provides an alternate means of output. *list* consists of a series of comma-separated strings and expressions; **print** displays these entities in the order of the list. It does not print a newline when it terminates. Expressions are evaluated, printed, and assigned to the special variable *last*. Strings (which may contain special characters, i.e., characters beginning with \) are simply printed. Special characters can be:

a	Alert or bell
b	Backspace
f	Form feed
n	Newline
r	Carriage return
q	Double quote
t	Tab
\	Backslash

continue	GNU extension. When within a **for** statement, jump to the next iteration.
halt	GNU extension. Cause the **bc** processor to quit.
limits	GNU extension. Print the limits enforced by the local version of **bc**.

Function keywords

define *f(args)* {	Begin the definition of function *f* having the arguments *args*. The arguments are separated by commas. Statements follow on successive lines. End with a }.
auto *x, y*	Set up *x* and *y* as variables local to a function definition, initialized to 0 and meaningless outside the function. Must appear first.
return(*expr***)**	Pass the value of expression *expr* back to the program. Return 0 if (*expr*) is left off. Used in function definitions.
sqrt(*expr***)**	Compute the square root of expression *expr*.

→

length(*expr*)

　　　　　　　　　Compute how many significant digits are in *expr*.

scale(*expr*)　　Same as **length**, but count only digits to the right of the decimal point.

read()　　　　　GNU extension. Read a number from standard input. Return value is the number read, converted via the value of **ibase**.

Math library functions

These are available when **bc** is invoked with **−l**. Library functions set **scale** to 20.

s(*angle*)　　　Compute the sine of *angle*, a constant or expression in radians.

c(*angle*)　　　Compute the cosine of *angle*, a constant or expression in radians.

a(*n*)　　　　　Compute the arctangent of *n*, returning an angle in radians.

e(*expr*)　　　　Compute **e** to the power of *expr*.

l(*expr*)　　　　Compute the natural log of *expr*.

j(*n*, *x*)　　　Compute the Bessel function of integer order *n*.

Operators

These consist of operators and other symbols. Operators can be arithmetic, unary, assignment, or relational:

　　　　　　arithmetic
　　　　　　　　+　−　*　　/　%　^

　　　　　　unary
　　　　　　　　−　++　− −

　　　　　　assignment
　　　　　　　　=+　=−　=*　=/　=%　=^　=

　　　　　　relational
　　　　　　　　<　<=　>　>=　==　!=

Other symbols

/* */　　　　　Enclose comments.

( )　　　　　　Control the evaluation of expressions (change precedence). Can also be used around assignment statements to force the result to print.

{ }　　　　　　Use to group statements.

| [ ] | Indicate array index. | **bc** |

| " *text* " | Use as a statement to print *text*. |

Examples

Note below that when you type some quantity (a number or expression), it is evaluated and printed, but assignment statements produce no display.

`ibase = 8`	*Octal input*
`20`	*Evaluate this octal number .*
`16`	*Terminal displays decimal value*
`obase = 2`	*Display output in base 2 instead of base 10*
`20`	*Octal input*
`10000`	*Terminal now displays binary value*
`ibase = A`	*Restore base 10 input*
`scale = 3`	*Truncate results to 3 decimal places*
`8/7`	*Evaluate a division*
`1.001001000`	*Oops! Forgot to reset output base to 10*
`obase=10`	*Input is decimal now, so A isn't needed*
`8/7`	
`1.142`	*Terminal displays result (truncated)*

The following lines show the use of functions:

`define p(r,n){`	*Function p uses two arguments*
`auto v`	*v is a local variable*
`v = r^n`	*r raised to the n power*
`return(v)}`	*Value returned*
`scale=5`	
`x=p(2.5,2)`	*x = 2.5 ^ 2*
`x`	*Print value of x*
`6.25`	
`length(x)`	*Number of digits*
`3`	
`scale(x)`	*Number of places right of decimal point*
`2`	

---

biff [*arguments*]   **biff**

Notifies user of mail arrival and sender's name. **biff** operates asynchronously. Mail notification works only if your system is running the **comsat(8)** server. The command **biff y** enables notification, and the command **biff n** disables notification. With no arguments, **biff** reports **biff**'s current status.

---

cal [*−jy*] [[*month*] *year*]   **cal**

Print a 12-month calendar (beginning with January) for the given *year* or a one-month calendar of the given *month* and *year*. *month* ranges from 1 to 12. *year* ranges from 1 to 9999. With no arguments, prints a calendar for the current month.

$\rightarrow$

cal	**Options**
←	−j Display Julian dates (days numbered 1 to 365, starting from January 1).

Options

−j   Display Julian dates (days numbered 1 to 365, starting from January 1).

−y   Display entire current year.

Examples

```
cal 12 1995
cal 1994 > year_file
```

---

cat

cat [*options*] [*files*]

Reads one or more *files* and prints them on standard output. Reads standard input if no *files* are specified or if − is specified as one of the files; input ends with *EOF*. You can use the > operator to combine several files into a new file or >> to append files to an existing file.

Options

−A, −−show-all
    Same as −vET.

−b, −−number-nonblank
    Number all nonblank output lines, starting with 1.

−e   Same as −vE.

−E, −−show-ends
    Print $ at the end of each line.

−n, −−number
    Number all output lines, starting with 1.

−s, −−squeeze-blank
    Squeeze down multiple blank lines to one blank line.

−t   Same as −vT.

−T, −−show-tabs
    Print TAB characters as ^I.

−u   Ignored; retained for Unix compatibility.

−v, −−show-nonprinting
    Display control and nonprinting characters, with the exception of LINEFEED and TAB.

Examples

```
cat ch1                    Display a file
cat ch1 ch2 ch3 > all      Combine files
cat note5 >> notes         Append to a file
```

```
cat > temp1            Create file at terminal; end with EOF
cat > temp2 << STOP    Create file at terminal; end with STOP
```

change [*options*] *user*   change

Change user password expiration date. With any option except -*l*, **change** can be used only by a privileged user. Without options, **change** prompts the user to keep or change the value of every field.

Options

−d *last_day*

> Set the *last_day* the password was changed. *last_day* may be the number of days since January 1, 1970 or a date of the format MM/DD/YY (or a regionally specific equivalent).

−l

> Return the date the user's password or account is due to expire.

−m *min_days*

> Set the minimum number of days between allowed password changes. If *min_days* is 0, user can change her password at any time.

−M *max_days*

> Set the maximum number of days during which a password is valid. When *max_days* plus *last_day* is less than the current day, the user will be required to change password.

−E *expire_date*

> Set a date on which a user's account will be made inaccessible. *expire_date* may be the number of days since January 1, 1970 or a date of the format MM/DD/YY (or a regionally-specific equivalent).

−I *inactive* Set a number of days of inactivity after a password has expired before the account is locked. A value of 0 means the account is locked as soon as the expire date is reached.

−W *warn_days*

> Warn the user of an approaching password expiration. *warn_days* is the number of days prior to password expiration that the user will be warned.

chattr	**chattr** [*options*] *mode files*
	Modify file attributes. Specific to Linux Second Extended File Systems. Behaves similarly to symbolic **chmod**, using +, −, and =; *mode* is in the form *opcode attribute*.
	Options

−R	Modify directories and their contents recursively.
−V	Print modes of attributes after changing them.
−v *version*	Set the file's version.

Opcodes

+	Add attribute.
−	Remove attribute.
=	Assign attributes (removing unspecified attributes).

Attributes

A	Don't update atime on modify.
a	Append only
c	Compressed
d	No dump
i	Immutable
s	Secure deletion
u	Undeletable
S	Synchronous updates

chfn	**chfn** [*options*] [*username*]
	Change the information that is stored in */etc/passwd* and displayed when a user is fingered. Without *options*, **chfn** will enter interactive mode and prompt for changes. To make a field blank, enter the keyword **none**.
	Options

−f, −−full-name	Specify new full name.
−h, −−home-phone	Specify new home phone number.
−o, −−office	Specify new office number.

−p, −−office-phone
>Specify new office phone number.

−u, −−help Print usage information.

−V, −−version
>Print version information.

---

chgrp *newgroup files*

Change the group of one or more *files* to *newgroup*. *newgroup* is either a group ID number or a group name located in */etc/group*. Only the owner of a file or a privileged user may change its group.

Options

−c, −−changes
>Print information about those files that are changed.

−f, −−silent, −−quiet
>Do not print error messages about files that cannot be changed.

−−help Print usage information.

−R, −−recursive
>Traverse subdirectories recursively, applying changes.

−v, −−verbose
>Verbosely describe ownership changes.

−−version Print version information.

---

chmod [*options*] *mode files*

Change the access *mode* (permissions) of one or more *files*. Only the owner of a file or a privileged user may change its mode. *mode* can be numeric or an expression in the form of *who opcode permission*. *who* is optional (if omitted, default is **a**); choose only one *opcode*. Multiple modes may be specified, separated by commas.

Options

−c, −−changes
>Print information about files that are changed.

−f, −−silent, −−quiet
>Do not notify user of files that **chmod** cannot change.

→

chmod	**-v, --verbose**	
←		Print information about each file, whether changed or not.
	-R, --recursive	
		Traverse subdirectories recursively, applying changes.
	--help	Print usage information.
	--version	Print version information.

Who

u	User
g	Group
o	Other
a	All (default)

Opcode

+	Add permission
–	Remove permission
=	Assign permission (and remove permission of the unspecified fields)

Permission

r	Read
w	Write
x	Execute
s	Set user (or group) ID
t	Sticky bit; save text (file) mode or prevent removal of files by nonowners (directory)
u	User's present permission
g	Group's present permission
o	Other's present permission
l	Mandatory locking

Alternatively, specify permissions by a three-digit octal number. The first digit designates owner permission; the second, group permission; and the third, other's permission. Permissions are calculated by adding the following octal values:

4	Read
2	Write
1	Execute

Note: A fourth digit may precede this sequence. This digit assigns the following modes:

4   Set user ID on execution

2   Set group ID on execution or set mandatory locking

1   Set sticky bit

Examples

Add execute-by-user permission to *file*:

```
chmod u+x file
```

Either of the following will assign read-write-execute permission by owner (7), read-execute permission by group (5), and execute-only permission by others (1) to *file*:

```
chmod 751 file
chmod u=rwx,g=rx,o=x file
```

Any one of the following will assign read-only permission to *file* for everyone:

```
chmod =r file
chmod 444 file
chmod a-wx,a+r file
```

Set the user ID, assign read-write-execute permission by owner, and assign read-execute permission by group and others:

```
chmod 4755 file
```

---

chown *newowner files*

Change the ownership of one or more *files* to *newowner*. *newowner* is either a user ID number or a login name located in */etc/passwd*. **chown** also accepts users in the form *newowner.newgroup* or *newowner.newgroup*. The last two forms change the group ownership as well. Only the current owner of a file, or a privileged user, may change its owner.

Options

−c, −−changes
        Print information about those files that are changed.

−f, −−silent, −−quiet
        Do not print error messages about files that cannot be changed.

→

chown
←
	−v, −−verbose
	      Print information about all files that **chown** attempts to change, whether or not they are actually changed.
	
	−R, −−recursive
	      Traverse subdirectories recursively, applying changes.
	
	−−help Print usage information.
	
	−−version Print version information.

chsh	**chsh** [*options*] [*username*]
	
	Change your login shell, interactively or on the command line. Warn if *shell* does not exist in */etc/shells*.
	
	Options
	
	−l, −−list-shells
	      Print valid shells, as listed in */etc/shells*, and exit.
	
	−s, −−shell Specify new login shell.
	
	−u, −−help Print usage information.
	
	−v, −−version
	      Print version information.

cksum	**cksum** [*files*] Compute a cyclic redundancy check (CRC) for all *files* to check for corruption. Read from standard input if the character − or no files are given. Display the result of the check, the number of bytes in the file, and (unless reading from standard input) the filename.
clear	**clear** Clear the terminal display.
cmp	**cmp** [*options*] *file1 file2* Compare *file1* with *file2*. Use standard input if *file1* is − or missing. See also **comm** and **diff**. *Options* **−c, −−print-chars** Print differing bytes as characters.

−i *num*, −−ignore-initial=*num*
> Ignore the first *num* bytes of input.

−l, −−verbose
> Print offsets and codes of all differing bytes.

−s, −−quiet, −−silent
> Work silently; print nothing, but return exit
> codes:
> 0   Files are identical
> 1   Files are different
> 2   Files are inaccessible

Example

Print a message if two files are the same (exit code is 0):

```
cmp -s old new && echo 'no changes'
```

col [*options*]

A postprocessing filter that handles reverse linefeeds and escape characters, allowing output from *tbl* or *nroff* to appear in reasonable form on a terminal.

Options

−b
> Ignore backspace characters; helpful when printing man pages.

−f
> Process half-line vertical motions, but not reverse line motion. (Normally, half-line input motion is displayed on the next full line.)

−l *n*
> Buffer at least *n* lines in memory. The default buffer size is 128 lines.

−x
> Normally, **col** saves printing time by converting sequences of spaces to tabs. Use −**x** to suppress this conversion.

Examples

Run *file* through *tbl* and *nroff,* then capture output on screen by filtering through **col** and **more**:

```
tbl file | nroff | col | more
```

Save man page output in *file*.**print**, stripping out backspaces (which would otherwise appear as ^H):

```
man file | col -b > file.print
```

colcrt	**colcrt** [*options*] [*files*]
	A postprocessing filter that handles reverse linefeeds and escape characters, allowing output from *tbl* (or *nroff*) files to appear in reasonable form on a terminal.
	− Do not underline.
	−2 Double space by printing all half lines.
colrm	**colrm** [*start* [*stop*]]
	Remove specified columns from a file, where a column is a single character in a line. Read from standard input and write to standard output. Columns are numbered starting with 1; begin deleting columns at (including) the *start* column, and stop at (including) the *stop* column. Entering a tab increments the column count to the next multiple of either the start or stop column; entering a backspace decrements it by 1.
column	**column** [*options*] [*file*]
	Format input into columns, filling rows first. Read from standard input if *file* is not specified.
	Options
	−c *num* Format output into *num* columns.
	−s *char* Delimit table columns with *char*. Meaningful only with **-t**.
	−t Format input into a table. Delimit with whitespace, unless an alternate delimiter has been provided with **-s**.
	−x Fill columns before filling rows.
comm	**comm** [*options*] *file1 file2*
	Compare lines common to the sorted files *file1* and *file2*. Three-column output is produced: lines unique to *file1*, lines unique to *file2*, and lines common to both files. **comm** is similar to **diff** in that both commands compare two files. But **comm** can also be used like **uniq**; that is, **comm** selects duplicate or unique lines between *two* sorted files, whereas **uniq** selects duplicate or unique lines within the *same* sorted file.
	Options
	− Read the standard input.

−*num*	Suppress printing of column num. Multiple columns may be specified and should not be space-separated.	**comm**

Example

Compare two lists of top-ten movies, and display items that appear in both lists:

```
comm -12 siskel_top10 ebert_top10
```

---

cp [*options*] *file1 file2*
cp [*options*] *files directory*
cp

Copy *file1* to *file2*, or copy one or more *files* to the same names under *directory*. If the destination is an existing file, the file is overwritten; if the destination is an existing directory, the file is copied into the directory (the directory is *not* overwritten).

Options

−a, −−archive
> Preserve attributes of original files where possible. Same as -dpR.

−b, −−backup
> Back up files that would otherwise be overwritten.

−d, −−no-dereference
> Do not dereference symbolic links; preserve hard link relationships between source and copy.

−f, −−force   Remove existing files in the destination.

−i, −−interactive
> Prompt before overwriting destination files.

−l, −−link   Make hard links, not copies, of nondirectories.

−p, −−preserve
> Preserve all information, including owner, group, permissions, and time stamps.

−r, −R, −−recursive
> Copy directories recursively.

−s, −−symbolic-link
> Make symbolic links instead of copying. Source filenames must be absolute.

→

cp ←	**−u, −−update** Do not copy a nondirectory that has an existing destination with the same or newer modification time. **−v, −−verbose** Before copying, print the name of each file. **−x, −−one-file-system** Ignore subdirectories on other filesystems. **−P, −−parents** Preserve intermediate directories in source. The last argument must be the name of an existing directory. For example, the command **cp −−parents jphekman/book/ch1 newdir** copies the file *jphekman/book/ch1* to *newdir/jphekman/book/ch1*, creating intermediate directories as necessary. **−S, −−suffix backup-suffix** Set suffix to be appended to backup files. This may also be set with the SIMPLE_BACKUP_SUFFIX environment variable. The default is ~. **−V, −−version-control {numbered | existing | simple}** Set the type of backups made. You may also use the VERSION_CONTROL environment variable. The default is **existing**. Valid arguments are: **t, numbered** Always make numbered backups. **nil, existing** Make numbered backups of files that already have them; otherwise, make simple backups. **never, simple** Always make simple backups.
cpio	**cpio** *flags* [*options*] Copy file archives in from or out to tape or disk, or to another location on the local machine. Each of the three flags −i, −o, or −p accepts different options: **−i** [*options*] [*patterns*] Copy in (extract) files whose names match selected *patterns*. Each pattern can include filename metacharacters from the Bourne shell. (Patterns should be quoted or escaped so they are interpreted by **cpio**, not by the shell.) If no

pattern is used, all files are copied in. During extraction, existing files are not overwritten by older versions in the archive (unless **–u** is specified).

–o [*options*]

Copy out a list of files whose names are given on the standard input.

–p [*options*] *directory*

Copy files to another directory on the same system. Destination pathnames are interpreted relative to the named *directory*.

Comparison of valid options

Options available to the **–i**, **–o**, and **–p** flags are shown respectively in the first, second, and third row below. (The **–** is omitted for clarity.)

```
i:   bcdf mnrtsuv B SVCEHMR IF
p: 0a  d lm    uv  L V     R
o: 0a  c       vABL VC HM O F
```

Options

–0, ––null Expect list of filenames to be terminated with null, not newline. This allows files with a newline in their names to be included.

–a, ––reset-access-time

Set access times of input files to now.

–A, ––append

Append files to an existing archive, which must be a disk file. Specify this archive with -O or -F.

–b, ––swap

Swap bytes and half-words.

–B Block input or output using 5120 bytes per record (default is 512 bytes per record).

–c Read or write header information as ASCII characters; useful when source and destination machines are of differing types.

–C *n*, **––io-size=***n*

Like **–B**, but block size can be any positive integer *n*.

–d, ––make-directories

Create directories as needed.

→

cpio
←

−E *file*, **−−pattern-file=***file*
> Extract filenames listed in *file* from the archives.

−f, **−−nonmatching**
> Reverse the sense of copying; copy all files *except* those that match *patterns*.

−F, **−−file=***file*
> Use *file* as archive, not **stdin** or **stdout**. *file* can exist on another machine, if given in the form *user@hostname:file*.

−−force-local
> Do not assume that *file* (provided by **-F**, **-I**, or **-O**) exists on remote machine, even if it contains a @.

−H *type*, **−−format=***type*
> Use *type* format. Default in copy-out is **bin**. Valid formats (all caps also accepted):

bin Binary

odc
> Old (POSIX.1) portable format

newc
> New (SVR4) portable format

crc New (SVR4) portable format with checksum added

tar Tar

ustar
> POSIX.1 tar (also recognizes GNU tar archives)

hpbin
> HP-UX's binary (obsolete)

hpodc
> HP-UX's portable format

−I *file*   Read *file* as an input archive. May be on a remote machine (see **-F**).

−k   Ignored. For backwards compatibility.

−l, **−−link**   Link files instead of copying.

−L, **−−dereference**
> Follow symbolic links.

−m, **−−preserve-modification-time**
> Retain previous file modification time.

−M *msg*, **−−message=***msg*
> Print *msg* when switching media, as a prompt before switching to new media. Use variable

%d in the message as a numeric ID for the next medium. **−M** is valid only with **−I** or **−O**.

−n, −−numeric-uid-gid
> When verbosely listing contents, show user ID and group ID numerically.

−−no-preserve-owner
> Make all copied files owned by yourself, instead of the owner of the original. Useful only if you are a privileged user.

−O *file*   Direct the output to *file*. May be a file on another machine (see **-F**).

−r   Rename files interactively.

−R [*user*][*:group*], **−−owner** [*user*][*:group*]
> Reassign file ownership and group information to the user's login ID (privileged users only).

−s, −−swap-bytes
> Swap bytes.

−S, −−swap-half-words
> Swap half-words.

−t, −−list   Print a table of contents of the input (create no files). When used with the **−v** option, resembles output of **ls −l**.

−u, −−unconditional
> Unconditional copy; old files can overwrite new ones.

−v   Print a list of filenames.

−V, −−dot   Print a dot for each file read or written (this shows **cpio** at work without cluttering the screen).

Examples

Generate a list of files whose names end in *.old* using **find**; use list as input to **cpio**:

```
find . -name "*.old" -print | cpio -ocBv\
    > /dev/rst8
```

Restore from a tape drive all files whose names contain **save** (subdirectories are created if needed):

```
cpio -icdv "*save*" < /dev/rst8
```

Move a directory tree:

```
find . -depth -print | cpio -padm /mydir
```

crontab	**crontab** [*options*] [*file*]

View, install, or uninstall your current crontab file. A privileged user can run **crontab** for another user by supplying −u *user*. A crontab file is a list of commands, one per line, that will execute automatically at a given time. Numbers are supplied before each command to specify the execution time. The numbers appear in five fields, as follows:

Minute	0-59
Hour	0-23
Day of month	1-31
Month	1-12
	Jan, Feb, Mar, ...
Day of week	0-6, with 0 = Sunday
	Sun, Mon, Tue, ...

Use a comma between multiple values, a hyphen to indicate a range, and an asterisk to indicate all possible values. For example, assuming the crontab entries below:

```
59 3 * * 5      find / -print | backup_program
0 0 1,15 * *    echo "Timesheets due" | mail user
```

The first command backs up the system files every Friday at 3:59 a.m., and the second command mails a reminder on the 1st and 15th of each month.

Options

−e	Edit the user's current crontab file (or create one).
−l	Display the user's crontab file on standard output.
−r	Delete the user's file in the crontab directory.
−u *user*	Indicates which *user*'s file will be acted upon.

csh	**csh** [*options*] [*file* [*arguments*]]

C shell, a command interpreter into which all other commands are entered. For more information, see Chapter 5, *csh and tcsh*.

csplit	**csplit** [*options*] *file arguments*

Separate *file* into sections and place sections in files named **xx00** through **xx**n (n < 100), breaking *file* at each pattern specified in *arguments*. See also **split**.

–   Read from standard input.

–b *suffix*, **– –suffix-format=***suffix*

Append *suffix* to output filename. *suffix* must specify how to convert the binary integer to readable form by including exactly one of the following: **%d**, **%i**, **%u**, **%o**, **%x**, or **%X**. The value of *suffix* determines the format for numbers as follows:

%d Signed decimal

%i Same as **%d**

%u Unsigned decimal

%o Octal

%x Hexadecimal

%X Same as **%x**.

This option causes **–n** to be ignored.

–f *prefix*, **– –prefix=***prefix*

Name new files *prefix***00** through *prefix**n* (default is **xx00** through **xx***n*).

–k, **– –keep-files**

Keep newly created files, even when an error occurs (which would normally remove these files). This is useful when you need to specify an arbitrarily large repeat argument, {*n*}, and you don't want an out of range error to cause removal of the new files.

–n *num*, **– –digits=***num*

Use output filenames with numbers *num* digits long. The default is 2.

–s, **–q**, **– –silent**, **– –quiet**

Suppress all character counts.

–z, **– –elide-empty-files**

Do not create empty output files. However, number as if those files had been created.

Arguments

Any one or a combination of the following expressions. Arguments containing blanks or other special characters should be surrounded by single quotes.

/ *expr***/** [*offset*]

Create file from the current line up to the line containing the regular expression *expr*. *offset*

→

should be of the form +*n* or −*n*, where *n* is the number of lines below or above *expr*.

%*expr*%[*offset*]
Same as /*expr*/ except no file is created for lines previous to line containing *expr*.

num
Create file from current line up to line number *num*. When followed by a repeat count (number inside {}), put the next *num* lines of input into another output file.

{*n*}
Repeat argument *n* times. May follow any of the above arguments. Files will split at instances of *expr* or in blocks of *num* lines. If * is given instead of *n*, repeat argument until input is exhausted.

Examples

Create up to 20 chapter files from the file **novel**:

```
csplit -k -f chap. novel '/CHAPTER/' '{20}'
```

Create up to 100 address files (**xx00** through **xx99**), each four lines long, from a database named **address_list**:

```
csplit -k address_list 4 {99}
```

---

cut

cut *options* [*files*]

Cut out selected columns or fields from one or more *files*. In the following options, *list* is a sequence of integers. Use a comma between separate values and a hyphen to specify a range (e.g., 1-10,15,20, or 50-). See also **paste** and **join**.

Options

−**b**, −−**bytes** *list*
Specify *list* of positions: only bytes in these positions will be printed.

−**c**, −−**characters** *list*
Cut the column positions identified in *list*.

−**d**, −−**delimiter** *c*
Use with −**f** to specify field delimiter as character *c* (default is tab); special characters (e.g., a space) must be quoted.

−**f**, −−**fields** *list*
Cut the fields identified in *list*.

−**n**
Don't split multi-byte characters.

−s, −−only-delimited

Use with **−f** to suppress lines without delimiters.

−−help Print usage information.

−−version Print version information.

Examples

Extract usernames and real names from **/etc/passwd**:

```
cut -d: -f1,5 /etc/passwd
```

Find out who is logged on, but list only login names:

```
who | cut -d" " -f1
```

Cut characters in the fourth column of *file*, and paste them back as the first column in the same file:

```
cut -c4 file | paste - file
```

---

date [*options*] [*+format*] [*date*]

Print the current date and time. You may specify a display *format*. *format* can consist of literal text strings (blanks must be quoted) as well as field descriptors, whose values will appear as described in the following entries (the listing shows some logical groupings). A privileged user can change the system's date and time.

Options

+format Display current date in a non-standard format. For example:

```
% date +"%A E %j %n%k %p"
Tuesday 248
15 PM
```

The default is **%a %b %e %T %Z %Y**—e.g., Tue Sep 5 14:59:37 EDT 1995.

−d *date*, **−−date** *date*

Print *date*, which may be in the format *d* **days** or *m* **months** *d* **days** to print a date in the future. Specify **ago** to print a date in the past. You may include formatting (see the "Format" section that follows).

−s *date*, **−−set** *date*

Set the date.

−u, **−−universal**

Set the date to Greenwich Mean Time, not local time.

→

date	Format	
←	%	Literal %.
	–	Do not pad fields (default: pad fields with zeroes).
	_	Pad fields with space (default: zeroes).
	%a	Abbreviated weekday.
	%b	Abbreviated month name.
	%c	Country-specific date and time format.
	%d	Day of month (01–31).
	%h	Same as %b.
	%j	Julian day of year (001–366).
	%k	Hour in 24-hour format, without leading zeroes (0–23).
	%l	Hour in 12-hour format, without leading zeroes (1–12).
	%m	Month of year (01–12).
	%n	Insert a newline.
	%p	String to indicate a.m. or p.m. (default is AM or PM).
	%r	Time in %I:%M:%S %p (12-hour) format.
	%s	Seconds since "The Epoch," 1970-01-01 00:00:00 UTC (a nonstandard extension).
	%t	Insert a tab.
	%w	Day of week (Sunday = 0).
	%x	Country-specific date format.
	%y	Last two digits of year (00–99).
	%A	Full weekday.
	%B	Full month name.
	%D	Date in %m/%d/%y format.
	%H	Hour in 24-hour format (00–23).
	%I	Hour in 12-hour format (01–12).
	%M	Minutes (00–59).
	%S	Seconds (00–59).
	%T	Time in %H:%M:%S format.
	%U	Week number in year (01–53); start week on Sunday.

%W	Week number in year (00–53); start week on Monday.
%X	Country-specific time format.
%Y	Four-digit year (e.g., 1996).
%Z	Time zone name.

Strings for setting date

Strings for setting the date may be numeric or nonnumeric. Numeric strings consist of time, day, and year in the format *MMddhhmmyy*, with an optional *.ss* appended. Non-numeric strings may include month strings, time zones, a.m., and p.m.

time	A two-digit hour and two-digit minute (*HHMM*); *HH* uses 24-hour format.
day	A two-digit month and two-digit day of month (*mmdd*); default is current day and month.
year	The year specified as either the full four digits or just the last two digits; default is current year.

Examples

Set the date to July 1 (**0701**), 4 a.m. (**0400**), 1995 (**95**):

```
date 0701040095
```

The command:

```
date +"Hello%t Date is %D %n%t Time is %T"
```

produces a formatted date as follows:

```
Hello           Date is 05/09/93
                Time is 17:53:39
```

dd [*option=value*]

Make a copy of an input file (**if=**) using the specified conditions, and send the results to the output file (or standard output if **of** is not specified). Any number of options can be supplied, although **if** and **of** are the most common and are usually specified first. Because **dd** can handle arbitrary block sizes, it is useful when converting between raw physical devices.

Options

| bs=*n* | Set input and output block size to *n* bytes; this option supersedes **ibs** and **obs**. |
| cbs=*n* | Set the size of the conversion buffer (logical record length) to *n* bytes. Use only if the con- |

version *flag* is **ascii**, **ebcdic**, **ibm**, **block**, or **unblock**.

conv=*flags*   Convert the input according to one or more (comma-separated) *flags* listed below. The first five *flags* are mutually exclusive.

ascii
EBCDIC to ASCII.

ebcdic
ASCII to EBCDIC.

ibm
ASCII to EBCDIC with IBM conventions.

block
Variable-length records (i.e., those terminated by a newline) to fixed-length records.

unblock
Fixed-length records to variable-length.

lcase
Uppercase to lowercase.

ucase
Lowercase to uppercase.

noerror
Continue processing when errors occur (up to 5 in a row).

notrunc
Don't truncate output file.

swab
Swap all pairs of bytes.

sync
Pad input blocks to **ibs**.

count=*n*   Copy only *n* input blocks.

files=*n*   Copy *n* input files (e.g., from magnetic tape), then quit.

ibs=*n*   Set input block size to *n* bytes (default is 512).

if=*file*   Read input from *file* (default is standard input).

obs=*n*   Set output block size to *n* bytes (default is 512).

of=*file*   Write output to *file* (default is standard output).

seek=*n*   Seek *n* blocks from start of output file.

skip=*n*   Skip *n* input blocks; useful with magnetic tape.

--help	Print usage information for this command.
--version	Print the version number of this command.

You can multiply size values (*n*) by a factor of 1024, 512, or 2 by appending the letter **k**, **b**, or **w**, respectively. You can use the letter **x** as a multiplication operator between two numbers.

Examples

Convert an input file to all lowercase:

```
dd if=caps_file of=small_file conv=lcase
```

Retrieve variable-length data; write it as fixed-length to **out**:

```
data_retrieval_cmd | dd of=out conv=sync,block
```

---

df [*options*] [*name*]   df

Report the amount of free disk space available on all mounted file systems or on the given *name*. (Cannot report on unmounted filesystems.) Disk space is shown in 1K blocks (default) or 512-byte blocks (if the variable POSIXLY_CORRECT is set). *name* can be a device name (e.g., */dev/hd**), the directory name of a mounting point (e.g., */usr*), or a directory name (in which case **df** reports on the entire filesystem in which that directory is mounted).

Options

-a, --all
Include empty filesystems (those with 0 blocks).

-i, --inodes
Report free, used, and percent-used inodes.

-k, --kilobytes
Print sizes in kilobytes, not 512 bytes.

-t, --type=*type*
Show only *type* filesystems.

-x, --exclude-type=*type*
Show only filesystems that are not of type *type*.

-P, --portability
Use POSIX output format, i.e., print information about each filesystem on exactly one line.

-T, --print-type
Display a type for each filesystem, for use as an argument to -t or -x.

diff

diff [*options*] [*diroptions*] *file1 file2*

Compare two text files. **diff** reports lines that differ between *file1* and *file2*. Output consists of lines of context from each file, with *file1* text flagged by a < symbol and *file2* text by a > symbol. Context lines are preceded by the **ed** command (**a**, **c**, or **d**) that would be used to convert *file1* to *file2*. If one of the files is –, standard input is read. If one of the files is a directory, **diff** locates the filename in that directory corresponding to the other argument (e.g., **diff my_dir junk** is the same as **diff my_dir/junk junk**). If both arguments are directories, **diff** reports lines that differ between all pairs of files having equivalent names (e.g., *olddir/program* and *newdir/program*); in addition, **diff** lists filenames unique to one directory, as well as subdirectories common to both. See also **cmp**.

Options

–b, ––ignore-space-change
    Ignore repeating blanks and end-of-line blanks; treat successive blanks as one.

–e, ––ed   Produce a script of commands (**a**, **c**, **d**) to recreate *file2* from *file1* using the **ed** editor.

–H   Speed output of large files by scanning for scattered small changes; long stretches with many changes may not show up.

–i, ––ignore-case
    Ignore case in text comparison. Upper- and lower-case are considered the same.

–w, ––ignore-all-space
    Ignore all whitespace in files for comparisons.

–B, ––ignore-blank-lines
    Ignore blank lines in files.

–I *regexp*, ––ignore-matching-lines=*regexp*
    Ignore lines in files that match the regular expression *regexp*.

–a, ––text Treat all files as text files. Useful for checking to see if binary files are identical.

–c   Context **diff**: print 3 lines surrounding each changed lines.

–u   Unified **diff**: print old and new versions of lines in a single block.

–q, ––brief Output only whether files differ.

–n, ––rcs Produce output in RCS diff format.

-y, --side-by-side
> Produce two-column output.

-w *n* For two-column output (-y), produce columns
> with *n* characters of maximum width. Default
> is 130.

--left-column
> For two-column output (-y), show only left
> column of common lines.

--suppress-common-lines
> For two-column output (-y), do not show com-
> mon lines.

-l, --paginate
> Paginate output by passing it to **pr**.

-t, --expand-tabs
> Produce output with tabs expanded to spaces.

-T, --initial-tab
> Insert initial tabs into output to line up tabs
> properly.

-r, --recursive
> Compare subdirectories recursively.

-N, --new-file
> Treat nonexistent files as empty.

-s, --report-identical-files
> Indicate when files do not differ.

-x *regexp*, --exclude=*regexp*
> Do not compare files in a directory whose
> names match *regexp*.

-X *filename*, --exclude-from=*filename*
> Do not compare files in a directory whose
> names match patterns described in the file *file-
> name*.

-S *filename* For directory comparisons, begin with the file
> *filename*.

-d, --minimal
> To speed up comparison, ignore segments of
> numerous changes and output a smaller set of
> changes.

---

diff3 [*options*] *file1 file2 file3*   diff3

Compare three files and report the differences with the following codes:

→

====	All three files differ.
====1	*file1* is different.
====2	*file2* is different.
====3	*file3* is different.

diff3 is also designed to merge changes in two differing files from a common ancestor file, i.e., when two people have made their own set of changes to the same file. **diff3** can find changes between the ancestor and one of the newer files, and generate output that adds those differences to the other new file. Unmerged changes are places where both of the newer files differ from each other, and at least one of them from the ancestor. Changes from the ancestor that are the same in both of the newer files are called merged changes. If all three files differ in the same place, it is called an overlapping change.

This scheme is used on the command line with the ancestor being *file2*, the second filename. Comparison is made between *file2* and *file3*, with those differences then applied to *file1*.

Options

-3
Create an **ed** script to incorporate into *file1* unmerged, nonoverlapping differences between *file1* and *file3*.

-a, --text   Treat files as text.

-A, --show-all
Create an **ed** script to incorporate all changes, showing conflicts in bracketed format.

-e, --ed   Create an **ed** script to incorporate into *file1* all unmerged differences between *file2* and *file3*.

-E, --show-overlap
Create an **ed** script to incorporate unmerged changes, showing conflicts in bracketed format.

-x, --overlap-only
Create an **ed** script to incorporate into *file1* all differences where all three files differ (overlapping changes).

-X
Same as -x, only show conflicts in overlapping the changes in bracketed format.

-m, --merge
Create file with changes merged (not an **ed** script).

−L *label*, **−−label=***label*
    Use *label* to replace filename in output.

−i   Append the **w** (save) and **q** (quit) commands
        to **ed** script output.

−T, −−initial-tab
    Begin lines with a tab instead of two spaces in
    output to line tabs up properly.

diff3

---

dirname *pathname*

Print *pathname* excluding last level. Useful for stripping the actual filename from a pathname. See also **basename**.

dirname

---

du [*options*] [*directories*]

Print disk usage, i.e., the number of 1K blocks used by each named directory and its subdirectories (default is current directory).

du

Options

−a, −−all   Print usage for all files, not just subdirectories.

−b, −−bytes
    Print sizes in bytes.

−c, −−total   In addition to normal output, print grand total
    of all arguments.

−k, −−kilobytes
    Print sizes in kilobytes (this is the default).

−l, −−count-links
    Count the size of all files, whether or not they
    have already appeared (i.e., via a hard link).

−r   Print `cannot open` message if a file or directory is inaccessible.

−s, −−summarize
    Print only the grand total for each named
    directory.

−x, −−one-file-system
    Display usage of files in current filesystem
    only.

−D, −−dereference-args
    Follow symbolic links, but only if they are
    command-line arguments.

−L, −−dereference
    Follow symbolic links.

→

du ←	−S, −−separate-dirs Do not include the sizes of subdirectories when totaling the size of parent directories.

dumpkeys

dumpkeys [*options*]

Print information about the keyboard driver's translation tables to standard output. Further information is available in the manual pages under *keytables*.

Options

    −c*charset*, −−charset=*charset*
> Specify character set with which to interpret character code values. Valid character sets are iso-8859-1 (default), iso-8859-2, iso-8859-3, iso-8859-4, and iso-8859-8.

    −−compose-only
> Print compose key combinations only.

    −f, −−full-table
> Output in canonical, not short, form: for each key, print a row with modifier combinations divided into columns.

    −−funcs-only
> Print function key string definitions only; do not print key bindings or string definitions.

    −i, −−short-info
> Print in short-info format, including information about acceptable keycode keywords in the keytable files; the number of actions that can be bound to a key; a list of the ranges of action codes (the values to the right of a key definition); and the number of function keys that the kernel supports.

    −−keys-only
> Print key bindings only; do not print string definitions.

    −l, −−long-info
> Print the same information as in −−short-info, plus a list of the supported action symbols and their numeric values.

    −n, −−numeric
> Print action code values in hexadecimal notation; do not attempt to convert them to symbolic notation.

echo [−n] [*string*]

This is the **/bin/echo** command. **echo** also exists as a command built into the C shell and Bourne shell. The following character sequences have special meanings.

\a Alert (bell)

\b Backspace

\c Suppress trailing newline

\f Form feed

\n Newline

\r Carriage return

\t Horizontal tab

\v Vertical tab

\\ Literal backslash

nnn
    The octal character whose ASCII code is *nnn*.

Options

−e   Enable character sequences with special mean-
            ing. (In some versions, this option is not
            required in order to make the sequences
            work.)

−n   Suppress printing of newline after text.

Examples

```
echo "testing printer" | lp
echo "TITLE\nTITLE" > file ; cat doc1 doc2 >> file
echo "Warning: ringing bell \07"
```

egrep [*options*] [*regexp*] [*files*]

Search one or more *files* for lines that match a regular expression *regexp*. **egrep** doesn't support the regular expressions \(, \), *n*, \<, \>, \{, or \}, but does support the other expressions, as well as the extended set +, ?, |, and ( ). Remember to enclose these characters in quotes. Regular expressions are described in Chapter 6, *Pattern Matching*. Exit status is 0 if any lines match, 1 if none match, and 2 for errors. See also **grep** and **fgrep**. **egrep** typically runs faster than those commands.

→

egrep
←
	Options
	
	    −*num* Print *num* lines of leading and trailing text.
	
	    −b, −−byte-offset
	          Print the byte offset within the input file before each line of output.
	
	    −c, −−count
	          Print only a count of matched lines. With **−v** or **−−revert-match** option, count non-matching lines.
	
	    −e *pattern*, −−regexp=*pattern*
	          Search for *pattern*. Same as specifying a pattern as an argument, but useful in protecting patterns beginning with −.
	
	    −f *file*, −−file=*file*
	          Take a list of patterns from *file*, one per line.
	
	    −h, −−no-filename
	          Print matched lines but not filenames (inverse of **−l**).
	
	    −i, −−ignore-case
	          Ignore uppercase and lowercase distinctions.
	
	    −l, −−files-with-matches
	          List the names of files with matches, but not individual matched lines; scanning per file stops on the first match.
	
	    −n, −−line-number
	          Print lines and their line numbers.
	
	    −q, −−quiet
	          Suppress normal output in favor of quiet mode; the scanning will stop on the first match.
	
	    −s, −−silent
	          Suppress error messages about nonexistent or unreadable files.
	
	    −u, −−unix-byte-offsets
	          Report Unix-style byte offsets. This option produces Unix-style results in DOS and Windows environments; must be used with **−b**.
	
	    −v, −−revert-match
	          Print all lines that *don't* match *pattern*.
	
	    −w, −−word-regexp
	          Match on whole words only. Words are divided by characters that are not letters, digits, or underscores.

-x, --line-regexp
> Print lines only if *pattern* matches the entire line.

-A *num*
> Print *num* lines of text that occur before the matching line.

-B *num*
> Print *num* lines of text that occur after the matching line.

-C, --context
> Print two lines of leading and trailing context. Same as -2.

-L, --files-without-match
> List files that contain no matching lines.

-U, --binary
> Treat the file(s) as binary; only supported in DOS and Windows.

-V, --version
> Print the version number to standard error.

Examples

Search for occurrences of *Victor* or *Victoria* in *file*:

```
egrep 'Victor(ia)*' file
egrep '(Victor|Victoria)' file
```

Find and print strings such as *old.doc1* or *new.doc2* in *files*, and include their line numbers:

```
egrep -n '(old|new)\.doc?' files
```

---

emacs [*options*] [*files*]

A text editor and all-purpose work environment. For more information, see Chapter 7, *The Emacs Editor*.

---

env [*option*] [*variable=value* ...] [*command*]

Display the current environment or, if an environment *variable* is specified, set it to a new *value* and display the modified environment. If *command* is specified, execute it under the modified environment.

Options

-, -i, --ignore-environment
> Ignore current environment entirely.

-u *name*, --unset *name*
> Unset the specified variable.

ex	**ex** [*options*] *file*
	An interactive command-based editor. For more information, see Chapter 9, *The ex Editor.*
expand	**expand** [*options*] *files*
	Convert tabs in given files (or standard input, if the file is named −) to appropriate number of spaces; write results to standard output.
	Options
	−*tabs*, −t, −−tabs *tabs*
	tabs is a comma-separated list of integers that specify the placement of tab stops. If exactly one integer is provided, the tab stops are set to every *integer* spaces. By default, tab stops are 8 spaces apart. With -t and −−tabs, the list may be separated by whitespace instead of commas.
	−i, −−initial
	Convert tabs only at the beginning of lines.
expr	**expr** *arg1 operator arg2* [*operator arg3* ...]
	Evaluate arguments as expressions and print the result. Arguments and operators must be separated by spaces. In most cases, an argument is an integer, typed literally or represented by a shell variable. There are three types of operators: arithmetic, relational, and logical. Exit status for **expr** is **0** (expression is nonzero and nonnull), **1** (expression is 0 or null), or **2** (expression is invalid).
	Arithmetic operators
	Use these to produce mathematical expressions whose results are printed.

+	Add *arg2* to *arg1.*
−	Subtract *arg2* from *arg1.*
*	Multiply the arguments.
/	Divide *arg1* by *arg2.*
%	Take the remainder when *arg1* is divided by *arg2.*

Addition and subtraction are evaluated last, unless they are grouped inside parentheses. The symbols *, (, and) have meaning to the shell, so they must be escaped (preceded by a backslash or enclosed in single quotes).

Relational operators

Use these to compare two arguments. Arguments can also be words, in which case comparisons are defined by the locale. If the comparison statement is true, the result is 1; if false, the result is 0. Symbols > and < must be escaped.

=, ==	Are the arguments equal?
!=	Are the arguments different?
>	Is *arg1* greater than *arg2*?
>=	Is *arg1* greater than or equal to *arg2*?
<	Is *arg1* less than *arg2*?
<=	Is *arg1* less than or equal to *arg2*?

Logical operators

Use these to compare two arguments. Depending on the values, the result can be *arg1* (or some portion of it), *arg2*, or 0. Symbols | and & must be escaped.

|	Logical OR; if *arg1* has a nonzero (and non-null) value, the result is *arg1*; otherwise, the result is *arg2*.
&	Logical AND; if both *arg1* and *arg2* have a nonzero (and nonnull) value, the result is *arg1*; otherwise, the result is 0.
:	Like **grep**; *arg2* is a pattern to search for in *arg1*. *arg2* must be a regular expression. If part of the *arg2* pattern is enclosed in \(\), the result is the portion of *arg1* that matches; otherwise, the result is simply the number of characters that match. By default, a pattern match always applies to the beginning of the first argument (the search string implicitly begins with a ^). Start the search string with .* to match other parts of the string.

match *string* **regex**
Same as *string : regex*.

substr *string start length*
Return a section of *string*, beginning with *start*, with a maximum length of *length* characters. Return null when given a negative or nonnumeric *start* or *length*.

index *string character-list*
Return the first position in *string* that matches the first possible character in *character-list*.

→

Continue through *character-list* until a match is found, or return 0.

length *string*

Return the length of *string*.

Examples

Division happens first; result is 10:

```
expr 5 + 10 / 2
```

Addition happens first; result is 7 (truncated from 7.5):

```
expr \( 5 + 10 \) / 2
```

Add 1 to variable **i**. This is how variables are incremented in shell scripts:

```
i=`expr $i + 1`
```

Print 1 (true) if variable **a** is the string "hello":

```
expr $a = hello
```

Print 1 (true) if **b** plus 5 equals 10 or more:

```
expr $b + 5 \>= 10
```

In the examples that follow, variable **p** is the string "version.100". This command prints the number of characters in **p**:

```
expr $p : '.*'        Result is 11
```

Match all characters and print them:

```
expr $p : '\(.*\)'         Result is "version.100"
```

Print the number of lowercase letters at the beginning of **p**:

```
expr $p : '[a-z]*'        Result is 7
```

Match the lowercase letters at the beginning of **p**:

```
expr $p : '\([a-z]*\)'        Result is "version"
```

Truncate **$x** if it contains five or more characters; if not, just print **$x**. (Logical OR uses the second argument when the first one is 0 or null; i.e., when the match fails.)

```
expr $x : '\(.....\)' \| $x
```

In a shell script, rename files to their first five letters:

```
mv $x `expr $x : '\(.....\)' \| $x`
```

(To avoid overwriting files with similar names, use **mv −i**.)

false   **false**

A null command that returns an unsuccessful (nonzero) exit status. Normally used in Bourne shell scripts. See also **true**.

---

fdformat [*options*] *device*   **fdformat**

Low-level format of a floppy disk. The device for a standard format is usually **/dev/fd0** or **/dev/fd1**.

Option

    −n   Do not verify format after completion.

---

fgrep [*options*] *pattern* [*files*]   **fgrep**

Search one or more *files* for lines that match a literal, text string *pattern*. Exit status is 0 if any lines match, 1 if not, and 2 for errors. See also **egrep** and **grep**.

Options

    −*num*   Print *num* lines of leading and trailing text.

    −b, −−byte-offset
            Print the byte offset within the input file before each line of output.

    −c, −−count
            Print only a count of matched lines. With −v or −−revert-match option, count non-matching lines.

    −e *pattern*, −−regexp=*pattern*
            Search for pattern *pattern*. Same as specifying a pattern as an argument, but useful in protecting patterns beginning with −.

    −f *file*, −−file=*file*
            Take a list of patterns from *file*, one per line.

    −h, −−no-filename
            Print matched lines but not filenames (inverse of −l).

    −i, −−ignore-case
            Ignore uppercase and lowercase distinctions.

    −l, −−files-with-matches
            List the names of files with matches, but not individual matched lines; scanning per file stops on the first match.

    −n, −−line-number
            Print lines and their line numbers.

→

fgrep

←

-q, --quiet

Suppress normal output in favor of quiet mode; the scanning will stop on the first match.

-s, --silent

Suppress error messages about nonexistent or unreadable files.

-u, --unix-byte-offsets

Report Unix-style byte offsets. This option produces Unix-style results in DOS and Windows environments; must be used with -b.

-v, --revert-match

Print all lines that *don't* match *pattern*.

-w, --word-regexp

Match on whole words only. Words are divided by characters that are not letters, digits, or underscores.

-x, --line-regexp

Print lines only if *pattern* matches the entire line.

-A *num*

Print *num* lines of text that occur before the matching line.

-B *num*

Print *num* lines of text that occur after the matching line.

-C, --context

Print two lines of leading and trailing context. Same as -2.

-L, --files-without-match

List files that contain no matching lines.

-U, --binary

Treat the file(s) as binary; only supported in DOS and Windows.

-V, --version

Print the version number to standard error.

Examples

Print lines in *file* that don't contain any spaces:

```
fgrep -v ' ' file
```

Print lines in *file* that contain the words in **spell_list**:

```
fgrep -f spell_list file
```

file [*options*] *files*

Classify the named *files* according to the type of data they contain. **file** checks the magic file (usually */etc/magic*, but sometimes */usr/lib/magic*) to identify some file types.

Options

−b	Brief mode; do not prepend filenames to output lines.
−c	Check the format of the magic file (*files* argument is invalid with **−c**).
−f *list*	Run **file** on the filenames in *list*.
−m *file*	Search for file types in *file* instead of */etc/magic*.
−v	Print the version of the program and exit.
−z	Attempt checking of compressed files.
−L	Follow symbolic links. By default, symbolic links are not followed.
−V	Display version information.

Many file types are understood. Output lists each filename, followed by a brief classification such as:

```
ascii text
c program text
c-shell commands
data
empty
iAPX 386 executable
directory
[nt]roff, tbl, or eqn input text
shell commands
symbolic link to ../usr/etc/arp
```

Example

List all files that are deemed to be troff/nroff input:

```
file * | grep roff
```

find [*pathnames*] [*conditions*]

An extremely useful command for finding particular groups of files (numerous examples follow this description). **find** descends the directory tree beginning at each *pathname* and locates files that meet the specified *conditions*. The default pathname is the current directory. The most useful conditions include **−print** (which is the default if no other expression is given), **−name** and **−type** (for general use), **−exec** and **−size** (for advanced users), and **−mtime** and **−user** (for administrators).

→

find

←

Conditions may be grouped by enclosing them in \(\) (escaped parentheses), negated with ! (use \! in the C shell), given as alternatives by separating them with −o, or repeated (adding restrictions to the match; usually only for −name, −type, −perm). Modification refers to editing of a file's contents. Change refers to modification, permission or ownership changes, etc.; therefore, for example, −ctime is more inclusive than −atime or −mtime.

Conditions and actions

−atime +*n* | −*n* | *n*
: Find files that were last accessed more than *n* (+*n*), less than *n* (−*n*), or exactly *n* days ago. Note that **find** changes the access time of directories supplied as *pathnames*.

−ctime +*n* | −*n* | *n*
: Find files that were changed more than *n* (+*n*), less than *n* (−*n*), or exactly *n* days ago. A change is anything that changes the directory entry for the file, such as a **chmod**.

−depth
: Descend the directory tree, skipping directories and working on actual files first (and *then* the parent directories). Useful when files reside in unwritable directories (e.g., when using **find** with **cpio**).

−exec *command* { } \;
: Run the Unix *command*, from the starting directory on each file matched by **find** (provided *command* executes successfully on that file; i.e., returns a 0 exit status). When *command* runs, the argument { } substitutes the current file. Follow the entire sequence with an escaped semicolon (\;).

−follow
: Follow symbolic links and track the directories visited (don't use this with −**type l**).

−group *gname*
: Find files belonging to group *gname*. *gname* can be a group name or a group ID number.

−inum *n*
: Find files whose inode number is *n*.

−links *n*
: Find files having *n* links.

−mount, −xdev
: Search for files that reside only on the same filesystem as *pathname*.

−mtime +*n* | −*n* | *n*

Find files that were last modified more than *n* (+*n*), less than *n* (−*n*), or exactly *n*, days ago. A modification is a change to a file's data, reflected in an **ls -l** listing.

−name *pattern*

Find files whose names match *pattern*. Filename metacharacters may be used, but should be escaped or quoted.

−newer *file* Find files that have been modified more recently than *file*; similar to **−mtime**. Affected by -follow only if it occurs after -follow on the command line.

−ok *command* { } \;

Same as **−exec**, but prompts user to respond with **y** before *command* is executed.

−perm *nnn* Find files whose permission flags (e.g., **rwx**) match octal number *nnn* exactly (e.g., 664 matches −rw−rw−r−−). Use a minus sign before *nnn* to make a "wildcard" match of any unspecified octal digit (e.g., −**perm** −**600** matches −rw−******, where * can be any mode).

−print Print the matching files and directories, using their full pathnames. Return **true**.

−regex *pattern*

Like **−path** but uses grep-style regular expressions instead of the shell-like globbing used in **−name** and **−path**.

−size *n*[c] Find files containing *n* blocks, or if **c** is specified, *n* characters long.

−type *c* Find files whose type is *c*. *c* can be **b** (block special file), **c** (character special file), **d** (directory), **p** (fifo or named pipe), **l** (symbolic link), **s** (socket), or **f** (plain file).

−user *user* Find files belonging to *user* (name or ID).

−daystart Calculate times from the start of the day today, not 24 hours ago.

−maxdepth *num*

Do not descend more than *num* levels of directories.

−mindepth *num*

Begin applying tests and actions only at levels deeper than *num* levels.

→

−noleaf   Normally, **find** assumes that each directory has
             at least two hard links that should be ignored
             (a hard link for its name and one for ".")—i.e.,
             two fewer "real" directories than its hard link
             count indicates. -noleaf turns off this assump-
             tion, a useful practice when **find** runs on non-
             Unix filesystems. This forces **find** to examine
             all entries, assuming that some might prove to
             be directories into which it must descend (a
             time-waster on Unix).

−amin +*n* | −*n* | *n*
             Find files last accessed more than *n* (+*n*), less
             than *n* (-*n*), or exactly *n*, minutes ago.

−anewer *file*
             Find files that were accessed after they were
             last modified. Affected by -**follow** when after
             -**follow** on the command line.

−cmin +*n* | −*n* | *n*
             Find files last changed more than *n* (+*n*), less
             than *n* (-*n*), or exactly *n* minutes ago.

−cnewer *file*
             Find files that were changed after they were
             last modified. Affected by -**follow** when after
             -**follow** on the command line.

−empty   Continue if file is empty. Applies to regular
             files and directories.

−false   Return false value for each file encountered.

−fstype *type*
             Match files only on *type* filesystems. Acceptable
             types are **ufs**, **4.2**, **4.3**, **nfs**, **tmp**, **mfs**, **S51K**,
             S52K.

−gid *num*   Find files with numeric group ID of *num*.

−ilname *pattern*
             A case-insensitive version of -**lname**.

−iname *pattern*
             A case-insensitive version of -**name**.

−ipath *pattern*
             A case-insensitive version of -**path**.

−iregex *pattern*
             A case-insensitive version of -**regex**.

−lname *pattern*
             Search for files that are symbolic links, pointing
             to files named *pattern*. *pattern* can include

shell metacharacters, and does not treat / or . specially. The match is case-insensitive.

−mmin +*n* | −*n* | *n*
Find files last modified more than *n* (+*n*), less than *n* (-*n*), or exactly *n* minutes ago.

−nouser The file's user ID does not correspond to any user.

−nogroup The file's group ID does not correspond to any group.

−path *pattern*
Find files whose names match *pattern*. Expect full pathnames relative to the starting pathname: i.e., do not treat / or . specially.

Examples

List all files (and subdirectories) in your home directory:

```
find $HOME -print
```

List all files named *chapter1* in the */work* directory:

```
find /work -name chapter1 -print
```

List all files beginning with *memo* owned by *ann*:

```
find /work -name 'memo*' -user ann -print
```

Search the filesystem (begin at root) for manpage directories:

```
find / -type d -name 'man*' -print
```

Search the current directory, look for filenames that *don't* begin with a capital letter, and send them to the printer:

```
find . \! -name '[A-Z]*' -exec lp {} \;
```

Find and compress files whose names *don't* end with **.gz**:

```
gzip `find . \! -name '*.gz' -print`
```

Remove all empty files on the system (prompting first):

```
find / -size 0 -ok rm {} \;
```

Search the system for files that were modified within the last two days (good candidates for backing up):

```
find / -mtime -2 -print
```

Recursively **grep** for a pattern down a directory tree:

```
find /book -print | xargs grep '[Nn]utshell'
```

If the files *kt1* and *kt2* exist in the current directory, their names can be printed with the command:

→

find
←
	``
	$ find . -name 'kt[0-9]'
	./kt1
	./kt2
	``

Since the command prints these names with an initial ./ path, you need to specify the ./ when using the **−path** option:

```
$ find . -path './kt[0-9]'
```

The **−regex** option uses a complete pathname, like **−path**, but treats the following argument as a regular expression rather than a glob pattern (although in this case the result is the same):

```
$ find . -regex './kt[0-9]'
```

---

finger

finger [*options*] *users*

Display data about one or more *users*, including information listed in the files .**plan** and .**project** in each *user*'s home directory. You can specify each *user* either as a login name (exact match) or as a first or last name (display information on all matching names). Networked environments recognize arguments of the form *user@host* and *@host*.

Options

−l	Force long format (default): everything included by the **−s** option, and home directory, home phone, login shell, mail status, .**plan**, .**project**, and .**forward**.
−m	Suppress matching of users' "real" names.
−p	Omit .**plan** and .**project** file from display.
−s	Show short format: login name, real name, terminal name, write status, idle time, office location, and office phone number.

---

fmt

fmt [*options*] [*files*]

Convert text to specified width by filling lines and removing newlines. Concatenate files on the command line, or text from standard input. By default, preserve blank lines, spacing, indentation. **fmt** attempts to break lines at the end of sentences, and to avoid breaking lines after a sentence's first word or before its last.

Options

−c, −−crown-margin

Crown margin mode. Do not change each paragraph's first two lines' indentation. Use the

second line's indentation as the default for subsequent lines.

−p *prefix*, **−−prefix=***prefix*
Format only lines beginning with *prefix*.

−s, −−split-only
Suppress line-joining.

−t, −−tagged-paragraph
Tagged paragraph mode. Same as crown mode
when the indentation of the first and second
lines differs. If the indentation is the same,
treat the first line as its own separate paragraph.

−u, −−uniform-spacing
Print exactly one space between words, and
two between sentences.

−width *width*, **−w** *width*, **−−width=***width*
Set column width to *width*. The default is 75.

---

fold [*option*] [*files*]

Break the lines of the named *files* so that they are no wider than
the specified width (default 80). **fold** breaks lines exactly at the
specified width, even in the middle of a word. Reads from standard input when given − as a file.

Options

−b, −−bytes
Count bytes, not columns; i.e., consider tabs,
backspaces, and carriage returns to be one column.

−s, −−spaces
Break at spaces only, if possible.

−w, −−width *width*
Set the maximum line width to *width*. Default
is 80.

---

formail [*options*]

Filter standard input into mailbox format. If no sender is appar-
ent, provide the sender *foo@bar*. By default, escape bogus **From**
lines with >.

fmt

fold

formail

→

formail	*Options*
←	

+*skip*   Do not split first *skip* messages.

−*total*   Stop after splitting *total* messages.

−a *headerfield*
> Append *headerfield* to header, unless it already exists. If *headerfield* is Message-ID or Resent-Message-ID with no contents, generate a unique message ID.

−b   Do not escape bogus **From** lines.

−c   When header fields are more than one line long, concatenate the lines.

−d   Do not assume that input must be in strict mailbox format.

−e   Allow messages to begin one immediately after the other; do not require empty space between them.

−f   Do not edit non-mailbox-format lines. By default, formail prepends **From** to such lines.

−i *headerfield*
> Append *headerfield* whether or not it already exists. Rename each existing *headerfield* to Old-*headerfield*, unless they are empty.

−k   For use only with −r. Keep the body as well as the fields specified by −r.

−m *minfields*
> Require at least *minfields* before recognizing the beginning of a new message. Default is 2.

−n   Allow simultaneous **formail** processes to run.

−p *prefix*   Escape lines with *prefix* instead of >.

−q   Do not display write errors, duplicate messages, and mismatched **Content-Length** fields. This is the default; use −q− to turn it off.

−r   Throw away all existing fields, retaining only **X-Loop**, and generate auto-reply header instead. You can preserve particular fields with the −i option.

−s   Must be the last option; everything following it will be assumed to be its arguments. Divide input to separate mail messages, and pipe them to the program specified, or concatenate them to standard output (by default).

| −t | Assume sender's return address to be valid. (By default, **formail** favors machine-generated addresses.) | formail |

−**u** *headerfield*
> Delete all but the first occurrence of *headerfield*.

−**x** *headerfield*
> Display the contents of *headerfield* on a single line.

−**z**
> When necessary, add a space between field names and contents. Remove ("zap") empty fields.

−**A** *headerfield*
> Append *headerfield* whether or not it already exists.

−**B**
> Assume that input is in BABYL **rmail** format.

−**D** *maxlen idcache*
> Remember old message IDs (in *idcache*, which will grow no larger than approximately *maxlen*). When splitting, refuse to output duplicate messages. Otherwise, return true on discovering a duplicate. With −**r**, look at the sender's mail address instead of the message ID.

−**I** *headerfield*
> Append *headerfield* whether or not it already exists. Remove existing fields.

−**R** *oldfield newfield*
> Change all fields named *oldfield* to *newfield*.

−**U** *headerfield*
> Delete all but the last occurrence of *headerfield*.

−**Y**
> Format in traditional Berkeley style; i.e., ignore **Content-Length:** fields.

−**X** *headerfield*
> Display the field name and contents of *headerfield* on a single line.

---

free
free

Display statistics about memory usage: total free, used, physical, swap, shared, and buffers used by the kernel.

→

free	*Options*
←	

<table>
<tr><td>−b</td><td>Calculate memory in bytes.</td></tr>
<tr><td>−k</td><td>Default. Calculate memory in kilobytes.</td></tr>
<tr><td>−m</td><td>Calculate memory in megabytes.</td></tr>
<tr><td>−o</td><td>Do not display "buffer adjusted" line. The −o switch disables the display "−/+ buffers" line.</td></tr>
<tr><td>−s time</td><td>Check memory usage every time seconds.</td></tr>
<tr><td>−t</td><td>Display all totals on one line at the bottom of output.</td></tr>
<tr><td>−V</td><td>Display version information.</td></tr>
</table>

ftp

ftp [*options*] [*hostname*]

Transfer files to and from remote network site *hostname*. **ftp** prompts the user for a command. The commands are listed below, following the options. Some of the commands are toggles, meaning they turn on a feature when it is off, and vice versa.

Options

<table>
<tr><td>−d</td><td>Enable debugging.</td></tr>
<tr><td>−g</td><td>Disable filename globbing.</td></tr>
<tr><td>−i</td><td>Turn off interactive prompting.</td></tr>
<tr><td>−n</td><td>No auto-login upon initial connection.</td></tr>
<tr><td>−v</td><td>Verbose. Show all responses from remote server.</td></tr>
</table>

Commands

![*command* [*args*]]
> Invoke an interactive shell on the local machine. If arguments are given, the first is taken as a command to execute directly, with the rest of the arguments as that command's arguments.

$ *macro-name* [*args*]
> Execute the macro *macro-name* that was defined with the **macdef** command. Arguments are passed to the macro unglobbed.

account [*passwd*]
> Supply a supplemental password that will be required by a remote system for access to resources once a login has been successfully completed. If no argument is given, the user

will be prompted for an account password in a
non-echoing mode.

append *local-file* [*remote-file*]

Append a local file to a file on the remote
machine. If *remote-file* is not given, the local
filename is used after being altered by any
ntrans or **nmap** setting. File transfer uses the
current settings for *type, format, mode,* and
structure.

ascii   Set the file transfer type to network ASCII
                 (default).

bell   Sound a bell after each file transfer command
                 is completed.

binary   Set file transfer type to support binary image
                 transfer.

bye   Terminate FTP session and exit **ftp**.

case   Toggle remote computer filename case map-
                 ping during **mget**. The default is **off**. When
                 case is **on**, files on the remote machine with
                 all-uppercase names will be copied to the local
                 machine with all-lowercase names.

cd *remote-directory*

Change working directory on remote machine
to *remote-directory*.

cdup   Change working directory of remote machine
                 to its parent directory.

chmod [*mode*] [*remote-file*]

Change file permissions of *remote-file*. If
options are omitted, the command prompts for
them.

close   Terminate FTP session and return to command
                 interpreter.

cr   Toggle carriage return stripping during ASCII-
                 type file retrieval.

delete *remote-file*

Delete file *remote-file* on remote machine.

debug [*debug-value*]

Toggle debugging mode. If *debug-value* is
specified, it is used to set the debugging level.

dir [*remote-directory*] [*local-file*]

Print a listing of the contents in the directory
remote-directory, and, optionally, place the
output in *local-file*. If no directory is specified,

→

the current working directory on the remote machine is used. If no local file is specified, or – is given instead of the filename, output comes to the terminal.

disconnect Synonym for **close**.

form *format*

Set the file transfer form to *format*. Default format is *file*.

get *remote-file* [*local-file*]

Retrieve the *remote-file* and store it on the local machine. If the local filename is not specified, it is given the same name it has on the remote machine, subject to alteration by the current **case**, **ntrans**, and **nmap** settings. If local file is –, output comes to the terminal.

glob Toggle filename expansion for **mdelete**, **mget**, and **mput**. If globbing is turned off, the filename arguments are taken literally and not expanded.

hash Toggle hash-sign (#) printing for each data block transferred.

help [*command*]

Print help information for *command*. With no argument, **ftp** prints a list of commands.

idle [*seconds*]

Get/set idle timer on remote machine. *seconds* specifies the length of the idle timer; if omitted, the current idle timer is displayed.

image Same as **binary**.

lcd [*directory*]

Change working directory on local machine. If *directory* is not specified, the user's home directory is used.

ls [*remote-directory*] [*local-file*]

Print listing of contents of directory on remote machine, in a format chosen by the remote machine. If *remote-directory* is not specified, current working directory is used.

macdef *macro-name*

Define a macro. Subsequent lines are stored as the macro *macro-name*; a null line terminates macro input mode. When **$i** is included in the macro, loop through arguments, substituting

the current argument for **$i** on each pass.
Escape **$** with \.

mdelete *remote-files*
> Delete the *remote-files* on the remote machine.

mdir *remote-files local-file*
> Like **dir**, except multiple remote files may be
> specified.

mget *remote-files*
> Expand the wildcard expression *remote-files* on
> the remote machine and do a **get** for each file-
> name thus produced.

mkdir *directory-name*
> Make a directory on the remote machine.

mls *remote-files local-file*
> Like **nlist**, except multiple remote files may be
> specified, and the local file must be specified.

mode [*mode-name*]
> Set file transfer mode to *mode-name*. Default
> mode is stream mode.

modtime [*file-name*]
> Show last modification time of the file on the
> remote machine.

mput [*local-files*]
> Expand wildcards in *local-files* given as argu-
> ments and do a **put** for each file in the result-
> ing list.

newer *remote-file* [*local-file*]
> Get file if remote file is newer than local file.

nlist [*remote-directory*] [*local-file*]
> Print list of files of a directory on the remote
> machine to *local-file* (or the screen if *local-file*
> is not specified). If *remote-directory* is unspeci-
> fied, the current working directory is used.

nmap [*inpattern outpattern*]
> Set or unset the filename mapping mechanism.
> The mapping follows the pattern set by *inpat-
> tern*, a template for incoming filenames, and
> *outpattern*, which determines the resulting
> mapped filename. The sequences $1 through
> $9 are treated as variables: for example, the
> *inpattern* **$1.$2**, along with the input file
> **readme.txt**, would set $1 to **readme** and $2 to
> **txt**. An *outpattern* of **$1.data** would result in
> an output file of **readme.data**. $0 corresponds

→

to the complete filename. **[string1, string2]** is replaced by *string1*, unless that string is null, in which case it's replaced by *string2*.

ntrans [*inchars* [*outchars*]]

Set or unset the filename character translation mechanism. Characters in a filename matching a character in *inchars* are replaced with the corresponding character in *outchars*. If no arguments are specified, the filename mapping mechanism is unset. If arguments are specified:

- Characters in remote filenames are translated during **mput** and **put** commands issued without a specified remote target filename.

- Characters in local filenames are translated during **mget** and **get** commands issued without a specified local target filename.

open *host* [*port*]

Establish a connection to the specified *host* FTP server. An optional *port* number may be supplied, in which case **ftp** will attempt to contact an FTP server at that port.

prompt   Toggle interactive prompting.

proxy *ftp-command*

Execute an FTP command on a secondary control connection—i.e., send commands to two separate remote hosts simultaneously.

put *local-file* [*remote-file*]

Store a local file on the remote machine. If *remote-file* is left unspecified, the local filename is used after processing according to any **ntrans** or **nmap** settings in naming the remote file. File transfer uses the current settings for *type, file, structure*, and *transfer mode*.

pwd   Print name of the current working directory on the remote machine.

quit   Synonym for **bye**.

quote *arg1 arg2...*

Send the arguments specified, verbatim, to the remote FTP server.

recv *remote-file* [*local-file*]

Synonym for **get**.

reget *remote-file* [*local-file*]
> Retrieve a file (like **get**), except it restarts at the end of *local-file*. Useful for restarting a dropped transfer.

remotehelp [*command-name*]
> Request help from the remote FTP server. If *command-name* is specified, remote help for that command is returned.

remotestatus [*filename*]
> Show status of the remote machine, or, if *filename* is specified, *filename* on remote machine.

rename [*from*] [*to*]
> Rename file *from* on remote machine to *to*.

reset
> Clear reply queue.

restart *marker*
> Restart the transfer of a file from a particular byte count.

rmdir [*directory-name*]
> Delete a directory on the remote machine.

runique
> Toggle storing of files on the local system with unique filenames. When this option is on, rename files as .1 or .2, etc., as appropriate, to preserve unique filenames, and report each such action. Default value is off.

send *local-file* [*remote-file*]
> Synonym for **put**.

sendport
> Toggle the use of **PORT** commands.

site [*command*]
> Get/set site-specific information from/on remote machine.

size *filename*
> Return size of *filename* on remote machine.

status
> Show current status of **ftp**.

struct [*struct-name*]
> Set the file transfer structure to *struct-name*. By default, **stream** structure is used.

sunique
> Toggle storing of files on remote machine under unique filenames.

system
> Show type of operating system running on remote machine.

→

ftp ←	**tenex**	Set file transfer type to that needed to talk to TENEX machines.
	trace	Toggle packet tracing.
	type [*type-name*]	
		Set file transfer **type** to *type-name*. If no type is specified, the current type is printed. The default type is network ASCII.
	umask [*mask*]	
		Set user file-creation mode mask on the remote site. If mask is omitted, the current value of the mask is printed.
	user *username* [*password*] [*account*]	
		Identify yourself to the remote FTP server. **ftp** will prompt the user for the password, if not specified and the server requires it, and the account field.
	verbose	Toggle verbose mode.
	? [*command*]	
		Same as **help**.

fuser	**fuser** [*options*] *filename* ... [–] **fuser** -*l*

Display the process IDs of all processes that are using particular files or filesystems. The information given can be interpreted in the following way:

c   Current directory

e   Executable

f   Open file; omitted in default display mode

r   Root directory

m   mmap'ed file or shared library

Options

–	Reset options and signal to defaults.
–*signal*	Send *signal* to process. (Default signal is SIGKILL.) **fuser** recognizes signals by name (as listed in **fuser –l**) and number.
–a	Show all specified files, not just those that are being accessed by at least one process.
–k	Terminate all processes accessing the file.

−l	Print a list of signal names; can be used without other arguments.	**fuser**
−m	Expect *filename* to refer to a mounted file system or block device, and list processes on this filesystem.	
−n *space*	Select a different name space (necessary in order to look up processes using TCP and UDP sockets). The name spaces file (filenames, the default), **udp** (local UDP ports), and **tcp** (local TCP ports) are supported. For ports, either the port number or the symbolic name can be specified. If there is no ambiguity, the shortcut notation **name/space** (e.g., **name/proto**) can be used.	
−s	Search silently—i.e., ignore -a, -u, and -v.	
−u	Print names of process owners.	
−v	Verbose: print process ID, user, command, and access fields.	
−V	Display version information.	

---

gawk [*options*] *'script' var=value... files*
gawk [*options*] *-f scriptfile var=value . . . files*

gawk

The GNU version of **awk**, a program that does pattern matching, record processing, and other forms of text manipulation. For more information, see Chapter 11, *The gawk Scripting Language*.

---

getkeycodes

getkeycodes

Print the kernel's scancode-to-keycode mapping table.

---

ghostscript [*options*] [*files*]
gs [*options*] [*files*]

ghostscript

A programming language similar to Adobe Systems' PostScript™ language, used for document processing. If − is used in place of *file*, standard input is used.

Options

−− *filename arg1 ...*
    Take the next argument as a filename, but use all remaining arguments to define ARGUMENTS in userdict (not systemdict) as an array of those strings, before running the file.

→

ghostscript
←

−g*number1*x*number2*
  Specify width and height of device; intended for systems like the X Window System.

−q
  Quiet startup (i.e., suppress normal startup messages, and also do the equivalent of −dQUIET).

−r*number*, −r*number1*x*number2*
  Specify X and Y resolutions (for the benefit of devices, such as printers, that support multiple X and Y resolutions). If only one number is given, it is used for both X and Y resolutions.

−D*name*=*token*, −d*name*=*token*
  Define a name in systemdict with the given definition. The token must be exactly one token (as defined by the token operator) and must not contain any whitespace.

−D*name*, −d*name*
  Define a name in systemdict with a null value.

−I*directories*
  Adds the designated list of directories at the head of the search path for library files.

−S*name*=*string*, −s*name*=*string*
  Define a name in systemdict with a given string as value.

Special names

−dDISKFONTS
  Causes individual character outlines to be loaded from the disk the first time they are encountered.

−dNOBIND Disables the **bind** operator. Useful only for debugging.

−dNOCACHE
  Disables character caching. Useful only for debugging.

−dNODISPLAY
  Suppresses the normal initialization of the output device. May be useful when debugging.

−dNOPAUSE
  Disables the prompt and pause at the end of each page.

−dNOPLATFONTS
  Disables the use of fonts supplied by the underlying platform (e.g., X Windows).

−dSAFER	Disables the *deletefile* and *renamefile* operators, and the ability to open files in any mode other than read-only.

−dWRITESYSTEMDICT
Leaves systemdict writable.

−sDEVICE=*device*
Selects an alternate initial output device.

−sOUTPUTFILE=*filename*
Selects an alternate output file (or pipe) for the initial output device.

---

grep [*options*] *pat* [*files*]

Search one or more *files* for lines that match a regular expression *regexp*. Regular expressions are described in Chapter 6, *Pattern Matching*. Exit status is 0 if any lines match, 1 if none match, and 2 for errors. See also **egrep** and **fgrep**.

Options

−*num*	Print *num* leading and trailing lines of context, but never print any given line more than once.

−b, −−byte-offset
Print the byte offset within the input file before each line of output.

−c, −−count
Print only a count of matched lines. With −v or −−revert-match option, count non-matching lines.

−e *pattern*, **−−regexp=***pattern*
Search for *pattern*. The −e option is useful in protecting patterns beginning with a −.

−f *file*, **−−file=***file*
Take a list of patterns from *file*, one per line.

−h, −−no-filename
Print matched lines but not filenames (inverse of −l).

−i, −−ignore-case
Ignore uppercase and lowercase distinctions.

−l, −−files-with-matches
List the names of files with matches, but not individual matched lines; scanning per file stops on the first match.

→

grep

←

−n, −−line-number

> Print lines and their line numbers.

−q, −−quiet

> Suppress normal output in favor of quiet mode; the scanning will stop on the first match.

−s, −−silent

> Suppress error messages about nonexistent or unreadable files.

−u, −−unix-byte-offsets

> Report Unix-style byte offsets. This option produces Unix-style results in DOS and Windows environments; must be used with **−b**.

−v, −−revert-match

> Print all lines that *don't* match *pattern*.

−w, −−word-regexp

> Match on whole words only. Words are divided by characters that are not letters, digits, or underscores.

−x, −−line-regexp

> Print lines only if *pattern* matches the entire line.

−A *num*   Print *num* lines of text that occur before the matching line.

−B *num*   Print *num* lines of text that occur after the matching line.

−C, −−context

> Print two lines of leading and trailing context. Same as **−2**.

−E   Parse pattern as extended regular expression. Similar to **egrep**. Treat ?, +, {, |, (, and) as special characters, even when they are not escaped.

−F   Same as **fgrep**.

−G   Default. Parse pattern as regular expression; i.e., do not extend special meaning to the characters ?, +, {, |, (, and), unless they are escaped with a \.

−L, −−files-without-match

> List files that contain no matching lines.

−U, −−binary

> Treat the file(s) as binary; only supported in DOS and Windows.

−V, −−version Print the version number to standard error.	**grep**

Examples

List the number of users who use *tcsh*:

```
grep -c /bin/tcsh /etc/passwd
```

List header files that have at least one **#include** directive:

```
grep -l '^#include' /usr/include/*
```

List files that don't contain *pattern*:

```
grep -c pattern files | grep :0
```

groff [*options*] [*files*] **troff** [*options*] [*files*]	**groff**

Front end to the **groff** document formatting system, which normally runs **troff** along with a postprocessor appropriate for the selected device. Options without arguments can be grouped after a single dash (-). A filename of − denotes standard input.

Devices

ascii	Typewriter-like device
dvi	TEX dvi format
latin1	Typewriter-like devices using the ISO Latin-1 character set
ps	PostScript
X75	75 dpi X11 previewer
X100	100 dpi X11 previewer
lj4	HP LaserJet4-compatible (or other PCL5-compatible) printer

Options

The following options are the same as for **troff**: −a, −b, −dcs, −i, −ffam, −mname, −olist, −nnum, −rcn, −wname, −C, −E, −Fdir, −Mdir, −Wname. **groff** also recognizes the following options:

−e	Preprocess with **eqn**.
−h	Print a help message.
−p	Preprocess with **pic**.
−s	Preprocess with **soelim**.

→

groff		
←	**−t**	Preprocess with **tbl**.
	−R	Preprocess with **refer**.
	−v	Make programs run by **groff** print out their version number.
	−V	Print the pipeline on stdout instead of executing it.
	−z	Suppress **troff** output (except error messages).
	−Z	Do not postprocess **troff** output. Normally **groff** automatically runs the appropriate postprocessor.
	−Parg	Pass *arg* to the postprocessor. Each argument should be passed with a separate **−P** option.
	−l	Send the output to a printer (as specified by the print command in the device description file).
	−Larg	Pass *arg* to the spooler. Each argument should be passed with a separate **−L** option.
	−Tdev	Prepare output for device *dev*; the default is **ps**.
	−N	Don't allow newlines with **eqn** delimiters; equivalent to **eqn**'s **−N** option.
	−S	Use safer mode (i.e., pass the **−S** option to **pic** and use the **−msafer** macros with **troff**).

Environment variables

GROFF_COMMAND_PREFIX
> If set to be X, **groff** will run **Xtroff** instead of **troff**.

GROFF_FONT_PATH
> Colon-separated list of directories in which to search for the *devname* directory.

GROFF_TMAC_PATH
> Colon-separated list of directories in which to search for the macro files.

GROFF_TMPDIR
> If set, temporary files will be created in this directory; otherwise, they will be created in TMPDIR (if set) or */tmp* (if TMPDIR is not set).

GROFF_TYPESETTER Default device. PATH Search path for commands that **groff** executes.	**groff**

groups [*user*]

Show the groups that *user* belongs to (default is your group).
Groups are listed in **/etc/passwd** and **/etc/group**.

groups

gzexe [*options*] [*file*]

gzexe

Compress executables. When run, these files will automatically
uncompress, thus trading time for space. **gzexe** creates backup
files (*filename~*) which should be removed after testing the original.

Option

    −d   Decompress files.

gzip [*options*] [*files*]
gunzip [*options*] [*files*]
zcat [*options*] [*files*]

gzip

Compress specified files (or read from standard input)
with Lempel-Ziv coding (LZ77). Rename compressed file
to *filename.gz*; keep ownership modes and access/modifi-
cation times. Ignore symbolic links. Uncompress with **gunzip**, which takes all of **gzip**'s options, except those
specified. **zcat** is identical to **gunzip** −c, and takes the
options −fhLV described below. Files compressed with the
compress command can be decompressed using these
commands.

Options

    −a, −−ascii Ascii text mode: convert end-of-lines using
                  local conventions. This option is supported
                  only on some non-Unix systems.

    −c, −−stdout, −−to-stdout
                  Print output to standard output, and do not
                  change input files.

    −d, −−decompress, −−uncompress
                  Same as **gunzip**.

    −f, −−force Force compression. **gzip** would normally
                  prompt for permission to continue when the
                  file has multiple links, its **.gz** version already

→

exists, or it is reading compressed data to or from a terminal.

-h --help Display a help screen and exit.

-l, --list Expects to be given compressed files as arguments. Files may be compressed by any of the following methods: **gzip, deflate, compress, lzh,** and **pack.** For each file, list uncompressed and compressed sizes (the latter being always -1 for files compressed by programs other than **gzip**), compression ratio, and uncompressed name. With **-v,** also print compression method, the 32-bit CRC of the uncompressed data, and the time stamp. With **-N,** look inside the file for the uncompressed name and time stamp.

-n, --no-name

When compressing, do not save the original filename and time stamp by default. When decompressing, do not restore the original filename if present, and do not restore the original time stamp if present. This option is the default when decompressing.

-q, --quiet

Print no warnings.

-r, --recursive

When given a directory as an argument, recursively compress or decompress files within it.

-t, --test Test compressed file integrity.

-v, --verbose

Print name and percent size reduction for each file.

-L, --license

Display the **gzip** license and quit.

-N, --name

Default. Save original name and time stamp. When decompressing, restore original name and time stamp.

-S *suffix,* **--suffix** *suffix*

Append *.suffix.* Default is **gz.** A null suffix while decompressing causes **gunzip** to attempt to decompress all specified files, regardless of suffix.

-V, --version

Display the version number and compilation options then exit.

−*n*, −−**fast**, −−**best**

 Regulate the speed of compression using the specified digit *n*, where −**1** or −−**fast** indicates the fastest compression method (less compression) and −**9** or −−**best** indicates the slowest compression method (most compression). The default compression level is −**6**.

gzip

---

head [*options*] [*files*]

head

Print the first few lines (default is 10) of one or more *files*. With no *files* defined or a − for *files*, read from standard input. With more than one file, print a header for each file.

Options

−**c** *num*[bkm], −−**bytes** *num*

 Print first *num* bytes; or, if *num* is followed by **b**, **k**, or **m**, first *num* 512-byte blocks, 1-kilobyte blocks, or 1-megabyte blocks.

−−**help** Display help and exit.

−**n** *num*, −−**lines** *num*

 Print first *num* lines. Default is 10.

−**q**, −−**quiet**, −−**silent**

 Quiet mode; never print headers giving filenames.

−**v**, −−**verbose**

 Print filename headers, even for only one file.

−−**version** Output version information and exit.

Examples

Display the first 20 lines of **phone_list**:

```
head -20 phone_list
```

Display the first ten phone numbers having a 202 area code:

```
grep '(202)' phone_list | head
```

---

hostid [−*v*] [*id*]

hostid

Print the ID number of the host. By default, the hexadecimal value is printed. With the −**v** option, the decimal value is printed, followed by the hexadecimal value in parentheses. The super-user may set the host ID by providing its decimal value.

hostname	**hostname** [*option*] [*nameofhost*]
	Set or print name of current host system. A privileged user can set the hostname with the *nameofhost* argument.
	Option
	−a, −−alias Display the alias name of the host (if used).
	−d, −−domain
	Print DNS domain name.
	−f, −−fqdn, −−long
	Print fully qualified domain name.
	−h, −−help Print a usage message and exit.
	−i, −−ip-address
	Display the IP address(es) of the host.
	−s, −−short Trim domain information from the printed name.
	−v, −−verbose
	Verbose mode.
	−y, −−yp, −−nis
	Display the NIS domain name.
	−F *file*, **−−file** *file*
	Consult *file* for hostname.
	−V, −−version
	Print version information and then exit.
id	**id** [*options*] [*username*]
	Display information about yourself, or another user: user ID, group ID, effective user ID and group ID if relevant, and additional group IDs.
	Options
	−g, −−group
	Print group ID only.
	−n, −−name
	With −u, −g, or −G, print user or group name, not number.
	−r, −−real With −u, −g, or −G, print real, not effective, user ID or group ID.
	−u, −−user Print user ID only.
	−G, −−groups
	Print supplementary groups only.

info [*options*] [*topics*]   '

GNU hypertext reader: displays online documentation previously
built from texinfo input. Info files are arranged in a hierarchy
and can contain menus for subtopics. When entered without
options, the command displays the top-level info file (usually
/usr/local/info/dir). When *topics* are specified, finds a subtopic
by choosing the first *topic* from the menu in the top-level info
file, the next *topic* from the new menu specified by the first
topic, and so on. The initial display can also be controlled by the
−f and −n options.

Options

 −d *directories*, −−directory *directories*
> Search *directories*, a colon-separated list, for
> info files. If this option is not specified, use the
> INFOPATH environment variable or the default
> directory (usually */usr/local/info*).

 −−dribble *file*
> Store each keystroke in *file*, which can be used
> in a future session with the −−restore option to
> return to this place in info.

 −f *file*, −−file *file*
> Display specified info file.

 −n *node*, −−node *node*
> Display specified node in the info file.

 −o *file*, −−output *file*
> Copy output to *file* instead of displaying it at
> the screen.

 −−help   Display brief help.

 −−restore *file*
> When starting, execute keystrokes in *file*.

 −−subnodes
> Display subtopics.

 −−version   Display version.

---

ispell [*options*] [*files*]

Compare the words of one or more named *files* with the system
dictionary. Display unrecognized words on the top of the
screen, accompanied by possible correct spellings, and allow
editing, via a series of commands.

→

ispell
←

Options

−b	Back up original file in *filename*.bak.
−d *file*	Search *file* instead of standard dictionary file.
−m	Suggest different root/affix combinations.
−n	Expect nroff or troff input file.
−p *file*	Search *file* instead of personal dictionary file.
−t	Expect TEX or LATEX input file.
−w *chars*	Consider *chars* to be legal, in addition to a–z and A–Z.
−x	Do not back up original file.
−B	Search for missing blanks (resulting in concatenated words) in addition to ordinary misspellings.
−C	Do not produce error messages in response to concatenated words.
−L *number*	Show *number* lines of context.
−M	List interactive commands at bottom of screen.
−N	Suppress printing of interactive commands.
−P	Do not attempt to suggest more root/affix combinations.
−S	Sort suggested replacements by likelihood that each is correct.
−T *type*	Expect all files to be formatted by *type*.
−W *n*	Never consider words that are *n* characters or less to be misspelled.
−V	Use hat notation (^L) to display control characters, and M- to display characters with the high bit set.

Interactive Commands

?	Display help screen.
space character	
	Accept the word in this instance.
number	Replace with suggested word corresponding to *number*.
!*command*	Invoke shell and execute *command* in it. Prompt before exiting.
a	Accept word as correctly spelled, but do not add it to personal dictionary.

i	Accept word and add it (capitalized, if so in file) to personal dictionary.	**ispell**
l	Search system dictionary for words.	
q	Exit without saving.	
r	Replace word.	
u	Accept word and add lowercase version of it to personal dictionary.	
x	Skip to the next file, saving changes.	
^L	Redraw screen.	
^Z	Suspend **ispell**.	

kbd_mode [*option*]   **kbd_mode**

Print or set current keyboard mode, which may be RAW, MEDI-UMRAW, or XLATE.

Options

−a	Set mode to XLATE (ASCII mode).
−k	Set mode to MEDIUMRAW (keycode mode).
−s	Set mode to RAW (scancode mode).
−u	Set mode to UNICODE (UTF-8 mode).

kill [*option*] *IDs*   **kill**

Send a signal to terminate one or more process *IDs*. You must own the process or be a privileged user. If no signal is specified, TERM is sent. This command is similar to the **kill** built into **bash** and other shells.

Options

−l	List all signals.
−p	Print the process ID of the named process, but don't send it a signal.
−*signal*	The signal number (from */usr/include/sys/signal.h*) or name (from **kill −l**). With a signal number of 9 (HUP), the kill cannot be caught by the process. The default is TERM.

killall [*options*] [*name*]   **killall**

Kill processes by name. If more than one process is running the specified command, kill all of them. Treat command names that contain a / as files: kill all processes that are executing that file.

→

killall ←	*Options*

    -signal   Send *signal* to process (default is TERM). *signal* may be a name or number.

    -e   Require an exact match to kill very long names (i.e., longer than 15 characters). Normally, **killall** will kill everything that matches within the first 15 characters. With **-e**, such entries are skipped. (**-v** specifies a message be printed for each skipped entry.)

    -i   Prompt for confirmation before killing processes.

    -l   List possible signal names.

    -q   Quiet; do not complain of processes not killed.

    -v   Verbose: after killing process, report success and process ID.

    -w   Wait for all killed processes to die. Note that **killall** may wait forever if the signal was ignored, had no effect, or if the process stays in zombie state.

---

killall5

killall5

The System V equivalent of **killall**, this command kills all processes except those on which it depends.

---

less

less [*options*] [*filename*]

less is a program for paging through files or other output. It was written in reaction to the perceived primitiveness of **more** (hence its name). Some commands may be preceded by a number.

Options

    -[z]*num*   Set number of lines to scroll to *num*. Default is one screenful. A negative *num* sets the number to *num* lines less than the current number.

    +[+]*command*
            Run *command* on startup. If *command* is a number, jump to that line. The option **++** applies this command to each file in the command-line list.

    -?   Print help screen. Ignore all other options; do not page through file.

-a	When searching, begin after last line displayed. (Default is to search from second line displayed.)
-b*buffers*	Use *buffers* buffers for each file (default is 10). Buffers are 1 kilobyte in size.
-c	Redraw screen from top, not bottom.
-d	Suppress dumb-terminal error messages.
-e	Automatically exit after reaching *EOF* twice.
-f	Force opening of directories and devices; do not print warning when opening binaries.
-g	Highlight only string found by past search command, not all matching strings.
-h*num*	Never scroll backward more than *num* lines at once.
-i	Make searches case-insensitive, unless the search string contains uppercase letters.
-j*num*	Position "target" line on *num*th line of screen. "Target" line can be the result of a search or a jump. Count lines beginning from 1 (top line). A negative *num* is counted back from bottom of screen.
-k*file*	Read *file* to define special key bindings.
-m	Display **more**-like prompt, including percent of file read.
-n	Do not calculate line numbers. Affects **-m** and **-M** options, and **=** and **v** commands (disables passing of line number to editor).
-o*file*	When input is from a pipe, copy output to *file* as well as to screen. (Prompt for overwrite authority if *file* exists.)
-p*pattern*	At startup, search for first occurrence of *pattern*.
m	Set medium prompt (specified by **-m**).
M	Set long prompt (specified by **-M**).
=	Set message printed by **=** command.
-q	Disable ringing of bell on attempts to scroll past *EOF* or before beginning of file. Attempt to use visual bell instead.
-r	Display "raw" control characters, instead of using ^*x* notation. Sometimes leads to display problems.

→

less	**−s**	Print successive blank lines as one line.
←	**−t**tag	Edit file containing tag. Consult ./tags (constructed by **ctags**).
	−u	Treat backspaces and carriage returns as printable input.
	−w	Print lines after EOF as blanks instead of tildes (~).
	−xn	Set tab stops to every n characters. Default is 8.
	−yn	Never scroll forward more than n lines at once.
	−B	Do not automatically allocate buffers for data read from a pipe. If −b specifies a number of buffers, allocate that many. If necessary, allow information from previous screens to be lost.
	−C	Redraw screen by clearing it and then redrawing from top.
	−E	Automatically exit after reaching EOF once.
	−G	Never highlight matching search strings.
	−I	Make searches case-insensitive, even when the search string contains uppercase letters.
	−M	Prompt more verbosely than with -m, including percentage, line number, and total lines.
	−N	Print line number before each line.
	−Ofile	Similar to −o, but does not prompt when overwriting file.
	−P[m,M,=]prompt	
		Set prompt (as defined by −m, −M, or =). Default is short prompt (-m).
	−Q	Never ring terminal bell.
	−S	Cut, do not fold, long lines.
	−Tfile	With the −t option or :t command, read file instead of ./tags.
	−U	Treat backspaces and carriage returns as control characters.
	−X	Do not send initialization and deinitialization strings from termcap to terminal.

Commands

Commands can be preceded by an argument.

SPACE, ^V, f, ^F

Scroll forward the default number of lines (usually one windowful).

z	Similar to SPACE, but allows the number of lines to be specified, in which case it resets the default to that number.

RETURN, ^N, e, ^E, j, ^J
> Scroll forward, a default of one line. Display all lines, even if the default is more lines than the screen size.

d, ^D	Scroll forward, a default of one half the screen size. The number of lines may be specified, in which case the default is reset.
b, ^B, ESC-v	Scroll backward, a default of one windowful.
w	Like **b**, but allows the number of lines to be specified, in which case it resets the default to that number.

y, ^Y, ^P, k, ^K
> Scroll backward, a default of 1 line. Display all lines, even if the default is more lines than the screen size.

u, ^U	Scroll backward, a default of one half the screen size. The number of lines may be specified, in which case the default is reset.
r, ^R, ^L	Redraw screen.
R	Like **r**, but discard buffered input.
F	Scroll forward. When an *EOF* is reached, continue trying to find more output, behaving similarly to **tail −f**.
g, <, ESC-<	Skip to a line, default 1.
G, >, ESC->	Skip to a line, default being the last one.
p, %	Prompt for a number between 0 and 100; then skip to a position *number* percent of the way into the file.
{	If the top line on the screen includes a {, find its matching }. If the top line contains multiple {, prompt for a number to determine which one to use in finding a match.
}	If the bottom line on the screen includes a }, find its matching {. If the bottom line contains multiple }, prompt for a number to determine which one to use in finding a match.
(	If the top line on the screen includes a (, find its matching). If the top line contains multiple (, prompt for a number to determine which one to use in finding a match.

→

less
←

)	If the bottom line on the screen includes a), find its matching (. If the bottom line contains multiple), prompt for a number to determine which one to use in finding a match.
[	If the top line on the screen includes a [, find its matching]. If the top line contains multiple [, prompt for a number to determine which one to use in finding a match.
]	If the bottom line on the screen includes a], find its matching [. If the bottom line contains multiple], prompt for a number to determine which one to use in finding a match.
ESC-^F	Behaves like {, but prompts for two characters, which it substitutes for { and } in its search.
ESC-^B	Behaves like }, but prompts for two characters, which it substitutes for { and } in its search.
m	Prompts for a lowercase letter, and then uses that letter to mark the current position.
'	Prompts for a lowercase letter, and then goes to the position marked by that letter. There are some special characters.
'	Return to position before last "large movement."
^	Beginning of file.
$	End of file.
^X^X	Same as '.
/pattern	Find next occurrence of *pattern*, starting at second line displayed. Some special characters can be entered before *pattern*.
!	Find lines that do not contain *pattern*.
*	If current file does not contain *pattern*, continue through the rest of the files in the command line list.
@	Search from the first line in the first file specified on the command line, no matter what the screen currently displays.
?pattern	Search backwards, beginning at the line before the top line. Treats !, *, and @ as special characters when they begin *pattern*, as / does.
ESC-/pattern	Same as /*.

ESC-?*pattern*
　　　　　　　Same as ?*.

n　　　　　　Repeat last *pattern* search.

N　　　　　　Repeat last *pattern* search, in the reverse direc-
　　　　　　　tion.

ESC-n　　　　Repeat previous search command, but as
　　　　　　　though it were prefaced by *.

ESC-N　　　　Repeat previous search command, but as
　　　　　　　though it were prefaced by *, and in the oppo-
　　　　　　　site direction.

ESC-u　　　　Toggle search highlighting.

:e [*filename*]
　　　　　　　Read in *filename* and insert it into the com-
　　　　　　　mand-line list of filenames. Without *filename*,
　　　　　　　re-read the current file. *filename* may contain
　　　　　　　special characters.

　　% Name of current file

　　# Name of previous file

^X^V, E　　　Same as :e.

:n　　　　　　Read in next file in command-line list.

:p　　　　　　Read in previous file in command-line list.

:x　　　　　　Read in first file in command-line list.

:f, =, ^G　　　Print filename, position in command-line list,
　　　　　　　line number on top of window, total lines, byte
　　　　　　　number, and total bytes.

−　　　　　　 Expects to be followed by a command-line
　　　　　　　option letter. Toggles the value of that option,
　　　　　　　or, if appropriate, prompts for its new value.

−+　　　　　　Expects to be followed by a command-line
　　　　　　　option letter. Resets that option to its default.

−−　　　　　　Expects to be followed by a command-line
　　　　　　　option letter. Resets that option to the opposite
　　　　　　　of its default, where "opposite" can be deter-
　　　　　　　mined.

−　　　　　　 Expects to be followed by a command-line
　　　　　　　option letter. Display that option's current set-
　　　　　　　ting.

+*cmd*　　　　Execute *cmd* each time a new file is read in.

q, :q, :Q, ZZ
　　　　　　　Exit.

→

v   Not valid for all versions. Invoke editor specified by $VISUAL or $EDITOR, or vi.

!   Not valid for all versions. Invoke $SHELL or sh. If *command* is given, run it and exit. Special characters:

%   Name of current file

Name of previous file

!!   Last shell command

| <*mark-letter*> *command*
     Not valid for all versions. Pipe fragment of file (from first line on screen to *mark-letter*) to *command. mark-letter* may also be:

^   Beginning of file

$ End of file

., newline
     Current screen is piped

Prompts

The prompt interprets certain sequences specially. Those beginning with % are always evaluated. Those beginning with ? are evaluated if certain conditions are true. Some prompts determine the position of particular lines on the screen. These sequences require that a method of determining that line be specified. There are five possibilities:

t   top of the screen

m   middle of the screen

b   bottom of the screen

B   line after the bottom of the screen

j   "target" line

%b{t,m,b,B,j}
     The byte offset into the file.

%B   Size of current file.

%E   Name of editor.

%f   Current file.

%i   Position of current file in command-line list.

%l{t,m,b,B,j}
     Line number in file of a specific line on screen.

%L   Line number of last line in current file.

%m	Total number of lines in all files.
%p{t,m,b,B,j}	
	Percent into current input file.
%s	Same as %B.
%t	Remove trailing spaces.
%x	Next input file in command-line list.
?a	True if prompt so far is nonnull.
?b{t,m,b,B,j}	
	True if specified line's byte offset can be determined.
?B	True if current file's size can be determined.
?e	True if *EOF* has been reached.
?f	True if reading from a file, not a pipe.
?l{t,m,b,B,j}	True if line number can be determined.
?L	True if final line number can be determined.
?m	True if there are multiple input files.
?n	True if this is the first prompt in the current file.
?p{t,m,b,B,j}	
	True if percent into current file can be determined.
?s	Same as ?B.
?x	True if current file is not the last one.

ln [*options*] *sourcename* [*destname*]
ln [*options*] *sourcenames destdirectory*

Create pseudonyms (links) for files, allowing them to be accessed by different names. In the first form, link *sourcename* to *destname*, where *destname* is usually a new filename, or (by default) the current directory. If *destname* is an existing file, it is overwritten; if *destname* is an existing directory, a link named *sourcename* is created in that directory. In the second form, create links in *destdirectory*, each link having the same name as the file specified.

Options

−b, −−backup
> Back up files before removing the originals.

−d, −F, −−directory
> Allow hard links to directories. Available to privileged users.

→

ln
←
	−f, −−force Force the link to occur (don't prompt for over-write permission).
	
	−−help Print a usage message and then exit.
	
	−i, −−interactive
	Prompt for permission before removing files.
	
	−n, −−no-dereference
	Replace symbolic links to directories instead of dereferencing them. **−−force** is useful with this option.
	
	−s, −−symbolic
	Create a symbolic link. This lets you link across file systems and also see the name of the link when you run **ls −l** (otherwise there's no way to know the name that a file is linked to).
	
	−v, −−verbose
	Verbose mode.
	
	−−version Print version information and then exit.
	
	−S *suffix*, **−−suffix** *suffix*
	Append *suffix* to files when making backups, instead of the default ˜.
	
	−V, −−version-control {numbered,existing,simple}
	Control the types of backups made.
	
	  t, numbered
	  Numbered
	
	  nil, existing
	  Simple (˜) unless a numbered backup exists; then make a numbered backup.
	
	  never, simple
	  Simple

locate	**locate** [*options*] *pattern*
	
	Search database(s) of filenames and print matches. *, ?, [, and] are treated specially; / and . are not. Matches include all files that contain *pattern*, unless *pattern* includes metacharacters, in which case **locate** requires an exact match.
	
	Option
	
	  −d *path*, **−−database=***path*
	    Search databases in *path*. *path* must be a colon-separated list.

--help	Print a usage message and then exit.	locate
--version	Print version information and then exit.	

lockfile [*options*] *filename*

lockfile

Create semaphore file(s), used to limit access to a file. When **lockfile** fails to create some of the specified files, it pauses for 8 seconds and tries the last one on which it failed. The command processes flags as they are encountered (i.e., a flag that is specified after a file will not affect that file).

Options

-*sleeptime* Time **lockfile** waits before retrying to create file it failed to. Default is 8 seconds.

-! Invert return value.

-l *lockout_time*
  Time (in seconds) after a lockfile was last modified at which it will be removed by force. See also -s

-m [l | u] If the permissions on the system mail spool directory allow it, or if **lockfile** is suitably setgid, it will be able to lock and unlock your system mailbox by using the options -**ml** and -**mu** respectively.

-r *retries* Stop trying to create *files* after *retries* retries. The default is -1 (never stop trying). When giving up, remove all created files.

-s *suspend_time*
  After a lockfile has been removed by force (see -l), a suspension of 16 seconds takes place by default. (This is intended to prevent the inadvertent immediate removal of any lockfile newly created by another program.) Use -s to change the default 16 seconds.

login [*name* | *option*]

login

Log in to the system. **login** asks for a username (*name* can be supplied on the command line), and password (if appropriate).

If successful, **login** updates accounting files, sets various environment variables, notifies users if they have mail, and executes startup shell files.

No user except **root** is able to log in when */etc/nologin* exists. That file will be displayed before the connection is terminated. **root** may connect only on a tty that is included in */etc/securetty*.

→

login
←
	If `~/.hushlogin` exists, execute a quiet login. If */var/adm/lastlog* exists, print the time of the last login.
	
	Options
	
	    -f Suppress second login authentication.
	
	    -h *host* Specify name of remote host. Normally used by servers, not humans; may be used only by **root**.
	
	    -p Preserve previous environment.

logname	**logname**
	
	Consult */etc/utmp* for user's login name. If found, print it; otherwise, exit with an error message.
	
	Options
	
	    --help Print a usage message and then exit.
	
	    --version Print version information and then exit.

look	**look** [*options*] *string* [*file*]
	
	Search for lines in *file* (*/usr/dict/words* by default) that begin with *string*.
	
	Options
	
	    -a Use alternate dictionary */usr/dict/web2*.
	
	    -d Compare only alphanumeric characters.
	
	    -f Search is not case-sensitive.
	
	    -t *character*
	              Examine only characters up to and including *character*.

lpq	**lpq** [*options*] [*name*] Check the print spool queue for status of print jobs. For each job, display username, rank in the queue, filenames, job number, and total file size (in bytes). If *name* is specified, display information only for that user. *Options* **-P***printer* Specify which printer to query. Without this option, *lpq* uses the default system printer or the printer set in the PRINTER environment variable.

−l	Print information about each file comprising a job.	lpq
#num	Check status for a particular job number.	

lpr [options] files

Send files to the printer spool queue.

Options

−c	Expect data produced by cifplot.
−d	Expect data produced by TEX in the DVI (device-independent) format.
−f	Use a filter that interprets the first character of each line as a standard carriage control character.
−g	Expect standard plot data as produced by the plot routines.
−l	Use a filter that allows control characters to be printed and suppresses page breaks.
−n	Expect data from ditroff (device-independent troff).
−p	Use pr to format the files (equivalent to print).
−t	Expect data from troff (cat phototypesetter commands).
−v	Expect a raster image for devices like the Benson Varian.
−Pprinter	Output to printer.
−h	Do not print the burst page.
−m	Mail on completion.
−r	Remove the file upon completion of spooling or printing (with the −s option).
−s	Use symbolic links instead of copying files to the spool directory. This can save time and disk space for large files. Files should not be modified or removed until they have been printed.
−#num	Print num copies of listed files.
−C string	Replace system name on the burst page with string.
−J string	Replace the printed file's name on the burst page with string.

→

lpr	−T *title*	Use *title* as the title name when using **pr**.
←	−i [*cols*]	Indent the output. Default is 8 columns. Specify number of columns to indent with the *cols* argument.
	−w *num*	Set *num* characters as the page width for **pr**.

lprm

lprm [*options*] [*jobnum*] [*user*]

Remove a print job from the print spool queue. You must specify a job number or numbers, which can be obtained from **lpq**. A privileged user may use the *user* parameter to remove all files belonging to a particular user or users.

Options

    −P*printer*   Specify printer name. Normally, the default printer or printer specified in the PRINTER environment variable is used.

    −   Remove all jobs in the spool owned by *user.*

ls

ls [*options*] [*names*]

List contents of directories. If no *names* are given, list the files in the current directory. With one or more *names*, list files contained in a directory *name* or that match a file *name*. *names* can include filename metacharacters. The options let you display a variety of information in different formats. The most useful options include −F, −R, −l, and −s. Some options don't make sense together; e.g., −u and −c.

Options

    −1, −−format=single-column
        Print one entry per line of output.

    −a   List all files, including the normally hidden files whose names begin with a period.

    −b, −−escape
        Display nonprinting characters in octal and alphabetic format.

    −c, −−time-ctime, −−time=status
        List files by status change time (not creation/modification time).

    −−color, −−colour, −−color=yes, −−colour=yes
        Colorize the names of files depending on the type of file.

--color=no, --colour=no
> Disables colorization. This is the default. Provided to override a previous color option.

--color=tty, --colour=tty
> Same as **--color**, but only if standard output is a terminal. Very useful for shell scripts and command aliases, especially if your favorite pager does not support color control codes.

-d, --directory
> Report only on the directory, not its contents.

-f
> Print directory contents in exactly the order in which they are stored, without attempting to sort them.

--full-time List times in full, rather than using the standard abbreviations.

--help Print a usage message and then exit.

-i, --inode
> List the inode for each file.

-k, --kilobytes
> If file sizes are being listed, print them in kilobytes. This option overrides the environment variable POSIXLY_CORRECT.

-l, --format=long, --format=verbose
> Long format listing (includes permissions, owner, size, modification time, etc.).

-m, --format=commas
> Merge the list into a comma-separated series of names.

-n, --numeric-uid-gid
> Like **-l**, but use group ID and user ID numbers instead of owner and group names.

-p Mark directories by appending **/** to them.

-q, --hide-control-chars
> Show nonprinting characters as **?**.

-r, --reverse
> List files in reverse order (by name or by time).

-s, --size Print size of the files in blocks.

-t, --sort=time
> Sort files according to modification time (newest first).

$\rightarrow$

−u, −−time=atime, −−time=access, −−time=use
> Sort files according to the file access time.

−−version Print version information on standard output, then exit.

−x, −−format=across, −−format=horizontal
> List files in rows going across the screen.

−A, −−almost-all
> List all files, including the normally hidden files whose names begin with a period. Does not include . and ..

−B, −−ignore-backups
> Do not list files ending in ˜, unless given as arguments.

−C, −−format=vertical
> List files in columns (the default format).

−F, −−classify
> Flag filenames by appending **/** to directories, * to executable files, @ to symbolic links, | to FIFOs, and = to sockets.

−G, −−no-group
> In long format, do not display group name.

−I, −−ignore *pattern*
> Do not list files whose names match the shell pattern *pattern*, unless they are given on the command line.

−L, −−dereference
> List the file or directory referenced by a symbolic link rather than the link itself.

−N, −−literal
> Do not list filenames.

−Q, −−quote-name
> Quote filenames with **"**; quote nongraphic characters with alphabetic and octal backslash sequences.

−R, −−recursive
> Recursively list subdirectories as well as the specified (or current) directory.

−S, −−sort=size
> Sort by file size, largest to smallest.

−T, −−tabsize *n_cols*
> Assume that each tabstop is *n_cols* columns wide. The default is 8.

−U, −−sort=none
> Do not sort files. Similar to −f, but displays in
> long format.

−X, −−sort=extension
> Sort by file extension.

Examples

List all files in the current directory and their sizes; use multiple
columns and mark special files:

```
ls -asCF
```

List the status of directories /bin and /etc:

```
ls -ld /bin /etc
```

List C source files in the current directory, the oldest first:

```
ls -rt *.c
```

Count the files in the current directory:

```
ls | wc -1
```

lsattr [options] [files]

lsattr

Print attributes of files on a Linux Second Extended File System.
See also **chattr**.

Options

−a
> List all files in specified directories.

−d
> List directories' attributes, not the attributes of
> the contents.

−R
> List directories and their contents recursively.

−v
> List version of files.

mail [options] [users]

mail

Read mail or send mail to other *users*. The **mail** utility allows
you to compose, send, receive, forward, and reply to mail. **mail**
has two main modes: compose mode, where you create a message; and command mode, where you manage your mail.

While **mail** is a powerful utility, it can be tricky for a novice
user. Most Linux distributions include **pine** and **elm**, which are
much easier to use.

This section presents **mail** commands, options, and files. To get
you started, here are two of the most basic commands.

→

mail	To enter interactive mail-reading mode, type:
←	

```
mail
```

To begin writing a message to *user*, type:

```
mail user
```

Command-line options

−b *list*	Set blind carbon copy field to comma-separated *list*.
−c *list*	Set carbon copy field to comma-separated *list*.
−f [*file*]	Process contents of *file*, or mbox, instead of */var/spool/mail/$user*.
−i	Do not respond to tty interrupt signals.
−n	Do not consult */etc/mail.rc* when starting up.
−p	Read mail in POP mode.
−s *subject*	Set subject to *subject*.
−u	Process contents of */var/spool/mail/$user*. Default.
−v	Verbose. Print information about mail delivery to standard out.
−I	Interactive—even when standard input has been redirected from the terminal.
−N	When printing a mail message or entering a mail folder, do not display message headers.
−P	Disable POP mode.

Compose-mode commands

˜!	Execute a shell escape from compose mode.
˜?	List compose mode escapes.
˜b*names*	Add names to or edit the *Bcc:* header.
˜c*names*	Add names to or edit the *Cc:* header.
˜d	Read in the *dead.letter* file.
˜e	Invoke text editor.
˜f*messages*	Insert *messages* into message being composed.
˜F*messages*	Similar to ˜f, but include message headers.
˜h	Add to or change all the headers interactively.
˜m*messages*	
	Similar to ˜f, but indent with a tab.

~M*messages*	Similar to ~m, but include message headers.
~p	Print message header fields and message being sent.
~q	Abort current message composition.
~r*filename*	Append file to current message.
~s*string*	Change *Subject:* header to *string*.
~t*names*	Add names to or edit the *To:* list.
~v	Invoke editor specified with the VISUAL environment variable.
~| *command*	Pipe message through *command*.
~:*mail-command*	Execute *mail-command*.
~~*string*	Insert *string* in text of message, prefaced by a single tilde (~). If string contains a ~, it must be escaped with a \.

Command-mode commands

?	List summary of commands (help screen).
!	Execute a shell command.
– *num*	Print *num*th previous message; defaults to immediately previous.
alias (a)	Print or create alias lists.
alternates (alt)	Specify remote accounts on remote machines that are yours. Tells mail not to reply to them.
chdir (c)	**cd** to home or specified directory.
copy (co)	Similar to save, but does not mark message for deletion.
delete (d)	Delete message.
dp	Delete current message and display next one.
edit (e)	Edit message.
exit (ex, x)	Exit mail without updating folder.
file (fi)	Switch folders.
folder (fold)	Read messages saved in a file. Files can be:

#	previous
%	system mailbox
%*user*	*user*'s system mailbox
&	mbox

+*folder*	File in *folder* directory.
folders	List folders.

→

mail

←

headers (h)	List message headers at current prompt.
headers+ (h+)	Move forward one window of headers.
headers- (h-)	Move back one window of headers.
help	Same as ?.
hold (ho)	Hold messages in system mailbox.
ignore	Append list of fields to ignored fields.
mail *user* (m)	Compose message to *user*.
mbox	Default. Move specified messages to mbox on exiting.
next (n)	Type next message, or next message that matches argument.
preserve (pr)	Synonym for **hold**.
print [*list*] (p)	Display each message in *list*.
Print [*list*] (P)	Similar to **print**, but include header fields.
quit (q)	Exit mail and update folder.
reply (r)	Send mail to all on distribution list.
Reply (R)	Send mail to author only.
respond	Same as **reply**.
retain	Always include this list of header fields when printing messages. With no arguments, list retained fields.
save (s)	Save message to folder.
saveignore	Remove ignored fields when saving.
saveretain	Override **saveignore** to retain specified fields.
set (se)	Set or print **mail** options.
shell (sh)	Enter a new shell.
size	Print size of each specified message.
source	Read commands from specified file.
top	Print first few lines of each specified message.
type (t)	Same as **print**.
Type (T)	Same as **Print**.
unalias	Discard previously defined aliases.
undelete (u)	Restore deleted message.
unread (U)	Mark specified messages as unread.
unset (uns)	Unset **mail** options.
visual (v)	Edit message with editor specified by the VISUAL environment vairable.
write (w)	Write message, without header, to file.
xit (x)	Same as **exit**.
z	Move **mail**'s attention to next windowful of text. Use **z-** to move it back.

mail options

These options are used inside of the *.mailrc* file. The syntax is "set *option*" or "unset *option*".

append	Append (do not prepend) messages to mbox.	**mail**
ask	Prompt for subject.	
askbcc	Prompt for blind carbon copy recipients.	
askcc	Prompt for carbon copy recipients.	
asksub	Prompt for **Subject:** line.	
autoprint	Print next message after a delete.	
chron	Display messages in chronological order, most recent last.	
debug	Same as **-d** on command line.	
dot	Interpret a solitary . as an *EOF.*	
folder	Define directory to hold mail folders.	
hold	Keep message in system mailbox upon quitting.	
ignore	Ignore interrupt signals from terminal. Print them as @.	
ignoreeof	Do not treat ^D as an *EOF.*	
metoo	Do not remove sender from groups when mailing to them.	
noheader	Same as **-N** on command line.	
nokerberos	Retrieve POP mail via POP3, not KPOP, protocol.	
nosave	Do not save aborted letters to *dead.letter.*	
pop-mail	Retrieve mail with POP3 protocol, and save it in *mbox.pop.*	
prompt	Set prompt to a different string.	
Replyall	Switch roles of **Reply** and **reply.**	
quiet	Do not print version at startup.	
searchheaders	When given the specifier */x:y,* expand all messages that contain the string *y* in the *x* header field.	
verbose	Same as **-v** on command line.	
verbose-pop	Display status while retrieving POP mail.	

Special files

calendar	Contains reminders that the operating system mails to you.
.maildelivery	Mail delivery configuration file.
.mailrc	Mail configuration file.
triplog	Keeps track of your automatic response recipients.
tripnote	Contains automatic message.

---

man [*options*] [*section*] [*title*]   **man**

Display information from the online reference manuals. **man** locates and prints the named *title* from the designated reference *section.*

$\rightarrow$

Options

−7, −−ascii   Expect a pure ASCII file, and format it for a 7-bit terminal or terminal emulator.

−a, −−all   Show all pages matching *title*.

−b   Leave blank lines in output.

−d, −−debug
Display debugging information. Suppress actual printing of manual pages.

−f, −−whatis
Same as **whatis** command.

−k, −−apropos
Same as **apropos** command.

−l, −−local-file
Search local files, not system files, for manual pages. If **i** is given as *filename*, search standard input.

−m *systems*, **−−systems=***systems*
Search *systems'* manual pages. *systems* should be a comma-separated list.

−p *preprocessors*, **−−preprocessor=***preprocessors*
Preprocess manual pages with *preprocessors* before turning them over to **nroff**, **troff**, or **groff**. Always runs **soelim** first.

−r *prompt*, **−−prompt=***prompt*
Set prompt if **less** is used as pager.

−t, −−troff   Format the manual page with */usr/bin/groff -Tgv -mandoc*. Implied by **−T** and **−Z**.

−u, −−update
Perform a consistency check between manual page cache and filesystem.

−w, −−where, −−location
Print pathnames of entries on standard output.

−D, −−default
Reset all options to their defaults.

−L *locale*, **−−locale=***locale*
Assume current locale to be *locale*; do not consult **setlocale( )**.

−M *path*, **−−manpath=***path*
Search for manual pages in *path*. Ignore **-m** option.

−P*pager*, −−pager=*pager*
> Select paging program *pager* to display the entry.

−T *device*, −−troff-device[=*device*]
> Format **groff** or **troff** output for *device*, such as **dvi**, **latin1**, **X75**, and **X100**.

−Z, −−ditroff
> Do not allow postprocessing of manual page after **groff** has finished formatting it.

Section names

Manual pages are divided into sections, depending on their intended audience.

1	Executable programs or shell commands
2	System calls (functions provided by the kernel)
3	Library calls (functions within system libraries)
4	Special files (usually found in */dev*)
5	File formats and conventions, e.g. */etc/passwd*
6	Games
7	Macro packages and conventions
8	System administration commands (usually only for a privileged user)
9	Kernel routines (nonstandard)

manpath [*options*]

Attempt to determine path to manual pages. Check $MANPATH first; if that is not set, consult */etc/manpath.conf,* user environment variables, and the current working directory.

Options

−q, −−quiet
> Do not print warning messages.

−d, −−debug
> Print debugging information.

−c, −−catpath
> Convert the determined **manpath** to its relative **catpath**.

−g, −−global
> Construct **manpath** from the list of paths that */etc/manpath.conf* designates as global.

→

manpath ←	**−m** *systems*, **−−systems=***systems* Search *systems* for the path.

merge

merge [*options*] *file1 file2 file3*

Perform a three-way file merge. **merge** incorporates all changes that lead from *file2* to *file3* into *file1*. The result ordinarily goes into *file1*. **merge** is useful for combining separate changes to an original. Suppose *file2* is the original, and both *file1* and *file3* are modifications of *file2*. Then merge combines both changes. A conflict occurs if both *file1* and *file3* have changes in a common segment of lines. If a conflict is found, merge normally outputs a warning and puts brackets around the conflict, with lines preceded by <<<<<<< and >>>>>>>. A typical conflict looks like this:

```
<<<<<<< file1
relevant lines from file1
=======
relevant lines from file3
>>>>>>> file3
```

If there are conflicts, the user should edit the result and delete one of the alternatives.

Options

−p	Send results to standard output instead of over-writing *file1*.
−q	Quiet; do not warn about conflicts.
−A	Output conflicts using the −A style of **diff3**, if supported by **diff3**. This merges all changes leading from *file2* to *file3* into *file1*, and generates the most verbose output.
−E	Output conflict information in a less verbose style than −A; this is the default.
−L *label*	Specify up to three labels to be used in place of the corresponding filenames in conflict reports. That is:

```
merge -L x -L y -L z file_a file_b file_c
```

generates output that looks like it came from *x*, *y*, and *z* instead of from *file_a*, *file_b*, and *file_c*.

mesg

mesg [*option*]

Change the ability of other users to send **write** messages to your terminal. With no options, display the permission status.

> n   Forbid **write** messages.
>
> y   Allow **write** messages (the default).

---

mimencode [*options*] [*filename*] [–o *output_file*]   mimencode
mimencode [*options*] [*filename*] [-o *output_file*]

Translate to and from MIME encoding formats, the pro-
posed standard for Internet multimedia mail formats. By
default, **mimencode** reads standard input and sends a
base64-encoded version of the input to standard output.

Options

> –b   Use the (default) base64 encoding.
>
> –o *output_file*
>   Send output to the named file rather than to
>   standard output.
>
> –p   Translate decoded CRLF sequences into the
>   local newline convention during decoding and
>   do the reverse during encoding; only mean-
>   ingful when the default base64 encoding is in
>   effect.
>
> –q   Use the quoted-printable encoding instead of
>   base64.
>
> –u   Decode the standard input rather than encode
>   it.

---

mkdir [*options*] *directories*   mkdir

Create one or more *directories*. You must have write permission
in the parent directory in order to create a directory. See also
rmdir. The default mode of the new directory is 0777, modified
by the system or user's **umask**.

Options

> –m, ––mode *mode*
>   Set the access *mode* for new directories. See
>   **chmod** for an explanation of acceptable for-
>   mats for *mode*.
>
> –p, ––parents
>   Create intervening parent directories if they
>   don't exist.

→

mkdir

←

Examples

Create a read-only directory named **personal**:

```
mkdir -m 444 personal
```

The following sequence:

```
mkdir work; cd work
mkdir junk; cd junk
mkdir questions; cd ../..
```

could be accomplished by typing this:

```
mkdir -p work/junk/questions
```

---

more

more [*options*] [*files*]

Display the named *files* on a terminal, one screenful at a time. See **less** for an alternative to **more**. Some commands can be preceded by a number.

Options

+*num*	Begin displaying at line number *num*.
+/*pattern*	Begin displaying two lines before *pattern*.
−c	Repaint screen from top instead of scrolling.
−d	Display the prompt "Hit space to continue, Del to abort" in reponse to illegal commands; disable bell.
−f	Count logical rather than screen lines. Useful when long lines wrap past the width of the screen.
−l	Ignore formfeed (**CTRL-L**) characters. Cause carriage return to be of the form **CTRL-M**.
−num *number*	Set screen size to *number* lines.
−p	Page through the file by clearing each window instead of scrolling. This is sometimes faster.
−r	Force display of control characters, in the form $\hat{}x$.
−s	Squeeze; display multiple blank lines as one.
−u	Suppress underline characters.

Commands

All commands in **more** are based on **vi** commands. An argument can be entered before many commands.

SPACE	Display next screen of text.
z	Display next *lines* of text, and redefine a screenful to *lines* lines. Default is one screenful.
RETURN	Display next *lines* of text, and redefine a screenful to *lines* lines. Default is one line.
d, ^D	Scroll *lines* of text, and redefine scroll size to *lines* lines. Default is one line.
q, Q, INTERRUPT	Quit.
s	Skip forward one line of text.
f	Skip forward one screen of text.
b, ^B	Skip backward one screen of text.
'	Return to point where previous search began.
=	Print number of current line.
/pattern	Search for *pattern*, skipping to *num*th occurrence if an argument is specified.
n	Repeat last search, skipping to *num*th occurrence if an argument is specified.
!cmd, :!cmd	Invoke shell and execute *cmd* in it.
v	Invoke **vi** editor on the file, at the current line.
^L	Redraw screen.
:n	Skip to next file.
:p	Skip to previous file.
:f	Print current filename and line number.
.	Re-execute previous command.

Examples

Page through *file* in "clear" mode, and display prompts:

```
more -cd file
```

Format *doc* to the screen, removing underlines:

```
nroff doc | more -u
```

View the man page for the **grep** command; begin near the word "BUGS" and compress extra whitespace:

```
man grep | more +/BUGS -s
```

mv	**mv** [*option*] *sources target*

Move or rename files and directories. The source (first column) and target (second column) determine the result (third column):

Source	Target	Result
File	*name* (nonexistent)	Rename file as *name*.
File	Existing file	Overwrite existing file with source file.
Directory	*name* (nonexistent)	Rename directory as *name*.
Directory	Existing directory	Move directory to be a subdirectory of existing directory.
One or more files	Existing directory	Move files to directory.

Options

−b, −−backup
: Back up files before removing.

−f
: Force the move, even if *target* file exists; suppress messages about restricted access modes.

−−help
: Print a usage message and then exit.

−i, −−interactive
: Query user before removing files.

−u, −−update
: Do not remove a file or link if its modification is the same as or newer than its replacement.

−v, −−verbose
: Print the name of each file before moving it.

−−version
: Print version information on standard output then exit.

−S, −−suffix *backup_suffix*
: Override the SIMPLE_BACKUP_SUFFIX environment variable, which determines the suffix used for making simple backup files. If the suffix is not set either way, the default is a tilde (˜).

−V, −−version-control {numbered,existing,simple}
: Override the VERSION_CONTROL environment variable, which determines the type of backups made. If the type is not set in either way, the default is **existing**. The acceptable values for the VERSION_CONTROL environment

variable and the argument to this option are
like the GNU Emacs "version-control" variable:

t, numbered
Always make numbered backups.

nil, existing
Make numbered backups of files that already
have them, simple backups of the others.

never, simple
Always make simple backups.

mv

---

namei [*options*] *pathname* [*pathname . . .*]

namei

Follow a pathname until a terminal point is found (e.g., a file,
directory, char device, etc). If **namei** finds a symbolic link, it
shows the link, and starts following it, indenting the output to
show the context. **namei** prints an informative message when
the maximum number of symbolic links this system can have
has been exceeded.

File type characters

For each line of output, **namei** prints the following characters to
identify the file types found:

–	A regular file
?	An error of some kind
b	A block device
c	A character device
d	A directory
f:	The pathname it's currently trying to resolve
l	A symbolic link (both the link and its contents are output as well)
s	A socket

Options

−m	Show the mode bits of each file type in the style of **ls**; for example: "rwxr-xr-x".
−x	Show mount point directories with a **D**, rather than a **d**.

---

newgrp [*group*]

newgrp

Similar to **login**. Changes user's group identification, by default
to the login group identification.

nice	**nice** [*option*] *command* [*arguments*]
	
	Execute a *command* and *arguments* with lower priority (i.e., be "nice" to other users). Without arguments, print the default scheduling priority (niceness). If **nice** is a child process, it prints the parent process's scheduling priority. Niceness has a range of −20 (highest priority) to 19 (lowest prority).
	
	Option
	
	    −−help Print a usage message and then exit.
	
	    −n *adjustment*, *−adjustment*, **−−adjustment**=*adjustment*
	        Run *command* with niceness incremented by *adjustment* (1–19); default is 10. A privileged user can raise priority by specifying a negative *adjustment* (e.g., −5).
	
	    −−version Print version information and then exit.

nohup	**nohup** *command* [*arguments*] Continue to execute the named *command* and optional command *arguments* after you log out (make command immune to hangups; i.e., **no hangup**). TTY output is appended to the file *nohup.out* by default. Modern shells preserve background commands by default; this command is necessary only in the original Bourne shell.
passwd	**passwd** [*user*] Create or change a password associated with a *user* name. Only the owner or a privileged user may change a password. Owners need not specify their *user* name.

paste	**paste** [*options*] *files*
	
	Merge corresponding lines of one or more *files* into vertical columns, separated by a tab. See also **cut**, **join**, and **pr**.
	
	Options
	
	    − Replace a filename with the standard input.
	
	    −d'*char*' Separate columns with *char* instead of a tab. Note: You can separate columns with different characters by supplying more than one *char*.
	
	    −−help Print a usage message and then exit.

--version   Print version information and then exit.

-s, --serial Merge subsequent lines from one file.

Examples

Create a three-column *file* from files *x*, *y*, and *z*:

```
paste x y z > file
```

List users in two columns:

```
who | paste - -
```

Merge each pair of lines into one line:

```
paste -s -d"\t\n" list
```

---

pathchk [*options*] *filenames*   **pathchk**

Determine validity and portability of *filenames*. Specifically, determine if all directories within the path are searchable, and if the length of the *filenames* is acceptable.

Option

  -p, --portability
       Check portability for all POSIX systems.

---

perl   **perl**

A powerful text-processing language that combines many of the most useful features of shell programs, C, **awk**, and **sed**, as well as adding extended features of its own. Chapter 14, *Perl 5 Quick Reference*, summarizes the features of the language. For more information, see *Learning Perl* by Randal L. Schwartz and *Programming Perl*, Second Edition, by Larry Wall, Tom Christiansen, and Randal L. Schwartz.

---

pidof [*options*] *programs*   **pidof**

Display the process IDs of the listed program or programs. **pidof** is actually a symbolic link to **killall5**.

Options

  -o *pids*   Omit all processes with the specified process
             ID. You may list several process IDs.

  -s   Return a single process ID.

  -x   Also return process IDs of shells running the
             named scripts.

pr

pr [*file*]

Convert a text file to a paginated, columned version, with headers. If − is provided as the filename, read from standard input.

Options

+*num_pag* Discard first *num_pag*-1 number of pages, and begin printing on page *num_pag*.

−*num_cols* Print in *num_cols* number of columns.

−a   Print columns horizontally, not vertically.

−b   At the end of the file, balance columns.

−c   Convert control characters to hat notation (such as ^C) and other unprintable characters to octal backslash.

−d   Double space.

−e[*tab-char*[*width*]]
         Convert tabs (or *tab-char*s) to spaces. If *width* is specified, convert tabs to *width* characters (default is 8).

−f, −F   Separate pages with formfeeds, not newlines.

−h *header* Use *header* for a header instead of the filename.

−i[*out-tab-char*[*out-tab-width*]]
         Replace spaces with tabs on output. Can specify alternative tab character (default is tab) and width (default is 8).

−l *lines* Set page length to *lines* (default 66). If *lines* is less than 10, omit headers and footers.

−m   Print one file per column.

−n[*delimiter*[*digits*]]
         Number columns, or, with the −m option, number lines. Append *delimiter* to each number (default is a tab) and limit the size of numbers to *digits* (default is 5).

−o *width* Set left margin to *width*.

−r   Continue silently when unable to open an input file.

−s[*delimiter*]
         Separate columns with *delimiter* (default is a tab) instead of spaces.

−t   Suppress headers, footers, and fills at end of pages.

−v	Convert unprintable characters to octal back-slash.	**pr**

−w *page_width*
        Set the page width to *page_width* columns. Default is 72.

---

printenv [*variables*]   **printenv**

Print values of all environment variables or, optionally, only the specified *variables*.

---

printf *formats* [*strings*]   **printf**

Print *strings* using the specified *formats*. *formats* can be ordinary text characters, C-language escape characters, or more commonly, a set of conversion arguments listed below.

Arguments

%s	Print the next *string*.
%*n*$s	Print the *n*th *string*.
%[-]*m*[.*n*]s	Print the next *string*, using a field that is *m* characters wide. Optionally limit the field to print only the first *n* characters of *string*. Strings are right-adjusted unless the left-adjustment flag, −, is specified.

Examples

```
printf '%s %s\n' "My files are in" $HOME
printf '%-25.15s %s\n' "My files are in" $HOME
```

---

ps [*options*]   **ps**

Report on active processes. Note that you do not need to include a − before options. In options, *list* arguments should either be separated by commas or be put in double quotes. In comparing the amount of output produced, note that −e prints more than −a and −l prints more than −f.

Options

pids	Include only specified processes, which are given in a comma-delimited list.
a	List all processes.
c	Consult **task_struct** for command name.
e	Include environment.

→

f	"Forest" family tree format.
h	Suppress header.
j	Jobs format.
l	Produce a long listing.
m	Memory format.
n	Print user IDs and WCHAN numerically.
r	Exclude processes that are not running.
s	Signal format.

--sort_delimiter_[+|-]_key_[,[+|-]_key_[,...]]
    Similar to O, but designed to protect multiletter sort keys. See _Sort keys_.

t_tty_	Display only processes running on _tty_.
u	Include username and start time.
v	_vm_ format.
w	Wide format. Don't truncate long lines.
x	Include processes without an associated terminal.

O[+|-]_key_[,[+|-]_key_[,...]]
    Sort processes. (See _Sort keys_.)

+	Return key to default direction.
–	Reverse default direction on key.
S	Include child processes' CPU time and page faults.

Sort keys

c, cmd	Name of executable.
C, cmdline	Whole command line.
f, flags	Flags.
g, pgrp	Group ID of process.
G, tpgid	Group ID of associated tty.
j, cutime	Cumulative user time.
J, cstime	Cumulative system time.
k, utime	User time.
K, stime	System time.
m, min_flt	Amount of minor page faults.
M, maj_flt	Amount of major page faults.

n, cmin_flt	Total minor page faults.
N, cmaj_flt	Total major page faults.
o, session	Session ID.
p, pid	Process ID.
P, ppid	Parent's process ID.
r, rss	Resident set size.
R, resident	Resident pages.
s, size	Kilobytes of memory used.
S, share	Number of shared pages.
t, tty	tty.
T, start_time	
	Process's start time.
U, uid	User ID.
u, user	User's name.
v, vsize	Bytes of VM used.
y, priority	Kernel's scheduling priority.

Fields

PRI	Process's scheduling priority. A higher number indicates lower priority.
NI	Process's nice value. A higher number indicates less CPU time.
SIZE	Size of virtual image.
RSS	Resident set size (amount of physical memory), in kilobytes.
WCHAN	Kernel function in which process resides.
STAT	Status.

	R	Runnable
	T	Stopped
	D	Asleep and not interruptible
	S	Asleep
	Z	Zombie
	W	No resident pages (second field)
	N	Positive nice value (third field)

| TT | Associated tty. |
| PAGEIN | Amount of major page faults. |

$\rightarrow$

ps	TRS	Size of resident text.
←	SWAP	Amount of swap used, in kilobytes.
	SHARE	Shared memory.

| pwd | **pwd** |
| | Print the full pathname of the current working directory. Note: The built-in versions **pwd** (Bourne and Korn shells) and **dirs** (C shell) are faster, so you might want to define the following C-shell alias: |
| | ```
alias pwd dirs -1
``` |

quota	quota [*options*] [*user	group*]
	Display the disk usage and total space allowed for a designated user or group. With no argument, the quota for the current user is displayed. This command reports quotas for all filesystems listed in */etc/fstab*.
	Options
	−g	Given with a *user* argument, display the quotas for the groups of which the user is a member, instead of the user's quotas.
	−q	Display information only on filesystems where the user is over quota.
	−u	The default behavior. When used together with **−g**, display both user and group quota information.
	−v	Display quotas on filesystems even when no storage is currently allocated.

rcp	rcp [*options*] *file1 file2* rcp [*options*] *file ... directory*
	Copy files between two machines. Each *file* or *directory* is either a remote filename of the form *rhost:path*, or a local filename.
	Options
	−k	Attempt to get tickets for remote host; query **krb_realmofhost** to determine realm.
	−p	Preserve modification times and modes of the source files.
```

−r	If any of the source files are directories, **rcp** copies each subtree rooted at that name.	**rcp**
−x	Turns on DES encryption for all data passed by **rcp**.	

rdate [*options*] [*hosts...*]

Retrieves the date and time from a host or hosts on the network. The function uses the RFC 868 protocol over TCP to retrieve the information. The date and time are returned in **ctime(3)** format, for example:

```
% rdate chambord sambuca
[chambord] Mon Dec 7 16:22:39 1998
[sambuca]  Mon Dec 7 16:21:53 1998
```

Options

−p	Print the date and time. Default behavior.
−s	Set the local system time from the host. Useful for root.

renice [*priority*] [*options*] [*target*]

Control the scheduling priority of various processes as they run. May be applied to a process, process group, or user (*target*). A privileged user may alter the priority of other users' processes. *priority* must, for ordinary users, lie between 0 and the environment variable PRIO_MAX (normally 20), with a higher number indicating increased niceness. A privileged user may set a negative priority, as low as PRIO_MIN, to speed up processes.

Options

+*num*	Specify number by which to increase current priority of process, rather than an absolute priority number.
−*num*	Specify number by which to decrease current priority of process, rather than an absolute priority number.
−g	Interpret *target* parameters as process group IDs.
−p	Interpret *target* parameters as process IDs (default).
−u	Interpret *target* parameters as usernames.

reset	**reset**
	Clear screen (reset terminal).
rev	**rev** [*file*]
	Reverses the lines of a file onto standard output. The order of characters for each line is reversed. If no file is specified, the function reads from standard input.
rlogin	**rlogin** *rhost* [*options*]
	Remote login. **rlogin** connects the terminal on the current local host system to the remote host system *rhost*. The remote terminal type is the same as your local terminal type. The terminal or window size is also copied to the remote system if the server supports it.

Options

−8	Allow an eight-bit input data path at all times.
−e*c*	Specify escape character *c* (default is ~).
−d	Debugging mode.
−k	Attempt to get tickets from remote host, requesting them in the realm as determined by **krb_realm-ofhost**.
−l *username*	
	Specify a different *username* for the remote login. Default is the same as your local username.
−x	Turns on DES encryption for all data passed via the **rlogin** session.
−E	Do not interpret any character as an escape character.
−K	Suppress all Kerberos authentication.
−L	Allow **rlogin** session to be run without any output postprocessing (in **litout** mode).

rm	**rm** [*options*] *files*
	Delete one or more *files*. To remove a file, you must have write permission in the directory that contains the file, but you need not have permission on the file itself. If you do not have write permission on the file, you will be prompted (**y** or **n**) to override.

> **−d, −−directory**
>> Remove directories, even if they are not empty; use **unlink**, not **rmdir**, to do so. Available only to a privileged user.
>
> **−f, −−force** Remove write-protected files without prompting.
>
> **−−help** Print a usage message and then exit.
>
> **−i, −−interactive**
>> Prompt for **y** (remove the file) or **n** (do not remove the file).
>
> **−r, −R, −−recursive**
>> If *file* is a directory, remove the entire directory and all its contents, including subdirectories. Be forewarned: use of this option can be dangerous.
>
> **−v, −−verbose**
>> Turn on verbose mode. (**rm** prints the name of each file before removing it.)
>
> **−−version** Print version information and then exit.
>
> **−−** Mark the end of options. Use this when you need to supply a filename beginning with −.

---

rmdir [*options*] *directories*

rmdir

Delete the named *directories* (not the contents). *directories* are deleted from the parent directory and must be empty (if not, **rm −r** can be used instead). See also **mkdir**.

Option

> **−p, −−parents**
>> Remove *directories* and any intervening parent directories that become empty as a result; useful for removing subdirectory trees.

---

rsh [*options*] *host* [*command*]

rsh

Execute *command* on remote host, or, if no command is specified, begin an interactive shell on the remote host using **rlogin**.

Options

> **−d** Enable socket debugging.
>
> **−k** Cause **rsh** to obtain tickets for the remote host in realm instead of the remote host's realm as determined by **krb_realmofhost(3)**.

→

rsh	**−l** *username*
←	Attempt to log in as *username*. By default, the name of the user executing **rsh** is used.
	−n Redirects the input to **rsh** from the special device */dev/null*. (This should be done when backgrounding **rsh** from a shell prompt, to direct the input away from the terminal.)
	−x Turns on DES encryption for all data exchange.
	−K Suppress Kerberos authentication.

rstat	**rstat** *host*
	Summarize *host*'s status: uptime, load averages, and current time.

run−parts	**run−parts** [*options*] *directory*
	Run scripts in specified directory. Consider every file with a filename consisting entirely of alphanumeric characters, underscores, and hyphens to be a script. Ignore others. Sort filenames lexically and run them in that order.
	Options
	−− Do not consider anything after this option to be an option. Useful for protecting filenames beginning with −.
	−−test Test mode. Print information about scripts which it would run, but do not actually run them.
	−−umask=*umask* Reset umask to *umask* (default is 022).

ruptime	**ruptime** [*options*]
	Show host status of local machines. These status lines are formed from packets broadcast by each host on the network once a minute. Machines for which no status report has been received for eleven minutes are shown as being down.
	Options
	−l Sort listing by load average.
	−r Reverse sort order.

−t	Sort listing by uptime.	**ruptime**
−u	Sort listing by number of users.	

rusers [*options*] [*host...*]   **rusers**

List who is logged in on local machines (RPC version). **rusers** produces output similar to the **who** command. When *host* arguments are given, **rusers** queries only the list of specified hosts. A remote host will respond only if it is running the **rusersd** daemon. Broadcasting does not work through gateways (this is a bug).

Options

−a   Give a report for a machine even if no users are logged on.

−l   Give a longer listing in the style of **who**.

rwall *hostname* [*file*]   **rwall**

Write to all users over a network. **rwall** reads a message from standard input until *EOF*. It then sends this message, preceded by the line `Broadcast Message . . .`, to all users logged in on *hostname*. If *file* is specified, it is sent instead of the standard input.

rwho [*option*]   **rwho**

Report who is logged on for all machines on the local network (similar to **who**).

Option

−a   List users even if they've been idle for more than one hour.

script [*option*] [*file*]   **script**

Copy all output from terminal to the file *typescript* or specified name. Stop copying when shell exits.

Option

−a   Append to file rather than overwriting.

sed [*options*] [*command*] [*files*]   **sed**

Stream editor—edit one or more *files* without user interaction. See Chapter 10, *The sed Editor*, for more information.

→

sed
←
	Options
	
	−e ' *instruction* ' , −−**expression=**' *instruction* '
	    Apply the editing *instruction* to the files.
	
	−f *script*, −−**file=***script*
	    Apply the set of instructions from the editing *script*.
	
	−n, −−**quiet**, −−**silent**
	    Suppress default output.

setfdprm	**setfdprm** [*options*] *device* [*name*]
	
	Load disk parameters used when auto-configuring floppy devices.
	
	Options
	
	    −c *device* Clear parameters of *device*.
	
	    −n *device* Disable format-configuring messages for *device*.
	
	    −p *device* [*name*
		parameter]
		        Permanently reset parameters of *device*. You may specify **dev**, **size**, **sect**, **heads**, **tracks**, **stretch**, **gap**, **rate**, **spec1**, or **fmt_gap**. Consult */etc/fdprm* for original values. *name* specifies the configuration.
		
		    −y *device* Enable format-configuring messages for *device*.

sh	**sh** [*options*] [*file* [*arguments*]] The standard Unix shell, a command interpreter into which all other commands are entered. On Linux, this is just another name for the **bash** shell. For more information, see Chapter 4, *bash: The Bourne Again Shell.*
shar	**shar** [*options*] *files* **shar** −S [*options*] Create shell archives (or shar files) that are in text format and can be mailed. These files may be unpacked later by executing them with */bin/sh*. Other commands may be required on the recipient's system, such as **compress**, **gzip**, and **uudecode**. The resulting archive is sent to standard output, unless the −o option is given.

Options have a short version starting with – or a long version
starting with ––. The exceptions are **––help**, **––version**,
––noi18n, and **––print-text-domain-dir**, which do not have a
short version.

–a, ––net-headers

Allows automatic generation of headers. The
–n option is required if the **–a** option is used.

–b *bits*, **––bits-per-code=***bits*

Use **–b** *bits* as a parameter to **compress** (when
doing compression). Default value is 12. The
–B option automatically turns on the **–Z**
option.

–c, ––cut-mark

Start the shar file with a line that says "Cut
here."

–d *delimiter*, **––here-delimiter=***delimiter*

Use *delimiter* for the files in the shar instead of
SHAR_EOF.

–f, ––basename

Causes only simple filenames to be used when
restoring, which is useful when building a shar
from several directories, or another directory.
(If a directory name is passed to **shar**, the sub-
structure of that directory will be restored
whether or not **–f** is used.)

–g *level*, **––level-for-gzip=***level*

Use *–level* as a parameter to **gzip** (when doing
compression). Default is 9. The **–g** option turns
on the **–z** option by default.

––help   Print a help summary on standard output, then
exit.

–l *nn*, **––whole-size-limit=***nn*

Limit the output file size to *nn*K bytes but
don't split input files. Requires use of **–o**.

–m, ––no-timestamp

Don't generate **touch** commands to restore the
file modification dates when unpacking files
from the archive.

–n *name*, **––-archive-name=***name*

Name of archive to be included in the header
of the shar files. Required if the **–a** option is
used.

→

—no-i18n Do not produce internationalized shell archives; use default English messages. By default, **shar** produces archives that will try to output messages in the unpacker's preferred language (as determined by LANG/LC_MES-SAGES).

−o *prefix*, −−output-prefix=*prefix*
Save the archive to files *prefix*.01 through *prefix.nn* (instead of sending it to standard output). This option must be used when either −l or −L is used.

−p, −−intermix-type
Allow positional parameter options. The options −B, −T, −z, and −Z may be embedded, and files to the right of the option will be processed in the specified mode.

−−print-text-domain-dir
Print the directory **shar** looks in to find messages files for different languages, then immediately exit.

−q, −−quiet, −−silent
Turn off verbose mode.

−s *who@where*, −−submitter=*who@where*
Supply submitter name and address, instead of allowing **shar** to determine it automatically.

−−version Print the version number of the program on standard output, then exit.

−w, −−no-character-count
Do *not* check each file with **wc** −c after unpacking. The default is to check.

−x, −−no-check-existing
Overwrite existing files without checking. Default is to check and not overwrite existing files. If −c is passed as a parameter to the script when unpacking (**sh** *archive* −c), existing files will be overwritten unconditionally. See also −X.

−z, −−gzip **gzip** and **uuencode** all files prior to packing. Must be unpacked with **uudecode** and **gunzip** (or **zcat**).

−B, −−uuencode
Treat all files as binary; use **uuencode** prior to packing. This increases the size of the archive, and it must be unpacked with **uudecode**.

−D, −−no-md5-digest shar

Do *not* use "md5sum" digest to verify the unpacked files. The default is to check.

−F, −−force-prefix

Force the prefix character to be prepended to every line even if not required. May slightly increase the size of the archive, especially if **−B** or **−Z** is used.

−L *nn,* **−−split-size-limit=***nn*

Limit output file size to *nn*K bytes and split files if necessary. The archive parts created with this option must be unpacked in correct order. Requires use of **−o**.

−M, −−mixed-uuencode

Pack files in mixed mode (the default). Distinguishes files as either text or binary; binaries are uuencoded prior to packing.

−P, −−no-piping

Use temporary files instead of pipes in the shar file.

−Q, −−quiet-unshar

Disable verbose mode.

−S, −−stdin-file-list

Read list of files to be packed from standard input rather than from the command line. Input must be in a form similar to that generated by the **find** command, with one filename per line.

−T, −−text-files

Treat all files as text.

−V, −−vanilla-operation

Produce "vanilla" shars that rely only upon the existence of **sed** and **echo** in the unsharing environment.

−X, −−query-user

Prompt user to ask if files should be overwritten when unpacking.

−Z, −−compress

Compress and uuencode all files prior to packing.

---

sleep *amount* [*units*] sleep

Wait a specified *amount* of time before executing another command. The default for *units* is seconds.

→

---

sleep	Time	Units
←	*s*	seconds
	m	minutes
	h	hours
	d	days

sort	

sort [*options*] [*files*]

Sort the lines of the named *files*. Compare specified fields for each pair of lines, or, if no fields are specified, compare them by byte, in machine collating sequence. See also **uniq**, **comm**, **join**.

Options

−b	Ignore leading spaces and tabs.
−c	Check whether *files* are already sorted, and if so, produce no output.
−d	Sort in dictionary order.
−f	"Fold"—ignore uppercase/lowercase differences.
−−help	Print a usage message and then exit.
−i	Ignore nonprinting characters (those outside ASCII range 040–176).
−m	Merge (i.e., sort as a group) input files.
−n	Sort in arithmetic order.
−o*file*	Put output in *file*.
−r	Reverse the order of the sort.
−t*c*	Separate fields with *c* (default is a tab).
−u	Identical lines in input file appear only one (unique) time in output.
−z*recsz*	Provide *recsz* bytes for any one line in the file. This option prevents abnormal termination of **sort** in certain cases.
+*n* [−*m*]	Skip *n* fields before sorting, and sort up to field position *m*. If *m* is missing, sort to end of line. Positions take the form *a.b*, which means character *b* of field *a*. If *.b* is missing, sort at the first character of the field.
−k *n*[,*m*]	Similar to +. Skip *n*−1 fields and stop at *m*−1 fields (i.e., start sorting at the *n*th field, where the fields are numbered beginning with 1).

--version	Print version information and then exit.
-M	Attempt to treat the first three characters as a month designation (JAN, FEB, etc). In comparisons, treat JAN < FEB < *invalid month name.*
-T *tempdir*	Directory pathname to be used for temporary files.

Examples

List files by decreasing number of lines:

```
wc -l * | sort -r
```

Alphabetize a list of words, remove duplicates, and print the frequency of each word:

```
sort -fd wordlist | uniq -c
```

Sort the password file numerically by the third field (user ID):

```
sort +2n -t: /etc/passwd
```

---

split [*option*] [*infile*] [*outfile*]

Split *infile* into a specified number of line segments. *infile* remains unchanged, and the results are written to *outfile*aa, *outfile*ab, etc. (default is **xaa**, **xab**, etc.). If *infile* is − (or missing), standard input is read. See also **csplit**.

Options

−*n*, −l *n*, --lines=*n*	
	Split *infile* into *n* line segments (default is 1000).
-b *n*[bkm], --bytes=*n*[bkm]	
	Split *infile*. By default, split it to *n* byte segements. Alternate block sizes may be specified:

b	512 bytes
k	1 kilobyte
m	1 megabyte

--help	Print a usage message and then exit.
-C *bytes*[bkm], --line-bytes=*bytes*[bkm]	
	Put a maximum of *bytes* into file; insist on adding complete lines.
--version	Print version information and then exit.
−	Take input from the standard input.

$\rightarrow$

split ←	**Examples** Break *bigfile* into 1000-line segments: ``` split bigfile ``` Join four files, then split them into ten-line files named *new.aa*, *new.ab*, etc. Note that without the −, **new.** would be treated as a nonexistent input file: ``` cat list[1-4]	split -10 - new. ```

stat	stat *filename* [*filenames* . . .]
	
	Print out the contents of an inode as they appear to stat(2) in a human-readable format. The error messages "Can't stat file" or "Can't lstat file" usually mean the file doesn't exist. "Can't read-link file" generally indicates that something is wrong with a symbolic link.
	
	Output
	
	Sample output from the command:
	
	``
	stat /
	
	  File: "/"
	  Size: 1024 Allocated Blocks: 2 Filetype: Directory
	  Mode: (0755/drwxr-xr-x) Uid: (0/ root) Gid: (0/ system)
	Device: 0,0 Inode: 2 Links: 20
	Access: Wed Jan 8 12:40:16 1986(00000.00:00:01)
	Modify: Wed Dec 18 09:32:09 1985(00021.03:08:08)
	Change: Wed Dec 18 09:32:09 1985(00021.03:08:08)
	``

strfile	strfile [*options*] *input_file* [*output_file*] unstr [-c *delimiter*] *input_file*[. *ext*] [*output_file*] **strfile** creates a random access file for storing strings. The input file should be a file containing groups of lines separated by a line containing a single percent '%' sign (or other specified delimiter character). **strfile** creates an output file that contains a header structure and a table of file offsets for each group of lines, allowing random access of the strings. The output file, if not specified on the command line, is named *sourcefile.dat*. **unstr** undoes the work of **strfile**, printing out the strings contained in the input file in the order that they are listed in the header file data. If no output file is specified, it prints to standard output; otherwise it prints to the file specified. **unstr** can also globally change the delimiter character in a strings file.

Options   strfile

Of the following options, only −c can be used with **unstr**. All other options apply to **strfile** alone.

−c *delimiter*

> Change the delimiting character from the percent sign to *delimiter*. Valid for both **strfile** and **unstr**.

−i   Ignore case when ordering the strings.

−o   Order the strings alphabetically.

−r   Randomize access to the strings.

−s   Run silently; don't give a summary message when finished.

−x   Set the STR_ROTATED bit in the header *str_flags* field.

---

stty [*options*] [*modes*]   stty

Set terminal I/O options for the current standard input device. Without options, **stty** reports the terminal settings that differ from those set by running **stty sane**, where a ˆ indicates the CONTROL key and ˆˆ indicates a null value. Most modes can be negated using an optional − (shown in brackets). The corresponding description is also shown in brackets. Some arguments use non-POSIX extensions; these are marked with a *.

```
stty [options] [modes] [< device]
```

Options

−a, −−all   Report all option settings.

−g   Report settings in hex.

Control modes

n   Set terminal baud rate to *n* (e.g., 2400).

[−]**clocal** [Enable]disable modem control.

[−]**cread**   [Disable]enable the receiver.

cs*bits*   Set character size to *bits*, which must be 5, 6, 7, or 8.

[−]**cstopb** [One]two stop bits per character.

[−]**hup**   [Do not]hang up connection on last close.

[−]**hupcl**   Same as previous.

ispeed *n* Set terminal input baud rate to *n*.

→

ospeed *n*   Set terminal output baud rate to *n*.

[−]parenb   [Disable]enable parity generation and detection.

[−]parodd   Use [even]odd parity.

[−]crtscts*   [Disable]enable RTS/CTS handshaking.

Flow control modes

The following flow control modes are available by combining the *ortsfl*, *ctsflow*, and *rtsflow* flags:

Flag settings	Flow control mode
ortsfl rtsflow ctsflow	Enable unidirectional flow control.
ortsfl rtsflow -ctsflow	Assert RTS when ready to send.
ortsfl -rtsflow ctsflow	No effect.
ortsfl -rtsflow -ctsflow	Enable bidirectional flow control.
-ortsfl rtsflow ctsflow	Enable bidirectional flow control.
-ortsfl rtsflow -ctsflow	No effect.
-ortsfl -rtsflow ctsflow	Stop transmission when CTS drops.
-ortsfl -rtsflow -ctsflow	Disable hardware flow control.

Input modes

[−]brkint   [Do not]signal INTR on break.

[−]icrnl   [Do not]map CR to NL on input.

[−]ignbrk   [Do not]ignore break on input.

[−]igncr   [Do not]ignore CR on input.

[−]ignpar   [Do not]ignore parity errors.

[−]inlcr   [Do not]map NL to CR on input.

[−]inpck   [Disable]enable input parity checking.

[−]istrip   [Do not]strip input characters to seven bits.

[−]iuclc*   [Do not]map uppercase to lowercase on input.

[−]ixany*   Allow [XON]any character to restart output.

[−]ixoff [−]tandem
    [Do not]send START/STOP characters when queue is nearly empty/full.

[−]ixon   [Disable]enable START/STOP output control.

[−]parmrk   [Do not]mark parity errors.

[−]imaxbel*
    When input buffer is too full to accept a new character, [flush the input buffer]beep; do not flush the input buffer.

bs*n*   Select style of delay for backspaces (0 or 1).

cr*n*   Select style of delay for carriage returns (0–3).

ff*n*   Select style of delay for formfeeds (0 or 1).

nl*n*   Select style of delay for linefeeds (0 or 1).

tab*n*   Select style of delay for horizontal tabs (0–3).

vt*n*   Select style of delay for vertical tabs (0 or 1).

[–]ocrnl*   [Do not]map CR to NL on output.

[–]ofdel*   Set fill character to [NULL]DEL.

[–]ofill*   Delay output with [timing]fill characters.

[–]olcuc*   [Do not]map lowercase to uppercase on out-
               put.

[–]onlcr*   [Do not]map NL to CR-NL on output.

[–]onlret*   On the terminal, NL performs [does not per-
               form] the CR function.

[–]onocr*   Do not [do] output CRs at column zero.

[–]opost   [Do not]postprocess output.

Local modes

[–]echo   [Do not]echo every character typed.

[–]echoe, [–]crterase
               [Do not]echo ERASE character as BS-space-BS
               string.

[–]echok   [Do not]echo NL after KILL character.

[–]echonl   [Do not]echo NL.

[–]icanon   [Disable]enable canonical input (ERASE, KILL,
               WERASE, and RPRINT processing).

[–]iexten   [Disable]enable extended functions for input
               data.

[–]isig   [Disable]enable checking of characters against
               INTR, SUSPEND, and QUIT.

[–]noflsh   [Enable]disable flush after INTR or QUIT.

[–]tostop*   [Do not]send SIGTTOU when background pro-
               cesses write to the terminal.

[–]xcase*   [Do not]change case on local output.

[–]echoprt, [–]prterase*
               When erasing characters, echo them backward,
               enclosed in \ and /.

→

[−]echoctl. [−]ctlecho*
> Do not echo control characters literally. Use hat notation (e.g. ˆZ).

[−]echoke [−]crtkill*
> Erase characters as specified by the **echoprt** and **echoe** settings (default **echoctl** and **echok** settings).

Control assignments

ctrl-char c
> Set control character to *c*. *ctrl-char* is: **dsusp** (flush input and then send stop), **eof**, **eol**, **eol2** (alternate end-of-line), **erase**, **intr**, **lnext** (treat next character literally), **kill**, **rprnt** (redraw line), **quit**, **start**, **stop**, **susp**, **swtch**, or **werase** (erase previous word). *c* can be a literal control character, a character in hat notation (e.g. ˆZ), in hex (must begin with 0x), in octal (must begin with 0), or in decimal. Disable the control character with values of ˆ− or **undef**.

min *n*
> Set the minimum number of characters that will satisfy a read until the time value has expired when –**icanon** is set.

time *n*
> Set the number of tenths of a second before reads time out if the **min** number of characters have not been read when –**icanon** is set.

line *i*
> Set line discipline to *i* (1–126).

Combination modes

cooked
> Same as −**raw**.

[−]evenp [−]parity
> Same as [-]**parenb** and cs[8]7.

[−]parity
> Same as [-]**parenb** and cs[8]7.

ek
> Reset ERASE and KILL characters to **CTRL-h** and **CTRL-u**, their defaults.

[−]lcase
> [Un]set **xcase**, **iuclc**, and **olcuc**.

[−]LCASE
> Same as [−]**lcase**.

[−]nl
> [Un]set **icrnl** and **onlcr**. −**nl** also unsets **inlcr**, **igncr**, **ocrnl**, and **onlret**, **icrnl**, **onlcr**.

[−]oddp
> Same as [−]**parenb**, [−]**parodd**, and cs7[8].

[−]raw
> [Disable]enable raw input and output (no ERASE, KILL, INTR, QUIT, EOT, SWITCH, or output postprocessing).

sane	Reset all modes to reasonable values.
[-]tabs*	[Expand to spaces]preserve output tabs.
[-]cbreak	Same as -icanon.
[-]pass8	Same as -parenb -istrip cs8.
[-]litout	Same as -parenb -istrip cs8.
[-]decctlq*	Same as -ixany.
crt	Same as **echoe echoctl echoke**.
dec	Same as **echoe echoctl echoke -ixany**. Additionally, set INTERRUPT to ^C, ERASE to DEL, and KILL to ^U.

Special settings

ispeed *speed*
> Specify input speed.

ospeed *speed*
> Specify output speed.

rows *rows*   Specify number of rows.

cols *columns*, **columns** *columns**
> Specify number of columns.

size*   Display current row and column settings.

line *discipline**
> Specify line discipline.

speed   Display terminal speed.

---

su [*option*] [*user*] [*shell_args*]

su

Create a shell with the effective user ID of another *user*. If no *user* is specified, create a shell for a privileged user (that is, become a superuser). Enter *EOF* to terminate. You can run the shell with particular options by passing them as *shell_args* (e.g., if the shell runs **sh**, you can specify −c *command* to execute *command* via **sh**, or −r to create a restricted shell).

Options

   −, −l, −−**login**
> Go through the entire login sequence (i.e., change to *user*'s environment).

−c *command*, −−**command**=*command*
> Execute *command* in new shell and exit immediately. If *command* is more than one word, it should be enclosed in quotes—for example:

```
su -c 'find / -name \*.c -print' nobody
```

→

su ←	**–f, – –fast** Start shell with -f option. In **csh** and **tcsh**, this suppresses the reading of the *.cshrc* file. In **bash**, this suppresses filename pattern expansion.
	–m, –p, – –preserve-environment Retain original values for HOME, USER, LOG-NAME, and SHELL. Execute $SHELL, not the shell specified in */etc/passwd*, unless $SHELL is a restricted shell.
	–s *shell*, **– –shell** *shell* Execute *shell*, not the shell specified in */etc/passwd*, unless *shell* is restricted.

---

sum

sum [*option*] *file*

Calculate and print a checksum and the number of (1 Kbyte) blocks for *file*. Useful for verifying data transmission.

Option

–r	The default setting. Use the BSD version checksum algorithm.
–s – –sysv	Use alternate checksum algorithm as used on System V. The block size is 512 bytes.
– –help	Print the usage information for this command.
– –version	Print the version number for this command.

---

symlinks

symlinks [*options*] *directories*

Provide listing of and information about symbolic links. Examine *directories* for symbolic links, and specify whether each is **relative**, **absolute**, **dangling**, or **other_fs**.

Options

–c	Convert absolute links to relative links, except absolute links from other filesystems.
–r	Recursively descend through subdirectories in search of symbolic links.
–v	Include relative links.

---

systat

systat [*options*] *host*

Query *host* for system information. Attempt to query the host's **systat** service; if unable to do so, use its **netstat** or **daytime** services.

−n, −−netstat
> Consult host's **netstat** service.

−p *port,* **−−port** *port*
> Direct query to host's *port.*

−s, −−systat
> Consult host's **systat** service (default).

−t, −−time   Consult host's **daytime** service.

---

tac [*options*] [*file*]   tac

Named for the common command **cat**, **tac** prints files in reverse. Without a filename, or with −, it reads from standard input. By default, it reverses the order of the lines, printing the last line first.

Options

−b, −−before
> Print separator (by default a newline) before string that it delimits.

−r, −−regex   Expect separator to be a regular expression.

−s *string,* **−−separator=***string*
> Specify alternate separator (default is newline).

---

tail [*options*] [*file*]   tail

Print the last ten lines of the named *file* (or standard input if − is specified) on standard output.

Options

−*n*[*k*]   Begin printing at *n*th item from end of file. *k* specifies the item to count: l (lines, the default), **b** (blocks), or **c** (characters).

−*k*   Same as −*n*, but use the default count of 10.

+*n*[*k*]   Like −*n*, but start at *n*th item from beginning of file.

+*k*   Like −*k*, but count from beginning of file.

−c *num*{bkm}, **−−bytes** *num*{bkm}
> Print last *num* bytes. An alternate block size may be specified:
>
> b   512 bytes

$\rightarrow$

tail ←	k 1 kilobyte m 1 megabyte **−f** Don't quit at the end of file; "follow" file as it grows. End with a **CTRL-C**. **−n** *num*, **−−lines** *num* Print last *num* lines. **−q**, **−−quiet**, **−−silent** Suppress filename headers. **−−version** Print version information and then exit. *Examples* Show the last 20 lines containing instances of **.Ah**: `grep '\.Ah' `*`file`*`	tail -20`  Show the last ten characters of variable **name**:     `echo "$name"	tail -c`  Print the last two blocks of **bigfile**:     `tail -2b bigfile`
talk	**talk** *person* [*ttyname*] Talk to another user. *person* is either the login name of someone on your own machine, or *user@host* on another host. To talk to a user who is logged in more than once, use *ttyname* to indicate the appropriate terminal name. Once communication has been established, the two parties may type simultaneously, with their output appearing in separate windows. To redraw the screen, type **CTRL-L**. To exit, type your interrupt character; **talk** then moves the cursor to the bottom of the screen and restores the terminal.
tcsh	**tcsh** [*options*] [*file* [*arguments*]] An extended version of the C shell, a command interpreter into which all other commands are entered. For more information, see Chapter 5, *csh and tcsh*.
tee	**tee** [*options*] *files* Accept output from another command and send it both to the standard output and to *files* (like a T or fork in a road).

Options

> **−a, −−append**
>> Append to *files*; do not overwrite.
>
> **−−help**   Print a usage message and then exit.
>
> **−i, −−ignore-interrupts**
>> Ignore interrupt signals.
>
> **−−version**   Print version information and then exit.

Example

> ```
> ls -l | tee savefile
> ```
> *View listing and save for later*

---

telnet [*options*] [*host* [*port*]]   **telnet**

Access remote systems. **telnet** is the user interface that communicates with another host using the TELNET protocol. If telnet is invoked without *host*, it enters command mode, indicated by its prompt, `telnet>`, and accepts and executes the commands listed after the following options. If invoked with arguments, **telnet** performs an **open** command (see the entry following) with those arguments. *host* indicates the host's official name. *port* indicates a port number (default is the TELNET port).

Options

> **−a**   Automatic login into the remote system.
>
> **−d**   Turn on socket-level debugging.
>
> **−e** [*escape_char*]
>> Set initial TELNET escape character to *escape_char*. If *escape_char* is omitted, there will be no predefined escape character.
>
> **−l** *user*   When connecting to remote system, and if remote system understands ENVIRON, send *user* to the remote system as the value for variable USER.
>
> **−n** *tracefile*
>> Open *tracefile* for recording the trace information.
>
> **−r**   Emulate **rlogin**: the default escape character is a tilde; an escape character followed by a dot causes **telnet** to disconnect from the remote host; a ^**Z** instead of a dot suspends **telnet**; and a] (the default **telnet** escape character) generates a normal **telnet** prompt. These codes are accepted only at the beginning of a line.

→

telnet	−8	Request 8-bit operation.
←	−E	Disable the escape character functionality.
	−L	Specify an 8-bit data path on output.
	−S *tos*	Set the IP type-of-service (TOS) option for the telnet connection to the value *tos*.

Commands

CTRL-Z Suspend **telnet**.

! [*command*]
  Execute a single command in a subshell on the local system. If *command* is omitted, an interactive subshell will be invoked.

? [*command*]
  Get help. With no arguments, print a help summary. If a command is specified, print the help information for just that command.

close Close a TELNET session and return to command mode.

display *argument* ...
  Display all, or some, of the **set** and **toggle** values.

environ [*arguments* [...]]
  Manipulate variables that may be sent through the TELNET ENVIRON option. Valid arguments for **environ** are:

  ? Get help for the **environ** command.

  define *variable value*
    Define *variable* to have a value of *value*.

  undefine *variable*
    Remove *variable* from the list of environment variables.

  export *variable*
    Mark *variable* to have its value exported to the remote side.

  unexport *variable*
    Mark *variable* to not be exported unless explicitly requested by the remote side.

  list Display current variable values.

logout If the remote host supports the **logout** command, close the **telnet** session.

mode [*type*]
>> Depending on state of TELNET session, *type* is one of several options:

> ? Print out help information for the **mode** command.

> character
>> Disable TELNET LINEMODE option, or, if remote side does not understand the option, enter "character at a time" mode.

> [–]edit
>> Attempt to [disable]enable the EDIT mode of the TELNET LINEMODE option.

> [–]isig
>> Attempt to [disable]enable the TRAPSIG mode of the LINEMODE option.

> line
>> Enable LINEMODE option, or, if remote side does not understand the option, attempt to enter "old line by line" mode.

> [–]softtabs
>> Attempt to [disable]enable the SOFT_TAB mode of the LINEMODE option.

> [–]litecho
>> [Disable]enable LIT_ECHO mode.

open [-l *user*] *host* [*port*]
>> Open a connection to the named *host*. If no *port* number is specified, attempt to contact a TELNET server at the default port.

quit   Close any open TELNET session and exit telnet.

status Show current status of **telnet**. This includes the peer one is connected to as well as the current mode.

send *arguments*
>> Send one or more special character sequences to the remote host. Following are the arguments that may be specified:

> ? Print out help information for **send** command.

> abort
>> Send TELNET ABORT sequence.

> ao Send TELNET AO sequence, which should cause the remote system to flush all output from the remote system to the user's terminal.

$\rightarrow$

telnet

←

ayt Send TELNET AYT (Are You There) sequence.

brk Send TELNET BRK (Break) sequence.

do *cmd*

dont *cmd*

will *cmd*

wont *cmd*
> Send TELNET DO *cmd* sequence, where *cmd* is a number between 0 and 255, or a symbolic name for a specific TELNET command. If *cmd* is ? or **help**, this command prints out help (including a list of symbolic names).

ec Send TELNET EC (Erase Character) sequence, which causes the remote system to erase the last character entered.

el Send TELNET EL (Erase Line) sequence, which causes the remote system to erase the last line entered.

eof Send TELNET EOF (End Of File) sequence.

eor Send TELNET EOR (End Of Record) sequence.

escape
> Send current TELNET escape character (initially ^).

ga Send TELNET GA (Go Ahead) sequence.

getstatus
> If the remote side supports the TELNET STATUS command, **getstatus** sends the subnegotiation request that the server send its current option status.

ip Send TELNET IP (Interrupt Process) sequence, which causes the remote system to abort the currently running process.

nop
> Send TELNET NOP (No OPeration) sequence.

susp
> Send TELNET SUSP (SUSPend process) sequence.

synch
> Send TELNET SYNCH sequence, which causes the remote system to discard all previously typed (but not read) input.

unset *argument value*

> Set any one of a number of telnet variables to a specific value or to "TRUE". The special value "off" disables the function associated with the variable. **unset** disables any of the specified functions. The values of variables may be interrogated with the aid of the **display** command. The variables which may be specified are:

?   Display legal **set** and **unset** commands.

ayt   If TELNET is in **localchars** mode, this character is taken to be the alternate AYT character.

echo

> This is the value (initially ˆ**E**) which, when in line-by-line mode, toggles between doing local echoing of entered characters and suppressing echoing of entered characters.

eof   If **telnet** is operating in LINEMODE or in the old line-by-line mode, entering this character as the first character on a line will cause the character to be sent to the remote system.

erase

> If **telnet** is in **localchars** mode and operating in the character-at-a-time mode, then when this character is entered, a TELNET EC sequence will be sent to the remote system.

escape

> This is the TELNET escape character (initially ˆ[), which causes entry into the TELNET command mode when connected to a remote system.

flushoutput

> If **telnet** is in **localchars** mode and the **flushoutput** character is entered, a TELNET AO sequence is sent to the remote host.

forw1

> If TELNET is in **localchars** mode, this character is taken to be an alternate end-of-line character.

forw2

> If TELNET is in **localchars** mode, this character is taken to be an alternate end-of-line character.

interrupt

> If TELNET AO is in **localchars** mode and the **interrupt** character is entered, a TELNET IP sequence is sent to the remote host.

→

telnet
←

kill   If TELNET IP is in **localchars** mode and operating in the "character-at-a-time" mode, then when this character is entered, a TELNET EL sequence is sent to the remote system.

lnext
If TELNET EL is in LINEMODE or in the old "line-by-line" mode, then this character is taken to be the terminal's **lnext** character.

quit
If TELNET EL is in **localchars** mode and the **quit** character is entered, a TELNET BRK sequence is sent to the remote host.

reprint
If TELNET BRK is in LINEMODE or in the old "line-by-line" mode, this character is taken to be the terminal's **reprint** character.

rlogin
Enable **rlogin** mode. Same as using **−r** command-line option.

start
If the TELNET TOGGLE-FLOW-CONTROL option has been enabled, this character is taken to be the terminal's **start** character.

stop
If the TELNET TOGGLE-FLOW-CONTROL option has been enabled, this character is taken to be the terminal's **stop** character.

susp
If TELNET is in **localchars** mode, or if the LINEMODE is enabled and the **suspend** character is entered, a TELNET SUSP sequence is sent to the remote host.

tracefile
File to which output generated by **netdata** is written.

worderase
If TELNET BRK is in LINEMODE or in the old "line-by-line" mode, this character is taken to be the terminal's **worderase** character. Defaults for these are the terminal's defaults.

slc [*state*]   Set state of special characters when TELNET LINEMODE option has been enabled.

?   List help on the **slc** command.

check

> Verify current settings for current special characters. If discrepancies are discovered, convert local settings to match remote ones.

export

> Switch to local defaults for the special characters.

import

> Switch to remote defaults for the special characters.

toggle *arguments* [...]

> Toggle various flags that control how TELNET responds to events. The flags may be set explicitly to TRUE or FALSE using the **set** and **unset** commands listed previously. The valid arguments are:

?   Display legal **toggle** commands.

autoflush

> If **autoflush** and **localchars** are both TRUE, then when the **ao** or **quit** characters are recognized, TELNET refuses to display any data on the user's terminal until the remote system acknowledges that it has processed those TELNET sequences.

autosynch

> If **autosynch** and **localchars** are both TRUE, then when the **intr** or **quit** character is entered, the resulting TELNET sequence sent is followed by the TELNET SYNCH sequence. Initial value for this **toggle** is FALSE.

binary

> Enable or disable the TELNET BINARY option on both the input and the output.

inbinary

> Enable or disable the TELNET BINARY option on the input.

outbinary

> Enable or disable the TELNET BINARY option on the output.

crlf

> If this **toggle** value is TRUE, carriage returns are sent as CR-LF. If FALSE, carriage returns are sent as CR-NUL. Initial value is FALSE.

→

telnet
←
	crmod
	   Toggle carriage return mode. Initial value is FALSE.
	
	debug
	   Toggle socket level debugging mode. Initial value is FALSE.
	
	localchars
	   If the value is TRUE, **flush, interrupt, quit, erase,** and **kill** characters are recognized locally, then transformed into appropriate TELNET control sequences. Initial value is TRUE.
	
	netdata
	   Toggle display of all network data. Initial value is FALSE.
	
	options
	   Toggle display of some internal **telnet** protocol processing pertaining to TELNET options. Initial value is FALSE.
	
	prettydump
	   When **netdata** is enabled, and if **prettydump** is enabled, the output from the **netdata** command is reorganized into a more user-friendly format; spaces are put between each character in the output, and an asterisk precedes any TELNET escape sequence.
	
	skiprc
	   Toggle whether to process ~/.telnetrc file. Initial value is FALSE, meaning the file is processed.
	
	termdata
	   Toggle printing of hexadecimal terminal data. Initial value is FALSE.
	
	    z Suspend **telnet**; only works for the *csh*.

test	**test** *expression* or [*expression*] Shell built-in also exists for most shells. Evaluate an *expression* and, if its value is true, return a zero exit status; otherwise, return a nonzero exit status. In shell scripts, you can use the alternate form [*expression*]. This command is generally used with conditional constructs in shell programs.

The syntax for all of these options is **test** *option file*. If the specified file does not exist, they return FALSE. Otherwise, they will test the file as specified in the option description.

−b	Is the file block special?
−c	Is the file character special?
−d	Is the file a directory?
−e	Does the file exist?
−f	Is the file a regular file?
−g	Does the file have the set group ID bit set?
−k	Does the file have the sticky bit set?
−L	Is the file a symbolic link?
−p	Is the file a named pipe?
−r	Is the file readable by the current user?
−s	Is the file nonempty?
−S	Is the file a socket?

−t [*file-descriptor*]

Is the file associated with *file-descriptor* (or 1, standard output, by default) connected to a terminal?

−u	Does the file have the set user ID bit set?
−w	Is the file writable by the current user?
−x	Is the file executable?
−O	Is the file owned by the process's effective user ID?
−G	Is the file owned by the process's effective group ID?

File comparisons

The syntax for file comparisons is **test** *file1 option file2*. A string by itself, without options, returns TRUE if it's at least one character long.

−nt	Is *file1* newer than *file2*? Check modification, not creation, date.
−ot	Is *file1* older than *file2*? Check modification, not creation, date.
−ef	Do the files have identical device and inode numbers?

→

test
←
	String tests
	
	The syntax for string tests is **test** *option string*.
	
	    −z Is the string zero characters long?
	
	    −n Is the string at least one character long?
	
	    = *string* Are the two strings equal? Strings with the same characters in different orders are considered equal.
	
	    != *string* Are the strings unequal?

String tests

The syntax for string tests is **test** *option string*.

−z	Is the string zero characters long?
−n	Is the string at least one character long?
= *string*	Are the two strings equal? Strings with the same characters in different orders are considered equal.
!= *string*	Are the strings unequal?

Expression tests

Note that an expression can consist of any of the previous tests.

! *expression*
    Is the expression false?

expression **−a** *expression*
    Are the expressions both true?

expression **−o** *expression*
    Is either expression true?

Integer tests

The syntax for integer tests is **test** *integer1 option integer2*. You may substitute **-l** *string* for an integer; this evaluates to *string's* length.

−eq	Are the two integers equal?
−ne	Are the two integers unequal?
−lt	Is *integer1* less than *integer2*?
−le	Is *integer1* less than or equal to *integer2*?
−gt	Is *integer1* greater than *integer2*?
−ge	Is *integer1* greater than or equal to *integer2*?

---

tftp

tftp [*host* [*port*]]

User interface to the TFTP (Trivial File Transfer Protocol) protocol, which allows users to transfer files to and from a remote machine. The remote *host* may be specified, in which case **tftp** uses *host* as the default host for future transfers.

Commands

Once **tftp** is running, it issues the prompt:

    `tftp>`

and recognizes the following commands:

tftp

? [*command-name...*]
> Print help information.

ascii   Shorthand for mode ASCII

binary   Shorthand for mode binary

connect *hostname* [*port*]
> Set the *hostname*, and optionally **port**, for transfers.

get *filename*

get *remotename localname*

get *filename1 filename2 filename3...filenameN*
> Get a file or set of files from the specified remote sources.

mode *transfer-mode*
> Set the mode for transfers. *transfer-mode* may be one of ASCII or binary. The default is ASCII.

put *filename*

put *localfile remotefile*

put *filename1 filename2...filenameN remote-directory*
> Transfer file or a set of files to the specified remote file or directory.

quit   Exit **tftp**.

rexmt *retransmission-timeout*
> Set the per-packet retransmission timeout, in seconds.

status   Print status information: whether **tftp** is connected to a remote host (i.e., whether a host has been specified for the next connection), the current mode, whether verbose and tracing modes are on, and the values for **retransmission timeout** and **total transmission timeout**.

timeout *total-transmission-timeout*
> Set the total transmission timeout, in seconds.

trace   Toggle packet tracing.

verbose   Toggle verbose mode.

---

tload [*options*] [*tty*]   **tload**

Display system load average in graph format. If *tty* is specified, print it to that tty.

$\rightarrow$

tload	*Options*
←	**−d** *delay* Specify the delay, in seconds, between updates.
	−s *scale* Specify scale (number of characters between each graph tick). A smaller number results in a larger scale.

top	**top**

Provide information (frequently refreshed) about the most CPU-intensive processes currently running. See **ps** for explanations of the field descriptors.

Options

−c	Display command line instead of the command name only.
−d *delay*	Specify delay between refreshes.
−i	Suppress display of idle and zombie processes.
−q	Refresh without any delay. As a privileged user, run with highest priority.
−s	Secure mode. Disable some (dangerous) interactive commands.
−S	Cumulative mode. Print total CPU time of each process, including dead children.

Interactive commands

c	Toggle display of command name or full command line.
f, F	Add fields to display or remove fields from the display.
h, ?	Display help about commands and the status of secure and cumulative modes.
k	Prompt for process ID to kill and signal to send (default is 15) to kill it.
i	Toggle suppression of idle and zombie processes.
l	Toggle display of load average and uptime information.
m	Toggle display of memory information.
n, #	Prompt for number of processes to show. If 0 is entered, show as many as will fit on the screen (default).

o, O	Change order of displayed fields.	top
q	Exit.	
r	Apply **renice** to a process. Prompt for PID and **renice** value. Suppressed in secure mode.	
s	Change delay between refreshes. Prompt for new delay time, which should be in seconds. Suppressed in secure mode.	
t	Toggle display of processes and CPU states information.	
^L	Redraw screen.	
M	Sort tasks by resident memory usage.	
P	Sort tasks by CPU usage (default).	
S	Toggle cumulative mode. (See the **-S** option.)	
T	Sort tasks by time/cumulative time.	
W	Write current setup to `~/.toprc`. This is the recommended way to write a **top** configuration file.	

touch [*options*] [*date*] *files*   touch

For one or more *files*, update the access time and modification time (and dates) to the current time and date, or update to the optional *date*. *date* is a date and time in the format *mmddhhmm*[*yy*]. **touch** is useful in forcing other commands to handle files a certain way; e.g., the operation of **make**, and sometimes **find**, relies on a file's access and modification time.

Options

  −a −−time=atime −−time=access −−time=use
      Update only the access time.

  −c −−no-create
      Do not create nonexistent files.

  −d *time*, −−date *time*
      Change the time value to the specified *time* instead of the current time. *time* can use several formats and may contain month names, timezones, am and pm strings, as well as others.

  −m −−time=mtime −−time=modify
      Update only the modification time.

  −r *file*, −−reference *file*
      Change times to be the same as those of the specified *file*, instead of the current time.

→

touch ←	**−t** *time*	Use the time specified in *time* instead of the current time. This argument must be of the format: *MMDDhhmm[[CC]YY][.ss]*, indicating month, date, hours, minutes, optional century and year, and optional seconds.
	−−help	Print the usage information for this command.
	−−version	Print the version number for this command.

tr	**tr** [*options*] [*string1* [*string2*]]

Translate characters—copy standard input to standard output, substituting characters from *string1* to *string2* or deleting characters in *string1*.

Options

   −c, −−complement
        Complement characters in *string1* with respect to ASCII 001-377.

   −d, −−delete
        Delete characters in *string1* from output.

   −s, −−squeeze-repeats
        Squeeze out repeated output characters in *string2*.

Special characters

\a	^G (bell)
\b	^H (backspace)
\f	^L (form feed)
\n	^J (newline)
\r	^M (carriage return)
\t	^I (tab)
\v	^K (vertical tab)
nnn	Character with octal value *nnn*.
\\	Literal backslash.

   char1−char2
        All of the characters in the range *char1* through *char2*. If *char1* does not sort before *char2*, produce an error.

   [*char**number] .
        The brackets should be literally included. Expand char to number occurrences. **[x*4]** expands to **xxxx**, for instance.

[:*class*:] The brackets should be literally included. Expand to all characters in *class*.

alnum
> Letters and digits

alpha
> Letters

blank
> Whitespace

cntrl
> Control characters

digit
> Digits

graph
> All printable characters except space

lower
> Lowercase letters

print
> All printable characters

punct
> Punctuation

space
> Whitespace (horizontal or vertical)

upper
> Uppercase letters

xdigit
> Hexadecimal digits

[=*char*=] The class of characters in which *char* belongs. Not fully implemented.

Examples

Change uppercase to lowercase in a file:

```
cat file | tr '[A-Z]' '[a-z]'
```

Turn spaces into newlines (ASCII code 012):

```
tr ' ' '\012' < file
```

Strip blank lines from **file** and save in **new.file** (or use **011** to change successive tabs into one tab):

```
cat file | tr -s "" "\012" > new.file
```

$\rightarrow$

tr ←	Delete colons from **file**; save result in **new.file**: `tr -d : < file > new.file`
troff	**troff** See **groff**.
true	**true** A null command that returns a successful (zero) exit status. See also **false**.

ul	**ul** [*options*] [*names*]
	
	Translate underscores to underlining. The correct sequence with which to do this will vary by terminal type. Some terminals are unable to handle underlining.
	
	Options
	
	    −i Translate −, when on a separate line, to underline, instead of _.
	
	    −t *terminal-type*
	           Specify terminal type. By default, TERM is consulted.

uname	**uname** [*options*]
	
	Print information about the machine and operating system. Without options, print the name of the operating system (Linux).
	
	Options
	
	    −a, −−all Combine all the system information from the other options.
	
	    −−help Display a help message.
	
	    −m, −−machine
	           Print the hardware the system is running on.
	
	    −n, −−nodename
	           Print the machine's fully qualified network hostname.
	
	    −r, −−release
	           Print the release number of the kernel.
	
	    −s, −−sysname
	           Print the name of the operating system (Linux).

−p, −−processor
>   Print the type of processor (not available on all
>   versions).

−v   Print build information about the kernel.

−−version Print version information about the command.

---

unexpand [*options*] [*files*]

Convert strings of initial whitespace, consisting of at least two
spaces and/or tabs, to tabs. Read from standard input if given no
file or a file named −.

Options

−, −t, −−tabs *tab-stops*
>   *tab-stops* is a comma-separated list of integers
>   that specify the placement of tab stops. If
>   exactly one integer is provided, the tab stops are
>   set to every *integer* space. By default, tab stops
>   are eight spaces apart. Implies −a. With −t and
>   −−tabs, the list may be separated by whitespace
>   instead of commas.

−a, −−all Convert all, not just initial, strings of spaces and
>   tabs.

---

uniq [*options*] [*file1* [*file2*]]

Remove duplicate adjacent lines from sorted *file1*, sending one
copy of each line to *file2* (or to standard output). Often used as
a filter. Specify only one of −c, −d, or −u. See also **comm** and
sort.

Options

−*n*, −f *n*, −−skip-fields=*n*
>   Ignore first *n* fields of a line. Fields are sepa-
>   rated by spaces or by tabs.

+*n*, −s *n*, −−skip-chars=*n*
>   Ignore first *n* characters of a field.

−c, −−count
>   Print each line once, counting instances of each.

−d, −−repeated
>   Print duplicate lines once, but no unique lines.

−−help   Print a usage message and then exit.

−u, −−unique
>   Print only unique lines (no copy of duplicate
>   entries is kept).

→

uniq ←	**--version** Print version information and then exit.
	-w *n*, **--check-chars=***n*
	Compare only first *n* characters per line (beginning after skipped fields and characters).

Examples

Send one copy of each line from **list** to output file **list.new**:

```
uniq list list.new
```

Show which names appear more than once:

```
sort names | uniq -d
```

Show which lines appear exactly three times:

```
sort names | uniq -c | grep "3 "
```

unshar	**unshar** [*options*] [*files*]

Unpack a shell archive (shar file). **unshar** scans mail messages looking for the start of a shell archive. It then passes the archive through a copy of the shell to unpack it. It will accept multiple files. If no files are given, standard input is used.

Options

Options have a short version starting with − or a long version starting with −−. The exceptions are **--help** and **--version**, which do not have a short version.

-c, **--overwrite**
Overwrite existing files.

-d *directory*, **--directory=***directory*
Change to *directory* before unpacking any files.

-e, **--exit-0**
Sequentially unpack multiple archives stored in same file; uses clue that many **shar** files are terminated by an exit 0 at the beginning of a line. (Option **-e** is internally equivalent to **-E** "**exit 0**".)

-E *string*, **--split-at=***string*
Like **-e**, but allows you to specify the string that separates archives if **exit 0** isn't appropriate.

-f, **--force**
Same as **-c**.

--help Print a help summary on standard output, then exit.

--version Print the version number of the program on standard output, then exit.	**unshar**

uptime

Print the current time, amount of time logged in, number of users logged in, and system load averages. This output is also produced by the first line of the **w** command.

uptime

users [*file*]

Print a space-separated list of each login session on the host. Note that this may include the same user multiple times. Consult *file* or, by default, */etc/utmp*.

users

usleep [*microseconds*]
usleep [*options*]

Sleep some number of microseconds (default 1).

Options

    --help   Print help information.

    -v   Print version information.

usleep

uudecode [*-o outfile*] [*file*]

Read a uuencoded file and recreate the original file with the permissions and name set in the file (see **uuencode**). The **-o** option specifies an alternate file to output to.

uudecode

uuencode [*-m*] [*file*] *name*

Encode a binary *file*. The encoding uses only printing ASCII characters and includes the permissions and *name* of the file. When *file* is reconverted via **uudecode**, the output will be sent to *name*. Without the *file* argument, **uuencode** can take standard input, so a single argument will be taken as the name to be given to the file when it is decoded. The **-m** option causes base64 encoding of a file. Commonly you will encode a file and save it with an identifying extension, such as *.uue*. This example encodes the binary file *flower12.jpg*, names it *rose.jpg*, and saves it to a *.uue* file:

uuencode

```
% uuencode flower12.jpg rose.jpg > rose.uue
```

vi	**vi** [*options*] [*files*] A screen-oriented text editor based on **ex**. For more information on **vi**, see Chapter 8, *The vi Editor*.
vrfy	**vrfy** [*options*] *address* [*host*] Query remote host to verify the accuracy of an email address. If *host* is provided, query that host directly; otherwise the query may go to a mail exchange. Print information about the address and, if provided by the remote host, about the user. With the -f and -p options, do not require the specification of an address on the command line.

Options

−a	Query each mail exchange host, not just primary.
−c *secs*	Timeout connection attempts after *secs* seconds. The default is 6.
−d	Enable debugging output.
−dd	Enable more verbose debugging output.
−e	Use EXPN, not VRFY, command when connected to the sendmail port on the remote host.
−f *file*	Consult file for list of email addresses to verify.
−l	Specify local error-handling mode.
−p *domain*	Determine whether domain's mail exchangers are presently accepting SMTP requests.
−s	Strip all comments from hosts' addresses.
−n	Use RCPT, not VRFY, command when connected to the sendmail port on the remote host. Disables recursion, as RCPT cannot support it.
−t *secs*	Time out read attempts after *secs* seconds. The default is 60.
−v	Verbose.
−vv	Very verbose.
−vvv	Amazingly verbose.
−L *levels*	Recursively verify *levels* levels of the address. -L recognizes mail loops and local users, and stops checking when it encounters them.
−R	Same as -L 17. 17 hops are the maximum in real mailings. Implies -s.

w [*options*] [*users*]

Print summaries of system usage, currently logged-in users, and what they are doing. **w** is essentially a combination of **uptime**, **who**, and **ps –a**. Display output for one user by specifying *user*.

Options

–f	Toggle printing the from (remote hostname) field.
–h	Suppress headings and **uptime** information.
–s	Use the short format.
–u	Ignore the username while figuring out the current process and cpu times.
–V	Display version information.

wc [*options*] [*files*]

Print a character, word, and line count for *files*. If no *files* are given, read standard input. See other examples under **ls** and **sort**.

Options

–c, –bytes, ––chars
:   Print character count only.

–l, ––lines
:   Print line count only.

–w, ––words
:   Print word count only.

Examples

Count the number of users logged in:

```
who | wc -l
```

Count the words in three essay files:

```
wc -w essay.[123]
```

Count lines in variable $file (don't display filename):

```
wc -l < $file
```

whatis *keyword* ...

Searches the short manual page descriptions in the *whatis* database for each *keyword* and prints a one-line description to standard output for each match. Like **apropos**, except that it only searches for complete words. Equivalent to **man –f**.

whereis	**whereis** [−bmsu] [−BMS *directories* −f] *filenames*
	Locate the binary, source, and manual page files for a specified command/file. The supplied names are first stripped of leading pathname components and any (single) trailing extension of the form *.ext* (for example, ".c"). Prefixes of "s." resulting from use of source code control are also dealt with. **whereis** then attempts to locate the desired program in a list of standard Linux directories (e.g., */bin, /etc, /usr/bin, /usr/local/bin/*, etc.).

Options

−b	Search only for binaries.
−f	Terminate the last directory list and signal the start of filenames; −f must be used when any of the −B, −M, or −S options are used.
−m	Search only for manual sections.
−s	Search only for sources.
−u	Search for unusual entries. A file is said to be unusual if it does not have one entry of each requested type. Thus **whereis −m −u *** asks for those files in the current directory that have no documentation.
−B *directory*	Change or otherwise limit the place where **whereis** searches for binaries.
−M *directory*	Change or otherwise limit the place where **whereis** searches for manual sections.
−S *directory*	Change or otherwise limit the place where **whereis** searches for sources.

Example

Find all files in */usr/bin* that are not documented in */usr/man/man1* but that have source in */usr/src*:

```
% cd /usr/bin
% whereis -u -M /usr/man/man1 -S /usr/src -f *
```

which	**which** [*commands*]
	Lists the full pathnames of the files that would be executed if the named *commands* had been run. **which** searches the user's **$PATH** environment variable.

```
$ which cc ls
/usr/ucb/cc
ls:      aliased to ls -sFC
```

who [*options*] [*file*]   who
who am i

Display information about the current status of the system. With no options, list the names of users currently
logged in to the system, their terminal, the time they have
been logged in, and the name of the host from which
they have logged on. An optional system *file* (default is
/etc/utmp) can be supplied to give additional information.

Options

 am i   Print the username of the invoking user.

 −−help Print a usage message and then exit.

 −i, −u, −−idle
      Include idle times. An idle time of . indicates
      activity within the last minute; one of **old** indi-
      cates no activity in more than a full day.

 −m   Same as **who am i**.

 −q, −−count
      "Quick." Display only the usernames and total
      number of users.

 −−version Print version information and then exit.

 −w, −T, −−mesg, −−message, −−writable
      Display user's message status.

    + mesg y (**write** messages allowed)

    − mesg n (**write** messages refused)

    ? cannot find terminal device

 −H, −−heading
      Print headings.

Example

This sample output was produced at 8 a.m. on April 17:

```
$ who -uH
NAME    LINE   TIME           IDLE   PID   COMMENTS
Earvin  ttyp3  Apr 16 08:14  16:25  2240
Larry   ttyp0  Apr 17 07:33   .     15182
```

Since Earvin has been idle since yesterday afternoon (16 hours),
it appears that Earvin isn't at work yet. He simply left himself
logged in. Larry's terminal is currently in use.

whoami	**whoami** Print current user ID. Equivalent to **who am i** and **id -un**.
write	**write** *user* [*tty*] *message* Initiate or respond to an interactive conversation with *user*. A **write** session is terminated with *EOF*. If the user is logged in to more than one terminal, specify a *tty* number. See also **talk**.

xargs	**xargs** [*options*] [*command*]
	
	Execute *command* (with any initial arguments), but read remaining arguments from standard input instead of specifying them directly. **xargs** passes these arguments in several bundles to *command*, allowing *command* to process more arguments than it could normally handle at once. The arguments are typically a long list of filenames (generated by **ls** or **find**, for example) that get passed to **xargs** via a pipe.
	
	Options
	
	   −0, −−null
	         Expect filenames to be terminated by NULL. Do not treat quotes or backlashes specially.
	
	   −e[*string*], **−−eof**[*=string*]
	         Set *EOF* to _ or, if specified, to *string*.
	
	   −−help Print a summary of the options to **xargs** and exit.
	
	   −i[*string*], **−−replace**[*=string*]
	         Edit all occurrences of {}, or *string*, to the names read in on standard input. Unquoted blanks are not considered argument terminators. Implies **-x** and **-l** 1.
	
	   −l[*lines*], **−−max-lines**[*=lines*]
	         Allow no more than 1, or *lines*, nonblank input lines on the command line. Implies **-x**.
	
	   −n *args*, **−−max-args**=*args*
	         Allow no more than *args* arguments on the command line. May be overridden by **-s**.
	
	   −p, −−interactive
	         Prompt for confirmation before running each command line. Implies **-t**.

−r, −−no-run-if-empty
> Do not run command if it is made up entirely of
> blanks.

−s *max,* **−−max-chars=***max*
> Allow no more than *max* characters per com-
> mand line.

−t, −−verbose
> Verbose mode. (Print command line on standard
> error before executing.)

−x, −−exit
> If the maximum size (as specified by -s) is
> exceeded, exit.

−−version Print the version number of **xargs** and exit.

−P *max,* **−−max-procs=***max*
> Allow no more than *max* processes to run at
> once. The default is 1. A maximum of 0 allows
> as many as possible to run at once.

Examples

grep for *pattern* in all files on the system:

```
find / -print | xargs grep pattern > out &
```

Run **diff** on file pairs (e.g., **f1.a** and **f1.b**, **f2.a** and **f2.b** ...):

```
echo $* | xargs -n2 diff
```

The previous line would be invoked as a shell script, specifying
filenames as arguments. Display *file*, one word per line (same as
deroff −w):

```
cat file | xargs -n1
```

Move files in *olddir* to *newdir*, showing each command:

```
ls olddir | xargs -i -t mv olddir/{} newdir/{}
```

---

yes *string*   yes
yes [−−help] [−−version]

Print the command-line arguments, separated by spaces
and followed by a newline, until killed. If no arguments
are given, print y followed by a newline until killed. Useful in scripts and in the background; its output can be
piped to a program that issues prompts.

Options

When **yes** is invoked with exactly one argument, the following
options are recognized:

$\rightarrow$

yes ←	--help	Print a usage message on standard output and exit successfully.
	--version	Print version information on standard output then exit successfully.

---

ypchfn

ypchfn [*options*] [*user*]

NFS/NIS command. Change the information that is stored in */etc/passwd* and is displayed when a user is fingered; distribute the change over NIS. Without options, **ypchfn** will enter interactive mode and prompt for changes. To make a field blank, enter the keyword **none**. See also **yppasswd** and **ypchsh**.

Options

-f	Behave like **ypchfn** (default).
-l	Behave like **ypchsh**.
-p	Behave like **yppasswd**.

---

ypchsh

ypchsh [*options*] [*user*]

NFS/NIS command. Change your login shell and distribute this information over NIS. Warn if *shell* does not exist in */etc/shells*. See also **yppasswd** and **ypchfn**.

Options

-f	Behave like **ypchfn**.
-l	Behave like **ypchsh** (default).
-p	Behave like **yppasswd**.

---

yppasswd

yppasswd [*options*] [*user*]

NFS/NIS command. Create or change a password associated with *user*, and distribute the new password over NIS. Only the owner or a privileged user may change a password. Owners need not specify their *user* name. See also **ypchfn** and **ypchsh**.

Options

-f	Behave like **ypchfn**.
-l	Behave like **ypchsh**.
-p	Behave like **yppasswd** (default).

---

zcat

zcat [*options*] [*files*]

Read one or more *files* that have been compressed with **gzip** or **compress** and write them to standard output. Read standard

input if no *files* are specified or if – is specified as one of the files; end input with *EOF*. **zcat** is identical to **gunzip –c**, and takes the options **–fhLV** described for **gzip/gunzip**.	zcat

zcmp [*options*] *files*

Read compressed files and pass them, uncompressed, to the **cmp** command, along with any command-line options. If a second file is not specified for comparison, look for a file called *file*.**gz**.

zcmp

zdiff [*options*] *files*

Read compressed files and pass them, uncompressed, to the **diff** command, along with any command-line options. If a second file is not specified for comparison, look for a file called *file*.**gz**.

zdiff

zforce [*names*]

Rename all **gzip**ped files to *filename*.**gz**, unless file already has a .**gz** extension.

zforce

zgrep [*options*] [*files*]

Uncompress files and pass to **grep**, along with any command-line arguments. If no files are provided, read from (and attempt to uncompress) standard input. May be invoked as **zegrep** or **zfgrep**, and will in those cases invoke **egrep** or **fgrep**.

zgrep

zmore [*files*]

Similar to **more**. Print compressed files, uncompressed, one screenful at a time.

zmore

Commands

space	Print next screenful.
i[*number*]	
	Print next screenful, or *number* lines. Set *i* to *number* lines.
^D	Print next *i*, or 11, lines.
d	Same as ^D.
*i*z	Print next *i* lines, or a screenful.
*i*s	Skip *i* lines. Print next screenful.
*i*f	Skip *i* screens. Print next screenful.

→

zmore ←	q, Q	Go to next file, or, if current file is the last, exit **zmore**.
	e, q	When the prompt —More—(Next file: *file*) is displayed, causes **zmore** to exit.
	s	Skip next file and continue.
	=	Print line number.
	i/expr	Search forward for *i*th occurrence (in all files) of *expr*, which should be a regular expression. Display occurrence, including the two previous lines of context.
	in	Search forward for the *i*th occurrence of the last regular expression searched for.
	!command	
		Execute *command* in shell. If *command* is not specified, execute last shell command. To invoke a shell without passing it a command, enter \!.
	:q, :Q	Skip to the next file. Same as q.
	.	Repeat the previous command.

---

znew

znew [*options*] [*files*]

Uncompress .Z files and recompress them in .gz format.

Options

−9	Optimal (and slowest) compression method.
−f	Recompress even if *filename*.gz already exists.
−t	Test .gz files before removing .Z files.
−v	Verbose mode.
−K	If the original file is smaller than the .gz file, keep it.
−P	Pipe data to conversion program. This saves disk space.

CHAPTER 3

The Unix Shells:
An Overview

The shell is a program that acts as a buffer between you and the operating system. In its role as a command interpreter, it should (for the most part) act invisibly. It can also be used for simple programming.

This section introduces three shells commonly used on Linux systems—the Bourne Again shell (**bash**), the C shell (**csh**), and **csh**'s enhanced version, **tcsh**—and summarizes the major differences between them. Details on them are provided in Chapter 4, *bash: The Bourne Again Shell*, and Chapter 5, *csh and tcsh*.

The following topics are presented in this chapter:

* Purpose of the shell
* Shell flavors
* Common features
* Differing features

Purpose of the Shell

There are three main uses for the shell:

* Interactive use
* Customization of your Linux session
* Programming

Interactive Use

When the shell is used interactively, it waits for you to issue commands, processes them (to interpret special characters, such as wildcards), and executes them. Shells also provide a set of commands, known as built-ins, to supplement Linux commands.

Customization of Your Linux Session

A Linux shell defines variables, such as the locations of your home directory and mail spool, to control the behavior of your session. Some variables are preset by the system; you can define others in startup files that your shell reads when you log in. Startup files can also contain Linux or shell commands or special shell commands, for execution immediately after login.

Programming

A series of individual commands (be they shell or other Linux commands available on the system) combined into one program is called a shell script. Batch files in MS-DOS are a similar concept. **bash** is considered a powerful programming shell, while scripting in **csh** is rumored to be hazardous to your health.

Shell Flavors

Many different Linux shells are available. This book describes the three most popular shells:

- The Bourne Again shell (**bash**), which is based on the Bourne shell and is standard for Linux

- The C shell (**csh**), which uses C syntax and has many conveniences

- **tcsh**, an extension of **csh** that appears instead of **csh** in many Linux distributions

Most systems have more than one shell, and people will often use one shell for writing shell scripts and another for interactive use.

When you log in, the system determines which shell to run by consulting your entry in */etc/passwd*. The last field of each entry calls a program to run as the default shell. For example:

If the program name is:	Your shell will be the:
/bin/sh	Bourne Again shell
/bin/bash	Bourne Again shell
/bin/csh	C shell
/bin/tcsh	tcsh

You can change to another shell by typing the program name at the command line. For example, to change from **bash** to **tcsh**, type:

```
$ exec tcsh
```

Common Features

The table below is a sampling of features that are common to **bash**, **csh**, and **tcsh**. Note that **tcsh** is an enhanced version of **csh**; therefore, **tcsh** includes all features of **csh**, plus some others.

Symbol/Command	Meaning/Action
>	Redirect output.
>>	Append output to file.
<	Redirect input.
<<	"Here" document (redirect input).
|	Pipe output.
&	Run process in background.
;	Separate commands on same line.
*	Match any character(s) in filename.
?	Match single character in filename.
!*n*	Repeat command number *n*.
[ ]	Match any characters enclosed.
( )	Execute in subshell.
` `	Substitute output of enclosed command.
" "	Partial quote (allows variable and command expansion).
' '	Full quote (no expansion).
\	Quote following character.
$*var*	Use value for variable.
$$	Process ID.
$0	Command name.
$*n*	*n*th argument ($0<n\le9$).
$*	All arguments as a simple word.
#	Begin comment.
bg	Background execution.
break	Break from loop statements.
cd	Change directories.
continue	Resume a program loop.
echo	Display output.
eval	Evaluate arguments.
exec	Execute a new shell or other program.
fg	Foreground execution.
jobs	Show active jobs.

Symbol/Command	Meaning/Action
kill	Terminate running jobs.
newgrp	Change to a new group.
shift	Shift positional parameters.
stop	Suspend a background job.
suspend	Suspend a foreground job.
umask	Set or list permissions on files to be created.
unset	Erase variable or function definitions.
wait	Wait for a background job to finish.

Differing Features

The table below is a sampling of features that are different among the three shells.

Meaning/Action	bash	csh	tcsh
Default prompt.	$	%	%
Force redirection.	>|	>!	>!
Force append.		>>!	>>!
Variable assignment.	var=value	set var=value	set var=value
Set environment variable.	export var	setenv var val	setenv var val
Number of arguments.	$#	$#argv	$#
Exit status.	$?	$status	$?
Execute commands in *file*.	. file	source file	source file
End a loop statement.	done	end	end
End case or switch.	esac	endsw	endsw
Loop through variables.	for/do	foreach	foreach
Sample if statement.	if [$i -eq 5]	if ($i==5)	if ($i==5)
End if statement.	fi	endif	endif
Set resource limits.	ulimit	limit	limit
Read from terminal.	read	$<	$<
Make a variable read-only.	readonly		set -r
File inquiry operator: tests for nonzero size.		-s	
Complete current word.	TAB		TAB
Ignore interrupts.	trap 2	onintr	onintr
Begin until loop.	until/do	until	until
Begin while loop.	while/do	while	while

CHAPTER 4

bash: The Bourne Again Shell

This chapter presents the following topics:

- Overview of features

- Invoking the shell

- Syntax

- Variables

- Arithmetic expressions

- Command history

- Built-in commands

- Job control

Overview of Features

bash is the standard shell and provides the following features:

- Input/output redirection

- Wildcard characters (metacharacters) for filename abbreviation

- Shell variables for customizing your environment

- Powerful programming capabilities

- Command-line editing (using **vi**- or Emacs-style editing commands)

- Access to previous commands (command history)

- Integer arithmetic

- Arithmetic expressions

- Command name abbreviation (aliasing)

- Job control

- Integrated programming features

- Control structures

- Directory stacking (using **pushd** and **popd**)

- Brace/tilde expansion

- Key bindings

Invoking the Shell

The command interpreter for **bash** can be invoked as follows:

   bash [*options*] [*arguments*]

bash can execute commands from a terminal (when −i is specified), from a file (when the first *argument* is an executable script), or from standard input (if no arguments remain or if −s is specified).

Options

−, −−	Treat all subsequent strings as arguments, not options.
−c *str*	Read commands from string *str*.
−i	Create an interactive shell (prompt for input).
−login	Behave like a login shell.

−nobraceexpansion
   Disable brace expansion.

−nolineediting
   Disable line editing with arrow and control keys.

−noprofile	Do not process */etc/profile*, ˜*/.bash_profile*, ˜*/.bash_login*, or ˜*/.profile* on startup.
−norc	Do not process ˜*/.bashrc* on startup.
−p	Start up as a privileged user; don't process *$HOME/.profile*.
−posix	Conform to POSIX standard.
−quiet	Default. Do not print startup information.
−rcfile *file*	Substitute *file* for *.bashrc* on startup.
−s	Read commands from standard input; output from built-in commands goes to file descriptor 1; all other shell output goes to file descriptor 2.

The remaining options to **bash** are listed under the **set** built-in command.

Arguments

Arguments are assigned, in order, to the positional parameters **$1**, **$2**, etc. If the first argument is an executable script, commands are read from it and remaining arguments are assigned to **$1**, **$2**, etc.

Syntax

This subsection describes the many symbols peculiar to **bash**. The topics are arranged as follows:

- Special files
- Filename metacharacters
- Command-line editing
- Quoting
- Command forms
- Redirection forms
- Coprocesses

Special Files

/etc/profile	Executed automatically at login.
$HOME/.bash_profile	Executed automatically at login.
$HOME/.bashrc	Executed automatically at shell startup.
$HOME/.bash_logout	Executed automatically at logout.
$HOME/.bash_history	Record of last session's commands.
/etc/passwd	Source of home directories for *˜name* abbreviations.

Filename Metacharacters

*	Match any string of zero or more characters.
?	Match any single character.
[*abc*...]	Match any one of the enclosed characters; a hyphen can be used to specify a range (e.g., a-z, A-Z, 0-9).
[!*abc*...]	Match any character *not* among the enclosed characters.
˜*name*	HOME directory of user *name*
˜+	Current working directory (PWD)
˜-	Previous working directory (OLDPWD)

Patterns can be a sequence of patterns separated by |; if any of the subpatterns match, the entire sequence is considered matching. This extended syntax resembles that available to **egrep** and **awk**.

Examples

```
$ ls new*       List new and new.1
$ cat ch?       Match ch9 but not ch10
$ vi [D-R]*     Match files that begin with uppercase D through R
```

Command-Line Editing

Command lines can be edited like lines in either Emacs or **vi**. Emacs is the default. See the section called "Line-Edit Mode" later in this chapter for more information.

vi mode has two sub-modes, insert mode and command mode. The default mode is insert; you can toggle modes by pressing ESC, or, in command mode, typing **a** (append) or **i** (insert) will return you to insert mode.

Table 4–1 through Table 4–14 show various Emacs and vi commands.

Table 4–1: Basic Emacs-Mode Commands

Command	Description
CTRL-B	Move backward one character (without deleting).
CTRL-F	Move forward one character.
DEL	Delete one character backward.
CTRL-D	Delete one character forward.

Table 4–2: Emacs-Mode Word Commands

Command	Description
ESC b	Move one word backward.
ESC f	Move one word forward.
ESC DEL	Kill one word backward.
ESC d	Kill one word forward.
CTRL-Y	Retrieve ("yank") last item killed.

Table 4–3: Emacs-Mode Line Commands

Command	Description
CTRL-A	Move to beginning of line.
CTRL-E	Move to end of line.
CTRL-K	Kill forward to end of line.

Table 4-4: Emacs-Mode Commands for Moving Through the History File

Command	Description
CTRL-P	Move to previous line.
CTRL-N	Move to next line.
CTRL-R	Search backward.
ESC <	Move to first line of history file.
ESC >	Move to last line of history file.

Table 4-5: Completion Commands

Command	Description
TAB	Attempt to perform general completion of the text.
ESC ?	List the possible completions.
ESC /	Attempt filename completion.
CTRL-X /	List the possible filename completions.
ESC ~	Attempt username completion.
CTRL-X ~	List the possible username completions.
ESC $	Attempt variable completion.
CTRL-X $	List the possible variable completions.
ESC @	Attempt hostname completion.
CTRL-X @	List the possible hostname completions.
ESC !	Attempt command completion.
CTRL-X !	List the possible command completions.
ESC TAB	Attempt completion from previous commands in the history list.

Table 4-6: Emacs-Mode Miscellaneous Commands

Command	Description
CTRL-J	Same as RETURN.
CTRL-L	Clear the screen, placing the current line at the top of the screen.
CTRL-M	Same as RETURN.
CTRL-O	Same as RETURN, then display next line in command history.
CTRL-T	Transposes character left of and under the cursor.
CTRL-U	Kill the line from the beginning to point.
CTRL-V	Insert keypress instead of interpreting it as a command.
CTRL-[	Same as ESC (most keyboards).
ESC c	Capitalize word under or after cursor.
ESC u	Change word under or after cursor to all capital letters.
ESC l	Change word under or after cursor to all lowercase letters.
ESC .	Insert last word in previous command line after point.
ESC _	Same as ESC.

Table 4-7: Editing Commands in vi Input Mode

Command	Description
DEL	Delete previous character.
CTRL-W	Erase previous word (i.e., erase until a blank).
CTRL-V	Insert keypress instead of interpreting it as a command.
ESC	Enter control mode (see next section).

Table 4-8: Basic vi Control Mode Commands

Command	Description
h	Move left one character.
l	Move right one character.
b	Move left one word.
w	Move right one word.
B	Move to beginning of preceding nonblank word.
W	Move to beginning of next nonblank word.
e	Move to end of current word.
E	Move to end of current nonblank word.
0	Move to beginning of line.
^	Move to first nonblank character in line.
$	Move to end of line.

Table 4-9: Commands for Entering vi Input Mode

Command	Description
i	Text inserted before current character (insert).
a	Text inserted after current character (append).
I	Text inserted at beginning of line.
A	Text inserted at end of line.
r	Text replaces current character.
R	Text overwrites existing text.

Table 4-10: Some vi-Mode Deletion Commands

Command	Description
dh	Delete one character backward.
dl	Delete one character forward.
db	Delete one word backward.
dw	Delete one word forward.
dB	Delete one nonblank word backward.
dW	Delete one nonblank word forward.
d$	Delete to end of line.
d0	Delete to beginning of line.

Table 4-11: Abbreviations for vi-Mode Delete Commands

Command	Description
D	Equivalent to **d$** (delete to end of line).
dd	Equivalent to **0d$** (delete entire line).
C	Equivalent to **c$** (delete to end of line, enter input mode).
cc	Equivalent to **0c$** (delete entire line, enter input mode).
X	Equivalent to **dl** (delete character backward).
x	Equivalent to **dh** (delete character forward).

Table 4-12: vi Control Mode Commands for Searching the Command History

Command	Description
k or −	Move backward one line.
j or +	Move forward one line.
G	Move to line given by repeat count.
/*string*	Search backward for *string*.
?*string*	Search forward for *string*.
n	Repeat search in same direction as previous.
N	Repeat search in opposite direction of previous.

Table 4-13: vi-Mode Character-Finding Commands

Command	Description
f*x*	Move right to next occurrence of *x*.
F*x*	Move left to previous occurrence of *x*.
t*x*	Move right to next occurrence of *x*, then back one space.
T*x*	Move left to previous occurrence of *x*, then forward one space.
;	Redo last character-finding command.
,	Redo last character-finding command in opposite direction.

Table 4-14: Miscellaneous vi-Mode Commands

Command	Description
~	Invert (toggle) case of current character(s).
_	Append last word of previous command, enter input mode.
CTRL-L	Clear the screen and redraw the current line on it; good for when your screen becomes garbled.
#	Prepend # (comment character) to the line and send it to the history file; useful for saving a command to be executed later, without having to retype it.

Quoting

Quoting disables a character's special meaning and allows it to be used literally, as itself. The following characters have special meaning to **bash**:

;	Command separator
&	Background execution
( )	Command grouping (enter a subshell)
{ }	Command block
|	Pipe
> < &	Redirection symbols
* ? [ ] ~ !	Filename metacharacters
**" ' **	Used in quoting other characters
`	Command substitution
$	Variable substitution (or command substitution)
newline space tab	Word separators
#	Comment

The following characters can be used for quoting:

" "   Everything between **"** and **"** is taken literally, except for the following characters that keep their special meaning:

         $ Variable substitution will occur.

         `   Command substitution will occur.

         "   This marks the end of the double quote.

' '   Everything between **'** and **'** is taken literally, except for another **'** .

**   The character following a **** is taken literally. Use within **" " to escape **"** , **$**, and **`** . Often used to escape itself, spaces, or newlines.

Examples

```
$ echo 'Single quotes "protect" double quotes'
Single quotes "protect" double quotes

$ echo "Well, isn't that \"special\"?"
Well, isn't that "special"?

$ echo "You have `ls|wc -l` files in `pwd`"
You have   43 files in /home/bob

$ echo "The value of \$x is $x"
The value of $x is 100
```

Command Forms

cmd **&**	Execute *cmd* in background.
cmd1 **;** cmd2	Command sequence; execute multiple *cmd*s on the same line.

`( cmd1 ; cmd2 )`	Subshell; treat *cmd1* and *cmd2* as a command group.
`cmd1	cmd2`	Pipe; use output from *cmd1* as input to *cmd2*.
`` cmd1 `cmd2` ``	Command substitution; use *cmd2* output as arguments to *cmd1*.
`cmd1 $(cmd2)`	Command substitution; nesting is allowed.
`cmd1 && cmd2`	AND; execute *cmd2* only if *cmd1* succeeds.
`cmd1 || cmd2`	OR; execute *cmd2* only if *cmd1* fails.
`{ cmd1 ; cmd2 }`	Execute commands in the current shell.

Examples

`$ nroff file &`	*Format in the background*
`$ cd; ls`	*Execute sequentially*
`$ (date; who; pwd) > logfile`	*All output is redirected*
`$ sort file	pr -3	lp`	*Sort file, page output, then print*
`` $ vi `grep -l ifdef *.c` ``	*Edit files found by grep*
`` $ egrep '(yes|no)' `cat list` ``	*Specify a list of files to search*
`$ egrep '(yes|no)' $(cat list)`	*bash version of previous*
`$ egrep '(yes|no)' $(<list)`	*Same, but faster*
`$ grep XX file && lp file`	*Print file if it contains the pattern*
`$ grep XX file || echo "XX not found"`	*Echo an error message if the pattern is not found*

Redirection Forms

File Descriptor	Name	Common Abbreviation	Typical Default
0	Standard input	stdin	Keyboard
1	Standard output	stdout	Terminal
2	Standard error	stderr	Terminal

The usual input source or output destination can be changed as shown in Table 4–15.

Table 4–15: I/O Redirectors

Redirector	Function
`> file`	Direct standard output to *file*.
`< file`	Take standard input from *file*.
`cmd1	cmd2`	Pipe; take standard output of *cmd1* as standard input to *cmd2*.
`>> file`	Direct standard output to *file*; append to *file* if it already exists.
`>| file`	Force standard output to *file* even if **noclobber** is set.
`n>| file`	Force output from the file descriptor *n* to *file* even if **noclobber** is set.
`<> file`	Use *file* as both standard input and standard output.

Table 4-15: I/O Redirectors (continued)

Redirector	Function
<< *text*	Read standard input up to a line identical to *text* (*text* can be stored in a shell variable). Input is usually typed on the screen or in the shell program. Commands that typically use this syntax include **cat**, **echo**, **ex**, and **sed**. If *text* is enclosed in quotes, standard input will not undergo variable substitution, command substitution, etc.
n> *file*	Direct file descriptor *n* to *file*.
n< *file*	Set *file* as file descriptor *n*.
>&*n*	Duplicate standard output to file descriptor *n*.
<&*n*	Duplicate standard input from file descriptor *n*.
&>*file*	Direct standard output and standard error to *file*.
<&-	Close the standard input.
>&-	Close the standard output.
n>&-	Close the output from file descriptor *n*.
n<&-	Close the input from file descriptor *n*.

Examples

```
$ cat part1 > book
$ cat part2 part3 >> book
$ mail tim < report

$ sed 's/^/XX /' << END_ARCHIVE
> This is often how a shell archive is "wrapped",
> bundling text for distribution. You would normally
> run sed from a shell program, not from the command line.
> END_ARCHIVE
XX This is often how a shell archive is "wrapped",
XX bundling text for distribution. You would normally
XX run sed from a shell program, not from the command line.
```

To redirect standard output to standard error:

```
$ echo "Usage error:  see administrator" 1>&2
```

The following command sends output (files found) to *filelist* and sends error messages (inaccessible files) to file *no_access*:

```
$ find / -print > filelist 2>no_access
```

Coprocesses

Coprocesses are a feature of **bash** only.

cmd1	*cmd2* |&	Coprocess; execute the pipeline in the background. The shell sets up a two-way pipe, allowing redirection of both standard input and standard output.

read -p *var*	Read coprocess input into variable *var*.
print -p *string*	Write *string* to the coprocess.
cmd **<&p**	Take input for *cmd* from the coprocess.
cmd **>&p**	Send output of *cmd* to the coprocess.

Examples

```
cat memo                    Print contents of file
Sufficient unto the day is
A word to the wise.
ed - memo |&               Start coprocess
print -p /word/            Send ed command to coprocess
read -p search             Read output of ed command into variable search
print "$search"            Show the line on standard output
A word to the wise.
```

Variables

This subsection describes:

* Variable substitution

* Built-in shell variables

Variable Substitution

Table 4–16: Substitution Operators

Operator	Substitution
${*varname:-word*}	If *varname* exists and isn't null, return its value; otherwise return *word*.
Purpose:	Returning a default value if the variable is undefined.
Example:	${**count**:-0} evaluates to 0 if **count** is undefined.
${*varname:=word*}	If *varname* exists and isn't null, return its value; otherwise set it to *word* and then return its value. Positional and special parameters cannot be assigned this way.
Purpose:	Setting a variable to a default value if it is undefined.
Example:	${**count**:=0} sets **count** to 0 if it is undefined.
${*varname: ?message*}	If *varname* exists and isn't null, return its value; otherwise print *varname*: followed by *message*, and abort the current command or script (non-interactive shells only). Omitting *message* produces the default message **parameter null or not set**.
Purpose:	Catching errors that result from variables being undefined.

Table 4-16: Substitution Operators (continued)

Operator	Substitution
Example:	{count:?"undefined!"} prints "count: undefined!" and exits if **count** is undefined.
${*varname*:+*word*}	If *varname* exists and isn't null, return *word*; otherwise return null.
Purpose:	Testing for the existence of a variable.
Example:	${count:+1} returns 1 (which could mean "true") if **count** is defined.

Table 4-17: Pattern-Matching Operators

Operator	Meaning
${*variable#pattern*}	If the pattern matches the beginning of the variable's value, delete the shortest part that matches and return the rest.
${*variable##pattern*}	If the pattern matches the beginning of the variable's value, delete the longest part that matches and return the rest.
${*variable%pattern*}	If the pattern matches the end of the variable's value, delete the shortest part that matches and return the rest.
${*variable%%pattern*}	If the pattern matches the end of the variable's value, delete the longest part that matches and return the rest.

Built-in Shell Variables

Built-in variables are automatically set by the shell and are typically used inside shell scripts. Built-in variables can make use of the variable substitution patterns already shown above. Variables are shown in Table 4-18 through Table 4-22 without them, but they are always needed when referencing them.

Table 4-18: Basic Shell Options

Option	Description
emacs	Enter Emacs editing mode (on by default).
ignoreeof	Don't allow use of a single **CTRL-D** to log off; use the **exit** command to log off. This has the same effect as setting the shell variable IGNOREEOF=1.
noclobber	Don't allow output redirection (>) to overwrite an existing file.
noglob	Don't expand filename wildcards like * and ? (wildcard expansion is sometimes called *globbing*).
nounset	Indicate an error when trying to use a variable that is undefined.
vi	Enter **vi** editing mode.

Table 4-19: Standard Variables

Variable	Meaning
COLUMNS	The number of columns your display has.
EDITOR	Pathname of your text editor.
LINES	The number of lines your display has.
SHELL	Pathname of the shell you are running.
TERM	The type of terminal that you are using.

Table 4-20: History Variables

Variable	Meaning
HISTCMD	The history number of the current command.
HISTCONTROL	If HISTCONTROL is set to the value of **ignorespace**, lines beginning with a space are not entered into the history list. If set to **ignoredups**, lines matching the last history line are not entered. Setting it to **ignoreboth** enables both options.
HISTFILE	Name of history file, on which the editing modes operate.
HISTFILESIZE	The maximum number of lines to store in the history file. The default is 500.
HISTSIZE	The maximum number of commands to remember in the command history. The default is 500.
FCEDIT	Pathname of editor to use with the **fc** command.

Table 4-21: Mail Variables

Variable	Meaning
MAIL	Name of file to check for incoming mail.
MAILCHECK	How often, in seconds, to check for new mail (default is 60 seconds).
MAILPATH	List of filenames, separated by colons (:), to check for incoming mail.

Table 4-22: Status Variables

Variable	Meaning
HOME	Name of your home (login) directory.
SECONDS	Number of seconds since the shell was invoked.
BASH	Pathname of this instance of the shell you are running.
BASH_VERSION	The version number of the shell you are running.
PWD	Current directory.
OLDPWD	Previous directory before the last **cd** command.

bash

Arithmetic Expressions

The **let** command performs integer arithmetic. **bash** provides a way to substitute integer values (for use as command arguments or in variables); base conversion is also possible:

$((expr))   Use the value of the enclosed arithmetic expression.

Operators

bash uses arithmetic operators from the C programming language; the following list is in decreasing order of precedence. Use parentheses to override precedence.

–	Unary minus
! ~	Logical negation; binary inversion (one's complement)
* / %	Multiplication; division; modulus (remainder)
+ -	Addition; subtraction
<< >>	Bitwise left shift; bitwise right shift
<= >=	Less than or equal to; greater than or equal to
< >	Less than; greater than
== !=	Equality; inequality (both evaluated left to right)
&	Bitwise AND
^	Bitwise exclusive OR
|	Bitwise OR
&&	Logical AND
||	Logical OR
=	Assign value.
+= -=	Reassign after addition/subtraction
*= /= %=	Reassign after multiplication/division/remainder
&= ^= |=	Reassign after bitwise AND/XOR/OR
<<= >>=	Reassign after bitwise shift left/right

Examples

See the **let** command for more information and examples.

```
let "count=0" "i = i + 1"      Assign i and count
let "num % 2"                  Test for an even number
```

Command History

bash lets you display or modify previous commands. This is similar to the C shell's history mechanism. Commands in the history list can be modified using:

- Line-edit mode

- The **fc** command

In addition, the command substitutions described in Chapter 5, *csh and tcsh*, also work in **bash**.

Line-Edit Mode

Line-edit mode lets you emulate many features of the **vi** or Emacs editors. The history list is treated like a file. When the editor is invoked, you type editing keystrokes to move to the command line you want to execute. You can also change the line before executing it. When you're ready to issue the command, press RETURN. See Table 4–23.

Line-edit mode can be started in several ways. For example, these are equivalent:

```
$ VISUAL=vi
$ EDITOR=vi
$ set -o vi          Overrides value of VISUAL or EDITOR
```

Note that **vi** starts in input mode; to type a **vi** command, press ESCAPE first.

Table 4–23: Common Editing Keystrokes

vi	Emacs	Result
k	**CTRL-P**	Get previous command.
j	**CTRL-N**	Get next command.
/string	**CTRL-R** string	Get previous command containing *string*.
h	**CTRL-B**	Move back one character.
l	**CTRL-F**	Move forward one character.
b	**ESC-B**	Move back one word.
w	**ESC-F**	Move forward one word.
X	**DEL**	Delete previous character.
x	**CTRL-D**	Delete one character.
dw	**ESC-D**	Delete word forward.
db	**ESC-H**	Delete word back.
xp	**CTRL-T**	Transpose two characters.

The fc Command

Use **fc −l** to list history commands and **fc −e** to edit them. See the entry under built-in commands for more information.

Examples

```
$ history              List the last 16 commands
$ fc -l 20 30          List commands 20 through 30
$ fc -l -5             List the last five commands
$ fc -l cat            List the last command beginning with cat
$ fc -ln 5 > doit      Save command 5 to file doit
```

```
$ fc -e vi 5 20          Edit commands 5 through 20 using vi
$ fc -e emacs            Edit previous command using Emacs.
$ !!                     Reexecute previous command
$ !cat                   Reexecute last cat command.
$ !cat foo-file          Reexecute last command, adding foo-file to the end of the
                         argument list
```

Command Substitution

!	Begin a history substitution.
!!	Previous command.
!*N*	Command number *N* in history list.
!*-N*	*N*th command back from current command.
!*string*	Most recent command that starts with *string*.
!?*string*?	Most recent command that contains *string*.
!?*string*?%	Most recent command argument that contains *string*.
!$	Last argument of previous command.
!!*string*	Previous command, then append *string*.
!*N string*	Command *N*, then append *string*.
!{*s1*}*s2*	Most recent command starting with string *s1*, then append string *s2*.
^*old*^*new*^	Quick substitution; change string *old* to *new* in previous command; execute modified command.

Built-in Commands

Examples to be entered as a command line are shown with the **$** prompt. Otherwise, examples should be treated as code fragments that might be included in a shell script. For convenience, some of the reserved words used by multiline commands are also included.

#	#
	Ignore all text that follows on the same line. # is used in shell scripts as the comment character, and is not really a command.

#!	#!*shell*
	Used as the first line of a script to invoke the named *shell* (with optional arguments). Some older, non-Linux systems do not support scripts starting with this line. For example: `#!/bin/bash`

:	:
	Null command. Returns an exit status of 0. Sometimes used as the first character in a file to denote a **bash** script. Shell variables can be placed after the : to expand them to their values.

Example

Check whether someone is logged in:

```
if who | grep $1 > /dev/null
then :                    # do nothing
                          # if pattern is found
else echo "User $1 is not logged in"
fi
```

. *file* [*arguments*]

Same as **source**.

alias [*name*[=`cmd`]]   alias

Assign a shorthand *name* as a synonym for *cmd*. If =`cmd` is omitted, print the alias for *name*; if *name* is also omitted, print all
aliases. If *cmd* is followed by a space, check subsequent command-
line argument for another alias. See also **unalias**.

bg [*jobIDs*]   bg

Put current job or *jobIDs* in the background. See "Job Control" later
in this chapter.

bind [*options*]   bind
bind [*options*] *keys*:*function*

Print or set key and function bindings.

Options

    −m *keymap*

        Specify a keymap for future bindings. Possible
        keymaps are **emacs**, **emacs-standard**, **emacs-meta**,
        emacs-ctlx, **vi**, **vi-move**, **vi-command**, and **vi-insert**.

    −l   Print all read-line functions.

    −v   Print all function names.

    −d   Display function names and bindings, suitable for
        rereading.

    −f *filename*

        Consult *filename* for bindings.

    −q *function*

        Display the bindings that invoke *function*.

bash

break	**break** [*n*] Exit from the innermost (most deeply nested) **for**, **while**, or **until** loop, or from the *n* innermost levels of the loop. Also exits from a **select** list.
built–in	**built–in** *command* [*arguments*] Execute *command*, which must be a shell built-in. Useful for invoking built-ins within scripts of the same name.

case	**case** *string*
	in
	   regex)
	   commands
	     ;;
	     . . .
	   esac
	
	If *string* matches regular expression *regex*, perform the following *commands*. Procede down the list of regular expressions until one is found (to catch all remaining strings, use * as *regex* at the end).

cd	**cd** [*dir*] With no arguments, change to home directory of user. Otherwise, change working directory to *dir*. If *dir* is a relative pathname but is not in the current directory, then the CDPATH variable is searched.

command	**command** [*options*] *command* [*arguments*]
	
	Execute *command*; do not perform function look up (i.e., refuse to run any command that is neither in PATH or a built-in). Set exit status to that returned by *command*, unless *command* cannot be found, in which case exit with a status of 127.
	
	   -p Search default path, ignoring the PATH variable's value.
	
	   -- Treat everything that follows as an argument, not an option.

continue	**continue** [*n*] Skip remaining commands in a **for**, **while**, or **until** loop, resuming with the next iteration of the loop (or skipping *n* loops).

declare [*options*] [*name*[*=value*]]
typeset [*options*] [*name*[*=value*]]
 	
Print or set variables. Options prefaced by + instead of – are inverted in meaning.
 	
    −f   Use only function names.
 	
    −r   Do not allow variables to be reset later.
 	
    −x   Mark variables for subsequent export.
 	
    −i   Expect variable to be an integer, and evaluate its assigned value.
	declare

dirs [*options*]
 	
Print directories currently remembered for **pushd/popd** operations.
 	
Options
 	
    +*entry*   Print *entry*th entry (starting with zero).
 	
    − *entry*   Print *entry*th entry from end of list.
 	
    −l   Long listing.
	dirs

echo [*options*] [*string*]
 	
Write *string* to standard output, terminated by a newline. If no *string* is supplied, echo a newline. In **bash**, **echo** is just an alias for **print −**. (See also **echo** in Chapter 2, *Linux User Commands.*)
 	
    −n   Do not append a newline to the output.
 	
    −e   Enable interpretation of escape characters.
 	
            \a Audible alert
 	
            \b Backspace
 	
            \c Suppress the terminating newline (same as **−n**)
 	
            \f Form feed
 	
            \n Newline
 	
            \r Carriage return
 	
            \t Horizontal tab
 	
            \v Vertical tab
	echo

bash

→

echo ←	\\ Backslash *nnn* The character whose ASCII code is the octal value *nnn*. −E Disable interpretation of escape characters.
enable	**enable** [−*n*] [−*a* │−*all*] [*built-in* ...] Enable (or when -*n* is specified, disable) built-in shell commands. Without *built-in*, print enabled built-ins; with -*a* or -*all* print the status of all built-ins. You can disable shell commands so as to define your own functions with the same names.
eval	**eval** [*command args...*] Perform *command*, passing *args*.
exec	**exec** [[−] *command*] Execute *command* in place of the current process (instead of creating a new process). **exec** is also useful for opening, closing, or copying file descriptors. If − is provided, pass − as zeroth argument to the new process. *Examples* `$ trap 'exec 2>&-' 0` *Close standard error when* *shell script exits (signal 0)* `$ exec /bin/tcsh` *Replace current shell with extended C shell* `$ exec < infile` *Reassign standard input to infile*

exit	**exit** [*n*]
	
	Exit a shell script with status *n* (e.g., **exit 1**). *n* can be 0 (success) or nonzero (failure). If *n* is not given, exit status will be that of the most recent command. **exit** can be issued at the command line to close a window (log out).
	
	Example
	
	``
	if [$# -eq 0]; then
	    echo "Usage: $0 [-c] [-d] file(s)"
	    exit 1 # Error status
	fi
	``

export	**export** [*options*] [*variables*] **export** [*options*] [*name=*[*value*]] ... Pass (export) the value of one or more shell *variables*, giving global meaning to the variables (which are local by default). For example, a variable defined in one shell script must be exported if its value

will be used in other programs called by the script. If no *variables* are given, **export** lists the variables exported by the current shell. If *name* and *value* are specified, assign *value* to a variable *name*.

Options

−−	Treat all subsequent strings as arguments, not options.
−f	Expect *variables* to be functions.
−n	Unexport variable.
−p	List variables exported by current shell.

---

fc [*options*] [*first*] [*last*]
fc −e − [*old=new*] [*command*]

bash

Display or edit commands in the history list. (Use only one of −1 or −e.) **fc** provides capabilities similar to the C shell's **history** and ! syntax. *first* and *last* are numbers or strings specifying the range of commands to display or edit. If *last* is omitted, **fc** applies to a single command (specified by *first*). If both *first* and *last* are omitted, **fc** edits the previous command or lists the last 16. The second form of **fc** takes a history *command*, replaces *old* string with *new* string, and executes the modified command. If no strings are specified, *command* is just reexecuted. If no *command* is given either, the previous command is reexecuted. *command* is a number or string like *first*. See examples under "Command History."

Options

−e [*editor*]
    Invoke *editor* to edit the specified history commands. The default *editor* is set by shell variable FCEDIT.

−1 [*first last*]
    List the specified command or range of commands, or list the last 16.

−n	Suppress command numbering from the −1 listing.
−r	Reverse the order of the −1 listing.

−s *pattern=newpattern*
    Edit command(s), replacing all occurrences of *pattern* with *newpattern*. Then reexecute.

---

fg [*jobIDs*]

Bring current job or *jobIDs* to the foreground. See "Job Control."

for	for *x* [in *list*]
	do
	    commands
	done
	
	Assign each word in list to *x* in turn and execute commands. If *list* is omitted, **$@** (positional parameters) is assumed.
	
	Examples
	
	Paginate all files in the current directory; save each result:
	
	<pre>for $file in *
	do
	     pr $file > $file.tmp
	done</pre>
	Search chapters for a list of words (like **fgrep −f**):
	
	<pre>for item in `cat program_list`
	do
	     echo "Checking chapters for"
	     echo "references to program $item..."
	     grep -c "$item.[co]" chap*
	done</pre>

function	function *command* { Define a function. Refer to arguments the same way as positional parameters in a shell script (**$1**, etc.) and terminate with }.
getopts	getopts *string name* [*args*] Process command-line arguments (or *args*, if specified) and check for legal options. **getopts** is used in shell script loops and is intended to ensure standard syntax for command-line options. *string* contains the option letters to be recognized by **getopts** when running the shell script. Valid options are processed in turn and stored in the shell variable *name*. If an option letter is followed by a colon, the option must be followed by one or more arguments. **getopts** uses the shell variables OPTARG and OPTIND.
hash	hash [−r] [*commands*] Search for *commands* and remember the directory in which each command resides. Hashing causes the shell to remember the association between a "name" and the absolute pathname of an executable, so that future executions don't require a search of PATH. With no arguments, **hash** lists the current

hashed commands. The display shows *hits* (the number of times the command is called by the shell) and *command* (the full pathname).

help [*string*]

Print help text on all built-in commands, or those matching *string*.

history [*options*]
history [*lines*]

Print a numbered command history, denoting modified commands with a *. Include commands from previous sessions. You may specify how many lines of history to print.

Options

    −a   **bash** maintains a file called *.bash_history* in the user's home directory, a record of previous sessions' commands. Ask **bash** to append the current session's commands to *.bash_history.*

    −n   Append to the history list those lines in the *bash_history* file that have not yet been included.

    −r   Use *.bash_history* as the history list, instead of the working history list.

    −w   Overwrite *.bash_history* with working history list.

if *test−cmds*

Begin a conditional statement. Possible formats are:

```
if test-cmds      if test-cmds      if test-cmds
then              then              then
    cmds1             cmds1             cmds1
fi                else              elif test-cmds
                      cmds2          then
                  fi                    cmds2
                                    ...
                                    else
                                        cmdsn
                                    fi
```

Usually, the initial **if** and any **elif** lines execute one **test** or [] command (although any series of commands is permitted). When **if** succeeds (that is, the last of its *test-cmds* returns zero), *cmds1* are performed; otherwise each succeeding **elif** or **else** line is tried.

jobs	**jobs** [*options*] [*jobIDs*]
	
	List all running or stopped jobs, or those specified by *jobIDs*. For example, you can check whether a long compilation or text format is still running. Also useful before logging out. See also "Job Control" later in this chapter.
	
	Options
	
	    −l List job IDs and process group IDs.
	
	    −n List only jobs whose status changed since last notification.
	
	    −p List process group IDs only.
	
	    −x *command* [*arguments*]
	         Execute *command*. If *jobIDs* are specified, replace them with *command*.

kill	**kill** [*options*] *IDs*
	
	Terminate each specified process *ID* or job *ID*. You must own the process or be a privileged user. See also "Job Control."
	
	Options
	
	    −*signal* The signal number (from **ps −f**) or name (from **kill −l**). With a signal number of 9, the kill cannot be caught. The default is TERM.
	
	    −− Consider all subsequent strings to be arguments, not options.
	
	    −l List the signal names. (Used by itself.)
	
	    −s *signal*
	         Specify *signal*. May be a name.

let	**let** *expressions* Perform arithmetic as specified by one or more integer *expressions*. *expressions* consist of numbers, operators, and shell variables (which don't need a preceding $). Expressions must be quoted if they contain spaces or other special characters. For more information and examples, see "Arithmetic Expressions" earlier in this section. See also **expr** in Chapter 2. *Examples* Both of the following examples add 1 to variable i: ```\nlet i=i+1\nlet "i = i + 1"\n```

local [*variable*[*=value*]] [*variable2*[*=value*]] ... ⎮ local

Without arguments, print all local variables. Otherwise, create
(and set, if specified) a local variable.

---

logout ⎮ logout

Exit shell. Can be used only if it is a login shell. Otherwise,
use **exit**.

---

popd [*options*] ⎮ popd

Manipulate the directory stack. By default, remove the top
directory and **cd** to it.

Options

   +*n*   Remove the *n*th directory in the stack, counting
             from 0.

   −*n*   Remove *n*th entry from the bottom of the stack,
             counting from 0.

---

pushd *directory* ⎮ pushd
pushd [*options*]

By default, switch top two directories on stack. If specified,
add a new directory to the top of the stack instead, and **cd** to
it.

Options

   +*n*   Rotate the stack to place the *n*th (counting from
             0) directory at the top.

   −*n*   Rotate the stack to place the *n*th directory from
             the bottom of the stack at the top.

---

pwd ⎮ pwd

Display the current working directory's absolute pathname. If
the built-in **-P** option is set, this pathname will not contain
symbolic links.

---

read [*options*] *variable1* [*variable2* ...] ⎮ read

Read one line of standard input, and assign each word (as
defined by IFS) to the corresponding *variable*, with all left-
over words assigned to the last variable. If only one variable
is specified, the entire line will be assigned to that variable.
See the following example; also see **case**. The return status is

→

read ←	0 unless *EOF* is reached. If no variable names are provided, read the entire string into the environment variable REPLY. *Options* **−r** Raw mode; ignore \ as a line continuation character. *Example* ```\n$ read first last address\nSarah Caldwell 123 Main Street\n$ echo "$last, $first\n$address"\nCaldwell, Sarah\n123 Main Street\n```

readonly	**readonly** [*options*] [*variable1 variable2 ...*]
	
	Prevent the specified shell variables from being assigned new values. Variables can be accessed (read) but not overwritten. In **bash**, the syntax *variable=value* can be used to assign a new value that cannot be changed.
	
	Options
	
	    −− Treat all subsequent strings as arguments, not options.
	
	    −f [*variable(s)*]
	          Set *variable(s)* to read-only, so that they cannot be changed.
	
	    −p Display all read-only variables (default).

return	**return** [*n*] Used inside a function definition. Exit the function with status *n* or with the exit status of the previously executed command.

select	**select** *name* [*in wordlist ;*]
	  do
	      commands
	  done
	
	Choose a value for *name* by displaying the words in *wordlist* to the user and prompting for a choice. Store user input in the variable **REPLY** and the chosen word in *name*. Then execute *commands* repeatedly until they execute a **break** or **return**.

set [*options*] [*arg1 arg2 ...*]

With no arguments, **set** prints the values of all variables
known to the current shell. Options can be enabled (−*option*)
or disabled (+*option*). Options can also be set when the shell
is invoked, via **bash**. Arguments are assigned in order to **$1**,
$2, etc.

Options

-      Turn off −**v** and −**x**, and turn off option processing.

--   Used as the last option; −− turns off option processing so that arguments beginning with − are
  not misinterpreted as options. (For example, you
  can set **$1** to −1.) If no arguments are given after
  −−, unset the positional parameters.

−**a**   From now on, automatically mark variables for
  export after defining or changing them.

−**b**   Report background job status at termination,
  instead of waiting for next shell prompt.

−**d**   Do not hash commands after looking them up.

−**e**   Exit if a command yields a nonzero exit status.

−**f**   Do not expand filename metacharacters (e.g., * ?
  [ ]).

−**h**   Locate commands as they are defined, and
  remember them.

−**k**   Assignment of environment variables (*var=value*)
  will take effect regardless of where they appear
  on the command line. Normally, assignments
  must precede the command name.

−**l**   When a **for** command uses a variable that is
  already bound, restore that variable's original
  value after the **for** command exits.

−**m**   Monitor mode. Enable job control; background
  jobs executes in a separate process group. −**m** is
  usually set automatically.

−**n**   Read commands but don't execute; useful for
  checking errors. Useful for noninteractive shells.

−**o** [*m*]
     List shell modes, or turn on mode *m*. Many modes
  can be set by other options. Modes are:

  allexport
     Same as −**a**.

bash

→

braceexpand
: Default. Enable brace expansion.

emacs
: Default. Enable Emacs-style command-line editing.

errexit
: Same as −e.

histexpand
: Same as −H.

ignoreeof
: Do not exit on *EOF*. To exit the shell, type **exit**.

interactive-comments
: Treat all words beginning with #, and all subsequent words, as comments.

monitor
: Same as −m.

noclobber
: Same as −C.

noexec
: Same as −n.

noglob
: Same as −f.

notify
: Same as −b.

nounset
: Same as −u.

physical
: Same as −P.

posix
: Match POSIX standard.

privileged
: Same as −p.

verbose
: Same as −v.

vi Enable **vi**-style command-line editing.

xtrace
: Same as −x.

−p
: Start up as a privileged user; don't process *$HOME/.profile*.

−t
: Exit after one command is executed.

−u	In substitutions, treat unset variables as errors.	**set**
−v	Show each shell command line when read.	
−x	Show commands and arguments when executed, preceded by a +. This provides step-by-step debugging of shell scripts. (Same as −o **xtrace**.)	
−C	Same as **noclobber**	
−H	Default. Enable ! and !! commands.	
−P	Print absolute pathnames in response to **pwd**. By default, **bash** includes symbolic links in its response to **pwd**.	

Examples

```
set -- "$num" -20 -30    Set $1 to $num, $2 to −20, $3 to −30.
set -vx                  Read each command line; show it;
                         execute it; show it again (with arguments)
set +x                   Stop command tracing
set -o noclobber         Prevent file overwriting
set +o noclobber         Allow file overwriting again
```

---

shift [*n*]

shift

Shift positional arguments (e.g., **$2** becomes **$1**). If *n* is given, shift to the left *n* places.

---

source *file* [*arguments*]

source

Read and execute lines in *file*. *file* does not have to be executable but must reside in a directory searched by PATH.

---

suspend [−f]

suspend

Same as **CTRL-Z**. Often used to stop an **su** command.

Option

−f	Force suspend, even if shell is a login shell.

---

test *condition*
or
[*condition*]

test

Evaluate a *condition* and, if its value is true, return a zero exit status; otherwise, return a nonzero exit status. An alternate form of the command uses [ ] rather than the word *test. condition* is constructed using the expressions below. Conditions are true if the description holds true.

$\rightarrow$

test

←

File conditions

−b *file*	*file* exists and is a block special file.
−c *file*	*file* exists and is a character special file.
−d *file*	*file* exists and is a directory.
−e *file*	*file* exists.
−f *file*	*file* exists and is a regular file.
−g *file*	*file* exists and its set-group-id bit is set.
−k *file*	*file* exists and its sticky bit is set.
−p *file*	*file* exists and is a named pipe (fifo).
−r *file*	*file* exists and is readable.
−s *file*	*file* exists and has a size greater than zero.
−t [*n*]	The open file descriptor *n* is associated with a terminal device; default *n* is 1.
−u *file*	*file* exists and its set-user-id bit is set.
−w *file*	*file* exists and is writable.
−x *file*	*file* exists and is executable.
−G *file*	*file* exists and its group is the process's effective group ID.
−L *file*	*file* exists and is a symbolic link.
−O *file*	*file* exists and its owner is the process's effective user ID.
−S *file*	*file* exists and is a socket.
f1 −ef *f2*	Files *f1* and *f2* are linked (refer to same file).
f1 −nt *f2*	File *f1* is newer than *f2*.
f1 −ot *f2*	File *f1* is older than *f2*.

String conditions

−n *s1*	String *s1* has nonzero length.
−z *s1*	String *s1* has zero length.
s1 = *s2*	Strings *s1* and *s2* are identical.
s1 != *s2*	Strings *s1* and *s2* are not identical.
string	*string* is not null.

Integer comparisons

n1 −eq *n2*	*n1* equals *n2*.

n1 −**ge** *n2*	*n1* is greater than or equal to *n2*.
n1 −**gt** *n2*	*n1* is greater than *n2*.
n1 −**le** *n2*	*n1* is less than or equal to *n2*.
n1 −**lt** *n2*	*n1* is less than *n2*.
n1 −**ne** *n2*	*n1* does not equal *n2*.

Combined forms

! *condition*	True if *condition* is false.
condition1 −**a** *condition2*	
	True if both conditions are true.
condition1 −**o** *condition2*	
	True if either condition is true.

Examples

Each of the following examples shows the first line of various statements that might use a test condition:

```
while test $# -gt 0          While there are arguments . . .
while [ -n "$1" ]            While the first argument is nonempty . . .
if [ $count -lt 10 ]         If $count is less than 10 . . .
if [ -d RCS ]                If the RCS directory exists . . .
if [ "$answer" != "y" ]      If the answer is not y . . .
if [ ! -r "$1" -o ! -f "$1" ]   If the first argument is not a
                                readable file or a regular file . . .
```

---

times

Print accumulated process times for user and system.

---

trap [−1] [[*commands*] *signals*]

Execute *commands* if any of *signals* is received. Common signals include 0, 1, 2, and 15. Multiple commands should be quoted as a group and separated by semicolons internally. If *commands* is the null string (i.e., **trap** "" *signals*), then *signals* will be ignored by the shell. If *commands* is omitted entirely, reset processing of specified signals to the default action. If both *commands* and *signals* are omitted, list current trap assignments. See examples at the end of this entry and under **exec**.

Option

−1   List signals.

Signals

Signals are listed along with what triggers them.

→

trap	0	Exit from shell (usually when shell script finishes)
←	1	Hangup (usually logout)
	2	Interrupt (usually **CTRL-C**)
	3	Quit
	4	Illegal instruction
	5	Trace trap
	6	Abort
	7	Unused
	8	Floating-point exception
	9	Termination
	10	User-defined
	11	Reference to invalid memory
	12	User-defined
	13	Write to a pipe without a process to read it
	14	Alarm timeout
	15	Software termination (usually via **kill**)
	16	Coprocessor stack fault
	17	Termination of child process
	18	Continue (if stopped)
	19	Stop process
	20	Stop typed at tty
	21	Background process has tty input
	22	Background process has tty output
	23	I/O error
	24	CPU time limit exceeded
	25	File size limit exceeded
	27	Profile
	28	Window resize

Examples

```
trap "" 2                    Ignore signal 2 (interrupts)
trap 2                       Obey interrupts again
```

Remove a **$tmp** file when the shell program exits, or if the user logs out, presses **CTRL-C**, or does a **kill**:

```
trap "rm -f $tmp; exit" 0 1 2 15
```

type [*options*] *commands*

Report absolute pathname of programs invoked for *commands*, and whether or not they are hashed.

`--`	Consider all subsequent strings to be arguments, not options.
`-a, -all`	Print all occurrences of *command*, not just that which would be invoked.
`-p, -path`	Print the hashed value of *command*, which may differ from the first appearance of *command* in the PATH.
`-t, -type`	Determine and state if *command* is an alias, keyword, function, built-in, or file.

Example

```
$ type mv read
mv is /bin/mv
read is a shell built-in
```

---

typeset

See **declare**.

---

ulimit [*options*] [*n*]

Print the value of one or more resource limits, or, if *n* is specified, set a resource limit to *n*. Resource limits can be either hard (**-H**) or soft (**-S**). By default, **ulimit** sets both limits or prints the soft limit. The options determine which resource is acted on.

Options

`--`	Consider all subsequent strings to be arguments, not options.
`-a`	Print all current limits.
`-H`	Hard resource limit.
`-S`	Soft resource limit.

Specific limits

These options limit specific resource sizes.

`-c`	Core files.
`-d`	Size of processes' data segments.
`-f`	Size of shell-created files.

$\rightarrow$

ulimit	−m	Resident set size.
←	−n	Number of file descriptors. On many systems, this cannot be set.
	−p	Pipe size, measured in blocks of 512 bytes.
	−s	Stack size.
	−t	Amount of CPU time, counted in seconds.
	−u	Number of processes per user.
	−v	Virtual memory used by shell.

umask	umask [*nnn*] umask [-*S*]

Display file creation mask or set file creation mask to octal value *nnn*. The file creation mask determines which permission bits are turned off (e.g., **umask 002** produces **rw−rw−r−−**).

Option

| | −S | Display **umask** symbolically, rather than in octal. |

unalias	unalias [−*a*] *names*

Remove *names* from the alias list. See also **alias**.

Option

| | −a | Remove all aliases. |

unset	unset [*options*] *names*

Erase definitions of functions or variables listed in *names*.

Options

| | −f | Expect *name* to refer to a function. |
| | −v | Expect *name* to refer to a variable (default). |

until	until
	   test-commands
	do
	   commands
	done

Execute *test-commands* (usually a **test** or [] command) and if the exit status is non-zero (that is, the test fails), perform *commands*; repeat.

wait [*ID*]

Pause in execution until all background jobs complete (exit status 0 will be returned), or pause until the specified background process *ID* or job *ID* completes (exit status of *ID* is returned). Note that the shell variable $! contains the process ID of the most recent background process. If job control is not in effect, *ID* can be only a process ID number. See "Job Control."

Example

> `wait $!` *Wait for last background process to finish*

wait

---

while
> *test-commands*

do
> *commands*

done

Execute *test-commands* (usually a **test** or [] command) and if the exit status is zero, perform *commands*; repeat.

while

Job Control

Job control lets you place foreground jobs in the background, bring background jobs to the foreground, or suspend (temporarily stop) running jobs. Job control is enabled by default. Once disabled, it can be reenabled by any of the following commands:

```
bash -m -i
set -m
set -o monitor
```

Many job control commands take *jobID* as an argument. This argument can be specified as follows:

%*n*	Job number *n*
%*s*	Job whose command line starts with string *s*
%?*s*	Job whose command line contains string *s*
%%	Current job
%+	Current job (same as above)
%–	Previous job

bash provides the following job control commands. For more information on these commands, see "Built-in Commands" earlier in this chapter.

bg	Put a job in the background.

fg	Put a job in the foreground.
jobs	List active jobs.
kill	Terminate a job.
stop	Suspend a background job.
stty tostop	Stop background jobs if they try to send output to the terminal.
wait	Wait for background jobs to finish.
CTRL-Z	Suspend a foreground job. Then use **bg** or **fg**. (Your terminal may use something other than **CTRL-Z** as the suspend character.)

CHAPTER 5

csh and tcsh

This chapter describes the C shell and its enhancement, **tcsh**. On some versions of Linux, **tcsh** is used as the C shell, so all the features in this chapter work even if you run **csh**. The C shell was so named because many of its programming constructs and symbols resemble those of the C programming language. The following topics are presented:

- Overview of features

- Invoking the shell

- Syntax

- Variables

- Expressions

- Command history

- Command-line manipulation

- Built-in commands

- Job control

Overview of Features

Features of the C shell include:

- Input/output redirection

- Wildcard characters (metacharacters) for filename abbreviation

- Shell variables for customizing your environment

- Integer arithmetic

- Access to previous commands (command history)

- Command-name abbreviation (aliasing)

- A built-in command set for writing shell programs

- Job control

The **tcsh** shell includes all of these features. In addition, it has some extensions:

- Command-line editing and editor commands

- Word completion (tab completion)

- Spell checking

- Extended history commands

- Extended handling of directory manipulation (**cd**, **pushd**, **popd**, **dirs**)

- Scheduled events, such as logout or terminal locking after a set idle period, and delayed commands

- New shell built-ins: **hup**, **ls-F**, **newgrp**, **printenv**, **which**, and **where**

- New shell variables (**gid**, **loginsh**, **oid**, **shlvl**, **tcsh**, **tty**, **uid**, and **version**) and environment variables (**HOST**, **REMOTEHOST**, **VENDOR**, **OSTYPE**, and **MACHTYPE**)

- New formatting sequences for the PROMPT variable, as well as two new prompts (in loops and spelling correction)

- Read-only variables

Invoking the Shell

A shell command interpreter can be invoked as follows:

> csh [*options*] [*arguments*]
> tcsh [*options*] [*arguments*]

csh and tcsh use syntax resembling C and execute commands from a terminal or a file. Options −n, −v, and −x are useful when debugging scripts.

Options

−b   Allow the remaining command-line options to be interpreted as options to a specified command, rather than as options to **csh** itself.

−c   Execute command specified following the argument.

−e   Exit if a command produces errors.

−f   Fast startup; start **csh** without executing *.cshrc* or *.login*.

−i   Invoke interactive shell (prompt for input).

−n	Parse commands but do not execute.
−s	Read commands from the standard input.
−t	Exit after executing one command.
−v	Display commands before executing them; expand history substitutions, but don't expand other substitutions (e.g., filename, variable, and command). Same as setting **verbose**.
−V	Same as −v, but also display *.cshrc*.
−x	Display commands before executing them, but expand all substitutions. Same as setting **echo**.
−X	Same as −x, but also display *.cshrc*.

Arguments

Arguments are assigned, in order, to the positional parameters $1, $2, etc. If the first argument is an executable script, commands are read from it and remaining arguments are assigned to $1, $2, etc.

Syntax

This section describes the many symbols peculiar to **csh** and **tcsh**. The topics are arranged as follows:

- Special files
- Filename metacharacters
- Quoting
- Command forms
- Redirection forms

Special Files

˜/.cshrc	Executed at each instance of shell startup
˜/.login	Executed by login shell after *.cshrc* at login
˜/.logout	Executed by login shell at logout
/etc/passwd	Source of home directories for *˜name* abbreviations

Filename Metacharacters

*	Match any string of zero or more characters.
?	Match any single character.
[abc...**]**	Match any one of the enclosed characters; a hyphen can be used to specify a range (e.g., a-z, A-Z, 0-9).
{abc,xxx, ...**}**	Expand each comma-separated string inside braces.

~	Home directory for the current user.
~name	Home directory of user *name*.

Examples

% **ls new***	*Match* new *and* new.1
% **cat ch?**	*Match* ch9 *but not* ch10
% **vi [D-R]***	*Match files that begin with uppercase D through R*
% **ls {ch,app}?**	*Expand, then match* ch1, ch2, app1, app2
% **cd ~tom**	*Change to* tom's *home directory*

Quoting

Quoting disables a character's special meaning and allows it to be used literally, as itself. The following characters have special meaning to the C shell:

;	Command separator
&	Background execution
( )	Command grouping
|	Pipe
* ? [ ] ~	Filename metacharacters
{ }	String expansion characters (usually don't require quoting)
> < & !	Redirection symbols
! ^	History substitution, quick substitution
**" ' **	Used in quoting other characters
`	Command substitution
$	Variable substitution
newline space tab	Word separators

The characters that follow can be used for quoting:

" "   Everything between " and " is taken literally, except for the following characters that keep their special meaning:

$	Variable substitution will occur.
`	Command substitution will occur.
"	This marks the end of the double quote.
****	Escape next character.
!	The history character
newline	The newline character

' '   Everything between ' and ' is taken literally except for ! (history) and another ', and newline.

****   The character following a \\ is taken literally. Use within " " to escape ", $, and `. Often used to escape itself, spaces, or newlines. Always needed to escape a history character (usually !).

Examples

```
% echo 'Single quotes "protect" double quotes'
Single quotes "protect" double quotes

% echo "Well, isn't that \"special\"?"
Well, isn't that "special"?

% echo "You have `ls|wc -l` files in `pwd`"
You have 43 files in /home/bob

% echo "The value of \$x is $x"
The value of $x is 100
```

Command Forms

cmd **&**	Execute *cmd* in background.
cmd1 **;** cmd2	Command sequence; execute multiple *cmd*s on the same line.
(cmd1 **;** cmd2)	Subshell; treat *cmd1* and *cmd2* as a command group.
cmd1 **|** cmd2	Pipe; use output from *cmd1* as input to *cmd2*.
cmd1 **`cmd2`**	Command substitution; use *cmd2* output as arguments to *cmd1*.
cmd1 **||** cmd2	OR; execute *cmd1* and then (if *cmd1* succeeds) *cmd2*.
cmd1 **&&** cmd2	AND; execute either *cmd1* or (if *cmd1* fails) *cmd2*.

Examples

`% nroff file &`	*Format in the background*
`% cd; ls`	*Execute sequentially*
`% (date; who; pwd) > logfile`	*All output is redirected*
`% sort file | pr -3 | lp`	*Sort file, page output, then print*
`% vi `grep -l ifdef *.c``	*Edit files found by* grep
`% egrep '(yes|no)' `cat list``	*Specify a list of files to search*
`% grep XX file || lp file`	*Print file if it contains the pattern*
`% grep XX file && echo XX not found`	*Echo an error message if* XX *not found*

Redirection Forms

File Descriptor	Name	Common Abbreviation	Typical Default
0	Standard input	stdin	Keyboard
1	Standard output	stdout	Terminal
2	Standard error	stderr	Terminal

The usual input source or output destination can be changed as follows:

Simple redirection

cmd **>** file	Send output of *cmd* to *file* (overwrite).
cmd **>!** file	Same as above, even if **noclobber** is set.
cmd **>>** file	Send output of *cmd* to *file* (append).

`cmd >>! file`	Same as above, even if **noclobber** is set.
`cmd < file`	Take input for *cmd* from `file`.
`cmd << text`	Read standard input up to a line identical to `text` (`text` can be stored in a shell variable). Input is usually typed on the screen or in the shell program. Commands that typically use this syntax include **cat**, **echo**, **ex**, and **sed**. If `text` is enclosed in quotes, standard input will not undergo variable substitution, command substitution, etc.

Multiple redirection

`cmd >& file`	Send both standard output and standard error to `file`.
`cmd >&! file`	Same as above, even if **noclobber** is set.
`cmd >>& file`	Append standard output and standard error to end of `file`.
`cmd >>&! file`	Same as above, even if **noclobber** is set.
`cmd1 |& cmd2`	Pipe standard error together with standard output.
`(cmd > f1) >& f2`	Send standard output to file `f1`, and standard error to file `f2`.
`cmd | tee files`	Send output of *cmd* to standard output (usually the terminal) and to `files`. (See the example in Chapter 2 under **tee**.)

Examples

`% cat part1 > book`	*Copy* part1 *to book*
`% cat part2 part3 >> book`	*Append parts 2 and 3 to same file as* part1
`% mail tim < report`	*Take input to message from* report
`% cc calc.c >& error_out`	*Store all messages, including errors*
`% cc newcalc.c >&! error_out`	*Overwrite old file*
`% grep Unix ch* |& pr`	*Pipe all messages, including errors*
`% (find / -print > filelist) >& no_access`	*Separate error messages from list of files*
`% sed 's/^/XX /' << "END_ARCHIVE"`	*Supply text right after command*

```
This is often how a shell archive is "wrapped",
bundling text for distribution. You would normally
run sed from a shell program, not from the command line
"END_ARCHIVE"
```

Variables

This subsection describes the following:

- Variable substitution

- Variable modifiers

- Predefined shell variables

- Sample *.cshrc* file

- Environment variables

Variable Substitution

In the following substitutions, braces ({ }) are optional, except when needed to separate a variable name from following characters that would otherwise be a part of it.

`${var}`	The value of variable *var*.
`${var[i]}`	Select word or words in position *i* of *var*. *i* can be a single number, a range *m-n*, a range *-n* (missing *m* implies 1), a range *m-* (missing *n* implies all remaining words), or * (select all words). *i* can also be a variable that expands to one of these values.
`${#var}`	The number of words in *var*.
`${#argv}`	The number of arguments.
`$0`	Name of the program.
`${#argv[n]}`	Individual arguments on command line (positional parameters); $1 \le n \le 9$.
`${n}`	Same as `${argv[n]}`.
`${#argv[*]}`	All arguments on command line.
`$*`	Same as `$argv[*]`.
`$argv[$#argv]`	The last argument.
`${?var}`	Return 1 if *var* is set, 0 if *var* is not set.
`$$`	Process number of current shell; useful as part of a filename for creating temporary files with unique names.
`$?0`	Return 1 if input filename is known, 0 if not.

Examples

Sort the third through last arguments and save the output in a file whose name is unique to this process:

```
sort $argv[3-] > tmp.$$
```

Process *.cshrc* commands only if the shell is interactive (i.e., the **prompt** variable must be set):

```
if ($?prompt) then
    set commands,
    alias commands,
    etc.
endif
```

Variable Modifiers

Except for $?var, $$, and $?0, the variable substitutions in the preceding section may be followed by one of these modifiers. When braces are used, the modifier goes inside them.

:r	Return the variable's root (the portion before the last dot).
:e	Return the variable's extension.
:h	Return the variable's header (the directory portion).
:t	Return the variable's tail (the portion after the last slash).
:gr	Return all roots.
:ge	Return all extensions.
:gh	Return all headers.
:gt	Return all tails.
:q	Quote a wordlist variable, keeping the items separate. Useful when the variable contains filename metacharacters that should not be expanded.
:x	Quote a pattern, expanding it into a wordlist.

Examples using pathname modifiers

The following table shows the use of pathname modifiers on the following variable:

```
set aa=(/progs/num.c /book/chap.ps)
```

Variable Portion	Specification	Output Result
Normal variable	echo $aa	/progs/num.c /book/chap.ps
Second root	echo $aa[2]:r	/book/chap
Second header	echo $aa[2]:h	/book
Second tail	echo $aa[2]:t	chap.ps
Second extension	echo $aa[2]:e	ps
Root	echo $aa:r	/progs/num /book/chap.ps
Global root	echo $aa:gr	/progs/num /book/chap
Header	echo $aa:h	/progs /book/chap.ps
Global header	echo $aa:gh	/progs /book
Tail	echo $aa:t	num.c /book/chap.ps
Global tail	echo $aa:gt	num.c chap.ps
Extension	echo $aa:e	c /book/chap.ps
Global extension	echo $aa:ge	c ps

Examples using quoting modifiers

Unless quoted, the shell expands variables to represent files in the current directory:

```
% set a="[a-z]*" A="[A-Z]*"
% echo "$a" "$A"
[a-z]* [A-Z]*

% echo $a $A
at cc m4 Book Doc

% echo $a:x $A
[a-z]* Book Doc

% set d=($a:q $A:q)
% echo $d
at cc m4 Book Doc

% echo $d:q
[a-z]* [A-Z]*

% echo $d[1] +++ $d[2]
at cc m4 +++ Book Doc

% echo $d[1]:q
[a-z]*
```

Predefined Shell Variables

Variables can be set in one of two ways, by assigning a value:

```
set var=value
```

or by simply turning the variable on:

```
set var
```

In the following list, variables that accept values are shown with the equal sign followed by the type of value they accept; the value is then described. (Note, however, that variables such as **argv**, **cwd**, or **status** are never explicitly assigned.) For variables that are turned on or off, the table describes what they do when set. **tcsh** automatically sets (and, in some cases, updates) the variables **addsuffix**, **argv**, **autologout**, **cwd**, **dirstack**, **echo-style**, **edit**, **gid**, **home**, **loginsh**, **logout**, **oid**, **owd**, **path**, **prompt**, **prompt2**, **prompt3**, **shell**, **shlvl**, **status**, **tcsh**, **term tty**, **uid**, **user**, and **version**. Variables in italics are specific to **tcsh**.

addsuffix	Append / to directories and a space to files during tab completion to indicate a precise match.
ampm	Display all times in 12-hour format.
argv=(*args*)	List of arguments passed to current command; default is ( ).
autocorrect	Check spelling before attempting to complete commands.
autoexpand	Expand history (such as ! references) during command completion.

`autolist[=ambiguous]`	Print possible completions when correct one is ambiguous. If **ambiguous** is specified, print possible completions only when completion adds no new characters.
`autologout=logout-` `minutes` `[locking-minutes]`	Log out after `logout-minutes` of idle time. Lock the terminal after `locking-minutes` of idle time, requiring a password before continuing.
`backslash_quote`	Always allow backslashes to quote \, ', and ".
`cdpath=dirs`	List of alternate directories to search when locating arguments for **cd**, **popd**, or **pushd**.
`complete=enhance`	When **enhance**, ignore case in completion, treat ., –, and _ as word separators, and consider _ and – to be the same.
`correct={cmd|` `complete|all}`	When `cmd`, spell-check commands. When `complete`, complete commands. When `all`, spell-check whole command line.
`cwd=dir`	Full pathname of current directory.
`dirsfile=file`	History file consulted by **dirs –S** and **dirs –L**. Default is `˜/.cshdirs`.
`dirstack`	Directory stack, in array format. `dirstack[0]` is always equivalent to **cwd**. The other elements can be artificially changed.
`dunique`	Make sure that each directory exists only once in the stack.
`echo`	Redisplay each command line before execution; same as **csh –x** command.
`echo_style={bsd|` `sysv|both|none}`	Don't echo a newline with **-n** option (bsd) | parse escaped characters (**sysv**) | do both | do neither.
`edit`	Enable command-line editor.
`ellipsis`	For use with **prompt** variable. Represent skipped directories with . . . .
`fignore=chars`	List of filename suffixes to ignore during filename completion (see **filec**).
`filec`	If set, a filename that is partially-typed on the command line can be expanded to its full name when ESC is pressed. If more than one filename would match, type *EOF* to list possible completions. Ignored in **tcsh**.
`gid`	User's group ID.
`histchars=ab`	A two-character string that sets the characters to use in history-substitution and quick-substitution (default is !ˆ).
`histdup={all|prev}`	Maintain a record only of unique history events (**all**), or do not enter new event when it is the same as the previous one (**prev**).

`histfile=file`	History file consulted by **history –S** and **history –L**. Default is `~/.history`.
`histlit`	Do not expand history lines when recalling them.
`history=n format`	The first word indicates the number of commands to save in the history list. The second indicates the format with which to display that list (**tcsh** only; see the prompt section for possible formats).
`home=dir`	Home directory of user, initialized from HOME. The ~ character is shorthand for this value.
`ignoreeof`	Ignore an end-of-file (*EOF*) from terminals; prevents accidental logout.
`inputmode=` `{insert|overwrite}`	Control editor's mode.
`listjobs=long`	When a job is suspended, list all jobs (in long format, if specified).
`listlinks`	In **ls –F** command, include type of file to which links point.
`listmax=num`	Do not allow **list-choices** to print more than *num* choices before prompting.
`listmaxrows=num`	Do not allow **list-choices** to print more than *num* rows of choices before prompting.
`loginsh`	Set if shell is a login shell.
`logout`	Indicates status of an imminent logout (**normal**, **automatic**, or **hangup**).
`mail=(n files)`	One or more files checked for new mail every five minutes or (if *n* is supplied) every *n* seconds.

`matchbeep=`
`{never|nomatch|`
`ambiguous|notunique}`
	Specifies cirumstances under which completion should beep: never, if no match exists, if multiple matches exist, or if multiple matches exist and one is exact.

`nobeep`	Disable beeping.
`noclobber`	Don't redirect output to an existing file; prevents accidental destruction of files.
`noglob`	Turn off filename expansion; useful in shell scripts.
`nokanji`	Disable Kanji (if supported).
`nonomatch`	Treat filename metacharacters as literal characters, if no match exists; e.g., **vi ch*** creates new file **ch*** instead of printing "No match."
`nostat=directory-` `list`	Do not stat `directory-list` during completion.
`notify`	Declare job completions when they occur.
`owd`	Old working directory.
`path=(dirs)`	List of pathnames in which to search for commands to execute. Initialized from PATH; the default is: `. /usr/ucb /usr/bin`

printexitvalue	Print all nonzero exit values.
prompt='str'	String that prompts for interactive input; default is %. See the section "Formatting for the Prompt Variable" later in this chapter for formatting information.
prompt2='str'	String that prompts for interactive input in **foreach** and **while** loops and continued lines (those with escaped newlines). See "Formatting for the Prompt Variable" for formatting information.
prompt3='str'	String that prompts for interactive input in automatic spelling correction. See "Formatting for the Prompt Variable" for formatting information.
pushdtohome	Change to home directory when **pushd** is invoked without arguments.
pushdsilent	Do not print directory stack when **pushd** and **popd** are invoked.
recexact	Consider completion to be concluded on first exact match.
recognize_only_ executables	When command completion is invoked, print only executable files.
rmstar	Prompt before executing the command **rm** *.
savedirs	Execute **dirs -S** before exiting.
savehist=max [merge]	Execute **history -S** before exiting. Save no more than *max* lines of history. If specified, merge those lines with previous history saves, and sort by time.
sched=string	Format for **sched**'s printing of events. See "Formatting for the Prompt Variable" for formatting information.
shell=file	Pathname of the shell program currently in use; default is */bin/csh*.
shlvl	Number of nested shells.
showdots[=-A]	Show hidden files with **ls** −**F**. If −**A** is specified, do not show **.** or **..** entries.
status=n	Exit status of last command. Built-in commands return 0 (success) or 1 (failure).
symlinks= {chase|ignore|expand}	Specify manner in which to deal with symbolic links. Expand them to real directory name in *cwd* (chase); treat them as real directories (ignore); or expand arguments that resemble pathnames (expand).
tcsh	Version of **tcsh**.
term	Terminal type.
time='n %c'	If command execution takes more than *n* CPU seconds, report user time, system time, elapsed time, and CPU percentage. Supply optional %c flags to show other data.

`tperiod`	Number of minutes between executions of **periodic** alias.
`tty`	Name of tty, if applicable.
`uid`	User ID.
`user`	Username.
`verbose`	Display a command after history substitution; same as the command **csh –v**.
`version`	Shell's version and additional information, including options set at compile time.
`visiblebell`	Flash screen instead of beeping.
`watch=( [n] user terminal . . . )`	Watch for `user` logging in at `terminal`, where `terminal` can be a tty name or **any**. Check every `n` minutes, or 10 by default.
`who=string`	Specify information to be printed by **watch**.
`wordchars=chars`	List of all nonalphanumeric characters that may be part of a word. Default is *?_–. [] ~=.

Formatting for the Prompt Variable

tcsh provides a list of substitutions that can be used in formatting the prompt. (**csh** allows only plain-string prompts and the ! history substitution below.) The list of available substitutions includes:

%%	Literal %
%/	The present working directory
%~	The present working directory, in ~ notation
%#	# for the superuser, > for others
%?	Previous command's exit status
%b	End boldfacing
%c[[0]*n*], %.[[0]*n*]	The last *n* (default 1) components of the present working directory. If 0 is specified, replace removed components with `/<skipped>`.
%d	Day of the week (e.g., Mon, Tue)
%h, %!, !	Number of current history event
%l	Current tty
%m	First component of hostname
%n	Username
%p	Current time, with seconds (12-hour mode)
%s	End standout mode (reverse video)
%t, %@	Current time (12-hour format)

%u	End underlining
%w	Month (e.g., Jan, Feb)
%y	Year (e.g., 94, 95)
%B	Begin boldfacing
%C	Similar to %c, but uses full pathnames instead of ~ notation
%D	Day of month (e.g., 09, 10)
%M	Fully-qualified hostname
%P	Current time, with seconds (24-hour format)
%S	Begin standout mode (reverse video)
%T	Current time (24-hour format)
%U	Begin underlining
%W	Month (e.g., 09, 10)
%Y	Year (e.g., 1994, 1995)

Sample .cshrc File

```
# PREDEFINED VARIABLES

set path=(~ ~/bin /usr/ucb /bin /usr/bin . )
set mail=(/usr/mail/tom)

if ($?prompt) then              # settings for interactive use
  set echo
  set noclobber ignoreeof

  set cdpath=(/usr/lib /usr/spool/uucp)
# Now I can type cd macros
# instead of cd /usr/lib/macros

  set history=100
  set prompt='tom \!% '         # includes history number
  set time=3

# MY VARIABLES

  set man1="/usr/man/man1"      # lets me do   cd $man1, ls $man1
  set a="[a-z]*"                # lets me do   vi $a
  set A="[A-Z]*"                # or           grep string $A

# ALIASES

  alias c "clear; dirs"         # use quotes to protect ; or |
  alias h "history|more"
  alias j jobs -l
  alias ls ls -sFC              # redefine ls command
  alias del 'mv \!* ~/tmp_dir'  # a safe alternative to rm
endif
```

Environment Variables

The C shell maintains a set of *environment variables*, which are distinct from shell variables and aren't really part of the C shell. Shell variables are meaningful only within the current shell, but environment variables are automatically exported, making them available globally. For example, C-shell variables are accessible only to a particular script in which they're defined, whereas environment variables can be used by any shell scripts, mail utilities, or editors you might invoke.

Environment variables are assigned as follows:

```
setenv VAR value
```

By convention, environment variable names are all uppercase. You can create your own environment variables, or you can use the predefined environment variables that follow.

These environment variables have corresponding C-shell variables. When either one changes, the value is copied to the other:

HOME   Home directory; same as **home**.

PATH   Search path for commands; same as **path**.

TERM   Terminal type; same as **term**.

Other environment variables include the following (italics means specific to **tcsh**):

EXINIT   A string of **ex** commands similar to those found in the startup *.exrc* file (e.g., **set ai**). Used by **vi** and **ex**.

IHOST   Name of machine.

LOGNAME   Another name for the USER variable.

MAIL   The file that holds mail. Used by mail programs. This is not the same as the C-shell **mail** variable, which only checks for new mail.

IOSTYPE   Operating system.

PWD   The current directory; the value is copied from **cwd**.

REMOTEHOST   Machine name of remote host.

SHELL   Undefined by default; once initialized to **shell**, the two are identical.

TERMCAP   The file that holds the cursor-positioning codes for your terminal type. Default is */etc/termcap*.

Expressions

Expressions are used in @, **if**, and **while** statements to perform arithmetic, string comparisons, file testing, etc. **exit** and **set** can also specify expressions. Expressions are formed by combining variables and constants with operators that resemble those in the C programming language. Operator precedence is the same as in C but can be remembered as follows:

1. `* / %`

2. `+ -`

Group all other expressions inside ( )s. Parentheses are required if the expression contains <, >, &, or |.

Operators

Operators can be one of the following types:

Assignment operators

`=`	Assign value
`+= -=`	Reassign after addition/subtraction
`*= /= %=`	Reassign after multiplication/division/remainder
`&= ^= |=`	Reassign after bitwise AND/XOR/OR
`++`	Increment
`--`	Decrement

Arithmetic operators

`* / %`	Multiplication; integer division; modulus (remainder)
`+ -`	Addition; subtraction

Bitwise and logical operators

`~`	Binary inversion (one's complement)
`!`	Logical negation
`<< >>`	Bitwise left shift; bitwise right shift
`&`	Bitwise AND
`^`	Bitwise exclusive OR
`|`	Bitwise OR
`&&`	Logical AND
`||`	Logical OR
`{ command }`	Return 1 if command is successful; 0 otherwise. Note that this is the opposite of *command*'s normal return code. The **$status** variable may be more practical.

Comparison operators

`== !=`	Equality; inequality
`<= >=`	Less than or equal to; greater than or equal to
`< >`	Less than; greater than

File inquiry operators

Command substitution and filename expansion are performed on *file* before the test is performed.

-d *file*	The file is a directory.
-e *file*	The file exists.
-f *file*	The file is a plain file.
-o *file*	The user owns the file.
-r *file*	The user has read permission.
-w *file*	The user has write permission.
-x *file*	The user has execute permission.
-z *file*	The file has zero size.
!	Reverse the sense of any inquiry above.

Examples

The following examples show @ commands and assume **n** = 4:

Expression	Value of $x
@ x = ($n > 10 || $n < 5)	1
@ x = ($n >= 0 && $n < 3)	0
@ x = ($n << 2)	16
@ x = ($n >> 2)	1
@ x = $n % 2	0
@ x = $n % 3	1

The following examples show the first line of **if** or **while** statements:

Expression	Meaning
while ($#argv != 0)	While there are arguments . . .
if ($today[1] == "Fri")	If the first word is "Fri". . .
if (-f $argv[1])	If the first argument is a plain file. . .
if (! -d $tmpdir)	If **tmpdir** is not a directory. . .

Command History

Previously executed commands are stored in a history list. The C shell lets you access this list so you can verify commands, repeat them, or execute modified versions of them. The **history** built-in command displays the history list; the predefined variables **histchars** and **history** also affect the history mechanism. There are three ways to use the history list:

- Making command substitutions (using ! and ˆ)

- Making argument substitutions (specific words within a command)

- Using modifiers to extract or replace parts of a command or word

Command Substitution

!	Begin a history substitution
!!	Previous command
!*N*	Command number *N* in history list
!-*N*	*N*th command back from current command
!*string*	Most recent command that starts with *string*
!?*string*?	Most recent command that contains *string*
!?*string*?%	Most recent command argument that contains *string*
!$	Last argument of previous command
!!*string*	Previous command, then append *string*
!*N string*	Command *N*, then append *string*
!{*s1*}*s2*	Most recent command starting with string *s1*, then append string *s2*
^*old*^*new*^	Quick substitution; change string *old* to *new* in previous command; execute modified command

Command Substitution Examples

The following command is assumed:

```
%3 vi cprogs/01.c ch002 ch03
```

Event Number	Command Typed	Command Executed
4	^00^0	vi cprogs/01.c ch02 ch03
5	nroff !*	nroff cprogs/01.c ch02 ch03
6	nroff !$	nroff ch03
7	!vi	vi cprogs/01.c ch02 ch03
8	!6	nroff ch03
9	!?01	vi cprogs/01.c ch02 ch03
10	!{nr}.new	nroff ch03.new
11	!!|lp	nroff ch03.new	lp
12	more !?pr?%	more cprogs/01.c

Word Substitution

Colons may precede any word specifier.

:0	Command name
:*n*	Argument number *n*
^	First argument
$	Last argument
:*n-m*	Arguments *n* through *m*

-m	Words 0 through m; same as :0-m
:n-	Arguments n through next-to-last
:n*	Arguments n through last; same as n-$
*	All arguments; same as ^-$ or 1-$
#	Current command line up to this point; fairly useless

Word Substitution Examples

The following command is assumed:

```
%13 cat ch01 ch02 ch03 biblio back
```

Event Number	Command Typed	Command Executed
14	ls !13^	ls ch01
15	sort !13:*	sort ch01 ch02 ch03 biblio back
16	lp !cat:3*	more ch03 biblio back
17	!cat:0-3	cat ch01 ch02 ch03
18	vi !-5:4	vi biblio

History Modifiers

Command and word substitutions can be modified by one or more of the following:

Printing, substitution, and quoting

:p	Display command but don't execute.
:s/old/new	Substitute string new for old, first instance only.
:gs/old/new	Substitute string new for old, all instances.
:&	Repeat previous substitution (:s or ^ command), first instance only.
:g&	Repeat previous substitution, all instances.
:q	Quote a wordlist.
:x	Quote separate words.

Truncation

:r	Extract the first available pathname root (the portion before the last period).
:gr	Extract all pathname roots.
:e	Extract the first available pathname extension (the portion after the last period).
:ge	Extract all pathname extensions.
:h	Extract the first available pathname header (the portion before the last slash).

:gh	Extract all pathname headers.
:t	Extract the first available pathname tail (the portion after the last slash).
:gt	Extract all pathname tails.
:u	Make first lowercase letter uppercase (**tcsh** only).
:l	Make first uppercase letter lowercase (**tcsh** only).
:a	Apply modifier(s) following a as many times as possible to a word. If used with g, a is applied to all words (**tcsh** only).

History Modifier Examples

From above, command number 17 is:

```
%17 cat ch01 ch02 ch03
```

Event Number	Command Typed	Command Executed
19	!17:s/ch/CH/	cat CH01 ch02 ch03
20	!17g&	cat CH01 CH02 CH03
21	!more:p	more cprogs/01.c *(displayed only)*
22	cd !$:h	cd cprogs
23	vi !mo:$:t	vi 01.c
24	grep stdio !$	grep stdio 01.c
25	^stdio^include stdio^:q	grep "include stdio" 01.c
26	nroff !21:t:p	nroff 01.c *(is that what I wanted?)*
27	!!	nroff 01.c *(execute it)*

Command-Line Manipulation

Completion

Both **tcsh** and **csh** provide word completion. **tcsh** automatically completes words and commands when the **TAB** key is hit; **csh** does so only when the *filec* variable is set, after the **ESC** key is hit. If the completion is ambiguous (i.e., more than one file matches the provided string), the shell completes as much as possible and beeps to notify you that the completion is not finished. You may request a list of possible completions with **CTRL-D**. **tcsh** will also notify you when a completion is finished by appending a space to complete filenames or commands and a / to complete directories.

Both **csh** and **tcsh** recognize ~ notation for home directories. The shells assume that words at the beginning of a line and subsequent to |, &, ;, ||, or && are commands, and modify their search paths appropriately. Completion can be done midword; only the letters to the left of the prompt are checked for completion. **CTRL-D** will list possible completions mid-word only in **vi** bindings, not Emacs bindings.

Related shell variables

- autolist
- fignore
- listmax
- listmaxrows

Related command-line editor commands

- complete-word-back
- complete-word-forward
- expand-glob
- list-glob

Related shell built-ins

- complete
- uncomplete

Command-Line Editing

tcsh lets you move your cursor around in the command line, editing it as you type it. There are two main modes for editing the command line, based on the two most common text editors: Emacs and **vi**. You can switch between them with:

```
bindkey -e          Select Emacs bindings
bindkey -v          Select vi bindings
```

The main difference between Emacs and **vi** bindings is that Emacs bindings are modeless; i.e., they always work. With **vi** bindings, you must switch between insert and command modes; different commands are useful in each mode. Additionally:

- Emacs mode is simpler; **vi** mode allows finer control.
- Emacs mode allows you to yank cut text and set a mark; **vi** mode does not.
- The command history searching capabilities differ.

Emacs mode

Tables 5-1 through 5-3 describe the various editing keystrokes available in Emacs mode.

Table 5-1: Cursor Positioning Commands (Emacs Mode)

Command	Description
CTRL-B	Move cursor back (left) one character.
CTRL-F	Move cursor forward (right) one character.
ESC b	Move cursor back one word.
ESC f	Move cursor forward one word.
CTRL-A	Move cursor to beginning of line.
CTRL-E	Move cursor to end of line.

Table 5-2: Text Deletion Commands (Emacs Mode)

Command	Description
DEL or CTRL-H	Delete character to left of cursor.
CTRL-D	Delete character under cursor.
ESC d	Delete word.
ESC DEL or ESC CTRL-H	Delete word backward.
CTRL-K	Delete from cursor to end of line.
CTRL-U	Delete entire line.

Table 5-3: Command Control (Emacs Mode)

Command	Description
CTRL-P	Previous command.
CTRL-N	Next command.
Up Arrow	Previous command.
Down Arrow	Next command.
cmd-fragment ESC p	Search history for cmd-fragment, which must be the beginning of a command.
cmd-fragment ESC n	Like ESC p, but search forward.
esc num	Repeat next command num times.
CTRL-Y	Yank previously deleted string.

vi mode

vi mode has two submodes, insert mode and command mode. The default mode is insert. You can toggle modes by hitting ESC; alternatively, in command mode, typing a (append) or i (insert) will return you to insert mode.

Tables 5-4 through 5-10 describe the editing keystrokes available in vi mode.

Table 5–4: Commands Available in Insert and Command Mode (vi Mode)

Command	Description
CTRL-P	Previous command
CTRL-N	Next command
Up Arrow	Previous command
Down Arrow	Next command
ESC	Toggle mode

Table 5–5: Editing Commands (vi Insert Mode)

Command	Description
CTRL-B	Move cursor back (left) one character.
CTRL-F	Move cursor forward (right) one character.
CTRL-A	Move cursor to beginning of line.
CTRL-E	Move cursor to end of line.
DEL or CTRL-H	Delete character to left of cursor.
CTRL-W	Delete word backward.
CTRL-U	Delete from beginning of line to cursor.
CTRL-K	Delete from cursor to end of line.

Table 5–6: Cursor Positioning Commands (vi Command Mode)

Command	Description
h or CTRL-H	Move cursor back (left) one character.
l or SPACE	Move cursor forward (right) one character.
w	Move cursor forward (right) one word.
b	Move cursor back (left) one word.
e	Move cursor to next word ending.
W, B, E	Like w, b, and e, but treats whitespace as word separator instead of all non-alphanumeric characters.
^ or CTRL-A	Move cursor to beginning of line (first nonwhitespace character).
0	Move cursor to beginning of line.
$ or CTRL-E	Move cursor to end of line.

Table 5–7: Text Insertion Commands (vi Command Mode)

Command	Description
a	Append new text after cursor until **ESC**.
i	Insert new text before cursor until **ESC**.
A	Append new text after end of line until **ESC**.
I	Insert new text before beginning of line until **ESC**.

Table 5–8: Text Deletion Commands (vi Command Mode)

Command	Description
x	Delete character under cursor.
X or **DEL**	Delete character to left of cursor.
d*m*	Delete from cursor to end of motion command *m*.
D	Same as **d$**.
CTRL-W	Delete word backward.
CTRL-U	Delete from beginning of line to cursor.
CTRL-K	Delete from cursor to end of line.

Table 5–9: Text Replacement Commands (vi Command Mode)

Command	Description
c*m*	Change characters from cursor to end of motion command *m* until **ESC**.
C	Same as **c$**.
r*c*	Replace character under cursor with character *c*.
R	Replace multiple characters until **ESC**.
s	Substitute character under cursor with characters typed until **ESC**.

Table 5–10: Character-Seeking Motion Commands (vi Command Mode)

Command	Description
f*c*	Move cursor to next instance of *c* in line.
F*c*	Move cursor to previous instance of *c* in line.
t*c*	Move cursor just before next instance of *c* in line.
T*c*	Move cursor just after previous instance of *c* in line.
;	Repeat previous **f** or **F** command.
,	Repeat previous **f** or **F** command in opposite direction.

Built-in csh and tcsh Commands

@ [*variable*[*n*]*=expression*]

Assign the value of the arithmetic *expression* to *variable*, or to the *n*th element of *variable* if the index *n* is specified. With no *variable* or *expression* specified, print the values of all shell variables (same as **set**). Expression operators as well as examples are listed under "Expressions," earlier in this chapter. Two special forms are also valid:

> **@** *variable++*   Increment *variable* by one.
>
> **@** *variable--*   Decrement *variable* by one.

#

Ignore all text that follows on the same line. # is used in shell scripts as the comment character, and is not really a command.

#!*shell*

Used as the first line of a script to invoke the named *shell* (with optional arguments). Not supported in all shells. For example:

```
#!/bin/csh -f
```

:

Null command. Returns an exit status of 0. The colon command is often put as the first character of a Bourne- or Korn-shell script to act as a place-holder to keep a # (hash) from accidentally becoming the first character.

---

alias [*name* [*command*]]

Assign *name* as the shorthand name, or alias, for *command*. If *command* is omitted, print the alias for *name*; if *name* is also omitted, print all aliases. Aliases can be defined on the command line, but they are more often stored in *.cshrc* so that they take effect upon logging in. (See the sample *.cshrc* file previously in this chapter.) Alias definitions can reference command-line arguments, much like the history list. Use \!* to refer to all command-line arguments, \!^ for the first argument, \!\!:2 for the second, \!$ for the last, etc. An alias *name* can be any valid Unix command; however, you lose the original command's meaning unless you type \ *name*. See also **unalias** and the "Special Aliases in tcsh" section.

→

csh and tcsh

alias ←	*Examples* Set the size for **xterm** windows under the X Window System: ``` alias R 'set noglob; eval `resize`; unset noglob' ``` Show aliases that contain the string **ls** : ``` alias	grep ls ``` Run **nroff** on all command-line arguments: ``` alias ms 'nroff -ms \!*' ``` Copy the file that is named as the first argument: ``` alias back 'cp \!^ \!^.ol'' ``` Use the regular **ls**, not its alias: ``` % \ls ```
alloc	**alloc** Print totals of used and free memory.
bg	**bg** [*jobIDs*] Put the current job or the *jobIDs* in the background. *Example* To place a time-consuming process in the background, you might begin with: ``` 4% nroff -ms report CTRL-Z ``` and then issue any one of the following: ``` 5% bg 5% bg % Current job 5% bg %1 Job number 1 5% bg %nr Match initial string nroff 5% % & ```
bindkey	**bindkey** [*options*] [*key*] [*command*] tcsh only. Display all key bindings, or bind a key to a command. −a List standard and alternate key bindings. −b *key* Expect *key* to be one of the following: a control character (in hat notation, e.g., ^B, or C notation, e.g., C-B); a metacharacter (e.g., M-B); a function key (e.g., F-*string*); or an extended prefix key (e.g., X-B).

−c *command*		**bindkey**
	Interpret *command* as a shell, not editor, command.	
−d *key*	Bind key to its original binding.	
−e	Bind to standard Emacs bindings.	
−k *key*	Expect *key* to refer to an arrow (**left**, **right**, **up**, or **down**).	
−l	List and describe all editor commands.	
−r *key*	Completely unbind *key*.	
−v	Bind to standard **vi** bindings.	

break	**break**
Resume execution following the **end** command of the nearest enclosing **while** or **foreach**.	

breaksw	**breaksw**
Break from a **switch**; continue execution after the **endsw**.	

built−ins	**built−ins**
tcsh only. Print all built-in shell commands.	

bye	**bye**
tcsh only. Same as **logout**.	

case *pattern* :	**case**
Identify a *pattern* in a **switch**.	

cd [*dir*]	**cd**
Change working directory to *dir*; default is home directory of user. If *dir* is a relative pathname but is not in the current directory, the **cdpath** variable is searched. See the sample *cshrc* file earlier in this chapter. **tcsh** includes some options for **cd**:	
− Change to previous directory.	
−l Explicitly expand ~ notation.	
−p Print directory stack.	

chdir	**chdir** [*dir*]
	Same as **cd**. Useful if you are redefining **cd**.

complete	**complete** [*string* [*word/pattern/list* [: *select*] / [*suffix*]]]

tcsh only. List all completions, or, if specified, all completions for *string* (which may be a pattern). Further options can be specified. Options for *word* are:

c	Complete current word only, and without referring to *pattern*.
C	Complete current word only, referring to *pattern*.
n	Complete previous word.
N	Complete word before previous word.
P	Expect *pattern* to be a range of numbers. Perform completion within that range.

Various *lists* of strings can be searched for possible completions. Some *list* options include:

(*string*)	Members of the list *string*
` command`	
	Output from *command*
a	Aliases
b	Bindings
c	Commands
C	External (not built-in) commands
d	Directories
D	Directories whose names begin with *string*
e	Environment variables
f	Filenames
F	Filenames that begin with *string*
g	Groups
t	Text files
T	Text files whose names begin with *string*
u	Users

select should be a glob-pattern. Completions are limited to words that match this pattern. *suffix* is appended to all completions.

continue

Resume execution of nearest enclosing **while** or **foreach**.

default :

Label the default case (typically last) in a **switch**.

dirs [*options*]

Print the directory stack, showing the current directory first. See also **popd** and **pushd**. All options except −l are **tcsh** extensions.

−l	Expand the home directory symbol (~) to the actual directory name.
−n	Wrap output.
−v	Print one directory per line.
−L *file*	Recreate stack from *file*, which should have been created by **dirs** -S *file*.
−S *file*	Print a series of **pushd** and **popd** commands, which will replicate the stack, to *file*.

echo [−n] *string*

Write *string* to standard output; if −n is specified, the output is not terminated by a newline. Unlike the Unix version (*/bin/echo*) and the Bourne-shell version, the C shell's **echo** doesn't support escape characters. See also **echo** in Chapter 2, *Linux User Commands*, and Chapter 4, *bash: The Bourne Again Shell*.

echotc [*options*] *arguments*

Display terminal capabilities, or move cursor on screen, depending on the argument. Some possible arguments are:

baud	Display current baud.
cols	Display current column.
cm *column row*	
	Move cursor to specified coordinates.
home	Move cursor to home position.
lines	Print number of lines per screen.
meta	Does this terminal have meta capacity (usually the ALT key)?
tabs	Does this terminal have tab capacity?

else	**else**
	Reserved word for interior of **if** ... **endif** statement.
end	**end**
	Reserved word that ends a **foreach** or **switch** statement.
endif	**endif**
	Reserved word that ends an **if** statement.
endsw	**endsw**
	Reserved word that ends a **switch** statement.
eval	**eval** *args*
	Typically, **eval** is used in shell scripts, and *args* is a line of code that may contain shell variables. **eval** forces variable expansion to happen first and then runs the resulting command. This "double-scanning" is useful any time shell variables contain input/output redirection symbols, aliases, or other shell variables. (For example, redirection normally happens before variable expansion, so a variable containing redirection symbols must be expanded first using **eval**; otherwise, the redirection symbols remain uninterpreted.)
	Examples
	The following line can be placed in the **.login** file to set up terminal characteristics:
	``
	set noglob eval `tset -s xterm` unset noglob
	``
	The following commands show the effect of **eval**:

```
% set b='$a'
% set a=hello
% echo $b                       Read the command line once
$a
% eval echo $b                  Read the command line twice
hello
```

	Another example of **eval** can be found under **alias**.
exec	**exec** *command*
	Execute *command* in place of current shell. This terminates the current shell, rather than creating a new process under it.

exit [(*expr*)]

Exit a shell script with the status given by *expr*. A status of zero means success; nonzero means failure. If *expr* is not specified, the exit value is that of the **status** variable. **exit** can be issued at the command line to close a window (log out).

---

fg [*jobIDs*]

Bring the current job or the *jobIDs* to the foreground. *jobID* can be %*job-number*.

Example

If you suspend a **vi** editing session (by pressing **CTRL-Z**), you might resume **vi** using any of these commands:

```
% %
% fg
% fg %
% fg %vi          Match initial string
```

fg

---

filetest −*op files*

tcsh only. Apply *op* file tester to *files*. Print results in a list. See "File inquiry operators" for a list of file testers.

filetest

---

foreach *name* (*wordlist*)
    commands
end

Assign variable *name* to each value in *wordlist* and execute *commands* between **foreach** and **end**. You can use **foreach** as a multi-line command issued at the C-shell prompt (first example below), or you can use it in a shell script (second example).

Examples

Rename all files that begin with a capital letter:

```
% foreach i ([A-Z]*)
? mv $i $i.new
? end
```

Check whether each command-line argument is an option or not:

```
foreach arg ($argv)
   # does it begin with - ?
   if ("$arg" =~ -*) then
      echo "Argument is an option"
   else
      echo "Argument is a filename"
```

foreach

$\rightarrow$

foreach	`endif` `end`
←	

glob	**glob** *wordlist*
	Do filename, variable, and history substitutions on *wordlist*. No \ escapes are recognized in its expansion, and words are delimited by null characters. **glob** is typically used in shell scripts to "hardcode" a value so that it remains the same for the rest of the script.

goto	**goto** *string*
	Skip to a line whose first nonblank character is *string* followed by a : and continue execution below that line. On the **goto** line, *string* can be a variable or filename pattern, but the label branched to must be a literal, expanded value and must not occur within a **foreach** or **while**.

hashstat	**hashstat**
	Display statistics that show the hash table's level of success at locating commands via the **path** variable.

history	**history** [*options*]
	Display the list of history events. (History syntax is discussed earlier, in "Command History.")
	Options

−c	tcsh only. Clear history list.
−h	Print history list without event numbers.
−r	Print in reverse order; show oldest commands last.
n	Display only the last *n* history commands, instead of the number set by the **history** shell variable.
−L *file*	tcsh only. Load series of **pushd** and **popd** commands from *file* in order to recreate a saved stack.
−M *file*	tcsh only. Merge the current directory stack and the stack saved in *file*. Save both, sorted by time, in *file*, as a series of **pushd** and **popd** commands.

−S *file*   tcsh only. Print a series of **pushd** and **popd** commands, which will replicate the stack, to *file*.

Example

To save and execute the last five commands:

```
history -h 5 > do_it
source do_it
```

hup [*command*]

tcsh only. Start *command* but make it exit when sent a hangup signal, which is sent when shell exits. By default, configure shell script to exit on hangup signal.

if

Begin a conditional statement. The simple format is:

```
if (expr) cmd
```

There are three other possible formats, shown side-by-side:

```
if (expr) then      if (expr) then      if (expr) then
   cmds                cmds1               cmds1
endif               else                else if (expr) then
                       cmds2               cmds2
                    endif               else
                                           cmds3
                                        endif
```

In the simplest form, execute *cmd* if *expr* is true; otherwise do nothing (redirection still occurs; this is a bug). In the other forms, execute one or more commands. If *expr* is true, continue with the commands after **then**; if *expr* is false, branch to the commands after **else** (or branch to after the **else if** and continue checking). For more examples, see "Expressions" earlier in this chapter, or **shift** or **while**.

Example

Take a default action if no command-line arguments are given:

```
if ($#argv == 0) then
    echo "No filename given. Sending to Report."
    set outfile = Report
else
    set outfile = $argv[1]
endif
```

jobs	jobs [-l]
	List all running or stopped jobs; -l includes process IDs. For example, you can check whether a long compilation or text format is still running. Also useful before logging out.

kill	kill [*options*] *ID*
	Terminate each specified process *ID* or job *ID*. You must own the process or be a privileged user. This built-in is similar to */bin/kill* described in Chapter 2 but also allows symbolic job names. Stubborn processes can be killed using signal 9.

Options

-l	List the signal names. (Used by itself.)
-*signal*	The signal number or name (obtained from **kill -l**). Default is TERM.

Signals

Signals are defined in */usr/include/sys/signal.h* and are listed here without the SIG prefix.

HUP	1	Hangup
INT	2	Interrupt
QUIT	3	Quit
ILL	4	Illegal instruction
TRAP	5	Trace trap
IOT	6	IOT instruction
EMT	7	EMT instruction
FPE	8	Floating point exception
KILL	9	Kill
BUS	10	Bus error
SEGV	11	Segmentation violation
SYS	12	Bad argument to system call
PIPE	13	Write to pipe, but no process to read it
ALRM	14	Alarm clock
TERM	15	Software termination (the default signal)
USR1	16	User-defined signal 1
USR2	17	User-defined signal 2
CLD	18	Child process died
PWR	19	Restart after power failure

Examples

If you've issued the following command:

```
44% nroff -ms report &
```
you can terminate it in any of the following ways:

```
45% kill 19536      Process ID
45% kill %          Current job
45% kill %1         Job number 1
45% kill %nr        Initial string
45% kill %?report   Matching string
```

---

limit [−h] [*resource* [*limit*]]

Display limits or set a *limit* on resources used by the current process and by each process it creates. If no *limit* is given, the current limit is printed for *resource*. If *resource* is also omitted, all limits are printed. By default, the current limits are shown or set; with −h, hard limits are used. A hard limit imposes an absolute limit that can't be exceeded. Only a privileged user may raise it. See also unlimit.

Option

   −h   Use hard, not current, limits.

Resource

   cputime   Maximum number of seconds the CPU can spend; can be abbreviated as cpu.

   filesize   Maximum size of any one file.

   datasize   Maximum size of data (including stack).

   stacksize   Maximum size of stack.

   coredumpsize Maximum size of a core dump file.

Limit

A number followed by an optional character (a unit specifier).

For cputime: nh (for n hours)
               nm (for n minutes)
               $mm:ss$ (minutes and seconds)

For others: nk (for n kilobytes, the default)
               nm (for n megabytes)

---

log

tcsh only. Consult **watch** variable for list of users being watched. Print list of those who are presently logged in. If

$\rightarrow$

log ←	– is entered as an option, reset environment as if user had logged in with new group.
login	**login** [*user*	**–p**] Replace *user*'s login shell with */bin/login*. **–p** is used to preserve environment variables.
logout	**logout** Terminate the login shell.
ls–F	**ls–F** [*options*] [*files*] **tcsh** only. Faster alternative to **ls -F**. If given any options, invokes **ls**.
newgrp	**newgrp** [–] [*group*] **tcsh** only. Change user's group ID to specified group ID, or, if none is specified, to original group ID. If – is entered as an option, reset environment as if user had logged in with new group.

nice	**nice** [**±***n*] *command*
	
	Change the execution priority for *command*, or, if none is given, change priority for the current shell. (See also **nice** in Chapter 2.) The priority range is –20 to 20, with a default of 4. The range seems backwards: –20 gives the highest priority (fastest execution); 20 gives the lowest. Only a privileged user may specify a negative number.
	
	    +*n* Add *n* to the priority value (lower job priority).
	
	    –*n* Subtract *n* from the priority value (raise job priority). Privileged users only.

nohup	**nohup** [*command*] "No hangup signals." Do not terminate *command* after terminal line is closed (i.e., when you hang up from a phone or log out). Use without *command* in shell scripts to keep script from being terminated. (See also **nohup** in Chapter 2.)

notify [*jobID*]

notify

Report immediately when a background job finishes (instead of waiting for you to exit a long editing session, for example). If no *jobID* is given, the current background job is assumed.

---

onintr *label*
onintr –
onintr

onintr

"On interrupt." Used in shell scripts to handle interrupt signals (similar to **bash**'s **trap 2** and **trap** "" **2** commands). The first form is like a **goto** *label*. The script will branch to *label*: if it catches an interrupt signal (e.g., **CTRL-C**). The second form lets the script ignore interrupts. This is useful at the beginning of a script or before any code segment that needs to run unhindered (e.g., when moving files). The third form restores interrupt handling that was previously disabled with **onintr –**.

Example

```
onintr cleanup      # go to "cleanup" on interrupt
    .
                    # shell script commands
    .
    .
cleanup:            # label for interrupts
   onintr -         # ignore additional interrupts
   rm -f $tmpfiles  # remove any files created
   exit 2           # exit with an error status
```

---

popd [*options*]

popd

Remove the current entry from the directory stack, or remove the *n*th entry from the stack. The current entry has number 0 and appears on the left. See also **dirs** and **pushd**.

Options

+*n*   Specify *n*th entry.

–l   Expand ~ notation.

–n   Wrap long lines.

–v   Print precisely one directory per line.

---

printenv [*variable*]

printenv

Print all (or one specified) environment variables and their values.

csh and tcsh

pushd	pushd *name* pushd [*options*] pushd The first form changes the working directory to *name* and adds it to the directory stack. The second form rotates the *n*th entry to the beginning, making it the working directory. (Entry numbers begin at 0.) With no arguments, **pushd** switches the first two entries and changes to the new current directory. The +*n*, -l, -n, and −*v* options behave the same as in popd. See also **dirs** and **popd**.

Examples

```
% dirs
/home/bob /usr
% pushd /etc                    Add /etc to directory stack
/etc /home/bob /usr
% pushd +2                      Switch to third directory
/usr /etc /home/bob
% pushd                         Switch top two directories
/etc /usr /home/bob
% popd                          Discard current entry; go to next
/usr /home/bob
```

rehash	rehash Recompute the hash table for the PATH variable. Use **rehash** whenever a new command is created during the current session. This allows the PATH variable to locate and execute the command. (If the new command resides in a directory not listed in PATH, add this directory to PATH before rehashing.) See also **unhash**.

repeat	repeat *n command* Execute *n* instances of *command*.

Examples

Print three copies of **memo**:

```
% repeat 3 pr memo | lp
```

Read 10 lines from the terminal and store in **item_list**:

```
% repeat 10 line > item_list
```

Append 50 boilerplate files to **report**:

```
% repeat 50 cat template >> report
```

sched [*options*]
sched *time command*

tcsh only. Without options, print all scheduled events. The second form schedules an event.

time should be specified in *hh:mm* form (e.g., 13:00).

Options

> +*hh:mm*   Schedule event to take place *hh:mm* from now.

> −*n*   Remove *n*th item from schedule.

---

set *variable* = *value*
set [*options*] *variable* [*n*] = *value*
set

Set *variable* to *value*, or if multiple values are specified, set the variable to the list of words in the value list. If an index *n* is specified, set the *n*th word in the variable to *value*. (The variable must already contain at least that number of words.) With no arguments, display the names and values of all set variables. See also "Predefined Shell Variables" earlier in this chapter.

Options

> −r   **tcsh** only. List only read-only variables, or set specified variable to read-only.

Examples

```
% set list=(yes no mabye)    Assign a wordlist
% set list[3]=maybe          Assign an item in existing wordlist
% set quote="Make my day"    Assign a variable
% set x=5 y=10 history=100    Assign several variables
% set blank                  Assign a null value to blank
```

---

setenv [*name* [*value*]]

Assign a *value* to an environment variable *name*. By convention, *name* is uppercase. *value* can be a single word or a quoted string. If no *value* is given, the null value is assigned. With no arguments, display the names and values of all environment variables. **setenv** is not necessary for the PATH variable because it is automatically exported from **path**.

csh and tcsh

settc	settc *capability value* Set terminal *capability* to *value*.

setty	setty [*options*] [+ I −*mode*]
	
	tcsh only. Do not allow shell to change specified tty modes. By default, act on execute set.
	
	Options
	
	    +*mode* Without arguments, list all modes in specified set that are on. Otherwise, set specified mode to on.
	
	    −*mode* Without arguments, list all modes in specified set that are off. Otherwise, set specified mode to on.
	
	    −a List all modes in specified set.
	
	    −d Act on edit set of modes (used when editing commands).
	
	    −q Act on quote set of modes (used when entering characters verbatim).
	
	    −x Act on execute set of modes (default) (used when executing examples).

shift	shift [*variable*]
	
	If *variable* is given, shift the words in a wordlist variable; i.e., *name*[2] becomes *name*[1]. With no argument, shift the positional parameters (command-line arguments); i.e., $2 becomes $1. **shift** is typically used in a **while** loop. See additional example under **while**.
	
	Example
	
	<pre>while ($#argv) # while there are arguments
	    if (-f $argv[1])
	        wc -l $argv[1]
	    else
	        echo "$argv[1] is not a regular file"
	    endif
	    shift # get the next argument
	end</pre>

source	source [−h] *script* Read and execute commands from a C-shell script. With −h, the commands are added to the history list but aren't executed.

Example	source
`source ~/.cshrc`	

---

stop [*jobIDs*]	**stop**
Suspend the current background jobs or the background jobs specified by *jobIDs*; this is the complement of **CTRL-Z** or **suspend**.	

---

suspend	**suspend**
Suspend the current foreground job; same as **CTRL-Z**. Often used to stop an **su** command.	

---

switch   **switch**

Process commands depending on the value of a variable. When you need to handle more than three choices, **switch** is a useful alternative to an **if-then-else** statement. If the *string* variable matches *pattern1*, the first set of *commands* is executed; if *string* matches *pattern2*, the second set of *commands* is executed, and so on. If no patterns match, execute commands under the **default** case. *string* can be specified using command substitution, variable substitution, or filename expansion. Patterns can be specified using the pattern-matching symbols *, ?, and [ ]. **breaksw** is used to exit the **switch**. If **breaksw** is omitted (which is rarely done), the **switch** continues to execute another set of commands until it reaches a **breaksw** or **endsw**. Below is the general syntax of **switch**, side-by-side with an example that processes the first command-line argument:

```
switch (string)                switch ($argv[1])
   case pattern1:                  case -[nN]:
      commands                        nroff $file | lp
      breaksw                         breaksw
   case pattern2:                  case -[Pp]:
      commands                        pr $file | lp
      breaksw                         breaksw
   case pattern3:                  case -[Mm]:
      commands                        more $file
      breaksw                         breaksw
      .                            case -[Ss]:
      .                               sort $file
      .                               breaksw
   default:                        default:
      commands                        echo "Error--no such option"
                                      exit 1
      breaksw                         breaksw
endsw                          endsw
```

telltc	**telltc** Print all terminal capabilities and their values.
time	**time** [*command*] Execute a *command* and show how much time it uses. With no argument, **time** can be used in a shell script to time the script.
umask	**umask** [*nnn*] Display file creation mask or set file creation mask to octal *nnn*. The file creation mask determines which permission bits are turned off. **umask** is also a standard command.
unalias	**unalias** *name* Remove *name* from the alias list. See **alias** for more information.
uncomplete	**uncomplete** *pattern* **tcsh** only. Remove completions (specified by **complete**).
unhash	**unhash** Remove internal hash table. The C shell will stop using hashed values and will spend time searching the **path** directories to locate a command. See also **rehash**.
unlimit	**unlimit** [*resource*] Remove the allocation limits on *resource*. If *resource* is not specified, remove limits for all resources. See **limit** for more information. With **-h**, specify removal of hard limits. This command can be run only by a privileged user.
unset	**unset** *variables* Remove one or more *variables*. Variable names may be specified as a pattern, using filename metacharacters. See **set**.
unsetenv	**unsetenv** *variable* Remove an environment variable. Filename matching is *not* valid. See **setenv**.

wait

Pause in execution until all child processes complete, or until an interrupt signal is received.

---

watchlog

Same as **log**.

---

where *command*

tcsh only. Display all aliases, built-ins, and executables named *command*.

---

which *command*

tcsh only. Report which version of command will be executed. Same as the executable **which**, but faster, and checks **tcsh** built-ins.

---

while (*expression*)
   commands
end

As long as *expression* is true (evaluates to nonzero), evaluate *commands* between **while** and **end**. **break** and **continue** can be used to terminate or continue the loop. See also example under **shift**.

Example

```
set user = (alice bob carol ted)
while ($argv[1] != $user[1])
    #Cycle through each user, checking for a match
    shift user
    #If we cycled through with no match...
    if ($#user == 0) then
      echo "$argv[1] is not on the list of users"
      exit 1
    endif
end
```

csh and tcsh

Special Aliases in tcsh

Certain special aliases can be set in **tcsh**. These are executed when specific events occur.

   beepcmd   At beep.

cwdcmd	When **cwd** changes.
periodic	Every few minutes. The exact amount of time is set by the *tperiod* shell variable.
precmd	Before printing a new prompt.
shell *shell*	If a script does not specify a shell, interpret it with *shell.*

Job Control

Job control lets you place foreground jobs in the background, bring background jobs to the foreground, or suspend (temporarily stop) running jobs. The C shell provides the following commands for job control. For more information on these commands, see "Built-in csh and tcsh Commands" earlier in this chapter.

bg	Put a job in the background.
fg	Put a job in the foreground.
jobs	List active jobs.
kill	Terminate a job.
notify	Notify when a background job finishes.
stop	Suspend a background job.
CTRL-Z	Suspend the foreground job.

Many job control commands take *jobID* as an argument. This argument can be specified as follows:

%*n*	Job number *n*.
%*s*	Job whose command line starts with string *s*.
%?*s*	Job whose command line contains string *s*.
%%	Current job.
%	Current job (same as above).
%+	Current job (same as above).
%-	Previous job.

CHAPTER 6

Pattern Matching

A number of Linux text-editing utilities let you search for, and in some cases change, text patterns rather than fixed strings. These utilities include the editing programs **ed**, **ex**, **vi**, and **sed**; the **awk** scripting language; and the commands **grep** and **egrep**. Text patterns (also called regular expressions) contain normal characters mixed with special characters (also called metacharacters).

Perl's regular expression support is so rich that it does not fit into the tables in this chapter; see Chapter 14 for a quick-ref to Perl. The Emacs editor also provides regular expressions similar to those shown in this chapter.

This chapter presents the following information:

- Filenames versus patterns
- List of metacharacters available to each program
- Description of metacharacters
- Examples

A thorough guide to pattern matching can be found in the Nutshell Handbook *Mastering Regular Expressions*, by Jeffrey E. F. Friedl.

Filenames Versus Patterns

Metacharacters used in pattern matching are different from those used for filename expansion. When you issue a command on the command line, special characters are seen first by the shell, then by the program; therefore, unquoted metacharacters are interpreted by the shell for filename expansion. The command:

```
$ grep [A-Z]* chap[12]
```

could, for example, be interpreted by the shell as:

```
$ grep Array.c Bug.c Comp.c chap1 chap2
```

and **grep** would then try to find the pattern "Array.c" in files *Bug.c*, *Comp.c*, *chap1*, and *chap2*. To bypass the shell and pass the special characters to **grep**, use quotes:

```
$ grep "[A-Z]*" chap[12]
```

Double quotes suffice in most cases, but single quotes are the safest bet.

Note also that * and ? have subtly different meanings in pattern matching and file-name expansion.

Metacharacters, Listed by Linux Program

Some metacharacters are valid for one program but not for another. Those that are available to a given program are marked by a bullet (•) in the following table. Full descriptions are provided after the table.

Symbol	ed	ex	vi	sed	awk	grep	egrep	Action
.	•	•	•	•	•	•	•	Match any character.
*	•	•	•	•	•	•	•	Match zero or more preceding.
^	•	•	•	•	•	•	•	Match beginning of line.
$	•	•	•	•	•	•	•	Match end of line.
\	•	•	•	•	•	•	•	Escape character following.
[ ]	•	•	•	•	•	•	•	Match one from a set.
\(\)	•	•		•				Store matched text for later replay.
{ }					•	•		Match a range of instances.
\{ \}	•			•			•	Match a range of instances.
\< \>		•	•					Match word's beginning or end.
+					•	•	•	Match one or more preceding.
?					•	•	•	Match zero or one preceding.
						•		•	Separate choices to match.
( )					•		•	Group expressions to match.

In **ed**, **ex**, and **sed**, note that you specify both a search pattern (on the left) and a replacement pattern (on the right). The metacharacters in this table are meaningful only in a search pattern.

In **awk**, { } is a GNU extension and is supported only if you run **awk** with the −Wre-interval option.

In **ed**, **ex**, and **sed**, the following additional metacharacters are valid only in a replacement pattern:

Symbol	ex	sed	ed	Action
\	•	•	•	Escape character following.
\n	•	•	•	Reuse matched text stored in \(\).
&	•	•		Reuse previous search pattern.
~	•			Reuse previous replacement pattern.
\u \U	•			Change characters to uppercase.
\l \L	•			Change characters to lowercase.
\E	•			Turn off previous \U or \L.
\e	•			Turn off previous \u or \l.

Metacharacters

The following characters have special meaning only in search patterns:

.   Match any *single* character except newline.

*   Match any number (or none) of the single character that immediately precedes it. The preceding character can also be a regular expression, e.g., since . (dot) means any character, .* means "match any number of any character" (except newlines).

^   Match the following regular expression at the beginning of the line.

$ Match the preceding regular expression at the end of the line.

[ ]   Match any *one* of the enclosed characters.

             A hyphen (–) indicates a range of consecutive characters. A circumflex (^) as the first character in the brackets reverses the sense: it matches any one character *not* in the list. A hyphen or close bracket ( ]) as the first character is treated as a member of the list. All other metacharacters are treated as members of the list.

[^]   Do not match enclosed character(s).

\{n,m\}   Match a range of occurrences of the single character that immediately precedes it. The preceding character can also be a regular expression. \{n\} matches exactly n occurrences, \{n,\} matches at least n occurrences, and \{n,m\} matches any number of occurrences between n and m. GNU **awk** with the **–Wre-interval** option recognizes { } without backslashes for this operation.

\   Turn off the special meaning of the character that follows.

\(\)   Save the matched text enclosed between \(and \) in a special holding space. Up to nine patterns can be saved on a single line. They can be "replayed" in substitutions by the escape sequences \1 to \9.

\< \>   Match characters at beginning (\<) or end (\>) of a word.

+   Match one or more instances of preceding regular expression.

?   Match zero or one instances of preceding regular expression.

| Match the regular expression specified before or after.

( )   Group regular expressions.

The following characters have special meaning only in replacement patterns:

\	Turn off the special meaning of the character that follows.
\n	Restore the *n*th pattern previously saved by \(and \). *n* is a number from 1 to 9, with 1 starting on the left.
&	Reuse the search pattern as part of the replacement pattern.
~	Reuse the previous replacement pattern in the current replacement pattern.
\u	Convert first character of replacement pattern to uppercase.
\U	Convert replacement pattern to uppercase.
\l	Convert first character of replacement pattern to lowercase.
\L	Convert replacement pattern to lowercase.

Examples of Searching

When used with **grep** or **egrep**, regular expressions are surrounded by quotes. (If the pattern contains a $, you must use single quotes; e.g., *'pattern'*.) When used with **ed**, **ex**, **sed**, and **awk**, regular expressions are usually surrounded by / (although any delimiter works). Here are some sample patterns:

Pattern	What does it match?
bag	The string *bag*.
^bag	*bag* at beginning of line.
bag$	*bag* at end of line.
^bag$	*bag* as the only word on line.
[Bb]ag	*Bag* or *bag*.
b[aeiou]g	Second letter is a vowel.
b[^aeiou]g	Second letter is a consonant (or uppercase or symbol).
b.g	Second letter is any character except newline.
^...$	Any line containing exactly three characters.
^\.	Any line that begins with a dot.
^\.[a-z][a-z]	Same, followed by two lowercase letters (e.g., troff requests).
^\.[a-z]\{2\}	Same as previous, **grep** or **sed** only.
^[^.]	Any line that doesn't begin with a dot.
bugs*	*bug*, *bugs*, *bugss*, etc.
"word"	A word in quotes.
"*word"*	A word, with or without quotes.
[A-Z][A-Z]*	One or more uppercase letters.
[A-Z]+	Same, **egrep** or **awk** only.
[A-Z].*	An uppercase letter, followed by zero or more characters.
[A-Z]*	Zero or more uppercase letters.
[a-zA-Z]	Any letter.
[0-9A-Za-z]*	Any alphanumeric sequence.

egrep or awk pattern	What does it match?
`[567]`	One of the numbers *5*, *6*, or *7*
`five|six|seven`	One of the words *five*, *six*, or *seven*
`80[23]?86`	*8086, 80286,* or *80386*
`compan(y|ies)`	*company* or *companies*

ex or vi pattern	What does it match?
`\<the`	Words like *theater* or *the*
`the\>`	Words like *breathe* or *the*
`\<the\>`	The word *the*

sed or grep pattern	What does it match?
`0\{5,\}`	Five or more zeros in a row
`[0-9]\{3\}-[0-9]\{2\}-[0-9]\{4\}`	Social security number (*nnn-nn-nnnn*)

Examples of Searching and Replacing

The following examples show the metacharacters available to **sed** or **ex**. Note that **ex** commands begin with a colon. A space is marked by a □; a tab is marked by *tab*.

Command	Result
`s/.*/(&)/`	Reproduce the entire line, but add parentheses.
`s/.*/mv & &.old/`	Change a wordlist (one word per line) into **mv** commands.
`/^$/d`	Delete blank lines.
`:g/^$/d`	Same as previous, in **ex** editor.
`/^[□tab]*$/d`	Delete blank lines, plus lines containing spaces or tabs.
`:g/^[□tab]*$/d`	Same as previous, in **ex** editor.
`s/□□*/□/g`	Turn one or more spaces into one space.
`:%s/□□*/□/g`	Same as previous, in **ex** editor.
`:s/[0-9]/Item &:/`	Turn a number into an item label (on the current line).
`:s`	Repeat the substitution on the first occurrence.
`:&`	Same as previous.
`:sg`	Same, but for all occurrences on the line.
`:&g`	Same as previous.
`:%&g`	Repeat the substitution globally.
`:.,$s/Fortran/\U&/g`	Change word to uppercase, on current line to last line.
`:%s/.*/\L&/`	Lowercase entire file.
`:s/\<./\u&/g`	Uppercase first letter of each word on current line. (Useful for titles.)
`:%s/yes/No/g`	Globally change a word (**yes**) to another word (**No**).
`:%s/Yes/~/g`	Globally change a different word to **No** (previous replacement).

Finally, here are some **sed** examples for transposing words. A simple transposition of two words might look like this:

```
s/die or do/do or die/          Transpose words
```

The real trick is to use hold buffers to transpose variable patterns. For example:

```
s/\([Dd]ie\) or \([Dd]o\)/\2 or \1/          Transpose, using hold buffers
```

CHAPTER 7

The Emacs Editor

This section presents the following topics:

- Introduction
- Typical problems
- Summary of Emacs commands by group
- Summary of Emacs commands by key
- Summary of Emacs commands by name

Introduction

Although Emacs is not part of Linux, this text editor is found on many Unix systems because it is a popular alternative to **vi**. Many versions are available. This book documents GNU Emacs, which is available from the Free Software Foundation in Cambridge, Massachusetts. For more information, see the Nutshell Handbook *Learning GNU Emacs*, Second Edition, by Debra Cameron, Bill Rosenblatt, and Eric Raymond.

To start an Emacs editing session, type:

emacs [*file*]

Typical Problems

A very common problem is that the DEL or Backspace key on the terminal does not delete the character before the cursor, as it should. Instead, it invokes a help prompt. This problem is caused by an incompatible terminal. A fairly robust fix is to create a file named *.emacs* in your home directory (or edit one that's already there) and add the following lines:

```
(keyboard-translate ?\C-h ?\C-?)
(keyboard-translate ?\C-\\ ?\C-h)
```

Now the DEL or Backspace kill should work, and you can invoke help by pressing C-\ (an arbitrarily chosen key sequence).

Another problem that could happen when you are logged in from a remote terminal is that C-s may cause the terminal to hang. This is caused by an old-fashioned handshake protocol between the terminal and the system. You can restart the terminal by pressing C-q, but that doesn't help you enter commands that contain the sequence C-s. The only solution (aside from using a more modern dial-in protocol) is to create new key-bindings that replace C-s.

Notes on the Tables

Emacs commands use the Control key and the Meta key. Most modern terminals provide a key named Alt that functions as a Meta key. In this section, the notation C- indicates that the Control key is pressed at the same time as the character that follows, while M- indicates that the Meta or Alt key is pressed along with the character that follows. (Instead of Meta, you can press the ESCAPE key, release it, and press the character.)

In the command tables that follow, the first column lists the keystroke and the last column describes it. When there is a middle column, it lists the command name. The command can be executed by typing M-x followed by the command name. If you're unsure of the name, you can type a space or a carriage return, and Emacs will list possible completions of what you've typed so far.

Because Emacs is such a comprehensive editor, containing hundreds of commands, some commands must be omitted for the sake of preserving a "quick" reference. You can browse the command set by typing C-h (for help) or M-x (for command names).

Absolutely Essential Commands

If you're just getting started with Emacs, here's a short list of the most important commands to know:

Binding	Action
C-h	Enter the online help system.
C-x C-s	Save the file.
C-x C-c	Exit Emacs.
C-x u	Undo last edit (can be repeated).
C-g	Get out of current command operation.
C-p	Up by line or character.
C-n	Down by line or character.
C-f	Forward by line or character.
C-b	Back by line or character.
C-v	Forward by one screen.

Binding	Action
M-v	Backward by one screen.
C-s	Search for characters.
C-d	Delete current character.
DEL	Delete previous character.
Backspace	Delete previous character.

Summary of Commands by Group

Reminder: Tables list keystrokes, command name, and description. C- indicates the Control key; M- indicates the Meta key.

File-Handling Commands

Binding	Command	Action
C-x C-f	find-file	Find file and read it.
C-x C-v	find-alternate-file	Read another file; replace the one read with C-x C-f.
C-x i	insert-file	Insert file at cursor position.
C-x C-s	save-buffer	Save file.
C-x C-w	write-file	Write buffer contents to file.
C-x C-c	save-buffers-kill-emacs	Exit Emacs.
C-z	suspend-emacs	Suspend Emacs (use **exit** or **fg** to restart).

Cursor Movement Commands

Some words are emphasized in the **Action** column to help you remember the binding for the command.

Binding	Command	Action
C-f	forward-char	Move *forward* one character (right).
C-b	backward-char	Move *backward* one character (left).
C-p	previous-line	Move to *previous* line (up).
C-n	next-line	Move to *next* line (down).
M-f	forward-word	Move one word *forward*.
M-b	backward-word	Move one word *backward*.
C-a	beginning-of-line	Move to beginning of line.
C-e	end-of-line	Move to *end* of line.
M-a	backward-sentence	Move backward one sentence.
M-e	forward-sentence	Move forward one sentence.
M-{	backward-paragraph	Move backward one paragraph.
M-}	forward-paragraph	Move forward one paragraph.
C-v	scroll-up	Move forward one screen.
M-v	scroll-down	Move backward one screen.
C-x [	backward-page	Move backward one page.
C-x]	forward-page	Move forward one page.

Binding	Command	Action
M->	end-of-buffer	Move to end of file.
M-<	beginning-of-buffer	Move to beginning of file.
(none)	goto-line	Go to line n of file.
(none)	goto-char	Go to character n of file.
C-l	recenter	Redraw screen with current line in the center.
M-n	digit-argument	Repeat the next command n times.
C-u n	universal-argument	Repeat the next command n times.

Deletion Commands

Binding	Command	Action
DEL	backward-delete-char	Delete previous character.
C-d	delete-char	Delete character under cursor.
M-DEL	backward-kill-word	Delete previous word.
M-d	kill-word	Delete the word the cursor is on.
C-k	kill-line	Delete from cursor to end of line.
M-k	kill-sentence	Delete sentence the cursor is on.
C-x DEL	backward-kill-sentence	Delete previous sentence.
C-y	yank	Restore what you've deleted.
C-w	kill-region	Delete a marked region (see next section).
(none)	backward-kill-paragraph	Delete previous paragraph.
(none)	kill-paragraph	Delete from the cursor to the end of the paragraph.

Paragraphs and Regions

Binding	Command	Action
C-@	set-mark-command	Mark the beginning (or end) of a region.
C-SPACE	(same as above)	(same as above)
C-x C-p	mark-page	Mark page.
C-x C-x	exchange-point-and-mark	Exchange location of cursor and mark.
C-x h	mark-whole-buffer	Mark buffer.
M-q	fill-paragraph	Reformat paragraph.
M-g	fill-region	Reformat individual paragraphs within a region.
M-h	mark-paragraph	Mark paragraph.
M-{	backward-paragraph	Move backward one paragraph.
M-}	forward-paragraph	Move forward one paragraph.
(none)	backward-kill-paragraph	Delete previous paragraph.
(none)	kill-paragraph	Delete from the cursor to the end of the paragraph.

Stopping and Undoing Commands

Binding	Command	Action
C-g	keyboard-quit	Abort current command.
C-x u	advertised-undo	Undo last edit (can be done repeatedly).

Binding	Command	Action
(none)	revert-buffer	Restore buffer to the state it was in when the file was last saved (or auto-saved).

Transposition Commands

Binding	Command	Action
C-t	transpose-chars	Transpose two letters.
M-t	transpose-words	Transpose two words.
C-x C-t	transpose-lines	Transpose two lines.
(none)	transpose-sentences	Transpose two sentences.
(none)	transpose-paragraphs	Transpose two paragraphs.

Capitalization Commands

Binding	Command	Action
M-c	capitalize-word	Capitalize first letter of word.
M-u	upcase-word	Uppercase word.
M-l	downcase-word	Lowercase word.
M- - M-c	negative-argument; capitalize-word	Capitalize previous word.
M- - M-u	negative-argument; upcase-word	Uppercase previous word.
M- - M-l	negative-argument; downcase-word	Lowercase previous word.
(none)	capitalize-region	Capitalize initial letters in region.
C-x C-u	upcase-region	Uppercase region
C-x C-l	downcase-region	Lowercase region.

Incremental Search Commands

Binding	Command	Action
C-s	isearch-forward	Start or repeat incremental search forward.
C-r	isearch-backward	Start or repeat incremental search backward.
Return	(none)	Exit a successful search.
C-g	keyboard-quit	Cancel incremental search; return to starting point.
DEL	(none)	Delete incorrect character of search string.
M-C-r	isearch-backward-regexp	Incremental search backward for regular expression.
M-C-s	isearch-forward-regexp	Incremental search forward for regular expression.

Word Abbreviation Commands

Binding	Command	Action
(none)	abbrev-mode	Enter (or exit) word abbreviation mode.
C-x -	inverse-add-global-abbrev	Type global abbreviation, then definition.
C-x C-h	inverse-add-local-abbrev	Type local abbreviation, then definition.
(none)	unexpand-abbrev	Undo the last word abbreviation.
(none)	write-abbrev-file	Write the word abbreviation file.
(none)	edit-abbrevs	Edit the word abbreviations.
(none)	list-abbrevs	View the word abbreviations.
(none)	kill-all-abbrevs	Kill abbreviations for this session.

Buffer Manipulation Commands

Binding	Command	Action
C-x b	switch-to-buffer	Move to specified buffer.
C-x C-b	list-buffers	Display buffer list.
C-x k	kill-buffer	Delete specified buffer.
(none)	kill-some-buffers	Ask about deleting each buffer.
(none)	rename-buffer	Change buffer name to specified name.
C-x s	save-some-buffers	Ask whether to save each modified buffer.

Window Commands

Binding	Command	Action
C-x 2	split-window-horizontally	Divide the current window horizontally into two.
C-x 3	split-window-vertically	Divide the current window vertically into two.
C-x >	scroll-right	Scroll the window right.
C-x <	scroll-left	Scroll the window left.
C-x o	other-window	Move to the other window.
C-x 0	delete-window	Delete current window.
C-x 1	delete-other-windows	Delete all windows but this one.
(none)	delete-windows-on	Delete all windows on a given buffer.
C-x ^	enlarge-window	Make window taller.
(none)	shrink-window	Make window shorter.
C-x }	enlarge-window-horizontally	Make window wider.
C-x {	shrink-window-horizontally	Make window narrower.
M-C-v	scroll-other-window	Scroll other window.
C-x 4 f	find-file-other-window	Find a file in the other window.
C-x 4 b	switch-to-buffer-other-window	Select a buffer in the other window.
(none)	compare-windows	Compare two buffers; show first difference.

Special Shell Mode Characters

Binding	Command	Action
C-c C-c	interrupt-shell-subjob	Terminate the current job.
C-c C-d	shell-send-eof	End of file character.
C-c C-u	kill-shell-input	Erase current line.
C-c C-w	backward-kill-word	Erase the previous word.
C-c C-z	stop-shell-subjob	Suspend the current job.

Indentation Commands

Binding	Command	Action
C-x .	set-fill-prefix	Prepend each line in paragraph with characters from beginning of line up to cursor column; cancel prefix by typing this command in column 1.
(none)	indented-text-mode	Major mode: each tab defines a new indent for subsequent lines.
(none)	text-mode	Exit indented text mode; return to text mode.
M-C-\	indent-region	Indent a region to match first line in region.
M-m	back-to-indentation	Move cursor to first character on line.
M-C-o	split-line	Split line at cursor; indent to column of cursor.
(none)	fill-individual-paragraphs	Reformat indented paragraphs, keeping indentation.

Centering Commands

Binding	Command	Action
M-s	center-line	Center line that cursor is on.
(none)	center-paragraph	Center paragraph that cursor is on.
(none)	center-region	Center currently defined region.

Macro Commands

Binding	Command	Action
C-x (	start-kbd-macro	Start macro definition.
C-x)	end-kbd-macro	End macro definition.
C-x e	call-last-kbd-macro	Execute last macro defined.
M-n C-x e	digit-argument and call-last-kbd-macro	Execute last macro defined, n times.
C-u C-x (	start-kbd-macro	Execute last macro defined, then add keystrokes.
(none)	name-last-kbd-macro	Name last macro you created (before saving it).
(none)	insert-last-keyboard-macro	Insert the macro you named into a file.
(none)	load-file	Load macro files you've saved.
(none)	*macroname*	Execute a keyboard macro you've saved.

Binding	Command	Action
C-x q	kbd-macro-query	Insert a query in a macro definition.
C-u C-x q	(none)	Insert a recursive edit in a macro definition.
M-C-c	exit-recursive-edit	Exit a recursive edit.

Detail Information Help Commands

Binding	Command	Action
C-h a	command-apropos	What commands involve this concept?
(none)	apropos	What commands, functions, and variables involve this concept?
C-h c	describe-key-briefly	What command does this keystroke sequence run?
C-h b	describe-bindings	What are all the key bindings for this buffer?
C-h k	describe-key	What command does this keystroke sequence run, and what does it do?
C-h l	view-lossage	What are the last 100 characters I typed?
C-h w	where-is	What is the key binding for this command?
C-h f	describe-function	What does this function do?
C-h v	describe-variable	What does this variable mean, and what is its value?
C-h m	describe-mode	Tell me about the mode the current buffer is in.
C-h s	describe-syntax	What is the syntax table for this buffer?

Help Commands

Binding	Command	Action
C-h t	help-with-tutorial	Run the Emacs tutorial.
C-h i	info	Start the info documentation reader.
C-h n	view-emacs-news	View news about updates to Emacs.
C-h C-c	describe-copying	View the Emacs General Public License.
C-h C-d	describe-distribution	View information on ordering Emacs from FSF.
C-h C-w	describe-no-warranty	View the (non)warranty for Emacs.

Summary of Commands by Key

Emacs commands are presented next in two alphabetical lists. Tables list keystrokes, command name, and description. C- indicates the Control key; M- indicates the Meta key.

Control-Key Sequences

Binding	Command	Action
C-@	set-mark-command	Mark the beginning (or end) of a region.

Binding	Command	Action
C-SPACE	(same as above)	(same as above)
C-]	(none)	Exit recursive edit and exit query-replace.
C-a	beginning-of-line	Move to beginning of line.
C-b	backward-char	Move *backward* one character (left).
C-c C-c	interrupt-shell-subjob	Terminate the current job.
C-c C-d	shell-send-eof	End of file character.
C-c C-u	kill-shell-input	Erase current line.
C-c C-w	backward-kill-word	Erase the previous word.
C-c C-z	stop-shell-subjob	Suspend the current job.
C-d	delete-char	Delete character under cursor.
C-e	end-of-line	Move to *end* of line.
C-f	forward-char	Move *forward* one character (right).
C-g	keyboard-quit	Abort current command.
C-h	help-command	Enter the online help system.
C-h a	command-apropos	What commands involve this concept?
C-h b	describe-bindings	What are all the key bindings for this buffer?
C-h C-c	describe-copying	View the Emacs General Public License.
C-h C-d	describe-distribution	View information on ordering Emacs from FSF.
C-h C-w	describe-no-warranty	View the (non)warranty for Emacs.
C-h c	describe-key-briefly	What command does this keystroke sequence run?
C-h f	describe-function	What does this function do?
C-h i	info	Start the info documentation reader.
C-h k	describe-key	What command does this keystroke sequence run, and what does it do?
C-h l	view-lossage	What are the last 100 characters I typed?
C-h m	describe-mode	Tell me about the mode the current buffer is in.
C-h n	view-emacs-news	View news about updates to Emacs.
C-h s	describe-syntax	What is the syntax table for this buffer?
C-h t	help-with-tutorial	Run the Emacs tutorial.
C-h v	describe-variable	What does this variable mean, and what is its value?
C-h w	where-is	What is the key binding for this command?
C-k	kill-line	Delete from cursor to end of line.
C-l	recenter	Redraw screen with current line in the center.
C-n	next-line	Move to *next* line (down).
C-p	previous-line	Move to *previous* line (up).
C-r	isearch-backward	Start or repeat nonincremental search backward.
C-r	(none)	Enter recursive edit (during query replace).
C-r	isearch-backward	Start incremental search backward.
C-s	isearch-forward	Start or repeat nonincremental search forward.
C-s	isearch-forward	Start incremental search forward.
C-t	transpose-chars	Transpose two letters.
C-u *n*	universal-argument	Repeat the next command *n* times.
C-u C-x (	start-kbd-macro	Execute last macro defined, then add keystrokes.
C-u C-x q	(none)	Insert recursive edit in a macro definition.
C-v	scroll-up	Move forward one screen.
C-w	kill-region	Delete a marked region.

Binding	Command	Action
C-x (	start-kbd-macro	Start macro definition.
C-x)	end-kbd-macro	End macro definition.
C-x [	backward-page	Move backward one page.
C-x]	forward-page	Move forward one page.
C-x ^	enlarge-window	Make window taller.
C-x {	shrink-window-horizontally	Make window narrower.
C-x }	enlarge-window-horizontally	Make window wider.
C-x <	scroll-left	Scroll the window left.
C-x >	scroll-right	Scroll the window right.
C-x -	inverse-add-global-abbrev	Type global abbreviation, then definition.
C-x .	set-fill-prefix	Prepend each line in paragraph with characters from beginning of line up to cursor column; cancel prefix by typing this command in column 1.
C-x 0	delete-window	Delete current window.
C-x 1	delete-other-windows	Delete all windows but this one.
C-x 2	split-window-horizon-tally	Divide current window horizontally into two.
C-x 4 b	switch-to-buffer-other-window	Select a buffer in the other window.
C-x 4 f	find-file-other-window	Find a file in the other window.
C-x 3	split-window-vertically	Divide current window vertically into two.
C-x b	switch-to-buffer	Move to the buffer specified.
C-x C-b	list-buffers	Display the buffer list.
C-x C-c	save-buffers-kill-emacs	Exit Emacs.
C-x C-f	find-file	Find file and read it.
C-x C-h	inverse-add-local-abbrev	Type local abbreviation, then definition.
C-x C-l	downcase-region	Lowercase region.
C-x C-p	mark-page	Place cursor and mark around whole page.
C-x C-q	(none)	Toggle read-only status of buffer.
C-x C-s	save-buffer	Save file.
C-x C-t	transpose-lines	Transpose two lines.
C-x C-u	upcase-region	Uppercase region.
C-x C-v	find-alternate-file	Read an alternate file, replacing the one read with C-x C-f.
C-x C-w	write-file	Write buffer contents to file.
C-x C-x	exchange-point-and-mark	Exchange location of cursor and mark.
C-x DEL	backward-kill-sentence	Delete previous sentence.
C-x e	call-last-kbd-macro	Execute last macro defined.
C-x h	mark-whole-buffer	Place cursor and mark around whole buffer.
C-x i	insert-file	Insert file at cursor position.

Binding	Command	Action
C-x k	kill-buffer	Delete the buffer specified.
C-x o	other-window	Move to the other window.
C-x q	kbd-macro-query	Insert a query in a macro definition.
C-x s	save-some-buffers	Ask whether to save each modified buffer.
C-x u	advertised-undo	Undo last edit (can be done repeatedly).
C-y	yank	Restore what you've deleted.
C-z	suspend-emacs	Suspend Emacs (use **exit** or **fg** to restart).

Meta-Key Sequences

Binding	Command	Action
M- - M-c	negative-argument; capitalize-word	Capitalize previous word.
M- - M-l	negative-argument; downcase-word	Lowercase previous word.
M- - M-u	negative-argument; upcase-word	Uppercase previous word.
M-$	spell-word	Check spelling of word after cursor.
M-<	beginning-of-buffer	Move to beginning of file.
M->	end-of-buffer	Move to end of file.
M-{	backward-paragraph	Move backward one paragraph.
M-}	forward-paragraph	Move forward one paragraph.
M-^	delete-indentation	Join this line to the previous one.
M-n	digit-argument	Repeat the next command n times.
M-n C-x e	digit-argument and call-last-kbd-macro	Execute the last defined macro n times.
M-a	backward-sentence	Move backward one sentence.
M-b	backward-word	Move one word *backward*.
M-C-\	indent-region	Indent a region to match first line in region.
M-C-c	exit-recursive-edit	Exit a recursive edit.
M-C-o	split-line	Split line at cursor; indent to column of cursor.
M-C-r	isearch-backward-regexp	Incremental search backward for regular expression.
M-C-s	isearch-forward-regexp	Incremental search forward for regular expression.
M-C-v	scroll-other-window	Scroll other window.
M-c	capitalize-word	Capitalize first letter of word.
M-d	kill-word	Delete word that cursor is on.
M-DEL	backward-kill-word	Delete previous word.
M-e	forward-sentence	Move forward one sentence.
M-f	forward-word	Move one word *forward*.
M-g	fill-region	Reformat individual paragraphs within a region.
M-h	mark-paragraph	Place cursor and mark around whole paragraph.
M-k	kill-sentence	Delete sentence the cursor is on.
M-l	downcase-word	Lowercase word.
M-m	back-to-indentation	Move cursor to first nonblank character on line.

Binding	Command	Action
M-q	fill-paragraph	Reformat paragraph.
M-s	center-line	Center line that cursor is on.
M-t	transpose-words	Transpose two words.
M-u	upcase-word	Uppercase word.
M-v	scroll-down	Move backward one screen.
M-x	(none)	Execute a command by typing its name.

Summary of Commands by Name

The Emacs commands below are presented alphabetically by command name. Use M-x to access the command name. Tables list command name, keystroke, and description. C- indicates the Control key; M- indicates the Meta key.

Command	Binding	Action
macroname	(none)	Execute a keyboard macro you've saved.
abbrev-mode	(none)	Enter (or exit) word abbreviation mode.
advertised-undo	C-x u	Undo last edit (can be done repeatedly).
apropos	(none)	What functions and variables involve this concept?
back-to-indentation	M-m	Move cursor to first nonblank character on line.
backward-char	C-b	Move backward one character (left).
backward-delete-char	DEL	Delete previous character.
backward-kill-paragraph	(none)	Delete previous paragraph.
backward-kill-sentence	C-x DEL	Delete previous sentence.
backward-kill-word	C-c C-w	Erase previous word.
backward-kill-word	M-DEL	Delete previous word.
backward-page	C-x [	Move backward one page.
backward-paragraph	M-{	Move backward one paragraph.
backward-sentence	M-a	Move backward one sentence.
backward-word	M-b	Move backward one word.
beginning-of-buffer	M-<	Move to beginning of file.
beginning-of-line	C-a	Move to beginning of line.
call-last-kbd-macro	C-x e	Execute last macro defined.
capitalize-region	(none)	Capitalize region.
capitalize-word	M-c	Capitalize first letter of word.
center-line	M-s	Center line that cursor is on.
center-paragraph	(none)	Center paragraph that cursor is on.
center-region	(none)	Center currently defined region.
command-apropos	C-h a	What commands involve this concept?
compare-windows	(none)	Compare two buffers; show first difference.
delete-char	C-d	Delete character under cursor.
delete-indentation	M-^	Join this line to previous one.
delete-other-windows	C-x 1	Delete all windows but this one.
delete-window	C-x 0	Delete current window.

Command	Binding	Action
delete-windows-on	(none)	Delete all windows on a given buffer.
describe-bindings	C-h b	What are all the key bindings for in this buffer?
describe-copying	C-h C-c	View the Emacs General Public License.
describe-distribution	C-h C-d	View information on ordering Emacs from FSF.
describe-function	C-h f	What does this function do?
describe-key	C-h k	What command does this keystroke sequence run, and what does it do?
describe-key-briefly	C-h c	What command does this keystroke sequence run?
describe-mode	C-h m	Tell me about the mode the current buffer is in.
describe-no-warranty	C-h C-w	View the (non)warranty for Emacs.
describe-syntax	C-h s	What is the syntax table for this buffer?
describe-variable	C-h v	What does this variable mean, and what is its value?
digit-argument	M-n	Repeat next command n times.
downcase-region	C-x C-l	Lowercase region.
downcase-word	M-l	Lowercase word.
edit-abbrevs	(none)	Edit word abbreviations.
end-kbd-macro	C-x)	End macro definition.
end-of-buffer	M->	Move to end of file.
end-of-line	C-e	Move to end of line.
enlarge-window	C-x ^	Make window taller.
enlarge-window-horizontally	C-x }	Make window wider.
exchange-point-and-mark	C-x C-x	Exchange location of cursor and mark.
exit-recursive-edit	M-C-c	Exit a recursive edit.
fill-individual-paragraphs	(none)	Reformat indented paragraphs, keeping indentation.
fill-paragraph	M-q	Reformat paragraph.
fill-region	M-g	Reformat individual paragraphs within a region.
find-alternate-file	C-x C-v	Read an alternate file, replacing the one read with C-x C-f.
find-file	C-x C-f	Find file and read it.
find-file-other-window	C-x 4 f	Find a file in the other window.
forward-char	C-f	Move forward one character (right).
forward-page	C-x]	Move forward one page.
forward-paragraph	M-}	Move forward one paragraph.
forward-sentence	M-e	Move forward one sentence.
forward-word	M-f	Move forward one word.
goto-char	(none)	Go to character n of file.
goto-line	(none)	Go to line n of file.
help-command	C-h	Enter the online help system.
help-with-tutorial	C-h t	Run the Emacs tutorial.
indent-region	M-C-\	Indent a region to match first line in region.

Emacs

Command	Binding	Action
indented-text-mode	(none)	Major mode: each tab defines a new indent for subsequent lines.
info	C-h i	Start the info documentation reader.
insert-file	C-x i	Insert file at cursor position.
insert-last-keyboard-macro	(none)	Insert the macro you named into a file.
interrupt-shell-subjob	C-c C-c	Terminate the current job.
inverse-add-global-abbrev	C-x -	Type global abbreviation, then definition.
inverse-add-local-abbrev	C-x C-h	Type local abbreviation, then definition.
isearch-backward	C-r	Start incremental search backward.
isearch-backward-regexp	M-C-r	Same, but search for regular expression.
isearch-forward	C-s	Start incremental search forward.
isearch-forward-regexp	M-C-s	Same, but search for regular expression.
kbd-macro-query	C-x q	Insert a query in a macro definition.
keyboard-quit	C-g	Abort current command.
kill-all-abbrevs	(none)	Kill abbreviations for this session.
kill-buffer	C-x k	Delete the buffer specified.
kill-line	C-k	Delete from cursor to end of line.
kill-paragraph	(none)	Delete from cursor to end of paragraph.
kill-region	C-w	Delete a marked region.
kill-sentence	M-k	Delete sentence the cursor is on.
kill-shell-input	C-c C-u	Erase current line.
kill-some-buffers	(none)	Ask about deleting each buffer.
kill-word	M-d	Delete word the cursor is on.
list-abbrevs	(none)	View word abbreviations.
list-buffers	C-x C-b	Display buffer list.
load-file	(none)	Load macro files you've saved.
mark-page	C-x C-p	Place cursor and mark around whole page.
mark-paragraph	M-h	Place cursor and mark around whole paragraph.
mark-whole-buffer	C-x h	Place cursor and mark around whole buffer.
name-last-kbd-macro	(none)	Name last macro you created (before saving it).
negative-argument; capitalize-word	M- - M-c	Capitalize previous word.
negative-argument; downcase-word	M- - M-l	Lowercase previous word.
negative-argument; upcase-word	M- - M-u	Uppercase previous word.
next-line	C-n	Move to next line (down).
other-window	C-x o	Move to the other window.
previous-line	C-p	Move to previous line (up).
query-replace-regexp	(none)	Query-replace a regular expression.
recenter	C-l	Redraw screen, with current line in center.
rename-buffer	(none)	Change buffer name to specified name.
replace-regexp	(none)	Replace a regular expression unconditionally.
re-search-backward	(none)	Simple regular expression search backward.
re-search-forward	(none)	Simple regular expression search forward.

Command	Binding	Action
revert-buffer	(none)	Restore buffer to the state it was in when the file was last saved (or auto-saved).
save-buffer	C-x C-s	Save file.
save-buffers-kill-emacs	C-x C-c	Exit Emacs.
save-some-buffers	C-x s	Ask whether to save each modified buffer.
scroll-down	M-v	Move backward one screen.
scroll-left	C-x <	Scroll the window left.
scroll-other-window	M-C-v	Scroll other window.
scroll-right	C-x >	Scroll the window right.
scroll-up	C-v	Move forward one screen.
set-fill-prefix	C-x .	Prepend each line in paragraph with characters from beginning of line up to cursor column; cancel prefix by typing this command in column 1.
set-mark-command	C-@ or C-SPACE	Mark the beginning (or end) of a region.
shell-send-eof	C-c C-d	End of file character.
shrink-window	(none)	Make window shorter.
shrink-window-horizontally	C-x {	Make window narrower.
spell-buffer	(none)	Check spelling of current buffer.
spell-region	(none)	Check spelling of current region.
spell-string	(none)	Check spelling of string typed in minibuffer.
spell-word	M-$	Check spelling of word after cursor.
split-line	M-C-o	Split line at cursor; indent to column of cursor.
split-window-horizontally	C-x 2	Divide current window horizontally into two.
split-window-vertically	C-x 3	Divide current window vertically into two.
start-kbd-macro	C-x (	Start macro definition.
stop-shell-subjob	C-c C-z	Suspend current job.
suspend-emacs	C-z	Suspend Emacs (use exit or fg to restart).
switch-to-buffer	C-x b	Move to the buffer specified.
switch-to-buffer-other-window	C-x 4 b	Select a buffer in the other window.
text-mode	(none)	Enter text mode.
transpose-chars	C-t	Transpose two letters.
transpose-lines	C-x C-t	Transpose two lines.
transpose-paragraphs	(none)	Transpose two paragraphs.
transpose-sentences	(none)	Transpose two sentences.
transpose-words	M-t	Transpose two words.
unexpand-abbrev	(none)	Undo the last word abbreviation.
universal-argument	C-u *n*	Repeat the next command *n* times.
upcase-region	C-x C-u	Uppercase region.
upcase-word	M-u	Uppercase word.
view-emacs-news	C-h n	View news about updates to Emacs.
view-lossage	C-h l	What are the last 100 characters I typed?
where-is	C-h w	What is the key binding for this command?
write-abbrev-file	(none)	Write the word abbreviation file.

Emacs

Command	Binding	Action
write-file	C-x C-w	Write buffer contents to file.
yank	C-y	Restore what you've deleted.

CHAPTER 8

The vi Editor

Linux systems usually provide an enhanced **vi** called **vim** or **nvi**. This chapter presents the following topics:

- Review of **vi** operations
- Movement commands
- Edit commands
- Saving and exiting
- Accessing multiple files
- Interacting with the shell
- Macros
- Miscellaneous commands
- Alphabetical list of keys
- Setting up **vi**

Review of vi Operations

This section provides a review of the following:

- Command-line syntax
- **vi** modes
- Syntax of **vi** commands
- Status-line commands

For more information on **vi**, refer to the Nutshell Handbook *Learning the vi Editor*, by Linda Lamb and Arnold Robbins.

Command-Line Syntax

The three most common ways of starting a **vi** session are:

> **vi** *file*
> **vi** +*n* *file*
> **vi** +/*pattern* *file*

You can open *file* for editing, optionally at line *n* or at the first line matching *pattern*. If no *file* is specified, **vi** opens with an empty buffer.

Command Mode

Once the file is opened, you are in command mode. From command mode, you can:

- Invoke insert mode
- Issue editing commands
- Move the cursor to a different position in the file
- Invoke **ex** commands
- Invoke a Linux shell
- Save or exit the current version of the file

Insert Mode

In insert mode, you can enter new text in the file. Press the ESCAPE key to exit insert mode and return to command mode. The following commands invoke insert mode:

a	Append after cursor.
A	Append at end of line.
c	Begin change operation.
C	Change to end of line.
i	Insert before cursor.
I	Insert at beginning of line.
o	Open a line below current line.
O	Open a line above current line.
R	Begin overwriting text.

| s | Substitute a character. |
| S | Substitute entire line. |

Syntax of vi Commands

In **vi**, commands have the following general form:

> [*n*] *operator* [*m*] *object*

The basic editing *operators* are:

c	Begin a change.
d	Begin a deletion.
y	Begin a yank (or copy).

If the current line is the object of the operation, then the operator is the same as the object: **cc**, **dd**, **yy**. Otherwise, the editing operators act on objects specified by cursor-movement commands or pattern-matching commands. *n* and *m* are the number of times the operation is performed, or the number of objects the operation is performed on. If both *n* and *m* are specified, the effect is $n \times m$.

An object can represent any of the following text blocks:

word	Includes characters up to a space or punctuation mark. A capitalized object is a variant form that recognizes only blank spaces.
sentence	Extends to ., !, ? followed by two spaces.
paragraph	Extends to next blank line or paragraph macro defined by **para=** option.
section	Extends to next section heading defined by **sect=** option.

Examples

2cw	Change the next two words.
d}	Delete up to next paragraph.
d^	Delete back to beginning of line.
5yy	Copy the next five lines.
y]]	Copy up to the next section.

Status-Line Commands

Most commands are not echoed on the screen as you input them. However, the status line at the bottom of the screen is used to echo input for the following commands:

| / | Search forward for a pattern. |
| ? | Search backward for a pattern. |

:	Invoke an **ex** command.
!	Invoke a shell command that takes as its input an object in the buffer and replaces it with output from the command.

Commands that are input on the status line must be entered by pressing the RETURN key. In addition, error messages and output from the **CTRL-G** command are displayed on the status line.

Movement Commands

A number preceding a command repeats the movement. Movement commands are also objects for change, delete, and yank operations.

Character

h, j, k, l	Left, down, up, right ($\leftarrow$, $\downarrow$, $\uparrow$, $\rightarrow$)
SPACEBAR	Right

Text

w, W, b, B	Forward, backward by word
e, E	End of word
), (	Beginning of next, current sentence
}, {	Beginning of next, current paragraph
]], [[	Beginning of next, current section

Lines

0, $	First, last position of current line
^	First nonblank character of current line
+, -	First character of next, previous line
RETURN	First character of next line
n|	Column n of current line
H	Top line of screen
M	Middle line of screen
L	Last line of screen
nH	n lines after top line
nL	n lines before last line

Screens

CTRL-F, CTRL-B	Scroll forward, backward one screen.
CTRL-D, CTRL-U	Scroll down, up one-half screen.
CTRL-E, CTRL-Y	Show one more line at bottom, top of window.
z RETURN	Reposition line with cursor to top of screen.

`z.`	Reposition line with cursor to middle of screen.
`z -`	Reposition line with cursor to bottom of screen.
CTRL-L, **CTRL-R**	Redraw screen (without scrolling).

Searches

`/pattern`	Search forward for *pattern*.
`/`	Repeat forward search.
`/pattern/+n`	Go to line *n* after *pattern*.
`?pattern`	Search backward for *pattern*.
`?`	Repeat previous search backward.
`?pattern?-n`	Go to line *n* before *pattern*.
`n`	Repeat previous search.
`N`	Repeat search in opposite direction.
`%`	Find match of current parenthesis, brace, or bracket.
`f`*x*	Move forward to *x* on current line.
`F`*x*	Move backward to *x* on current line.
`t`*x*	Move forward to just before *x* in current line.
`T`*x*	Move back to just after *x* in current line.
`,`	Reverse search direction of last **f**, **F**, **t**, or **T**.
`;`	Repeat last character search (**f**, **F**, **t**, or **T**).

Line numbering

CTRL-G	Display current line number.
n`G`	Move to line number *n*.
G	Move to last line in file.
`:`*n*	Move to line number *n*.

Marking position

`m`*x*	Mark current position with character *x*.
`` ` ``*x*	(backquote) Move cursor to mark *x*.
`'`*x*	(apostrophe) Move to start of line containing *x*.
`` `` ``	(backquotes) Return to previous mark (or to location prior to a search).
`''`	(apostrophes) Like above, but return to start of line.

Edit Commands

Recall that **c**, **d**, and **y** are the basic editing operators.

Inserting New Text

`a`	Append after cursor.
`A`	Append to end of line.

i	Insert before cursor.
I	Insert at beginning of line.
o	Open a line below cursor.
O	Open a line above cursor.
ESC	Terminate insert mode.
TAB	Insert a tab.
BACKSPACE	Move back one character.
RETURN	Move down one line.
CTRL-J	Move down one line.
CTRL-I	Insert a tab.
CTRL-T	Move to next tab setting.
CTRL-D	Move to previous tab setting.
CTRL-H	Move back one character.
CTRL-U	Delete current line.
CTRL-V	Insert next character verbatim.
CTRL-W	Move back one word.

The last four control characters are set by **stty**. Your terminal settings may differ.

Changing and Deleting Text

cw	Change word.
cc	Change line.
c	Change text from current position to end of line.
dd	Delete current line.
*n*dd	Delete *n* lines.
D	Delete remainder of line.
dw	Delete a word.
d}	Delete up to next paragraph.
d^	Delete back to beginning of line.
d/*pat*	Delete up to first occurrence of pattern.
dn	Delete up to next occurrence of pattern.
df*a*	Delete up to and including *a* on current line.
dt*a*	Delete up to (not including) *a* on current line.
dL	Delete up to last line on screen.
dG	Delete to end of file.
p	Insert last deleted text after cursor.
P	Insert last deleted text before cursor.
r*x*	Replace character with *x*.
R*text*	Replace *text* beginning at cursor.
s	Substitute character.
*n*s	Substitute *n* characters.
S	Substitute entire line.
u	Undo last change.
U	Restore current line.
x	Delete current cursor position.
X	Delete back one character.
*n*X	Delete previous *n* characters.

.	Repeat last change.
~	Reverse case.

Copying and moving

Y	Copy current line to new buffer.
yy	Copy current line.
"xyy	Yank current line to buffer x.
"xd	Delete into buffer x.
"Xd	Delete and append into buffer x.
"xp	Put contents of buffer x.
y]]	Copy up to next section heading.
ye	Copy to end of word.

Saving and Exiting

Writing a file means saving the edits and updating the file's modification time.

ZZ	Quit vi, writing the file only if changes were made.
:x	Same as ZZ.
:wq	Write and quit file.
:w	Write file.
:w file	Save copy to file.
:n1,n2w file	Write lines n1 to n2 to new file.
:n1,n2w >> file	Append lines n1 to n2 to existing file.
:w!	Write file (overriding protection).
:w! file	Overwrite file with current buffer.
:w %.new	Write current buffer named file as file.new.
:q	Quit file.
:q!	Quit file (discarding edits).
Q	Quit vi and invoke ex.
:vi	Return to vi after Q command.
:e file2	Edit file2 without leaving vi.
:n	Edit next file.
:e!	Return to version of current file at time of last write.
:e#	Edit alternate file.
%	Current filename.
#	Alternate filename.

Accessing Multiple Files

:e file	Edit another file; current file becomes alternate.
:e!	Restore last saved version of current file.
:e + file	Begin editing at end of file.
:e +n file	Open file at line n.
:e #	Open to previous position in alternate file.

`:ta` *tag*	Edit file at location *tag*.
`:n`	Edit next file.
`:n!`	Force next file.
`:n` *files*	Specify new list of *files*.
`CTRL-G`	Show current file and line number.
`:args`	Display multiple files to be edited.
`:rew`	Rewind list of multiple files to top.

Interacting with the Shell

`:r` *file*	Read in contents of *file* after cursor.
`:r !`*command*	Read in output from *command* after current line.
`:nr !`*command*	Like above, but place after line *n* (0 for top of file).
`:!`*command*	Run *command*, then return.
`!`*object command*	Send buffer *object* to *command*; replace with output.
`:n1,n2!` *command*	Send lines *n1 - n2* to *command*; replace with output.
`n!!`*command*	Send *n* lines to *command*; replace with output.
`!!`	Repeat last system command.
`:sh`	Create subshell; return to file with *EOF*.
`CTRL-Z`	Suspend editor, resume with **fg**.
`:so` *file*	Read and execute commands from *file*.

Macros

`:ab` *in out*	Use *in* as abbreviation for *out*.
`:unab` *in*	Remove abbreviation for *in*.
`:ab`	List abbreviations.
`:map` *c sequence*	Map character *c* as *sequence* of commands.
`:unmap` *c*	Disable map for character *c*.
`:map`	List characters that are mapped.
`:map!` *c sequence*	Map character *c* to input mode *sequence*.
`:unmap!` *c*	Disable input mode map (you may need to quote the character with **CTRL-V**).
`:map!`	List characters that are mapped to input mode.

The following characters are unused in command mode and can be mapped as user-defined commands.

Letters: g K q V v

Control keys: ^A ^K ^O ^T ^W ^X

Symbols: _ * \ =

(Note: The = is used by **vi** if Lisp mode is set.)

Miscellaneous Commands

J	Join two lines.
:j!	Join two lines, preserving blank spaces.
<<	Shift this line left one shift width (default is 8 spaces).
>>	Shift this line right one shift width (default is 8 spaces).
>}	Shift right to end of paragraph.
<%	Shift left until matching parenthesis, brace, bracket, etc. (Cursor must be on the matching symbol.)

Alphabetical List of Keys

For brevity, control characters are marked by ^.

a	Append text after cursor.
A	Append text at end of line.
^A	Unused.
b	Back up to beginning of word in current line.
B	Back up one word, ignoring punctuation.
^B	Scroll backward one window.
c	Change operator.
C	Change to end of current line.
^C	Unused in command mode; ends insert mode.
d	Delete operator.
D	Delete to end of current line.
^D	Scroll down half-window; in insert mode, unindent to **shiftwidth** if **autoindent** is set.
e	Move to end of word.
E	Move to end of word, ignoring punctuation.
^E	Show one more line at bottom of window.
f	Find next character typed forward on current line.
F	Find next character typed backward on current line.
^F	Scroll forward one window.
g	Unused.
G	Go to specified line or end of file.
^G	Print information about file on status line.
h	Left arrow cursor key.
H	Move cursor to Home position.
^H	Left arrow cursor key; Backspace key in insert mode.
i	Insert text before cursor.
I	Insert text before first nonblank character on line.
^I	Unused in command mode; in insert mode, same as TAB key.
j	Down arrow cursor key.

J	Join two lines.
^J	Down arrow cursor key; in insert mode, move down a line.
k	Up arrow cursor key.
K	Unused.
^K	Unused.
l	Right arrow cursor key.
L	Move cursor to Last position in window.
^L	Redraw screen.
m	Mark the current cursor position in register (a-z).
M	Move cursor to Middle position in window.
^M	Carriage return.
n	Repeat the last search command.
N	Repeat the last search command in reverse direction.
^N	Down arrow cursor key.
o	Open line below current line.
O	Open line above current line.
^O	Unused.
p	Put yanked or deleted text after or below cursor.
P	Put yanked or deleted text before or above cursor.
^P	Up arrow cursor key.
q	Unused.
Q	Quit **vi** and invoke **ex**.
^Q	Unused. (On some terminals, resume data flow.)
r	Replace character at cursor with the next character you type.
R	Replace characters.
^R	Redraw the screen.
s	Change the character under the cursor to typed characters.
S	Change entire line.
^S	Unused. (On some terminals, stop data flow.)
t	Move cursor forward to character before next character typed.
T	Move cursor backward to character after next character typed.
^T	Unused in command mode; in insert mode, move to next tab setting.
u	Undo the last change made.
U	Restore current line, discarding changes.
^U	Scroll the screen upward a half-window.
v	Unused.
V	Unused.
^V	Unused in command mode; in insert mode, insert next character verbatim.
w	Move to beginning of next word.
W	Move to beginning of next word, ignoring punctuation.
^W	Unused in command mode; in insert mode, back up to beginning of word.

x	Delete character under cursor.
X	Delete character before cursor.
^X	Unused.
y	Yank or copy operator.
Y	Make copy of current line.
^Y	Show one more line at top of window.
z	Reposition line containing cursor. **z** must be followed either by: RETURN (reposition line to top of screen), . (reposition line to middle of screen), or – (reposition line to bottom of screen).
ZZ	Exit the editor, saving changes.
^Z	Suspend **vi**.

Setting Up vi

This section describes the following:

- The :**set** command

- Options available with :**set**

- Sample *.exrc* file

The :set Command

The :**set** command lets you specify options that change characteristics of your editing environment. Options may be put in the *.exrc* file or set during a **vi** session.

The colon should not be typed if the command is put in *.exrc*.

:**set** *x*	Enable option *x*.
:**set nox**	Disable option *x*.
:**set** *x=val*	Give *value* to option *x*.
:**set**	Show changed options.
:**set all**	Show all options.
:**set** *x?*	Show value of option *x*.

Options Used by :set

The following table describes the options to :**set**. The first column includes the optional abbreviation, if there is one, and uses an equal sign to show that the option takes a value. The second column gives the default, and the third column describes the behavior of the enabled option.

Option	Default	Description
autoindent (ai)	noai	In insert mode, indent each line to the same level as the line above or below. Use with **shiftwidth** option.

Option	Default	Description
autoprint (ap)	ap	Display changes after each editor command. (For global replacement, display last replacement.)
autowrite (aw)	noaw	Automatically write (save) file if changed, before opening another file with :n or before giving Linux command with :!.
beautify (bf)	nobf	Ignore all control characters during input (except tab, newline, or formfeed).
directory= (dir)	/tmp	Name the directory in which **ex** stores buffer files. (Directory must be writable.)
edcompatible	noed-compatible	Use **ed**-like features on substitute commands.
errorbells (eb)	errorbells	Sound bell when an error occurs.
exrc (ex)	noexrc	Allow the execution of *.exrc* files that reside outside the user's home directory.
hardtabs= (ht)	8	Define boundaries for terminal hardware tabs.
ignorecase (ic)	noic	Disregard case during a search.
lisp	nolisp	Insert indents in appropriate Lisp format. ( ), { }, [[, and]] are modified to have meaning for Lisp.
list	nolist	Print tabs as ^I; mark ends of lines with $. (Use **list** to tell if end character is a tab or a space.)
magic	magic	Wildcard characters . (dot), * (asterisk), and [ ] (brackets) have special meaning in patterns.
mesg	mesg	Permit system messages to display on terminal while editing in **vi**.
number (nu)	nonu	Display line numbers on left of screen during editing session.
open	open	Allow entry to open mode from **ex**.
optimize (opt)	noopt	Abolish carriage returns at the end of lines when printing multiple lines; speeds output on dumb terminals when printing lines with leading white space (blanks or tabs).

Option	Default	Description
paragraphs= (para)	IPLPPPQPLI pplpipbp	Define paragraph delimiters for movement by { or }. The pairs of characters in the value are the names of nroff/troff macros that begin paragraphs.
prompt	prompt	Display the **ex** prompt (:) when vi's **Q** command is given.
readonly (ro)	noro	Any writes (saves) of a file will fail unless you use ! after the write (works with **w**, **ZZ**, or **autowrite**).
redraw (re)	noredraw	Terminal redraws screen whenever edits are made (in other words, insert mode pushes over existing characters, and deleted lines immediately close up). Default depends on line speed and terminal type. **noredraw** is useful at slow speeds on a dumb terminal: deleted lines show up as @, and inserted text appears to overwrite existing text until you press ESC.
remap	remap	Allow nested map sequences.
report=	5	Display a message on the prompt line whenever you make an edit that affects at least a certain number of lines. For example, **6dd** reports the message "6 lines deleted."
scroll=	<1/2 window>	Amount of screen to scroll.
sections= (sect)	SHNHH HU	Define section delimiters for [[ ]] movement. The pairs of characters in the value are the names of nroff/troff macros that begin sections.
shell= (sh)	/bin/sh	Pathname of shell used for shell escape (:!) and shell command (:sh). Default value is derived from SHELL variable.
shiftwidth= (sw)	8	Define number of spaces used by the indent commands (^T, ^D, >>, and <<).
showmatch (sm)	nosm	In **vi**, when) or } is entered, cursor moves briefly to matching (or {. (If the match is not on the screen, rings the error message bell.) Very useful for programming.

Option	Default	Description
showmode	noshowmode	In insert mode, displays a message on the prompt line indicating the type of insert you are making. For example, "Open Mode" or "Append Mode."
slowopen (slow)		Hold off display during insert. Default depends on line speed and terminal type.
tabstop= (ts)	8	Define number of spaces that a tab indents during editing session. (Printer still uses system tab of 8.)
taglength= (tl)	0	Define number of characters that are significant for tags. Default (zero) means that all characters are significant.
tags=	tags /usr/lib/tags	Define pathname of files containing tags (see the **ctags** command in Chapter 12). By default, the system looks for files **tags** (in the current directory) and */usr/lib/tags*.
term=		Set terminal type.
terse	noterse	Display shorter error messages.
timeout (to)	timeout	Keyboard maps "time out" after 1 second.
ttytype=		Set terminal type. Default is inherited from TERM environment variable.
warn	warn	Display the message, "No write since last change."
window= (w)		Show a certain number of lines of the file on the screen. Default depends on line speed and terminal type.
wrapmargin= (wm)	0	Define right margin. If greater than zero, automatically insert carriage returns to break lines.
wrapscan (ws)	ws	Searches wrap around either end of file.
writeany (wa)	nowa	Allow saving to any file.

Sample .exrc File

```
set nowrapscan wrapmargin=7
set sections=SeAhBhChDh nomesg
map q :w^M:n^M
map v dwElp
ab ORA O'Reilly & Associates, Inc.
```

CHAPTER 9

The ex Editor

ex is a line editor that serves as the foundation for the screen editor **vi**. **ex** commands work on the current line or on a range of lines in a file. On Linux, **ex** is often called **hex**.

Most often, you use **ex** from within **vi**. In **vi**, **ex** commands are preceded by a colon and entered by pressing RETURN.

But you can invoke **ex** on its own—from the command line—just as you would invoke **vi**. (You could execute an **ex** script this way.) You can also use the **vi** command **Q** to quit the **vi** editor and enter **ex**.

This chapter presents the following topics:

* Syntax of **ex** commands

* Alphabetical summary of commands

For more information, see the Nutshell Handbook *Learning the vi Editor* by Linda Lamb.

Syntax of ex Commands

To enter an **ex** command from **vi**, type:

    :[*address*] *command* [*options*]

An initial : indicates an **ex** command. As you type the command, it is echoed on the status line. Enter the command by pressing RETURN. *address* is the line number or range of lines that are the object of *command*. *options* and *addresses* are described in the following sections. **ex** commands are described in the alphabetical summary.

You can exit **ex** in several ways:

:**x**	Exit (save changes and quit).
:**q!**	Quit without saving changes.
:**vi**	Enter the **vi** editor.

Options

!	Indicates a variant command form, overriding the normal behavior.
count	The number of times the command is to be repeated. Unlike **vi** commands, **ex** commands cannot be preceded by *count*, because a number preceding an **ex** command is treated as a line address. For example, **d3** deletes three lines beginning with the current line; **3d** deletes line 3.
file	The name of a file that is affected by the command. % stands for current file; # stands for previous file.

Addresses

If no address is given, the current line is the object of the command. If the address specifies a range of lines, the format is:

x,y

where x and y are the first and last addressed lines (x must precede y in the buffer). x and y may be line numbers or symbols. Using ; instead of , sets the current line to x before interpreting y. The notation 1,$ addresses all lines in the file, as does %.

Address Symbols

1,$	All lines in the file
%	All lines; same as **1,$**
x,y	Lines x through y
$x;y$	Lines x through y, with current line reset to x
0	Top of file
.	Current line
n	Absolute line number n
$	Last line
$x-n$	n lines before x
$x+n$	n lines after x
–[n]	One or n lines previous
+[n]	One or n lines ahead
$'x$	Line marked with x
$''$	Previous mark
/*pattern*/	Forward to line matching *pattern*
?*pattern*?	Backward to line matching *pattern*

See Chapter 6, *Pattern Matching*, for more information on using patterns.

Alphabetical Summary of ex Commands

ex commands can be entered by specifying any unique abbreviation. In this listing, the full name appears in the margin, and the shortest possible abbreviation is used in the syntax line. Examples are assumed to be typed from **vi**, so they include the : prompt.

abbrev	**ab** [*string text*]
	
	Define *string* when typed to be translated into *text*. If *string* and *text* are not specified, list all current abbreviations.
	
	Examples
	
	Note: ˆM appears when you type **CTRL-V** followed by RETURN.
	
	    `:ab ora O'Reilly & Associates, Inc.`
	    `:ab id Name:ˆMRank:ˆMPhone:`

append	*[address]* a[!] *text* . Append *text* at specified *address*, or at present address if none is specified. Add a ! to switch the **autoindent** setting that will be used during input (e.g., if **autoindent** was enabled, ! disables it).
args	**ar** Print filename arguments (the list of files to edit). The current argument is shown in brackets ([ ]).
change	*[address]* c[!] *text* . Replace the specified lines with *text*. Add a ! to switch the **autoindent** setting during input of *text*.
copy	*[address]* co *destination* Copy the lines included in *address* to the specified *destination* address. The command **t** is the same as **copy**. ***Example*** `:1,10 co 50` *Copy first 10 lines to just after line 50*

[address] d *[buffer]*	delete

Delete the lines included in *address*. If *buffer* is specified, save or append the text to the named buffer.

Examples

```
:/Part I/,/Part II/-1d        Delete to line above "Part II"
:/main/+d                     Delete line below "main"
:.,$d                         Delete from this line to last line
```

e[!] [+*n*] *[file]*	edit

Begin editing *file*. Add a ! to discard any changes to the current file. If no *file* is given, edit another copy of the current file. With the +*n* argument, begin editing on line *n*.

Examples

```
:e file
:e#                   Return to editing the previous file
:e!                   Discard edits since last save
```

f *[filename]*	file

Change the name of the current file to *filename*, which is considered "not edited." If no *filename* is specified, print the current status of the file.

Example

```
:f %.new
```

[address] g[!]/*pattern*/[*commands*]	global

Execute *commands* on all lines that contain *pattern* or, if *address* is specified, on all lines within that range. If *commands* are not specified, print all such lines. If ! is used, execute *commands* on all lines that don't contain *pattern*. See **v**.

Examples

```
:g/Unix/p                Print all lines containing "Unix"
:g/Name:/s/tom/Tom/      Change "tom" to "Tom" on all lines
                         containing "Name:"
```

address i[!]	insert
text	

.

Insert *text* at line before the specified *address*, or at present address if none is specified. Add a ! to switch the **autoindent** setting during input of *text*.

join	*[address]* j[!] *[count]*
	Place the text in the specified *address* on one line, with whitespace adjusted to provide two blank characters after a period (.), no blank characters after a), and one blank character otherwise. Add a ! to prevent whitespace adjustment.
	Example
	`:1,5j!` *Join first five lines, preserving whitespace*
k	*[address]* k *char*
	Mark the given *address* with *char*. Return later to the line with *char*.
list	*[address]* l *[count]*
	Print the specified lines so that tabs display as ^I, and the ends of lines display as $. l is a temporary version of :**set list**.
map	map[!] *[char commands]*
	Define a keyboard macro named *char* as the specified sequence of *commands*. *char* is usually a single character, or the sequence #*n*, representing a function key on the keyboard. Use a ! to create a macro for input mode. With no arguments, list the currently defined macros.
	Examples
	`:map K dwwP` *Transpose two words*
	`:map q :w^M:n^M` *Write current file; go to next*
	`:map! + ^[bi(^[ea)` *Enclose previous word in parentheses*
mark	*[address]* ma *char*
	Mark the specified line with *char*, a single lowercase letter. Return later to the line with *char*. Same as **k**.
move	*[address]* m *destination*
	Move the lines specified by *address* to the *destination* address.
	Example
	`:.,/Note/m /END/` *Move text block after line containing "END"*

n[!] [[+*command*] *filelist*] —

Edit the next file from the command-line argument list. Use **args** to list these files. If *filelist* is provided, replace the current argument list with *filelist* and begin editing on the first file; if *command* is given (containing no spaces), execute *command* after editing the first such file.

Example

```
:n chap*          Start editing all "chapter" files
```

[*address*] nu [*count*] — number

Print each line specified by *address*, preceded by its buffer line number. Use **#** as an alternate abbreviation for **number**. *count* specifies the number of lines to show, starting with *address*.

[*address*] o [/*pattern*/] — open

Enter **vi**'s open mode at the lines specified by *address*, or at the lines matching *pattern*. Enter and exit open mode with **Q**. Open mode lets you use the regular **vi** commands, but only one line at a time. May be useful on slow dialup lines.

---

pre — preserve

Save the current editor buffer as though the system had crashed.

[*address*] p [*count*] — print

Print the lines specified by *address*. *count* specifies the number of lines to print, starting with *address*. **P** is another abbreviation.

Example

```
:100;+5p          Show line 100 and the next five lines
```

[*address*] pu [*char*] — put

Restore the lines that were previously deleted or yanked from named buffer *char*, and put them after the line specified by *address*. If *char* is not specified, restore the last deleted or yanked text.

quit	**q[!]** Terminate current editing session. Use ! to discard changes made since the last save. If the editing session includes additional files in the argument list that were never accessed, quit by typing **q!** or by typing **q** twice.
read	*[address]* **r** *file* Copy in the text from *file* on the line below the specified *address*. If *file* is not specified, the current filename is used. *Example* `:0r $HOME/data` *Read file in at top of current file*
read	*[address]* **r** *!command* Read the output of Linux *command* into the text after the line specified by *address*. *Example* `:$r !cal` *Place a calendar at end of file*
recover	**rec** *[file]* Recover *file* from system save area.
rewind	**rew[!]** Rewind argument list and begin editing the first file in the list. The ! flag rewinds, discarding any changes to the current file that haven't been saved.

set	**se** *parameter1 parameter2* ...
	
	Set a value to an option with each *parameter*, or if no *parameter* is supplied, print all options that have been changed from their defaults. For Boolean-valued options, each *parameter* can be phrased as *option* or **no***option*; other options can be assigned with the syntax *option=value*. Specify **all** to list current settings.
	
	Examples
	
	`:set nows wm=10`
	`:set all`

sh	shell

Create a new shell. Resume editing when the shell is terminated.

---

so *file*	source

Read and execute **ex** commands from *file*.

Example

```
:so $HOME/.exrc
```

[address] **s** *[/pattern/replacement/]* *[options]* *[count]*	substitute

Replace each instance of *pattern* on the specified lines with *replacement*. If *pattern* and *replacement* are omitted, repeat last substitution. *count* specifies the number of lines on which to substitute, starting with *address*. For more examples, see "Examples of Searching and Replacing" in Chapter 6.

Options

c	Prompt for confirmation before each change.
g	Substitute all instances of *pattern* on each line.
p	Print the last line on which a substitution was made.

Examples

```
:1,10s/yes/no/g          Substitute on first 10 lines
:%s/[Hh]ello/Hi/gc       Confirm global substitutions
:s/Fortran/\U&/ 3        Uppercase first instance of "Fortran"
                         on next three lines
```

[address] **t** *destination*	t

Copy the lines included in *address* to the specified *destination* address. **t** is an alias for **copy**.

Example

```
:%t$     Copy the file and add it to the end
```

[address] **ta** *tag*	tag

Switch the editing session to the file containing *tag*.

**ex
Editor**

→

tag
←
	Example
	Run **ctags**, then switch to the file containing *myfunction*:
	
	`:!ctags *.c`
	`:tag myfunction`

unabbreviate	**una** *word* Remove *word* from the list of abbreviations.
undo	**u** Reverse the changes made by the last editing command.
unmap	**unm**[!] *char* Remove *char* from the list of keyboard macros. Use ! to remove a macro for input mode.
v	*[address]* **v**/*pattern/*[*commands*] Execute *commands* on all lines *not* containing *pattern*. If *commands* are not specified, print all such lines. **v** is equivalent to **g**!. *Example* `:v/#include/d` *Delete all lines except "#include" lines*
version	**ve** Print the editor's current version number.
visual	*[address]* **vi** [*type*] [*count*] Enter visual mode (**vi**) at the line specified by *address*. Exit with **Q**. *type* can be one of −, ^, or . (See the **z** command.) *count* specifies an initial window size.
vi	**vi** [+*n*] file Begin editing *file* in visual mode (**vi**), optionally at line *n*.
write	*[address]* **w**[!] [[>>] *file*] Write lines specified by *address* to *file*, or write full contents of buffer if *address* is not specified. If *file* is also omitted, save the contents of the buffer to the current filename. If >> *file* is used, write contents to the end of an

existing *file*. The ! flag forces the editor to write over any current contents of *file*.

	write

[address] **w** *!command*

Write lines specified by *address* to *command*.

Examples

```
:1,10w name_list          Copy first 10 lines to name_list
:50w >> name_list         Now append line 50
```

	write

---

wq[!]

Write and quit the file in one command. The ! flag forces the editor to write over any current contents of *file*.

	wq

---

x

Write the file if it was changed since the last write; then quit.

	xit

[address] **ya** *[char] [count]*

Place lines specified by *address* in named buffer *char*. If no *char* is given, place lines in general buffer. *count* specifies the number of lines to yank, starting with *address*.

Example

```
:101,200 ya a
```

	yank

[address] **z** *[type] [count]*

Print a window of text, with the line specified by *address* at the top. *count* specifies the number of lines to be displayed.

Type

+	Place specified line at top of window (the default).
-	Place specified line at bottom of window.
.	Place specified line in center of window.
^	Move up one window.
=	Place specified line in center of window, and leave this line as the current line.

	z

!	*[address]* ! *command*
	Execute Linux *command* in a shell. If *address* is specified, apply the lines contained in *address* as standard input to *command*, and replace the lines with the output.
	Examples
| | ```
:!ls                      List files in the current directory
:11,20!sort -f            Sort lines 11–20 of current file
``` |
=	*[address]* =
	Print the line number of the next line matching *address*. If no address is given, print the number of the last line.
<>	*[address]* < *[count]* *[address]* > *[count]*
	Shift lines specified by *address* either left (<) or right (>). Only blanks and tabs are removed in a left shift. *count* specifies the number of lines to shift, starting with *address*.
address	*address*
	Print the line specified in *address*.
RETURN	RETURN
	Print the next line in the file.
&	& *[options]* *[count]*
	Repeat the previous substitution (**s**) command. *count* specifies the number of lines on which to substitute, starting with *address*.
	Examples
| | ```
:s/Overdue/Paid/          Substitute once on current line
:g/Status/&               Redo substitution on all "Status" lines
``` |
| ~ | *[address]* ~ *[count]* |
| | Replace the previous regular expression with the previous replacement pattern from a substitute (**s**) command. |

CHAPTER 10

The sed Editor

This chapter presents the following topics:

- Conceptual overview of **sed**

- Command-line syntax

- Syntax of **sed** commands

- Group summary of **sed** commands

- Alphabetical summary of **sed** commands

For more information, see the Nutshell Handbook *sed & awk*, Second Edition, by Dale Dougherty and Arnold Robbins.

Conceptual Overview

sed is a noninteractive, or stream-oriented, **editor**. It interprets a script and performs the actions in the script. **sed** is stream-oriented because, as with many Unix programs, input flows through the program and is directed to standard output. For example, **sort** is stream-oriented; **vi** is not. **sed**'s input typically comes from a file, but can be directed from the keyboard. Output goes to the screen by default, but can be captured in a file instead.

Typical uses of **sed** include:

- Editing one or more files automatically

- Simplifying repetitive edits to multiple files

- Writing conversion programs

sed operates as follows:

- Each line of input is copied into a pattern space.

- All editing commands in a **sed** script are applied in order to each line of input.

- Editing commands are applied to all lines (globally) unless line addressing restricts the lines affected.

- If a command changes the input, subsequent commands are applied to the changed line, not to the original input line.

- The original input file is unchanged because the editing commands modify a copy of the original input line. The copy is sent to standard output (but can be redirected to a file).

Command-Line Syntax

The syntax for invoking **sed** has two forms:

> **sed** [*options*] '*command*' *file(s)*
> **sed** [*options*] **−f** *scriptfile file(s)*

The first form allows you to specify an editing command on the command line, surrounded by single quotes. The second form allows you to specify a *scriptfile*, a file containing **sed** commands. If no files are specified, **sed** reads from standard input.

The following *options* are recognized:

−e *cmd*   Next argument is an editing command; not needed unless specifying two or more editing commands.

−f *file*   Next argument is a file containing editing commands.

−n   Suppress the default output; **sed** displays only those lines specified with the **p** command, or with the **p** flag of the **s** command.

Syntax of sed Commands

sed commands have the general form:

> [*address*][*, address*][!]*command* [*arguments*]

sed commands consist of *addresses* and editing *commands. commands* consist of a single letter or symbol; they are described later, alphabetically and by group. *arguments* include the label supplied to **b** or **t**, the filename supplied to **r** or **w**, and the substitution flags for **s**. *addresses* are described in the next section.

Pattern Addressing

A **sed** command can specify zero, one, or two addresses. An address can be a line number, the symbol **$** (for last line), or a regular expression enclosed in slashes

(*/pattern/*). Regular expressions are described in Chapter 6, *Pattern Matching*. Additionally, \n can be used to match any newline in the pattern space (resulting from the N command), but not the newline at the end of the pattern space.

If the command specifies:	Then the command is applied to:
No address	Each input line.
One address	Any line matching the address. Some commands accept only one address: **a**, **i**, **r**, **q**, and **=**.
Two comma-separated addresses	First matching line and all succeeding lines up to and including a line matching the second address.
An address followed by **!**	All lines that do *not* match the address.

Examples

```
s/xx/yy/g           Substitute on all lines (all occurrences)
/BSD/d              Delete lines containing BSD
/^BEGIN/,/^END/p    Print between BEGIN and END, inclusive
/SAVE/!d            Delete any line that doesn't contain SAVE
/BEGIN/,/END/!s/xx/yy/g    Substitute on all lines, except between BEGIN
                    and END
```

Braces ({}) are used in **sed** to nest one address inside another or to apply multiple commands at the same address:

> [*/address/*][,*/address/*]{
> *command1*
> *command2*
> }

The opening curly brace must end a line, and the closing curly brace must be on a line by itself. Be sure there are no blank spaces after the braces.

Group Summary of sed Commands

In the lists below, the **sed** commands are grouped by function and are described tersely. Full descriptions, including syntax and examples, can be found afterward in the alphabetical summary.

Basic Editing

a	Append text after a line.
c	Replace text (usually a text block).
i	Insert text before a line.
d	Delete lines.
s	Make substitutions.
y	Translate characters (like **tr** in Chapter 2, *Linux User Commands*).

Line Information

=	Display line number of a line.
l	Display control characters in ASCII.
p	Display the line.

Input/Output Processing

n	Skip current line and go to line below.
r	Read another file's contents into the input.
w	Write input lines to another file.
q	Quit the **sed** script (no further output).

Yanking and Putting

h	Copy pattern space into hold space; wipe out what's there.
H	Copy pattern space into hold space; append to what's there.
g	Get the hold space back; wipe out the pattern space.
G	Get the hold space back; append to pattern space.
x	Exchange contents of hold space and pattern space.

Branching Commands

b	Branch to *label* or to end of script.
t	Same as **b**, but branch only after substitution.
: *label*	Label branched to by **t** or **b**.

Multiline Input Processing

N	Read another line of input (creates embedded newline).
D	Delete up to the embedded newline.
P	Print up to the embedded newline.

Alphabetical Summary of sed Commands

:	:*label*
	Label a line in the script for the transfer of control by **b** or **t**. *label* may contain up to seven characters.
=	[/*pattern*/]=
	Write to standard output the line number of each line containing *pattern*.

[*address*]a\
text

a

Append *text* following each line matched by *address*. If *text* goes over more than one line, newlines must be "hidden" by preceding them with a backslash. The *text* will be terminated by the first newline that is not hidden in this way. The *text* is not available in the pattern space, and subsequent commands cannot be applied to it. The results of this command are sent to standard output when the list of editing commands is finished, regardless of what happens to the current line in the pattern space.

Example

```
$a\
This goes after the last line in the file\
(marked by $). This text is escaped at the\
end of each line, except for the last one.
```

[*address1*][,*address2*]b[*label*]

b

Transfer control unconditionally to :*label* elsewhere in script. That is, the command following the *label* is the next command applied to the current line. If no *label* is specified, control falls through to the end of the script, so no more commands are applied to the current line.

Example

Ignore lines between .**TS** and .**TE**; resume script after .**TE**:

```
/^\.TS/,/^\.TE/b
```

[*address1*][,*address2*]c\
text

c

Replace the lines selected by the address with *text*. When a range of lines is specified, all lines as a group are replaced by a single copy of *text*. The newline following each line of *text* must be escaped by a backslash, except the last line. The contents of the pattern space are, in effect, deleted and no subsequent editing commands can be applied.

Example

Replace first 100 lines in a file:

```
1,100c\
\
<First 100 names to be supplied>
```

d	*[address1][, address2]***d** Delete the addressed line (or lines) from the pattern space. Thus, the line is not passed to standard output. A new line of input is read, and editing resumes with the first command in the script. ***Example*** Delete all blank lines: `/^$/d`
D	*[address1][, address2]***D** Delete first part (up to embedded newline) of multiline pattern space created by **N** command, and resume editing with first command in script. If this command empties the pattern space, then a new line of input is read, as if the **d** had been executed. ***Example*** Strip multiple blank lines, leaving only one: <code>/^$/{ N /^\n$/D }</code>
g	*[address1][, address2]***g** Paste the contents of the hold space (see **h** or **H** command) back into the pattern space, wiping out the previous contents of the pattern space. The example shows a simple way to copy lines. ***Example*** This script collects all lines containing the word *Item:* and copies them to a place marker later in the file. The place marker is overwritten. <code>/Item:/H /<Replace this line with the item list>/g</code>
G	*[address1][, address2]***G** Same as **g**, except that the hold space is pasted below the address instead of overwriting it. The example shows a simple way to "cut and paste" lines. ***Example*** This script collects all lines containing the word *Item:* and moves them after a place marker later in the file. The original *Item:* lines are deleted.

```
/Item:/{
H
d
}
/Summary of items:/G
```

---

*[address1][,address2]*h

Copy the pattern space into the hold space, a special temporary buffer. The previous contents of the hold space are obliterated. You can use **h** to save a line before editing it.

Example

```
# Edit a line; print the change; replay the original
/Linux/{
h
s/.* Linux \(.*\) .*/\1:/
p
x
}
```

Sample input:

```
This describes the Linux ls command.
This describes the Linux cp command.
```

Sample output:

```
ls:
This describes the Linux ls command.
cp:
This describes the Linux cp command.
```

---

*[address1][,address2]*H

Append the contents of the pattern space (preceded by a newline) to the contents of the hold space. Even if the hold space is empty, **H** still appends a newline. **H** is like an incremental copy. See examples under **g** and **G**.

---

*[address1]*i\
text

Insert *text* before each line matched by *address*. (See **a** for details on *text*.)

Example

```
/Item 1/i\
The five items are listed below:
```

l	*[address1][,address2]*l

List the contents of the pattern space, showing nonprinting characters as ASCII codes. Long lines are wrapped.

n	*[address1][,address2]*n

Read next line of input into pattern space. The current line is sent to standard output, and the next line becomes the current line. Control passes to the command following **n** instead of resuming at the top of the script.

Example

In the **ms** macros, a section header occurs on the line below an .NH macro. To print all lines of header text, invoke this script with sed −n:

```
/^\.NH/{
n
p
}
```

N	*[address1][,address2]*N

Append next input line to contents of pattern space; the two lines are separated by an embedded newline. (This command is designed to allow pattern matches across two lines.) Using \n to match the embedded newline, you can match patterns across multiple lines. See example at **D**.

Examples

Like previous example, but print .NH line as well as header title:

```
/^\.NH/{
N
p
}
```

Join two lines (replace newline with space):

```
/^\.NH/{
N
s/\n/ /
p
}
```

p	*[address1][,address2]*p

Print the addressed lines. Unless the −n command-line option is used, this command will cause duplicate lines to be output. Also, it is typically used before commands that change flow control (**d**, **N**,

b) and that might prevent the current line from being output. See examples at **h**, **n**, and **N**.

p

---

*[address1][,address2]*P

P

Print first part (up to embedded newline) of multiline pattern created by **N** command. Same as **p** if **N** has not been applied to a line.

---

*[address]*q

q

Quit when *address* is encountered. The addressed line is first written to output (if default output is not suppressed), along with any text appended to it by previous **a** or **r** commands.

Examples

Delete everything after the addressed line:

```
/Garbled text follows:/q
```

Print only the first 50 lines of a file:

```
50q
```

---

*[address]*r *file*

r

Read contents of *file* and append after the contents of the pattern space. Exactly one space must be put between the **r** and the filename.

Example

```
/The list of items follows:/r item_file
```

---

*[address1][,address2]*s/*pattern*/*replacement*/*[flags]*

s

Substitute *replacement* for *pattern* on each addressed line. If pattern addresses are used, the pattern // represents the last pattern address specified. The following flags can be specified:

n	Replace *n*th instance of /*pattern*/ on each addressed line. *n* is any number in the range 1 to 512; the default is 1.
g	Replace all instances of /*pattern*/ on each addressed line, not just the first instance.
p	Print the line if a successful substitution is done. If several successful substitutions are done, multiple copies of the line will be printed.

$\rightarrow$

w *file*   Write the line to a *file* if a replacement was done.

Examples

Here are some short, commented scripts:

```
# Change third and fourth quote to ( and ):
/function/{
s/"/(/3
s/")/4
}

# Remove all quotes on a given line:
/Title/s/"//g

# Remove first colon or all quotes; print resulting lines:
s/://p
s/"//gp

# Change first "if" but leave "ifdef" alone:
/ifdef/!s/if/    if/
```

[address1][,address2]t [label]

Test if any substitutions have been made on addressed lines, and if so, branch to line marked by :*label*. (See **b** and :.) If *label* is not specified, control falls through to bottom of script. The **t** command is like a case statement in the C programming language or the shell programming languages. You test each case: when it's true, you exit the construct.

Example

Suppose you want to fill empty fields of a database. You have this:

```
ID: 1   Name: greg   Rate: 45
ID: 2   Name: dale
ID: 3
```

You want this:

```
ID: 1   Name: greg   Rate: 45   Phone: ??
ID: 2   Name: dale   Rate: ??   Phone: ??
ID: 3   Name: ????   Rate: ??   Phone: ??
```

You need to test the number of fields already there. Here's the script (fields are tab-separated):

```
/ID/{
s/ID: .* Name: .* Rate: .*/&    Phone: ??/p
t
s/ID: .* Name: .*/&    Rate: ??    Phone: ??/p
t
s/ID: .*/&    Name: ??    Rate: ??    Phone: ??/p
}
```

[address1][,address2]w file

Append contents of pattern space to *file*. This action occurs when the command is encountered, rather than when the pattern space is output. Exactly one space must separate the **w** and the filename. This command will create the file if it does not exist; if the file exists, its contents will be overwritten each time the script is executed. Multiple write commands that direct output to the same file append to the end of the file.

Example

```
# Store tbl and eqn blocks in a file:
/^\.TS/,/^\.TE/w troff_stuff
/^\.EQ/,/^\.EN/w troff_stuff
```

[address1][,address2]x   x

Exchange contents of the pattern space with the contents of the hold space. See **h** for an example.

[address1][,address2]y/abc/xyz/   y

Translate characters. Change every instance of *a* to *x*, *b* to *y*, *c* to *z*, etc.

Example

```
# Change item 1, 2, 3 to Item A, B, C ...
/^item [1-9]/y/123456789/ABCDEFGHI/
```

CHAPTER 11

The gawk Scripting Language

gawk is the GNU version of **awk**, a powerful pattern-matching program for processing text files that may be composed of fixed or variable length records separated by some delineator (by default, a newline character). **gawk** may be used from the command line or in **gawk** scripts. Normally you should be able to invoke this utility using either **awk** or **gawk** on the shell command line.

This chapter presents the following topics:

- Conceptual overview

- Command-line syntax

- Patterns and procedures

- System variables

- Operators

- Variable and array assignment

- Group listing of commands

- Alphabetical summary of commands

For more information, see the Nutshell Handbook *sed & awk*, Second Edition, by Dale Dougherty and Arnold Robbins.

Conceptual Overview

With **gawk**, you can:

- Conveniently process a text file as though it were made up of records and fields in a textual database.

- Use variables to change the database.

- Execute shell commands from a script.

- Perform arithmetic and string operations.

- Use programming constructs such as loops and conditionals.

- Define your own functions.

- Process the result of shell commands.

- Process command-line arguments more gracefully.

- Produce formatted reports.

Command-Line Syntax

gawk's syntax has two forms:

> **gawk** [*options*] '*script*' *var=value file(s)*
> **gawk** [*options*] **–f** *scriptfile var=value file(s)*

You can specify a *script* directly on the command line, or you can store a script in a *scriptfile* and specify it with **–f**. Multiple **–f** options are allowed.

gawk operates on one or more input *files*. If none are specified (or if **–** is specified), **gawk** reads from the standard input.

Variables can be assigned a value on the command line. The *value* assigned to a variable can be a literal, a shell variable ($*name*), or a command substitution (`cmd`), but the value is available only after a line of input is read (i.e., after the **BEGIN** statement).

For example, to print the first three (colon-separated) fields of the password file, use **–F** to set the field separator to a colon:

```
gawk -F: '{print $1; print $2; print $3}' /etc/passwd
```

Numerous examples are shown later in this section under "Patterns and Procedures."

Options

All options exist in both traditional POSIX (one-letter) format and GNU-style (long) format. Some recognized *options* are:

––
: Treat all subsequent text as commands or filenames, not options.

–f *file*, **––file-program=***file*
: Read **gawk** commands from *file* instead of command line.

–v *var=value*, **––assign=***var=value*
: Assign a *value* to variable *var*. This allows assignment before the script begins execution.

−F*c*, **−−field-separator=***c*

Set the field separator to character *c*. This is the same as setting the variable **FS**. *c* may be a regular expression. Each input line, or record, is divided into fields by whitespace (blanks or tabs) or by some other user-definable record separator. Fields are referred to by the variables **$1**, **$2**, . . . , **$***n*. **$0** refers to the entire record.

−W *option*

All −W options are specific to **gawk**, as opposed to **awk**. An alternate syntax is **−−***option* (i.e., **−−compat**). *option* may be one of:

compat
> Same as **traditional**.

copyleft
> Print copyleft notice and exit.

copyright
> Same as **copyleft**.

help
> Print syntax and list of options, then exits.

lint Warn about commands that might not port to other versions of **awk**, or that **gawk** considers problematic.

lint-old
> Like **lint** but compares to an older version of **awk**.

posix
> Expect exact compatibility with POSIX; additionally, ignore *x* escape sequences, the synonym function, ******, and ****=**.

re-interval
> Allow use of {*n,m*} intervals in regular expressions.

source=*program*
> Treat *program* as **gawk** commands. Like the '*script*' argument, but lets you mix commands from files (using −**f** options) with commands on the **gawk** command line.

traditional
> Behave exactly like traditional (non-GNU) **awk**.

usage
> Same as **help**.

version
> Print version information and exit.

Patterns and Procedures

gawk scripts consist of patterns and procedures:

> *pattern* {*procedure*}

Both are optional. If *pattern* is missing, {*procedure*} is applied to all lines. If {*procedure*} is missing, the matched line is printed.

Patterns

A pattern can be any of the following:

> /*regular expression*/
> *relational expression*
> *pattern-matching expression*
> *pattern,pattern*
> **BEGIN**
> **END**

- Expressions can be composed of quoted strings, numbers, operators, functions, defined variables, or any of the predefined variables described later under "gawk System Variables."

- Regular expressions use the extended set of metacharacters, and are described in Chapter 6, *Regular Expressions*.

- In addition, ^ and $ can be used to refer to the beginning and end of a field, respectively, rather than the beginning and end of a line.

- Relational expressions use the relational operators listed under "Operators" later in this chapter. Comparisons can be either string or numeric. For example, **$2 > $1** selects lines for which the second field is greater than the first.

- Pattern-matching expressions use the operators ~ (match) and !~ (don't match). See "Operators" later in this chapter.

- The **BEGIN** pattern lets you specify procedures that take place *before* the first input line is processed. (Generally, you set global variables here.)

- The **END** pattern lets you specify procedures that take place *after* the last input record is read.

- If there are multiple **BEGIN** or **END** patterns, their associated actions are taken in the order in which they appear in the script.

- *pattern,pattern* specifies a range of lines.

Except for **BEGIN** and **END**, patterns can be combined with the Boolean operators || (or), **&&** (and), and ! (not).

In addition to other regular expression operators, GNU **awk** supports POSIX character lists, which are useful for matching non-ASCII characters in languages other than English. These lists are recognized only within [ ] ranges. A typical use would be [[:lower:]], which in English is the same as [a-z].

The following table lists POSIX character lists.

Notation	Action
[:alnum:]	Alphanumeric characters
[:alpha:]	Alphabetic characters, uppercase and lowercase
[:blank:]	Printable whitespace: spaces and tabs but not control characters
[:cntrl:]	Control characters, such as ^A through ^Z
[:digit:]	Decimal digits
[:graph:]	Printable characters, excluding whitespace
[:lower:]	Lowercase alphabetic characters
[:print:]	Printable characters, including whitespace but not control characters
[:punct:]	Punctuation, a subclass of printable characters
[:space:]	Whitespace, including spaces, tabs, and some control characters
[:upper:]	Uppercase alphabetic characters
[:xdigit:]	Hexadecimal digits

Procedures

Procedures consist of one or more commands, functions, or variable assignments, separated by newlines or semicolons, and contained within curly braces. Commands fall into four groups:

- Variable or array assignments

- Printing commands

- Built-in functions

- Control-flow commands

Simple Pattern-Procedure Examples

1. Print first field of each line (no pattern specified):

   ```
   { print $1 }
   ```

2. Print all lines that contain *pattern*:

   ```
   /pattern/
   ```

3. Print first field of lines that contain *pattern*:

   ```
   /pattern/{ print $1 }
   ```

4. Print records containing more than two fields:

   ```
   NF > 2
   ```

5. Interpret each group of lines up to a blank line as a single input record:

   ```
   BEGIN { FS = "\n"; RS = "" }
   ```

6. Print fields 2 and 3 in switched order, but only on lines whose first field matches the string "URGENT":

```
$1 ~ /URGENT/ { print $3, $2 }
```

7. Count and print the number of *pattern* found:

```
/pattern/ { ++x } END { print x }
```

8. Add numbers in second column and print total:

```
{total += $2 }; END { print "column total is", total}
```

9. Print lines that contain fewer than 20 characters:

```
length($0) < 20
```

10. Print each line that begins with *Name:* and that contains exactly seven fields:

```
NF == 7 && /^Name:/
```

11. Reverse the order of fields:

```
{ for (i = NF; i >= 1; i--) print $i }
```

gawk System Variables

Variable	Description
$n	nth field in current record; fields are separated by **FS**
$0	Entire input record
ARGC	Number of arguments on command line
ARGIND	Current file's place in command line (starting with 0)
ARGV	An array containing the command-line arguments
CONVFMT	Conversion format for numbers (default is %.**6g**)
ENVIRON	An associative array of environment variables
ERRNO	Description of last system error
FIELDWIDTHS	List of field widths (whitespace separated)
FILENAME	Current filename
FNR	Like **NR**, but relative to the current file
FS	Field separator (default is any whitespace; null string separates into individual characters)
IGNORECASE	If true, make case-insensitive matches
NF	Number of fields in current record
NR	Number of the current record
OFMT	Output format for numbers (default is %.**6g**)
OFS	Output field separator (default is a blank)
ORS	Output record separator (default is a newline)
RLENGTH	Length of the string matched by **match** function
RS	Record separator (default is a newline)
RSTART	First position in the string matched by **match** function
SUBSEP	Separator character for array subscripts (default is \034)

Operators

The table below lists the operators, in order of increasing precedence, that are available in **gawk**.

Symbol	Meaning
`= += -= *= /= %= ^= **=`	Assignment
`? :`	C conditional expression
`||`	Logical OR
`&&`	Logical AND
`~  !~`	Match regular expression and negation
`< <= > >= != ==`	Relational operators
(blank)	Concatenation
`+ -`	Addition, subtraction
`* / %`	Multiplication, division, and modulus
`+ - !`	Unary plus and minus, and logical negation
`^ **`	Exponentiation
`++ --`	Increment and decrement, either prefix or postfix
`$`	Field reference

Variables and Array Assignments

Variables can be assigned a value with an = sign. For example:

```
FS = ","
```

Expressions using the operators +, −, /, and % (modulo) can be assigned to variables.

Arrays can be created with the **split** function (see the listing in the "Alphabetical Summary of Commands"), or they can simply be named in an assignment statement. Array elements can be subscripted with numbers (*array*[1], ..., *array*[*n*]) or with names. For example, to count the number of occurrences of a pattern, you could use the following script:

```
/pattern/ { array["/pattern/"]++ }
END { print array["/pattern/"] }
```

In **gawk**, variables need not be declared previous to their use, nor do arrays need to be dimensioned; they are activated upon first reference. All variables are stored as strings, but may be used either as strings or numbers. **gawk** will use the program script context to determine whether to treat a variable as a string or a number, but the distinction can also be forced by the user. To force a variable to be treated as a string, catenate a null to the variable:

```
var ""
```

To force a variable to be treated as a number, add zero to it:

```
var + 0
```

Group Listing of gawk Commands

gawk commands may be classified as follows:

Arithmetic Functions	String Functions	Control Flow Statements	Input/Output Processing	Time Functions	Miscellaneous
atan2	gensub	break	close	systime	delete
cos	gsub	continue	fflush	strftime	function
exp	index	do/while	getline		system
int	length	exit	next		
log	match	for	nextfile		
rand	split	if	print		
sin	sub	return	printf		
sqrt	substr		sprintf		
srand	tolower		while		
	toupper				

Alphabetical Summary of Commands

The following alphabetical list of statements and functions includes all that are available in **gawk** in Linux.

---

atan2 (*y,x*)

Return the arctangent of y/x in radians.

atan2

---

break

Exit from a **while** or **for** loop.

break

---

close (*filename–expr*)

close(*command-expr*)

Close a file read by a **getline** command or a pipe; takes as an argument the same expression that opened the pipe or file.

close

---

continue

Begin next iteration of **while** or **for** loop without reaching the bottom.

continue

---

cos (*x*)

Return the cosine of x, an angle in radians.

cos

---

delete	**delete** (*array*[*element*]) Delete *element* of *array*.
do	**do** *body* **while** (*expr*) Looping statement. Execute statements in *body*, then evaluate *expr*. If *expr* is true, execute *body* again.
exit	**exit** Do not execute remaining instruction, and read no new input. END procedures will be executed.
exp	**exp** (*arg*) Return the natural exponent of *arg* (the inverse of **log**).
for	**for** (*i*=*lower*; *i*<=*upper*; *i*++) *command* While the value of variable *i* is in the range between *lower* and *upper*, do *command*. A series of commands must be put within braces. <= or any relational operator can be used; ++ or – – can be used to increment or decrement the variable.
for	**for** (*item* in *array*) *command* For each *item* in an associative *array*, do *command*. Multiple commands must be put inside braces. Refer to each element of the array as *array*[*item*]. Elements of **gawk** arrays are stored in an order that enables access of any element in essentially equivalent time. This order may appear to be indiscriminate; if the output is desired in sorted order, you must pipe it through the **sort** command.
fflush	**fflush** (*filename*) Flushes output to *filename*; default is the standard output.

function	**function** *name*(*parameter–list*) {
	
	    statements
	 }

Create *name* as a user-defined function consisting of **gawk** *statements* that apply to the specified list of parameters.	function

getline [*var*] [<*file*] *command* | **getline** [*var*] The first form reads input from *file* or the next file on the command line, and the second form reads the output of *command*. Both forms read one line at a time, and each time the statement is executed it gets the next line of input. The line of input is assigned to $0 and is parsed into fields, setting **NF**, **NR**, and **FNR**. If *var* is specified, the result is assigned to *var*, and the $0 is not changed. Thus, if the result is assigned to a variable, the current line does not change. **getline** is actually a function, and it returns 1 if it reads a record successfully, 0 at *EOF*, and −1 if for some reason it is otherwise unsuccessful.	getline

gensub (*r, s, n, t*) Substitute *s* for the *n*th match of regular expression *r* in the string *t*. Leave *t* unchanged but return new string as the result. If *n* is **g** or **G**, change all matches. If *t* is not supplied, it defaults to $0. .	gensub

gsub (*r, s, t*) Globally substitute *s* for each match of the regular expression *r* in the string *t*. Return the number of substitutions. If *t* is not supplied, it defaults to $0.	gsub

if (*condition*)
 	
    command1
[**else**]
    [*command2*]
 	
If *condition* is true, do *command1*; otherwise do *command2*. Condition can be an expression using any of the relational operators <, <=, ==, !=, >=, or >, as well as the pattern-matching operator ~. A series of commands must be put within braces. The following lines determine whether the first word in each line starts with A, uppercase or lowercase:
 	
``
if ($1 ~ /[Aa]*/)
    ...begins with A or a
``
	if

index	**index** (*substr,str*)
	Return the position of a substring in a string. Returns 0 if *substr* is not contained in *str*.
int	**int** (*arg*)
	Return the integer part of *arg*.
length	**length** (*arg*)
	Return the length of *arg*. If *arg* is not supplied, **$0** is assumed. Therefore, **length** can be used as a predefined variable that contains the length of the current record.
log	**log** (*arg*)
	Return the natural logarithm of *arg* (the inverse of **exp**).
match	**match** (*s,r*)
	Return position in *s* where regular expression *r* first matches or 0 if no occurrences are found. Sets the value of **RSTART** and **RLENGTH**.
next	**next**
	Read next input line and start new cycle through pattern/procedures statements.
nextfile	**nextfile**
	Skip to the next file on the **gawk** command line and start new cycle through pattern/procedures statements.
print	**print** [*args*] [*destination*]
	Print *args* on output. Literal strings must be quoted. Fields are printed in the order they are listed. If separated by commas in the argument list, they are separated in the output by the character specified by **OFS**. If separated by spaces, they are concatenated in the output. *destination* is a shell redirection or pipe expression (e.g., > *file*) that redirects the default output.
printf	**printf** [*format* [, *expressions*]]
	Formatted **print** statement. Expressions or variables can be formatted according to instructions in the *format* argument. The number of *expressions* must correspond to the number specified in the format sections.

format follows the conventions of the C-language **printf** statement. Here are a few of the most common formats:

%s	A string.
%d	A decimal number.
%*n.m*f	A floating point number; *n* = total number of digits. *m* = number of digits after decimal point.
%[-]*nc*	*n* specifies minimum field length for format type *c*, while - justifies value in field; otherwise value is right-justified.

The field width may be specified. For example, %3.2f limits a floating point number to three digits before the decimal point and two after.

format can also contain embedded escape sequences, \n (newline) and \t (tab) being the most common. Spaces and literal text can be placed in the *format* argument by quoting the entire argument. If there are multiple expressions to be printed, multiple formats should be specified.

Example

Using the script:

```
{printf ("The sum on line %s is %d.\n", NR, $1+$2)}
```

the following input line:

```
5    5
```

produces this output, followed by a newline:

```
The sum on line 1 is 10.
```

---

rand ( )

Generate a random number between 0 and 1. This function returns the same series of numbers each time the script is executed, unless the random number generator is seeded using the **srand()** function.

---

return [*expr*]

Used at end of user-defined functions to exit function, returning the value of *expr.*

---

sin (*x*)

Return the sine of *x,* an angle in radians.

split	**split** (*string,array*[*,sep*]) Split *string* into elements of array *array*[1], . . . ,*array*[*n*]. The string is split at each occurrence of separator *sep*. If *sep* is not specified, **FS** is used. If *sep* is a null string, a split is performed on every character. The number of array elements created is returned.
sprintf	**sprintf** [*format* [, *expression(s)*]] Return the value of one or more *expressions*, using the specified *format* (see **printf**). Data is formatted but not printed.
sqrt	**sqrt** (*arg*) Return square root of *arg*.
srand	**srand** (*expr*) Use *expr* to set a new seed for random number generator. Default is time of day.
strftime	**strftime** (*format, time*) Return time (which should be input in same format as that returned by **systime()**) in specified format, which uses the same % tokens as the C function **strftime** or the **date** command discussed in Chapter 2. The *format* argument defaults to that used by the **date** command (see Chapter 2); the *time* argument defaults to current time.
sub	**sub** (*r,s,t*) Substitute *s* for first match of the regular expression *r* in the string *t*. Return 1 if successful; 0 otherwise. If *t* is not supplied, defaults to $0.
substr	**substr** (*string,m*[*,n*]) Return substring of *string* beginning at character position *m* and consisting of the next *n* characters. If *n* is omitted, include all characters to the end of string.
system	**system** (*command*) Execute the specified shell *command* and return its status. The status of the command that is executed typically indicates its success (1), completion (0), or unexpected error (−1). The output of the command is not available for processing within the **gawk** script. Use "*command*	**getline**" to read the output of a command into the script.

systime () Return number of seconds since midnight UTC, January 1, 1970.	systime
tolower (*str*) Translate all uppercase characters in *str* to lowercase and return the new string.	tolower
toupper (*str*) Translate all lowercase characters in *str* to uppercase and return the new string.	toupper
while (*condition*) *command* Do *command* while *condition* is true (see **if** for a description of allowable conditions). A series of commands must be put within braces.	while

gawk

CHAPTER 12

Programming Overview
and Commands

This chapter lists tables of commonly used programming commands.

Common Commands

Following are tables of commonly used software development commands. These commands, and more, are covered in detail in the next section, "Alphabetical Summary of Commands."

Creating Programs

ar	Create and update library files.
as	Generate object file.
bison	Generate parsing tables.
cpp	Preprocess C code.
g++	GNU C++ compiler.
gcc	GNU C compiler.
ld	Link editor.
flex	Lexical analyzer.
m4	Macro processor.
make	Create programs.
rpcgen	Translate RPC to C code.
yacc	Generate parsing tables.

Maintaining Programs

ctags	Generate symbol list for use with the **vi** editor.
etags	Generate symbol list for use with the Emacs editor.
gdb	GNU debugger.

gprof	Display object file's profile data.
imake	Generate makefiles for use with **make**.
make	Maintain, update, and regenerate related programs and files.
nm	Display object file's symbol table.
patch	Apply patches to source code.
size	Print the size of an object file in bytes.
strip	Strip symbols from an object file.

Alphabetical Summary of Commands

ar [−V] *key* [*args*] [*posname*] *archive* [*files*]   **ar**

Programming

Maintain a group of *files* that are combined into a file *archive*. Used most commonly to create and update library files as used by the link editor (**ld**). Only one key letter may be used, but each can be combined with additional *args* (with no separations between). *posname* is the name of a file in *archive*. When moving or replacing *files*, you can specify that they be placed before or after *posname*. −V prints the version number of **ar** on standard error.

Key

d	Delete *files* from *archive*.
m	Move *files* to end of *archive*.
p	Print *files* in *archive*.
q	Append *files* to *archive*.
r	Replace *files* in *archive*.
t	List the contents of *archive* or list the named *files*.
x	Extract contents from *archive* or only the named *files*.

Args

a	Use with **r** or **m** key to place *files* in the archive after *posname*.
b	Same as **a** but before *posname*.
c	Create *archive* silently.
i	Same as **b**.
l	For backwards compatibility; meaningless in Linux.
o	Preserve original time stamps.

→

ar ←	s	Force regeneration of *archive* symbol table (useful after running **strip**).
	u	Use with **r** to replace only *files* that have changed since being put in *archive*.
	v	Verbose; print a description of actions taken.

Example

Replace **mylib.a** with object files from the current directory:

```
ar r mylib.a `ls *.o`
```

---

as

as [*options*] *files*

Generate an object file from each specified assembly language source *file*. Object files have the same root name as source files but replace the .s suffix with .o. There may be some additional system-specific options.

Options

−− [| *files*]
: Read input files from standard input, or from *files* if the pipe is used.

−a[**dhlns**][=*file*]
: With only the −a option, list source code, assembler listing, and symbol table. The other options specify additional things to list or omit:

  −ad
  : Omit debugging directives.

  −ah
  : Include the high level source code, if available.

  −al Include an assembly listing.

  −an
  : Suppress forms processing.

  −as Include a symbol listing.

  =*file*
  : Set the listing filename to *file*.

−**defsym** *symbol=value*
: Define the *symbol* to have the value *value*, which must be an integer.

−f
: Skip preprocessing.

−o *objfile* Place output in object file *objfile* (default is *file*.o).

−v	Display the version number of the assembler.	**as**
−I *path*	Include *path* when searching for .**include** directives.	
−K	Warn before altering difference tables.	
−L	Do not remove local symbols, which begin with L.	
−R	Combine both data and text in text section.	
−W	Quiet mode.	

bison [*options*] *file*

Given a *file* containing context-free grammar, convert into tables for subsequent parsing while sending output to *file.c*. This utility is both to a large extent compatible with **yacc** and named for it. All input files should use the suffix *.y*; output files will use the original prefix. All long options (those preceded by −−) may instead be preceded by +.

Options

−b *prefix*, −−**file-prefix**=*prefix*
> Use *prefix* for all output files.

−d, −−**defines**
> Generate *file.h*, producing **#define** statements that relate **bison**'s token codes to the token names declared by the user.

−r, −−**raw** Use **bison** token numbers, not **yacc**-compatible translations, in *file.h*.

−k, −−**token-table**
> Include token names and values of YYNTO-KENS, YYNNTS, YYNRULES, and YYNSTATES in *file.c*.

−l, −−**no-lines**
> Exclude **#line** constructs from code produced in *file.c*. (Use after debugging is complete.)

−n, −−**no-parser**
> Suppress parser code in output, allowing only declarations. Assemble all translations into a switch statement body and print it to *file.act*.

−o *file*, −−**output-file**=*file*
> Output to *file*.

−p *prefix*, −−**name-prefix**=*prefix*
> Substitute *prefix* for **yy** in all external symbols.

→

bison
←
	−t, −−debug
	    Compile runtime debugging code.
	
	−v, −−verbose
	    Verbose mode. Print diagnostics and notes about parsing tables to *file.output*.
	
	−V, −−version
	    Display version number.
	
	−y, −−yacc, −−fixed-output-files
	    Duplicate **yacc**'s conventions for naming output files.

c++	**c++** [*options*] *files* See **g++**.
cc	**cc** [*options*] *files* See **gcc**.

cpp	**cpp** [*options*] [*ifile* [*ofile*]]
	
	GNU C language preprocessor. **cpp** is invoked as the first pass of any C compilation by the **gcc** command. The output of **cpp** is a form acceptable as input to the next pass of the C compiler, and **cpp** normally invokes **gcc** after it finishes processing. *ifile* and *ofile* are, respectively, the input and output for the preprocessor; they default to standard input and standard output.
	
	Options
	
	    −$** Do not allow **$ in identifiers.
	
	    −dM Suppress normal output. Print series of **#defines** that create the macros used in the source file.
	
	    −dD Similar to **−dM**, but excludes predefined macros and includes results of preprocessing.
	
	    −idirafter *dir*
	        Search *dir* for header files when a header file is not found in any of the included directories.
	
	    −imacros *file*
	        Process macros in *file* before processing main files.
	
	    −include *file*
	        Process *file* before main file.
	
	    −iprefix *prefix*
	        When adding directories with **−iwithprefix**, prepend *prefix* to the directory's name.

−iwithprefix *dir*

> Append *dir* to the list of directories to be searched when a header file cannot be found in the main include path. If **−iprefix** has been set, prepend that prefix to the directory's name.

−lang-c, −lang-c++, −lang-objc, −lang-objc++

> Expect the source to be in C, C++, Objective C, or Objective C++, respectively.

−lint   Display all lint commands in comments as **#pragma lint** *command.*

−nostdinc   Search only specified, not standard, directories for header files.

−nostdinc++

> Suppress searching of directories believed to contain C++−specific header files.

−pedantic   Warn verbosely.

−pedantic-errors

> Produce a fatal error in every case in which **−pedantic** would have produced a warning.

−traditional

> Behave like traditional C, not ANSI.

−undef   Suppress definition of all nonstandard macros.

−C   Pass along all comments (except those found on **cpp** directive lines). By default, **cpp** strips C-style comments.

−D*name*[*=def*]

> Define *name* with value *def* as if by a **#define**. If no *=def* is given, *name* is defined with value 1. **−D** has lower precedence than **−U**.

−H   Print pathnames of included files, one per line, on standard error.

−I*dir*   Search in directory *dir* for **#include** files whose names do not begin with / before looking in directories on standard list. **#include** files whose names are enclosed in double quotes and do not begin with / will be searched for first in the current directory, then in directories named on **−I** options, and last in directories on the standard list.

−M [**−MG**]

> Suppress normal output. Print a rule for **make** that describes the main source file's dependencies. If **−MG** is specified, assume that missing

$\rightarrow$

header files are actually generated files, and look for them in the source file's directory.

−MD *file*   Similar to **−M**, but output to *file*; also compile the source.

−MM   Similar to **−M**. Describe only those files included as a result of #**include** "*file*".

−MMD *file*

Similar to **−MD**, but describe only the user's header files.

−P   Preprocess input without producing line control information used by next pass of C compiler.

−U*name*   Remove any initial definition of *name*, where *name* is a reserved symbol predefined by the preprocessor or a name defined on a **−D** option. Names predefined by **cpp** are **unix** and **i386** (for Intel systems).

−Wcomment, −Wcomments

Warn when encountering the beginning of a nested comment.

−Wtraditional

Warn when encountering constructs that are interpreted differently in ANSI from traditional C.

Special names

cpp understands various special names, some of which are:

__DATE__
Current date (e.g., Oct 10 1997)

__FILE__
Current filename (as a C string)

__LINE__
Current source line number (as a decimal integer)

__TIME__
Current time (e.g., 12:00:00)

These special names can be used anywhere, including macros, just like any other defined names. **cpp**'s understanding of the line number and filename may be changed using a #**line** directive.

Directives

All **cpp** directive lines start with # in column 1. Any number of blanks and tabs is allowed between the # and the directive. The directives are:

#define *name token-string*
> Defines a macro called *name*, with a value of *token-string*. Subsequent instances of *name* are replaced with *token-string*.

#define *name(arg, ... , arg) token-string*
> This allows substitution of a macro with arguments. *token-string* will be substituted for *name* in the input file. Each call to *name* in the source file includes arguments that are plugged into the corresponding *args* in *token-string*.

#undef *name*
> Remove definition of the macro *name*. No additional tokens are permitted on the directive line after *name*.

#ident *string*
> Put *string* into the comment section of an object file.

#include *"filename"*, **#include<***filename***>**
> Include contents of *filename* at this point in the program. No additional tokens are permitted on the directive line after the final " or >.

#line *integer-constant "filename"*
> Causes **cpp** to generate line-control information for the next pass of the C compiler. The compiler behaves as if *integer-constant* is the line number of the next line of source code and *filename* (if present) is the name of the input file. No additional tokens are permitted on the directive line after the optional *filename*.

#endif   End a section of lines begun by a test directive (**#if**, **#ifdef**, or **#ifndef**). No additional tokens are permitted on the directive line.

#ifdef *name*
> Lines following this directive and up to matching **#endif** or next **#else** or **#elif** will appear in the output if *name* is currently defined. No additional tokens are permitted on the directive line after *name*.

#ifndef *name*
> Lines following this directive and up to matching **#endif** or next **#else** or **#elif** will appear in the output if *name* is not currently defined. No additional tokens are permitted on the directive line after *name*.

Programming

→

#if *constant-expression*

Lines following this directive and up to matching **#endif** or next **#else** or **#elif** will appear in the output if *constant-expression* evaluates to nonzero.

#elif *constant-expression*

An arbitrary number of **#elif** directives are allowed between a **#if**, **#ifdef**, or **#ifndef** directive and a **#else** or **#endif** directive. The lines following the **#elif** and up to the next **#else**, **#elif**, or **#endif** directive will appear in the output if the preceding test directive and all intervening **#elif** directives evaluate to zero, and the *constant-expression* evaluates to nonzero. If *constant-expression* evaluates to nonzero, all succeeding **#elif** and **#else** directives will be ignored.

#else   Lines following this directive and up to the matching **#endif** will appear in the output if the preceding test directive evaluates to zero, and all intervening **#elif** directives evaluate to zero. No additional tokens are permitted on the directive line.

#error   Report fatal errors.

#warning Report warnings, but then continue processing.

---

ctags

ctags [*options*] *files*

Create a list of function and macro names that are defined in the specified C, Pascal, FORTRAN, **yacc**, or **lex** source *files*. The output list (named **tags** by default) contains lines of the form:

     name   *file*   *context*

where *name* is the function or macro name, *file* is the source file in which *name* is defined, and *context* is a search pattern that shows the line of code containing *name*. After the list of tags is created, you can invoke **vi** on any file and type:

```
:set tags=tagsfile
:tag name
```

This switches the **vi** editor to the source file associated with the *name* listed in *tagsfile* (which you specify with −**t**).

etags produces an equivalent file for tags to be used with Emacs.

  −a, −−append
    Append tag output to existing list of tags.

  −d, −−defines
    Include tag entries for C preprocessor defini-
    tions.

  −o *file*, **−−output=***file*
    Write to *file*.

  −t, −−typedefs
    Include tag entries for **typedefs**.

  −u, −−update
    Update tags file to reflect new locations of func-
    tions (e.g., when functions are moved to a dif-
    ferent source file). Old tags are deleted; new
    tags are appended.

  −v, −−vgrind
    Print to standard output a listing (index) of each
    function, source file, and page number (1 page
    = 64 lines).

  −w, −−no-warn
    Suppress warning messages.

  −x, −−cxref
    Produce a listing of each function, and its line
    number, source file, and context.

  −B, −−backward-search
    Search for tags backward through files.

  −C, −−c++
    Expect *.c* and *.h* files to contain C++, not C,
    code.

  −S, −−ignore-indentation
    Normally **ctags** uses indentation to parse the tag
    file; this option tells it to rely on it less.

  −T, −−typedefs-and-c++
    Include tag entries for typedefs, structs, enums,
    unions, and C++ member functions.

---

etags [*options*] *files*

Create a list of function and macro names that are defined in the
specified C, Pascal, FORTRAN, **yacc**, or **flex** source *files*. The output list (named **tags** by default) contains lines of the form:

       name   *file*   *context*

where *name* is the function or macro name, *file* is the source file

Programming

→

in which *name* is defined, and *context* is a search pattern that shows the line of code containing *name*. After the list of tags is created, you can invoke Emacs on any file and type:

```
ESC-x visit-tags-table
```

You will be prompted for the name of the tag table; the default is TAGS. To switch to the source file associated with the *name* listed in *tagsfile*, type:

```
ESC-x find-tag
```

You will be prompted for the tag you would like Emacs to search for. **ctags** produces an equivalent tags file for use with **vi**.

Options

−a, −−append

Append tag output to existing list of tags.

−d, −−defines

Include tag entries for C preprocessor definitions.

−i *file,* **−−include=***file*

Add a note to the tags file that *file* should be consulted in addition to the normal input file.

−l *language,* **−−language=***language*

Consider the files that follow this option to be written in *language*. Use the **−h** option for a list of languages and their default filename extensions.

−o *file,* **−−output=***file*

Write to *file*.

−r *regexp,* **−−regex=***regexp*

Include a tag for each line that matches *regexp* in the files following this option.

−C, −−c++

Expect *.c* and *.h* files to contain C++, not C, code.

−D, −−no-defines

Do not include tag entries for C preprocessor definitions.

−H, −−help

Print usage information.

−R, −−noregex

Don't include tags based on regular-expression matching for the files that follow this option.

−S, −−ignore-indentation

    Normally **etags** uses indentation to parse the tag file; this option tells it to rely on it less.

−V, −−version

    Print the version number.

---

flex [*options*] [*file*]

flex (Fast Lexical Analyzer Generator) is a faster variant of **lex**. It generates a lexical analysis program (named *lex.yy.c*) based on the regular expressions and C statements contained in one or more input *files*. See also **bison**, **yacc**, and the Nutshell Handbook *lex & yacc*, by John Levine, Tony Mason, and Doug Brown.

Options

−b   Generate backup information to *lex.backup*.

−d   Debug mode.

−f   Use faster compilation (limited to small programs).

−h   Help summary.

−i   Scan case-insensitively.

−l   Maximum **lex** compatibility.

−o *file*   Write output to *file* instead of *lex.yy.c*.

−p   Print performance report.

−s   Exit if the scanner encounters input that does not match any of its rules.

−t   Print to standard out. (By default, **flex** prints to *lex.yy.c*.)

−v   Print a summary of statistics.

−w   Suppress warning messages.

−B   Generate batch (non-interactive) scanner.

−F   Use the fast scanner table representation.

−I   Generate an interactive scanner (default).

−L   Suppress **#line** directives in *lex.yy.c*.

−P *prefix*

    Change default **yy** prefix to *prefix* for all globally visible variable and function names.

−V   Print version number.

−7   Generate a 7-bit scanner.

−8   Generate an 8-bit scanner (default).

Programming

→

flex	−+	Generate a C++ scanner class.
←	−C	Compress scanner tables but do not use equivalence classes.
	−Ca	Align tables for memory access and computation. This creates larger tables, but gives faster performance.
	−Ce	Construct equivalence classes. This creates smaller tables and sacrifices little performance (default).
	−Cf	Generate full scanner tables, not compressed.
	−CF	Generate faster scanner tables, like -F.
	−Cm	Construct meta-equivalence classes (default).
	−Cr	Bypass use of the standared I/O library. Instead use **read( )** system calls.

g++

g++ [*options*] *files*

Invoke **gcc** with the options necessary to make it recognize C++. **g++** recognizes all the file extensions **gcc** does, in addition to C++ source files (*.C, .cc,* or *.cxx* files) and C++ preprocessed files (*.ii* files). See also **gcc**.

gcc

gcc [*options*] *files*

Compile one or more C source files (*file.c*), assembler source files (*file.s*), or preprocessed C source files (*file.i*). If the file suffix is not recognizable, assume that the file is an object file or library. **gcc** automatically invokes the link editor **ld** (unless −c, −S, or −E is supplied). In some cases, **gcc** generates an object file having a *.o* suffix and a corresponding root name. By default, output is placed in *a.out*. **gcc** accepts many system specific options, not covered here.

Note: **gcc** is the GNU form of **cc**; on most Linux systems, the command **cc** will invoke **gcc**. The command **g++** will invoke **gcc** with the appropriate options for interpreting C++.

Options

−a	Provide profile information for basic blocks.
−ansi	Enforce full ANSI conformance.
−b *machine*	Compile for use on *machine* type.
−c	Create linkable object file for each source file, but do not call linker.

−dD	Print #defines.
−dM	Suppress normal output. Print series of #defines that are in effect at the end of preprocessing.
−dN	Print #defines with macro names only, not arguments or values.
−fno-asm	Do not recognize asm, inline, or typeof as keywords. Implied by −ansi.

−fno-builtin

Do not recognize built-in functions unless they begin with two underscores.

−fno-gnu-keywords

Do not recognize classof, headof, signature, sigof, or typeof as keywords.

−fno-ident Do not respond to #ident commands.

−fsigned-bitfields

−funsigned-bitfields

−fno-signed-bitfields

−fno-unsigned-bitfields

Set default control of bitfields to signed or unsigned if not explicitly declared.

−fsigned-char

Cause the type **char** to be signed.

−fsyntax-only

Check for syntax errors. Do not attempt to actually compile.

−funsigned-char

Cause the type **char** to be unsigned.

−g	Include debugging information for use with **gdb**.
−g*level*	Provide *level* amount of debugging information. *level* must be 1, 2, or 3, with 1 providing the least amount of information. The default is 2.

−idirafter *dir*

Include *dir* in the list of directories to search when an include file is not found in the normal include path.

−include *file*

Process *file* before proceeding to the normal input file.

−imacros *file*

Process the macros in *file* before proceeding to the normal input file.

→

−iprefix *prefix*
> When adding directories with −iwithprefix, prepend *prefix* to the directory's name.

−isystem *dir*
> Add *dir* to the list of directories to be searched when a system file cannot be found in the main include path.

−iwithprefix *dir*
> Append *dir* to the list of directories to be searched when a header file cannot be found in the main include path. If −iprefix has been set, prepend that prefix to the directory's name.

−l*lib*   Link to *lib*.

−nostartfiles
> Force linker to ignore standard system startup files.

−nostdinc   Search only specified, not standard, directories for header files.

−nostdinc++
> Suppress searching of directories believed to contain C++-specific header files.

−nostdlib   Suppress linking to standard library files.

−o *file*   Specify output file as *file*. Default is *a.out*.

−p   Provide profile information for use with **prof**.

−pedantic   Warn verbosely.

−pedantic-errors
> Err in every case in which −pedantic would have produced a warning.

−pg   Provide profile information for use with **gprof**.

−pipe   Transfer information between stages of compiler by pipes instead of temporary files.

−s   Remove all symbol table and relocation information from the executable.

−save-temps
> Save temporary files in current directory when compiling.

−static   Suppress linking to shared libraries.

−traditional
> Attempt to behave like a traditional C compiler.

−traditional-cpp
> Cause the preprocessor to attempt to behave like a traditional C preprocessor.

−trigraphs Include trigraph support.

−u *symbol*

> Force the linker to search libraries for a definition of *symbol* and to link to them, if found.

−undef Define only those constants required by the language standard, not system-specific constants like "unix."

−v Verbose mode. Display commands as they are executed, **gcc** version number, and preprocessor version number.

−w Suppress warnings.

−x *language*

> Expect input file to be written in *language*, which may be **c**, **objective-c**, **c-header**, **c++**, **cpp-output**, **assembler**, or **assembler-with-cpp**. If **none** is specified as *language*, guess the language by filename extension.

−A*question(answer)*

> If the preprocessor encounters a conditional such as **#if** *question*, assert *answer* in response. To turn off standard assertions, use **−A−**.

−B*path* Specify the *path* directory where the compiler files are located.

−C Retain comments during preprocessing. Meaningful only with **−E**.

−D*name*[*=def*]

> Define *name* with value *def* as if by a **#define**. If no *=def* is given, *name* is defined with value 1. **−D** has lower precedence than **−U**.

−E Preprocess the source files, but do not compile. Print result to standard output.

−I*dir* Include *dir* in list of directories to search for include files. If *dir* is **−**, search those directories that were specified by **−I** *before* the **−I−** only when **#include "file"** is specified, not **#include <file>**.

−L*dir* Search *dir* in addition to standard directories.

−M Instead of compiling, print a rule suitable for inclusion in a makefile that describes dependencies of the source file based on its **#include** directives. Implies **−E**.

Programming

→

gcc
←

−MD	Similar to **−M**, but sends dependancy information to files ending in "*.d*" in addition to ordinary compilation.
−MG	Used with **−M** or **−MM**. Suppresses error messages if an included file does not exist; useful if the included file is automatically generated by a build.
−MMD	Similar to **−MD**, but record only user header file information, and not system header file information.
−MM	Similar to **−M**, but limits the rule to non-standard **#include** files; that is, only files declared through **#include** "*file*" and not those declared through **#include** <*file*>.
−H	Print pathnames of included files, one per line, on standard error.
−O[*level*]	Optimize. *level* should be 1, 2, 3, or 0. The default is 1. 0 turns off optimization; 3 optimizes the most.
−P	Preprocess input without producing line control information used by next pass of C compiler. Meaningful only with **-E**.
−S	Compile source files into assembler code, but do not assemble.
−U*name*	Remove any initial definition of *name*, where *name* is a reserved symbol predefined by the preprocessor or a name defined on a **−D** option. Names predefined by **cpp** are **unix** and **i386**.
−V *version*	
	Attempt to run **gcc** version *version*.
−W	Warn more verbosely than normal.
−Wl,*option*	
	Invoke linker with *option*, which may be a comma-separated list.
−Wa,*option*	
	Call assembler with *option*, which may be a comma-separated list.
−Waggregate-return	
	Warn if any functions return structures or unions are defined or called.
−Wall	Enable **−W**, **−Wchar-subscripts**, **−Wcomment**, **−Wformat**, **−Wimplicit**, **−Wparentheses**, **−Wre-**

turn-type, −Wswitch, −Wtemplate-debugging, −Wtrigraphs, −Wuninitialized, and −Wunused.

−Wcast-align

> Warn when encountering instances in which pointers are cast to types that increase the required alignment of the target from its original definition.

−Wcast-qual

> Warn when encountering instances in which pointers are cast to types that lack the type qualifier with which the pointer was originally defined.

−Wchar-subscripts

> Warn when encountering arrays with subscripts of type **char**.

−Wcomment

> Warn when encountering the beginning of a nested comment.

−Wconversion

> Warn in particular cases of type conversions.

−Werror Exit at the first error.

−Wformat Warn about inappropriately formatted **printfs** and **scanfs**.

−Wimplicit

> Warn when encountering implicit function or parameter declarations.

−Winline Warn about illegal inline functions.

−Wmissing-declarations

> Warn if a global function is defined without a previous declaration.

−Wmissing-prototypes

> Warn when encountering global function definitions without previous prototype declarations.

−Wnested-externs

> Warn if an **extern** declaration is encountered within a function.

−Wno-import

> Don't warn about use of **#import**.

−Wp,*options*

> Pass *options* to the preprocessor. Multiple options are separated by commas. Not a warning parameter.

$\rightarrow$

−Wparentheses

    Enable more verbose warnings about omitted parentheses.

−Wpointer-arith

    Warn when encountering code that attempts to determine the size of a function or void.

−Wredundant-decls

    Warn if anything is declared more than once in the same scope.

−Wreturn-type

    Warn about functions defined without return types, or with improper return types.

−Wshadow

    Warn when a local variable shadows another local variable.

−Wstrict-prototypes

    Insist that argument types be specified in function declarations and definitions.

−Wswitch Warn about switches that skip the index for one of their enumerated types.

−Wtemplate-debugging

    Warn if debugging is not available for C++ templates.

−Wtraditional

    Warn when encountering code that produces different results in ANSI C and traditional C.

−Wtrigraphs

    Warn when encountering trigraphs.

−Wuninitialized

    Warn when encountering uninitialized automatic variables.

−Wunused

    Warn about unused variables and functions.

−Xlinker *option*

    Pass an *option* to the linker. A linker option with an argument requires two −**X**'s, the first specifying the option and the second specifying the argument.

Pragma directives

#pragma interface [*header-file*]

    Used in header files to force object files to provide definition information via references, instead of including it locally in each file. C++-specific.

#pragma implementation [*header-file*]

Used in main input files to force generation of full output from *header-file* (or, if it is not specified, from the header file with the same base name as the file containing the pragma directive). This information will be globally visible. Normally the specified header file contains a **#pragma interface** directive.

gdb [*options*] [*program* [*core* |*pid*]]

GDB (GNU DeBugger) allows you to step through C, C++, and Modula-2 programs in order to find the point at which they break. The program to be debugged is normally specified on the command line; you can also specify a core, or, if you want to investigate a running program, a process ID.

Options

−s *file*, −**symbols**=*file*

Consult *file* for symbol table. With −**e**, also uses *file* as the executable.

−e *file*, −**exec**=*file*

Use *file* as executable, to be read in conjunction with source code. May be used in conjunction with −**s** to read symbol table from the executable.

−c *file*, −**core**=*file*

Consult *file* for information provided by a core dump.

−x *file*, −**command**=*file*

Read **gdb** commands from *file*.

−d *directory*, −**directory**=*directory*

Include *directory* in path that is searched for source files.

−n, −**nx**   Ignore *.gdbinit* file.

−q, −**quiet**

Suppress introductory and copyright messages.

−**batch**   Exit after executing all the commands specified in *.gdbinit* and -**x** files. Print no startup messages.

−**cd**=*directory*

Use *directory* as **gdb**'s working directory.

→

−f, −fullname

Show full filename and line number for each stack frame.

−b *bps*   Set line speed of serial device used by GDB to *bps*.

−tty=*device*

Set standard in and standard out to *device*.

Common commands

These are just some of the more common **gdb** commands; there are too many commands to list all of them here.

backtrace   Print the current location within the program and a stack trace showing how the current location was reached. (**where** does the same thing.)

breakpoint

Set a breakpoint in the program.

cd   Change the current working directory.

clear   Delete the breakpoint where you just stopped.

commands

List commands to be executed when breakpoint is hit.

continue   Continue execution from a breakpoint.

delete   Delete a breakpoint or a watchpoint; also used in conjunction with other commands.

display   Cause variables or expressions to be displayed when program stops.

down   Move down one stack frame to make another function the current one.

frame   Select a frame for the next **continue** command.

info   Show a variety of information about the program. For instance, **info breakpoints** shows all outstanding breakpoints and watchpoints.

jump   Start execution at another point in the source file.

kill   Abort the process running under **gdb**'s control.

list   List the contents of the source file corresponding to the program being executed.

next   Execute the next source line, executing a function in its entirety.

print   Print the value of a variable or expression.

pwd	Show the current working directory.	**gdb**
ptype	Show the contents of a data type, such as a structure or C++ class.	
quit	Exit **gdb**.	
reverse-search		
	Search backward for a regular expression in the source file.	
run	Execute the program.	
search	Search for a regular expression in the source file.	
set variable		
	Assign a value to a variable.	
signal	Send a signal to the running process.	
step	Execute the next source line, stepping into a function if necessary.	
undisplay	Reverse the effect of the **display** command; keep expressions from being displayed.	
until	Finish the current loop.	
up	Move up one stack frame to make another function the current one.	
watch	Set a watchpoint (i.e., a data breakpoint) in the program.	
whatis	Print the type of a variable or function.	

gprof [*options*] [*object_file*]

Display the profile data for an object file. The file's symbol table is compared with the call graph profile file *gmon.out* (previously created by compiling with **gcc -pg**).

Options

-a   Do not display statically declared functions. Since their information might still be relevant, append it to the information about the functions loaded immediately before.

-b   Do not display information about each field in the profile.

-c   Consult the object file's text area to attempt to determine the program's static call graph. Display static-only parents and children with call counts of 0.

→

gprof
←
	−e *routine*
	    Do not display entries for *routine* and its descendants.
	
	−f *routine*
	    Print only *routine*, but include time spent in all routines.
	
	−k *from to*
	    Remove arcs between the routines *from* and *to*.
	
	−s Summarize profile information in the file *gmon.sum*.
	
	−v Print version and exit.
	
	−z Include zero-usage calls.
	
	−E *routine*
	    Do not display entries for *routine* and its descendants, or include time spent on them in calculations for total time.
	
	−F *routine*
	    Print only information about *routine*. Do not include time spent in other routines.

imake	**imake** *options* C preprocessor (**cpp**) interface to the **make** utility. **imake** (for *include make*) solves the portability problem of **make** by allowing machine dependencies to be kept in a central set of configuration files, separate from the descriptions of the various items to be built. The targets are contained in the *Imakefile*, a machine-independent description of the targets to be built, written as **cpp** macros. **imake** uses **cpp** to process the configuration files and the *Imakefile*, and to generate machine-specific *Makefile*s, which can then be used by **make**. One of the configuration files is a template file, a master file for **imake**. This template file (default is *Imake.tmpl*) #includes the other configuration files that contain machine dependencies such as variable assignments, site definitions, and **cpp** macros, and directs the order in which the files are processed. Each file affects the interpretation of later files and sections of *Imake.tmpl*. Comments may be included in **imake** configuration files, but the initial # needs to be preceded with an empty C comment: `/**/#` For more information, see **cpp** and **make**. Also check out the Nutshell Handbook *Sofware Portability with imake*, by Paul DuBois.

     −D*define*   Set directory-specific variables. This option is passed directly to **cpp**.

     −e   Execute the generated *Makefile*. Default is to leave this to the user.

     −f *filename*

            Name of per-directory input file. Default is *Imakefile*.

     −I*directory*

            Directory in which **imake** template and configuration files may be found. This option is passed directly to **cpp**.

     −s *filename*

            Name of **make** description file to be generated. If filename is a dash, the output is written to **stdout**. The default is to generate, but not execute, a *Makefile*.

     −T*template*

            Name of master template file used by **cpp**. This file is usually located in the directory specified with the −I option. The default file is *Imake.tmpl*.

     −v   Print the **cpp** command line used to generate the *Makefile*.

Tools

Following is a list of tools used with **imake**:

     makedepend [*options*] *files*

            Create header file dependencies in *Makefiles*. **make- depend** reads the named input source *files* in sequence and parses them to process **#include**, **#define**, **#undef**, **#ifdef**, **#ifndef**, **#endif**, **#if**, and **#else** directives so it can tell which **#include** directives would be used in a compilation. **makedepend** determines the dependencies and writes them to the *Makefile*. **make** then knows which object files must be recompiled when a dependency has changed. **makedepend** has the following options:

         −− *options* −−

            Ignore any unrecognized options following double hyphen. A second double hyphen terminates this action. Recognized options between the hyphens are processed normally.

→

imake
←

-a Append dependencies to any existing ones instead of replacing existing ones.

−f *filename*
Write dependencies to *filename* instead of to *Makefile*.

−m Print a warning when encountering a multiple inclusion.

−s *string*
Use *string* as delimiter in file, instead of # DO NOT DELETE THIS LINE — make depend depends on it.

−v Verbose. List all files included by main source file.

−D *name=value*

−D *name*
Define *name* with the given value (first form) or with value 1 (second form).

−I *dir*
Add directory *dir* to the list of directories searched.

−Y *dir*
Search only *dir* for include files. Ignore standard include directories.

mkdirhier *dir...*
Create directory *dir* and all missing parent directories during file installation operations.

xmkmf [*option*] [*topdir*] [*curdir*]
Bootstrap a *Makefile* from an *Imakefile*. *topdir* specifies the location of the project root directory. *curdir* (usually omitted) is specified as a relative pathname from the top of the build tree to the current directory. The −a option is equivalent to the following command sequence:

```
% xmkmf
% make Makefiles
% make includes
% make depend
```

Configuration files

Following is a list of the **imake** configuration files:

Imake.tmpl
Master template for **imake**. *Imake.tmpl* includes all the other configuration files, plus the *Imakefile* in the current directory.

Imake.params

    Contains definitions that apply across sites and vendors.

Imake.rules

    Contains **cpp** macro definitions that are configured for the current platform. The macro definitions are fed into **imake**, which runs **cpp** to process the macros. Newlines (line continuations) are indicated by the string @@\ (double at-sign, backslash).

site.def   Contains site-specific (as opposed to vendor-specific) information, such as installation directories, what set of programs to build, and any special versions of programs to use during the build. The *site.def* file changes from machine to machine.

Project.tmpl

    File containing X-specific variables.

Library.tmpl

    File containing library rules.

Server.tmpl

    File containing server-specific rules.

.cf   The *.cf* files are the vendor-specific *VendorFiles* that live in *Imake.vb*. A *.cf* file contains platform-specific definitions, such as version numbers of the operating system and compiler, and workarounds for missing commands. The definitions in *.cf* files override the defaults, defined in *Imake.params*.

The Imakefile

The *Imakefile* is a per-directory file that indicates targets to be built and installed, and rules to be applied. **imake** reads the *Imakefile* and expands the rules into *Makefile* target entries. An *Imakefile* may also include definitions of **make** variables, and list the dependencies of the targets. The dependencies are expressed as **cpp** macros, defined in *Imake.rules*. Whenever you change an *Imakefile*, you need to rebuild the *Makefile* and regenerate header file dependencies. For more information on **imake**, see the Nutshell Handbook *Software Portability with imake*, by Paul DuBois.

---

ld [*options*] *objfiles*

Combine several *objfiles*, in the specified order, into a single executable object module (*a.out* by default). **ld** is the link editor and

$\rightarrow$

is often invoked automatically by compiler commands.

Options

−c *file*   Consult *file* for commands.

−d, −dc, −dp
> Force the assignment of space to common symbols.

−defsym *symbol = expression*
> Create the global *symbol* with the value *expression*.

−e *symbol* Set *symbol* as the address of the output file's entry point.

−i   Produce a linkable output file; attempt to set its magic number to OMAGIC.

−l*arch*   Include the archive file *arch* in the list of files to link.

−m *linker* Emulate *linker*.

−n   Make text read only; attempt to set NMAGIC.

−noinhibit-exec
> Produce output file even if errors are encountered.

−o *output* Place output in *output*, instead of *a.out*.

−oformat *format*
> Specify output format.

−r   Produce a linkable output file; attempt to set its magic number to OMAGIC.

−s   Do not include any symbol information in output.

−sort-common
> Do not sort global common symbols by size.

−t   Announce each input file's name as it is processed.

−u *symbol*
> Force *symbol* to be undefined.

−v, −−version
> Show version number.

−−verbose
> Print information about **ld**; print the names of input files while attempting to open them.

−warn-common
> Warn when encountering common symbols combined with other constructs.

−warn-once
: Provide only one warning per undefined symbol.

−x
: With −s or −S, delete all local symbols beginning with L.

−L *dir*
: Search directory *dir* before standard search directories (this option must precede the −l option that searches that directory).

−M
: Display a link map on standard out.

−Map *file*
: Print a link map to *file*.

−N
: Allow reading of and writing to both data and text; mark ouput if it supports Unix magic numbers; do not page-align data.

−R *file*
: Obtain symbol names and addresses from *file*, but suppress relocation of *file* and its inclusion in output.

−S
: Do not include debugger symbol information in output.

−Tbss *address*
: Begin bss segment of output at *address*.

−Tdata *address*
: Begin data segment of output at *address*.

−Ttext *address*
: Begin text segment of output at *address*.

−Ur
: Synonymous with −r except when linking C++ programs, where it resolves constructor references.

−X
: With −s or −S, delete local symbols beginning with L.

−V
: Show version number and emulation linkers for -m option.

---

ldd [*options*] *programs*

Display a list of the shared libraries each *program* requires.

Options

−v
: Display **ldd**'s version.

−V
: Display the linker's version.

Programming

m4

m4 [*options*] [*macros*] [*files*]

Macro processor for C and other files.

Options

    −e
        Operate interactively, ignoring interrupts.

    −d*flags*, −−debug=*flags*
        Specify *flag*-level debugging.

    −l*n*, −−arglength=*n*
        Specify the length of debugging output.

    −o *file*, −−error-output=*file*
        Place output in *file*. Despite the name, print error messages on standard error.

    −p, −−prefix-built-ins
        Prepend m4_ to all built-in macro names.

    −s, −−synclines
        Insert **#line** directives for the C preprocessor.

    −B*n*
        Set the size of the push-back and argument collection buffers to *n* (default is 4,096).

    −D*name*[=*value*], −−define=*name*[=*value*]
        Define *name* as *value* or, if *value* is not specified, define *name* as null.

    −E, −−fatal-warnings
        Consider all warnings to be fatal, and exit after the first of them.

    −F*file*, −−freeze-state *file*
        Record m4's frozen state in *file*, for subsequent reloading.

    −G, −−traditional
        Behave like traditional **m4**, ignoring GNU extensions.

    −H*n*, −−hashsize=*n*
        Set symbol-table hash array to *n* (default is 509).

    −I*directory*, −−include=*directory*
        Search *directory* for include files.

    −Q, −−quiet, −−silent
        Suppress warning messages.

    −R*file*, −−reload-state *file*
        Load state from *file* before starting execution.

    −U*name*, −−undefine=*name*
        Undefine *name*.

make [*options*] [*targets*] [*macro definitions*]

Update one or more *targets* according to dependency instructions in a description file in the current directory. By default, this file is called *makefile* or *Makefile*. Options, targets, and macro definitions can be in any order. Macros definitions are typed as:

```
name=string
```

For more information on **make**, see the Nutshell Handbook *Managing Projects with make*, by Andrew Oram and Steve Talbott.

Options

    -b   Ignored, out of date.

  -d, -dd, --debug
                Print detailed debugging information.

  -e, --environment-overrides
                Override **makefile** macro definitions with environment variables.

  -f *makefile*, **--file** *makefile*, **--makefile** *makefile*
                Use *makefile* as the description file; a filename of - denotes standard input.

  -h, --help   Print options to **make** command.

  -i, --ignore-errors
                Ignore command error codes (same as .IGNORE).

  -j [*jobs*], **--jobs** [*jobs*]
                Attempt to execute *jobs* jobs simultaneously, or, if no number is specified, as many jobs as possible.

  -k, --keep-going
                Abandon the current target when it fails, but keep working with unrelated targets.

  -l [*load*], **--load-average** [*load*], **--max-load** [*load*]
                Attempt to keep load below *load*, which should be a floating-point number. Used with -j.

  -m   Ignored, out of date.

  -n, --just-print, --dry-run, --recon
                Print commands but don't execute (used for testing).

  -o *file*, **--old-file** *file*, **--assume-old** *file*
                Never remake *file*, or cause other files to be remade on account of it.

Programming

→

make

←

-p, --print-data-base
   Print rules and variables in addition to normal execution.

-q, --question
   Query; return 0 if file is up to date; nonzero otherwise.

-r, --no-built-in-rules
   Do not use default rules.

-s, --silent, --quiet
   Do not display command lines (same as .SILENT).

-t, --touch   Touch the target files, without remaking them.

-v, --version
   Show version of **make**.

-w, --print-directory
   Display the current working directory before and after execution.

--warn -undefined -variables
   Print warning if a macro is used without being defined.

-C *directory*, --directory *directory*
   cd to *directory* before beginning **make** operations. A subsequent -C directive will cause **make** to attempt to **cd** into a directory relative to the current working directory.

-I *directory*, --include-dir *directory*
   Include *directory* in list of directories that contain included files.

-S, --no-keep-going, --stop
   Cancel previous -k options. Useful in recursive **make**s.

-W *file*, --what-if *file*, --new-file *file assume-new file*
   Behave as though *file* has been recently updated.

Description file lines

Instructions in the description file are interpreted as single lines. If an instruction must span more than one input line, use a backslash (\) at the end of the line so that the next line is considered as a continuation. The description file may contain any of the following types of lines:

blank lines
   Blank lines are ignored.

comment lines

> A pound sign (#) can be used at the beginning of a line or anywhere in the middle. **make** ignores everything after the #.

dependency lines

> Depending on one or more targets, certain commands that follow will be executed. Possible formats include:

```
targets : dependencies
targets : dependencies ; command
```

> Subsequent commands are executed if *dependency* files (the names of which may contain wildcards) do not exist or are newer than a target. If no prerequisites are supplied, then subsequent commands are *always* executed (whenever any of the targets are specified). No tab should precede any *targets.*

suffix rules

> These specify that files ending with the first suffix can be prerequisites for files ending with the second suffix (assuming the root filenames are the same). Either of these formats can be used:

```
.suffix.suffix:
.suffix:
```

> The second form means that the root filename depends on the filename with the corresponding suffix.

commands

> Commands are grouped below the dependency line and are typed on lines that begin with a tab. If a command is preceded by a hyphen (–), **make** ignores any error returned. If a command is preceded by an at-sign (@), the command line won't echo on the display (unless **make** is called with **–n**).

macro definitions

> These have the following form:

```
name = string
     or
define name
string
endef
```

> Blank space is optional around the =.

→

Programming

include statements
> Similar to the C include directive, these have the form:

```
include files
```

Internal macros

$?
> The list of prerequisites that have been changed more recently than the current target. Can be used only in normal description file entries—not suffix rules.

$@
> The name of the current target, except in description file entries for making libraries, where it becomes the library name. Can be used both in normal description file entries and in suffix rules.

$<
> The name of the current prerequisite that has been modified more recently than the current target.

$*
> The name—without the suffix—of the current prerequisite that has been modified more recently than the current target. Can be used only in suffix rules.

$%
> The name of the corresponding .o file when the current target is a library module. Can be used both in normal description file entries and in suffix rules.

$^
> A space-separated list of all dependencies, with no duplications.

$+
> A space-separated list of all dependencies, including duplications.

Pattern rules

These are a more general application of the idea behind suffix rules. If a target and a dependency both contain %, GNU **make** will substitute any part of an existing filename. For instance, the standard suffix rule:

```
$(cc) -o $@ $<
```

can be written as the following pattern rule:

```
%.o : %.c
     $(cc) -o $@ $<
```

D   The directory portion of any internal macro
                  name except $?. Valid uses are:

                  $(*D) $$(@D) $(?D) $(<D)
                  ${%D} $(@D) $(^D)

F   The file portion of any internal macro name
                  except $?. Valid uses are:

                  $(*F) $$(@F) $(?F) $(<F)
                  ${%F} $(@F) $(^F)

Functions

$(subst *from, to, string*)
                  Replace all occurrences of *from* with *to* in *string*.

$(patsubst *pattern, to, string*)
                  Similar to **subst**, but treats % as a wildcard within
                  pattern. Substitutes *to* for any word in *string* that
                  matches *pattern*.

$(strip *string*)
                  Remove all extraneous whitespace.

$(findstring *substring, mainstring*)
                  Return *substring* if it exists within *mainstring*;
                  otherwise, return null.

$(filter *pattern, string*)
                  Return those words in *string* that match at least
                  one word in *pattern*. *pattern*s may include the
                  wildcard %.

$(filter-out *pattern, string*)
                  Remove those words in *string* that match at least
                  one word in *pattern*. *pattern*s may include the
                  wildcard %.

$(sort *list*)   Return *list*, sorted in lexical order.

$(dir *list*)   Return the directory part (everything up to the
                  last slash) of each filename in *list*.

$(notdir *list*)
                  Return the nondirectory part (everything after
                  the last slash) of each filename in *list*.

$(suffix *list*)
                  Return the suffix part (everything after the last
                  period) of each filename in *list*.

$(basename *list*)
                  Return everything but the suffix part (everything
                  up to the last period) of each filename in *list*.

$\rightarrow$

Programming

$(addsuffix *suffix,list*)

  Return each filename given in *list* with *suffix* appended.

$(addprefix *prefix,list*)

  Return each filename given in *list* with *prefix* prepended.

$(join *list1,list2*)

  Return a list formed by concatenating the two arguments, word by word; e.g., $(join a b,.c .o) becomes a.c b.o

$(word *n,string*)

  Return the *n*th word of *string*.

$(words *string*)

  Return the number of words in *string*.

$(firstword *list*)

  Return the first word in the list *list*.

$(wildcard *pattern*)

  Return a list of existing files in the current directory that match *pattern*.

$(origin *variable*)

  Return one of the following strings that describes how *variable* was defined: **undefined, default, environment, environment override, file, command line, override,** or **automatic.**

$(shell *command*)

  Return the results of *command*. Any newlines in the result are to be converted to spaces. This function works similarly to backquotes in most shells.

Macro string substitution

${*macro:s1=s2*}

  Evaluates to the current definition of ${*macro*}, after substituting the string *s2* for every occurrence of *s1* that occurs either immediately before a blank or tab, or at the end of the macro definition.

Special target names

  .DEFAULT: Commands associated with this target are executed if **make** can't find any description file entries or suffix rules with which to build a requested target.

.EXPORT_ALL_VARIABLES:
> If this target exists, export all macros to all child processes.

.IGNORE: Ignore error codes. Same as the −i option.

.PHONY: Always execute commands under a target, even if it is an existing, up-to-date file.

.PRECIOUS: Files you specify for this target are not removed when you send a signal (such as an interrupt) that aborts **make**, or when a command line in your description file returns an error.

.SILENT: Execute commands but do not echo them. Same as the −s option.

.SUFFIXES: Suffixes associated with this target are meaningful in suffix rules. If no suffixes are listed, the existing list of suffix rules is effectively "turned off."

Programming

nm [*options*] [*objfiles*]

Print the symbol table (name list) in alphabetical order for one or more object files. If no object files are specified, perform operations on *a.out*. Output includes each symbol's value, type, size, name, etc. A key letter categorizing the symbol can also be displayed. If no object file is given, use *a.out*.

Options

−a, −−debug-syms
> Print debugger symbols.

−f *format*   Specify output format (**bsd**, **sysv**, or **posix**). Default is **bsd**.

−g, −−extern-only
> Print external symbols only.

−n, −v, −−numeric-sort
> Sort the external symbols by address.

−p, −−no-sort   Don't sort the symbols at all.

−r, −−reverse-sort
> Sort in reverse, alphabetically or numerically.

−−size-sort   Sort by size.

−u, −−undefined-only
> Report only the undefined symbols.

→

nm ←	**−A, −o, −print-file-name** Print input filenames before each symbol. **−C, −−demangle** Translate low-level symbol names into readable versions. **−D, −−dynamic** Print dynamic, not normal, symbols. Useful only when working with dynamic objects (some kinds of shared libraries, for example). **−P, −−portability** Same as **-f posix**. **−V, −−version** Print **nm**'s version number on standard error.

patch	**patch** [*options*] [*original* [*patchfile*]]
	
	Apply the patches specified in *patchfile* to *original*. Replace the original with the new, patched version; move the original to *original.orig* or *original˜*.
	
	Options
	
	+ [*options*] [*original2*]
	Apply patches again, with different options or a different original file.
	
	−b *suffix*, **−−suffix**=*suffix*
	Back up the original file in *original.suffix*.
	
	−B *prefix*, **−−prefix**=*prefix*
	Prepend *prefix* to the backup filename.
	
	−c, **−−context** Interpret *patchfile* as a context diff.
	
	−d *dir*, **−−directory**=*dir*
	cd to *directory* before beginning **patch** operations.
	
	−D *string*, **−−ifdef**=*string*
	Mark all changes with:
	
	`#ifdef`
	string
	`#endif`
	
	−e, **−−ed** Treat the contents of *patchfile* as **ed** commands.
	
	−E, **−−remove-empty-files**
	If **patch** creates any empty files, delete them.

−f, −−force	Force all changes, even those that look incorrect. Skip patches if the original file does not exist; force patches for files with the wrong version specified; assume patches are never reversed.
−t, −−batch	Skip patches if the original file does not exist.

−F *num*, −−fuzz=*num*
> Specify the maximum number of lines that may be ignored (fuzzed over) when deciding where to install a hunk of code. The default is 2. Meaningful only with context diffs.

−l, −−ignore-whitespace
> Ignore whitespace while pattern matching.

−n, −−normal	Interpret patch file as a normal diff.
−N, −−forward	Ignore patches that appear to be reversed or to have already been applied.

−o *file*, −−output=*file*
> Print output to *file*.

−p[*num*], −−strip[=*num*]
> Specify how much of preceding pathname to strip. A *num* of 0 strips everything, leaving just the filename. 1 strips the leading /; each higher number after that strips another directory from the left.

−r *file*, −−reject-file=*file*
> Place rejects (hunks of the patch file that **patch** fails to place within the original file) in *file*. Default is *original.rej*.

−R, −−reverse	Do a reverse patch: attempt to undo the damage done by patching with the old and new files reversed.

−s, −−silent, −−quiet
> Suppress commentary.

−S, −−skip	Skip to next patch in the patch file.
−u, −−unified	Interpret patch file as a unified context diff.

−V *method*, −−version-control=*method*
> Specify method for creating backup files (overridden by −B):

→

patch	**t, numbered** Make numbered backups.
←	**nil, existing** Back up files according to preexisting backup schemes, with simple backups as the default. This is **patch**'s default behavior.
	never, simple Make simple backups.
	TMPDIR Specify the directory for temporary files, */tmp* by default.
	SIMPLE_BACKUP_SUFFIX Suffix to append to backup files instead of *.orig* or ˜.
	VERSION_CONTROL Specify what method to use in naming backups (see −**V**).

rpcgen	**rpcgen** [*options*] *file*

Parse *file*, which should be written in the RPC language, and produce a program written in C that implements the RPC code. Place header code generated from *file.x* in *file.h*, XDR routines in *file_xdr.c*, server code in *file_svc.c*, and client code in *file_clnt.c*. Lines preceded by % are not parsed. By default, **rpcgen** produces SunOS 4.1-compatible code.

−**a**   Produce all files (client and server).

−**5**   Produce SVR4-compatible code.

−**c**   Create XDR routines. Cannot be used with other options.

−**C**   Produce ANSI C code (default).

−**k**   Produce K&R C code.

−**D***name*[=*value*]
            Define the symbol *name*, and set it equal to *value* or 1.

−**h**   Produce a header file. With −**T**, make the file support RPC dispatch tables. Cannot be used with other options.

−**I**   Produce an **inetd**-compatible server.

−**K** *secs* Specify amount of time that the server should wait after replying to a request and before exiting. Default is 120. A *secs* of -1 prevents the program from ever exiting.

−1	Produce client code. Cannot be used with other options.	**rpcgen**
−m	Produce server code only, suppressing creation of a "main" routine. Cannot be used with other options.	
−N	New style. Allow multiple arguments for procedures. Not necessarily backwards compatible.	
−o [*file*]	Print output to *file* or standard output.	
−Ss	Create skeleton server code only.	
−t	Create RPC dispatch table. Cannot be used with other options.	
−T	Include support for RPC dispatch tables.	

size [*options*] [*objfile...*]

size

Print the number of bytes of each section of *objfile*, and its total size. If *objfile* is not specified, *a.out* is used.

Options

−d   Display the size in decimal and hexadecimal.

−−**format** *format*
     Imitate the **size** command from either System V (−−**format sysv**) or BSD (−−**format berkeley**).

−o   Display the size in octal and hexadecimal.

−−**radix** *num*
     Specify how to display the size: in hexadecimal and decimal (if *num* is **10** or **16**) or hexadecimal and octal (if *num* is **8**.)

−x   Display the size in hexadecimal and decimal.

−A   Imitate System V's **size** command.

−B   Imitate BSD's **size** command.

strip [*options*] *files*

strip

Remove symbols from object *files*, thereby reducing file sizes and freeing disk space.

Options

−F *format*, −−**target**=*format*
     Expect the input file to be in the format *format*.

−O *format*, −−**output-target**=*format*
     Write output file in *format*.

→

strip ←	−R *section*, −−remove-section=*section*
	    Delete *section*.
	
	−s, −−strip-all
	    Strip all symbols.
	
	−S, −g, −−strip-debug
	    Strip debugging symbols.
	
	−x, −−discard-all
	    Strip nonglobal symbols.
	
	−X, −−discard-locals
	    Strip local symbols that were generated by the compiler.
	
	−v, −−verbose
	    Verbose mode.

yacc	**yacc** [*options*] *file* Given a *file* containing context-free grammar, convert *file* into tables for subsequent parsing and send output to *y.tab.c*. This command name stands for yet another compiler-compiler. See also **flex**, **bison**, and the Nutshell Handbook *lex & yacc*, by John Levine, Tony Mason, and Doug Brown. *Options* −b *prefix* Prepend *prefix*, instead of *y*, to the output file. −d Generate *y.tab.h*, producing **#define** statements that relate **yacc**'s token codes to the token names declared by the user. −l Exclude **#line** constructs from code produced in *y.tab.c*. (Use after debugging is complete.) −t Compile runtime debugging code. −v Generate *y.output*, a file containing diagnostics and notes about the parsing tables.

RCS and CVS

The RCS Utility

The Revision Control System (RCS) is designed to keep track of multiple file revisions, thereby reducing the amount of storage space needed. With RCS you can automatically store and retrieve revisions, merge or compare revisions, keep a complete history (or log) of changes, and identify revisions using symbolic keywords. This chapter describes Version 5.7, although we note important differences between versions 4 and 5.

Overview of Commands

The three most important RCS commands are:

ci   Check in revisions (put a file under RCS control).

co   Check out revisions.

rcs   Set up or change attributes of RCS files.

Two commands provide information about RCS files:

ident   Extract keyword values from an RCS file.

rlog   Display a summary (log) about the revisions in an RCS file.

You can compare RCS files with these commands:

rcsdiff Report differences between revisions.

rcsmerge

        Incorporate changes from two RCS files into a third RCS file.

The following command helps with configuration management:

rcsclean Remove working files that have not been changed.

Basic Operations

Normally, you maintain RCS files in a subdirectory called **RCS**, so the first step in using RCS should be:

```
mkdir RCS
```

Next, you place an existing file (or files) under RCS control by running the check-in command:

```
ci file
```

This creates a file called *file,*v in directory **RCS**. *file,*v is called an RCS file, and it will store all future revisions of *file.* When you run **ci** on a file for the first time, you are prompted to describe the contents. **ci** then deposits *file* into the RCS file as revision 1.1.

To edit a new revision, check out a copy:

```
co -l file
```

This causes RCS to extract a copy of *file* from the RCS file. You must lock the file with −l to make it writable by you. This copy is called a working file. When you're done editing, you can record the changes by checking the working file back in again:

```
ci file
```

This time, you are prompted to enter a log of the changes made, and the file is deposited as revision 1.2. Note that a check-in normally removes the working file. To retrieve a read-only copy, do a check-out without a lock:

```
co file
```

This is useful when you need to keep a copy on hand for compiling or searching. As a shortcut to the previous **ci/co**, you could type:

```
ci -u file
```

This checks in the file but immediately checks out a read-only copy. To compare changes between a working file and its latest revision, you can type:

```
rcsdiff file
```

Another useful command is **rlog**, which shows a summary of log messages. System administrators can use the **rcs** command to set up default behavior of RCS.

General RCS Specifications

This section discusses:

- Keyword substitution
- Revision numbering
- Specifying the date
- Specifying states
- Standard options and environment variables

Keyword Substitution

RCS lets you place keyword variables in your working files. These variables are later expanded into revision notes. You can then use the notes either as embedded comments in the input file, or as text strings that appear when the output is printed. To create revision notes via keyword substitution, follow this procedure:

1. In your working file, type any of the keywords listed below.

2. Check the file in.

3. Check the file out again. Upon checkout, the **co** command expands each keyword to include its value. That is, **co** replaces instances of:

   `$keyword$`

   with:

   `$keyword:value$`.

4. Subsequent check-in and check-out of a file will update any existing keyword values. Unless otherwise noted below, existing values are replaced by new values.

Note: In RCS Version 5, many commands have a **−k** option that provides more flexibility during keyword substitution.

Keywords

$Author$
> Username of person who checked in revision.

$Date$ Date and time of check-in.

$Header$
> A title that includes the RCS file's full pathname, revision number, date, author, state, and (if locked) the person who locked the file.

Id Same as **$Header$**, but exclude the full pathname of the RCS file.

$Locker$
> Username of person who locked the revision. If the file isn't locked, this value is empty.

Log The message that was typed during check-in to describe the file, preceded by the RCS filename, revision number, author, and date. Log messages accumulate rather than being overwritten.

$RCSfile$
The RCS filename, without its pathname.

$Revision$
The assigned revision number.

$Source$
The RCS filename, including its pathname.

$State$ The state assigned by the −s option of **ci** or **rcs**.

Example values

Let's assume that the file **/projects/new/chapter3** has been checked in and out by a user named **daniel**. Here's what keyword substitution would produce for each keyword, for the second revision of the file:

```
$Author: daniel $

$Date: 92/03/18 17:51:36 $

$Header: /projects/new/chapter3,v 1.2 92/03/18 17:51:36 daniel \
    Exp Locker: daniel $

$Id: chapter3,v 1.2 92/03/18 17:51:36 daniel Exp Locker: daniel $

$Locker: daniel $

$Log:      chapter3,v $
# Revision 1.2  92/03/18  17:51:36  daniel
# Added section on error-handling
#
# Revision 1.1  92/03/18  16:49:59  daniel
# Initial revision
#

$RCSfile: chapter3,v $

$Revision: 1.2 $

$Source: /projects/new/chapter3,v $

$State: Exp $
```

Revision Numbering

Unless told otherwise, RCS commands typically operate on the latest revision. Some commands have a −r option that is used to specify a revision number. In addition, many options accept a revision number as an optional argument. (In the command summary, this argument is shown as [R].) Revision numbers consist of up to four fields: release, level, branch, and sequence, but most revisions consist of only the release and level.

For example, you can check out revision 1.4 as follows:

```
co -l -r1.4 ch01
```

When you check it in again, the new revision will be marked as 1.5. But suppose the edited copy needs to be checked in as the next release. You would type:

```
ci -r2 ch01
```

This creates revision 2.1. You can also create a branch from an earlier revision. The following command creates revision 1.4.1.1:

```
ci -r1.4.1 ch01
```

Numbers are not the only way to specify revisions, though. You can assign a text label as a revision name, using the −n option of **ci** or **rcs**. You can also specify this name in any option that accepts a revision number for an argument. For example, you could check in each of your C programs, using the same label regardless of the current revision number:

```
ci -u -nPrototype *.c
```

In addition, RCS Version 5.6 lets you specify a $, which means the revision number is extracted from the keywords of a working file. For example:

```
rcsdiff -r$ ch01
```

compares **ch01** to the revision that is checked in. You can also combine names and symbols. The command:

```
rcs -nDraft:$ ch*
```

assigns a name to the revision numbers associated with several chapter files.

Specifying the Date

Revisions are timestamped by time and date of check-in. Several keyword strings include the date in their values. Dates can be supplied in options to **ci**, **co**, and **rlog**. RCS uses the following date format as its default:

```
1995/10/16 02:00:00 (year/month/day  time)
```

The default timezone is Greenwich Mean Time (GMT), which is also referred to as Coordinated Universal Time (UTC). Dates can be supplied in free format. This lets you specify many different styles. Here are some of the more common ones, which show the same time as in the example above:

```
6:00 pm lt                        (assuming today is Oct. 16, 1995)
2:00 AM, Oct. 16, 1995
Mon Oct 16 18:00:00 1995 LT
Mon Oct 16 18:00:00 PST 1995
```

The uppercase or lowercase "lt" indicates local time (here, Pacific Standard Time). The third line shows **ctime** format (plus the "LT"); the fourth line is the **date** command format.

Specifying States

In some situations, particularly programming environments, you want to know the status of a set of revisions. RCS files are marked by a text string that describes their *state*. The default state is **Exp** (experimental). Other common choices include **Stab** (stable) or **Rel** (released). These words are user-defined and have no special internal meaning. Several keyword strings include the state in their values. In addition, states can be supplied in options to **ci**, **co**, **rcs**, and **rlog**.

Standard Options

RCS Version 5.6 defines an environment variable RCSINIT, which is used to set up default options for RCS commands. If you set RCSINIT to a space-separated list of options, they will be prepended to the command-line options you supply to any RCS command. Three options are useful to include in RCSINIT: $-q$, $-V$, and $-x$. They can be thought of as standard options because most RCS commands accept them. Note that $-V$ is new in RCS Version 5 and that $-x$ is new in Version 5.6.

$-q[R]$ Quiet mode; don't show diagnostic output. R specifies a file revision.

$-Vn$ Emulate version n of RCS; useful when trading files between systems that run different versions. n can be 3, 4, or 5.

$-x$*suffixes*

     Specify an alternate list of *suffixes* for RCS files. Each suffix is separated by a /. On UNIX systems, RCS files normally end with the characters ,v. The $-x$ option provides a workaround for systems that don't allow a comma (,) character in filenames.

For example, when depositing a working file into an RCS file, the command:

```
ci -x,v/ ch01                    (second suffix is blank)
```

searches in order for the RCS filenames:

```
RCS/ch01,v
ch01,v
RCS/ch01
```

Alphabetical Summary of Commands

For details on the syntax of keywords, revision numbers, dates, states, and standard options, refer to the previous discussions.

ci	**ci** [*options*] *files* Check in revisions. **ci** stores the contents of the specified working *files* into their corresponding RCS files. Normally, **ci** deletes the working file after storing it. If no RCS file exists, then the working file is an initial revision. In this case, the RCS file is created and you are prompted to enter a description of the file. If an RCS file exists, **ci** increments the revision number and prompts you to enter a message that logs the changes made. In RCS Version 5.6, if a working file is

checked in without changes, the file reverts to the previous revision. In older RCS versions, you may end up having to check in a new revision that contains no changes.

The mutually exclusive options −u, −l, and −r, are the most common. Use −u to keep a read-only copy of the working file (for example, so that the file can be compiled or searched). Use −l to update a revision and then immediately check it out again with a lock. This allows you to save intermediate changes but continue editing (for example, during a long editing session). Use −r to check in a file with a different release number. ci accepts the standard options −q, −V, and −x.

Options

−d[*date*]
> Check the file in with a timestamp of *date* or, if no date is specified, with the time of last modification.

−f[*R*]   Force a check-in even if there are no differences.

−I[*R*]   Interactive mode; prompt user even when standard input is not a terminal (e.g., when ci is part of a command pipeline). −I is new in RCS Version 5.

−i[*R*]   Create (initialize) an RCS file and check it in. A warning is reported if the RCS file already exists.

−j[*R*]   Check in a file without initializing. Will report an error if file does not already exist.

−k[*R*]   Assign a revision number, creation date, state, and author from keyword values that were placed in the working file, instead of computing the revision information from the local environment. −k is useful for software distribution: the preset keywords serve as a timestamp shared by all distribution sites.

−l[*R*]   Do a co −l after checking in. This leaves a locked copy of the next revision.

−m*msg*   Use the *msg* string as the log message for all files checked in. When checking in multiple files, ci normally prompts whether to reuse the log message of the previous file. −m bypasses this prompting.

−M[*R*]   Set the working file's modification time to that of the retrieved version. Use of −M can confuse **make** and should be used with care. (New in RCS Version 5.6.)

−n*name*
> Associate a text *name* with the new revision number.

−N*name*
> Same as −n, but override a previous *name*.

ci	−r[*R*]	Check the file in as revision *R*.
←	−r	By itself, reverts to default behavior when releasing a lock and removing the working file. This option overrides any −l or −u options that have been initialized by shell aliases or scripts. This behavior for −r is specific to **ci**.
	−s*state*	Set the *state* of the checked-in revision.
	−T	Set the RCS file's modification time to the time of the latest revision if the RCS file's time precedes the new revision.
	−t*file*	Replace RCS file description with contents of *file*. As of Version 5, this works only for initial check-in.
	−t−*string*	Replace RCS file description with *string*. As of Version 5, this works only for initial check-in.
	−u[*R*]	Do a **co** −u after checking in. This leaves a read-only copy.
	−w*user*	Set the author field to *user* in the checked-in revision.
	−z[*zone*]	Specify the format of the date in keyword substitution. If empty, the default is to output the UTC time with no zone indication. With an argument of **LT**, the local time zone will be used to output an ISO 8601 format, with an indication of the separation from UTC. You may also specify a numeric UTC offset. For example, −z+4:30 would output a string such as: 1998-11-24 02:30:00+4:30.

Examples

Check in chapter files using the same log message:

```
ci -m'First round edits' chap*
```

Check in edits to **prog.c**, leaving a read-only copy:

```
ci -u prog.c
```

Start revision level 2; refer to revision 2.1 as "Prototype":

```
ci -r2 -nPrototype prog.c
```

co	**co** [*options*] *files*

Retrieve a previously checked-in revision, and place it in the corresponding working file (or print to standard output if −p is specified). If you intend to edit the working file and check it in again, specify −l to lock the file. **co** accepts the standard options −q, −V, and −x.

−d*date*   Retrieve latest revision whose check-in timestamp is on or before *date*.

−f[*R*]   Force the working file to be overwritten.

−I[*R*]   Interactive mode; prompt user even when standard input is not a terminal. (New in RCS Version 5.)

−j*R2:R3*

This works like **rcsmerge**. *R2* and *R3* specify two revisions whose changes are merged into a third file: either the corresponding working file or a third revision (any *R* specified by other **co** options).

−k*c*   Expand keyword symbols according to flag *c*. *c* can be:

 b Like **o**, but performs its operations in binary mode, generating the previous revision's keywords and values in binary.

 k Expand symbols to keywords only (no values). This is useful for ignoring trivial differences during file comparison.

 kv Expand symbols to keyword and value (the default). Insert the locker's name only during a **ci −l** or **co −l**.

 kvl Like **kv**, but always insert the locker's name.

 o Expand symbols to keyword and value present in previous revision. This is useful for binary files that don't allow substring changes.

 v Expand symbols to values only (no keywords). This prevents further keyword substitution and is not recommended.

−l[*R*]   Same as −**r**, but also lock the retrieved revision.

−M[*R*]   Set the working file's modification time to that of the retrieved version. Use of −**M** can confuse **make** and should be used with care. (New in RCS Version 5.6.)

−p[*R*]   Send retrieved revision to standard output instead of to a working file. Useful for output redirection or filtering.

−r[*R*]   Retrieve the latest revision or, if *R* is given, retrieve the latest revision that is equal to or lower than *R*.

−s*state*   Retrieve the latest revision having the given *state*.

−T   Preserve the modification time of the RCS file even if a lock is added or removed.

−u[*R*]   Same as −**r**, but also unlock the retrieved revision if you locked it previously.

RCS and CVS

→

co

←

-w[*user*]
> Retrieve the latest revision that was checked in either by the invoking user or by the specified *user*.

Examples

Sort the latest stored version of *file*:

```
co -p file | sort
```

Check out (and lock) all uppercase filenames for editing:

```
co -l [A-Z]*
```

Note that filename expansion fails unless a working copy resides in the current directory. Therefore, this example works only if the files were previously checked in via **ci** −**u**. Finally, here are some different ways to extract the working files for a set of RCS files (in the current directory):

```
co -r3 *,v                    Latest revisions of release 3
co -r3 -wjim *,v              Same, but only if checked in by jim
co -d'May 5, 2 pm LT' *,v     Latest revisions that were
                              modified on or before the date
co -rPrototype *,v            Latest revisions named Prototype
```

---

ident

ident [*option*] [*files*]

Extract keyword/value symbols from *files*. *files* can be text files, object files, or dumps.

Option

-q   Suppress warning message when no keyword patterns are found.

Examples

If file **prog.c** is compiled, and it contains this line of code:

```
char rcsID[] = "$Author: george $
```

then the following output is produced:

```
% ident prog.c prog.o
prog.c:
     $Author: george $
prog.o:
     $Author: george $
```

Show keywords for all RCS files (suppress warnings):

```
co -p RCS/*,v | ident -q
```

An administrative command for setting up or changing the default
attributes of RCS files. Among other things, **rcs** lets you set strict locking (−L), delete revisions (−o), and override locks set by **co** (−l and
−u). RCS files have an access list (created via −a); anyone whose
username is on the list can run **rcs**. The access list is often empty,
meaning that **rcs** is available to everyone. In addition, you can always
invoke **rcs** if you own the file, if you're a privileged user, or if you
run **rcs** with −i. **rcs** accepts the standard options −q, −V, and −x.

Options

−a*users* Append the comma-separated list of *users* to the access
list.

−A*otherfile*

Append *otherfile*'s access list to the access list of *files*.

−b[*R*] Set the default branch to *R* or, if *R* is omitted, to the
highest branch on the trunk.

−c'*s*' The comment character for **$Log** keywords is set to
string *s*. By default, **co** expands embedded **$Log** key-
words into comments preceded by #. You could, for
example, set *s* to . \" for troff files or set *s* to * for C
programs. (You would need to manually insert an
enclosing /* and */ before and after **$Log**.)

−e[*users*]

Erase everyone (or only the specified *users*) from the
access list.

−i Create (initialize) an RCS file but don't deposit a revision.

−I Interactive mode; prompt user even when standard
input is not a terminal. (New in RCS Version 5.)

−k*c* Use *c* as the default style for keyword substitution. (See
co for values of *c*.) −k**kv** restores the default substitution style; all other styles create incompatibilities with
RCS Version 4 or earlier.

−l[*R*] Lock revision *R* or the latest revision. −l "retroactively
locks" a file and is useful if you checked out a file
incorrectly by typing **co** instead of **co** −l.

−L Turn on strict locking (the default). This means that
everyone, including the owner of the RCS file, must use
co −l to edit files. Strict locking is recommended when
files are to be shared. (See −U.)

−m*R*:*msg*

Use the *msg* string to replace the log message of revision *R*. (New in RCS Version 5.6.)

→

-M   Disable email notification when breaking a lock on a file with **rcs −u**. This should only be used when there is another means to warn users that their files have been unlocked.

−n*flags* Add or delete an association between a revision and a name. *flags* can be:

name:*R*
    Associate *name* with revision *R*.

name:
    Associate *name* with latest revision.

name
    Remove association of *name*.

−N*flags* Same as −**n** but overwrite existing *names*.

−o*R_list*
        Delete (outdate) revisions listed in *R_list*. *R_list* can be specified as: *R1*, *R1−R2*, *R1−*, or *−R2*. When a branch is given, −**o** deletes only the latest revision on it. RCS Version 5.6 has changed the range separator character to :, although − is still valid.

−s*state*[:*R*]
        Set the state of revision *R* (or the latest revision) to the word *state*.

−t[*file*] Replace RCS file description with contents of *file* or, if no file is given, with standard output.

−t−*string*
        Replace RCS file description with *string*. Preserves the time of modification on an RCS file unless a revision is removed.

−u[*R*]   The complement of −**l**: unlock a revision that was previously checked out via **co** −**l**. If someone else did the check-out, you are prompted to state the reason for breaking the lock. This message is mailed to the original locker.

−U   Turn on non-strict locking. Everyone except the file owner must use **co** −**l** to edit files. (See −**L**.)

−V   Print the RCS version number.

−z*zone* Sets the default time zone for timestamp options performed by the **ci** and **co** commands.

Examples

Associate the label **To_customer** with the latest revision of all RCS files:

```
rcs -nTo_customer: RCS/*
```

Add three users to the access list of file **beatle_deals**:

```
rcs -ageorge,paul,ringo beatle_deals
```

Delete revisions 1.2 through 1.5:

```
rcs -o1.2-1.5 doc
```

Replace an RCS file description with the contents of a variable:

```
echo "$description" | rcs -t file
```

rcsclean [options] [files]

Compares checked-out files against the corresponding latest revision or revision *R* (as given by the options). If no differences are found, the working file is removed. (Use **rcsdiff** to find differences.) **rcsclean** is useful in makefiles. For example, you could specify a "clean up" target to update your directories. **rcsclean** is also useful prior to running **rcsfreeze**. **rcsclean** accepts the standard options −q, −V, and −x.

Options

−k*c*   When comparing revisions, expand keywords using style *c*. (See **co** for values of *c*.)

−n[*R*]   Show what would happen but don't actually execute.

−r[*R*]   Compare against revision *R*. *R* can be supplied as arguments to other options, so −r is redundant.

−T   Preserve the modification time of the RCS file even if a lock is added or removed.

−u[*R*]   Unlock the revision if it's the same as the working file.

−z[*zone*]
          Set the time zone format for the keyword substitution.

Examples

Remove unchanged copies of program and header files:

```
rcsclean *.c *.h
```

rcsdiff [options] [diff_options] files

Compare revisions via **diff**. Specify revisions using −r as follows:

Number of Revisions specified:	Comparison made:
None	Working file against latest revision
One	Working file against specified revision
Two	One revision against the other

rcsdiff accepts the standard options −q, −T, −V, −x, and −z, as well

→

rcsdiff
←
	as *diff_options*, which can be any valid **diff** option. **rcsdiff** exits with a status of 0 (no differences), 1 (some differences), or 2 (unknown problem).
	
	Options
	
	  −k*c* When comparing revisions, expand keywords using style *c*. (See **co** for values of *c*.)
	
	  −r*R1* Use revision *R1* in the comparison.
	
	  −r*R2* Use revision *R2* in the comparison. (−r*R1* must also be specified.)

rcsmerge	**rcsmerge** [*options*] *file*
	
	Perform a three-way merge of file revisions, taking two differing versions and incorporating the changes into the working *file*. You must provide either one or two revisions to merge (typically with −**r**). Overlaps are handled the same as with **merge**, by placing warnings in the resulting file. **rcsmerge** accepts the standard options −**q**, −**V**, −**x**, and −**z**. **rcsmerge** exits with a status of 0 (no overlaps), 1 (some overlaps), or 2 (unknown problem).
	
	Options
	
	  −k*c* When comparing revisions, expand keywords using style *c*. (See **co** for values of *c*.)
	
	  −p[*R*] Send merged version to standard output instead of overwriting *file*.
	
	  −r[*R*] Merge revision *R* or, if no *R* is given, merge the latest revision.
	
	Examples
	
	Suppose you need to add updates to an old revision (1.3) of **prog.c**, but the current file is already at revision 1.6. To incorporate the changes:
	
	```\nco -l prog.c\n```
	(edit latest revision by adding revision 1.3 updates, then:)
	```\nrcsmerge -p -r1.3 -r1.6 prog.c > prog.updated.c\n```
	
	Undo changes between revisions 3.5 and 3.2, and overwrite the working file:
	
	```\nrcsmerge -r3.5 -r3.2 chap08\n```

rlog	**rlog** [*options*] *files* Display identification information for RCS *files*, including the log message associated with each revision, the number of lines added or removed, date of last check-in, etc. With no options, **rlog** displays all

information. Use options to display specific items. **rlog** accepts the standard options −**T**, −**V**, −**x**, and −**z**.

Options

−**b**   Prune the display; print only about the default branch.

−**d***dates* Display information for revisions whose check-in timestamp falls in the range of *dates* (a list separated by semicolons). Be sure to use quotes. Each date can be specified as:

d1 < *d2*
Select revisions between *date1* and *date2*, inclusive.

d1 <
Select revisions made on or after *date1*.

d1 >
Select revisions made on or before *date1*.

−**h**   Display the beginning of the normal **rlog** listing.

−**l**[*users*]
Display information only about locked revisions or, if *lockers* is specified, only about revisions locked by the list of *users*.

−**L**   Skip files that aren't locked.

−**N**   Don't display symbolic names.

−**r**[*list*] Display information for revisions in the comma-separated *list* of revision numbers. If no *list* is given, the latest revision is used. Items can be specified as:

R1 Select revision *R1*. If *R1* is a branch, select all revisions on it.

R1.
If *R1* is a branch, select its latest revision.

R1−*R2*
Select revisions *R1* through *R2*.

−*R1*
Select revisions from beginning of branch through *R1*.

R1−
Select revisions from *R1* through end of branch.

RCS Version 5.6 has changed the range separator character to :, although − is still valid.

−**R**   Display only the name of the RCS file.

−**s***states* Display information for revisions whose state matches one from the comma-separated list of *states*.

→

rlog	−t	Same as −**h**, but also display the file's description.
←	−**w**[*users*]	
		Display information for revisions checked in by anyone in the comma-separated list of *users*. If no *users* are supplied, assume the name of the invoking user.

Examples

Display a file's revision history:

```
rlog RCS/*,v | more
```

Display names of RCS files that are locked by user **daniel**:

```
rlog -R -L -ldaniel RCS/*
```

Display the "title" portion (no revision history) of a working file:

```
rlog -t calc.c
```

The CVS Utility

CVS (Concurrent Version Control) is a front end to the RCS revision control system. Whereas RCS controls changes and versions of files from a single directory, CVS expands the control structure to a hierarchical collection of directories containing revision-controlled files. CVS can manage the concurrent editing of files among multiple users, and can produce a software release from the collection of directories and files.

CVS keeps a single copy of the master sources called the source *repository*. It contains all the information required to extract a previous release based on either a symbolic revision tag or a specific date. Users maintain private copies of the files they need, usually in their home directories. CVS commands update the source repository with the changes a user makes in the working directory.

CVS Overview

The CVS repository contains all the files and directories for your controlled sources and the administrative files for CVS. You create a repository with the **init** function. By default, the repository is created in the directory defined by the CVSROOT environment variable. You can set up this variable for your default root or use the −**d** option to specify a different root directory. For example:

```
%cvs -d /work/projects/cvsroot init
```

will set up a CVS repository in the */work/projects/cvsroot* directory. When using CVS to edit source files, you will not be working in the repository directory, but one of your choice. You will need to make sure you have CVSROOT set to the proper directory, or use the −**d** option when checking out files (the repository location will be remembered for subsequent activities in the working directory).

Administrative files are stored in the $CVSROOT/CVSROOT directory. The most useful file here is the *modules* file. Each line of this file defines a module, or group of files in the repository. The name of the module is given first, followed by whitespace and the directory where the files are. The path for the directory is relative to CVSROOT. You can use either module names or directory names when using **checkout** to create a working directory.

CVS Commands

CVS provides a number of commands with a rich set of options to support a wide variety of needs for distributed software development. Basic use of CVS control requires only five commands.

All commands start with **cvs** at the beginning of the line, followed by a CVS command and any options. CVS commands have the following syntax:

> % **cvs** [*cvs–options*] *command* [*command–options*] *files*

A command is always required unless you are requesting help with **cvs –H** or checking the version with **cvs –v**. The options to the **cvs** function must be placed before the command and any command options to avoid confusion and errors.

The following commands perform the basic functions of the CVS system:

checkout
> Creates your private copy of the source for modules, which are named collections of source files. This is your working copy that you edit without interfering with others' work.

update
> Updates your copies of source files from changes that others have checked in to the source repository.

add   Adds new files to the modules in your working directory. These files will be added to the source respository when you run **cvs commit** to check in your changes. To add new files to the source repository that aren't in a module you are working on, use **cvs import** instead.

remove
> Eliminates files from the source repository. Make sure you erase the files from your private copy before you use this command. Respository files will be removed when you run **cvs commit**.

commit
> Publishes your changes to the source repository. Similar to checking in your files in RCS.

Unlike RCS, CVS does not implement file locking by default. This means that multiple changes can be made to the same file simultaneously. CVS will coordinate these changes when you **update** (or, if you try to **commit** and new source revisions exist, you are forced to **update**). When you **update** your working directory and there is a new revision, CVS will compare the source and working files and merge the changes from the new revisions into your working files. If no conflicts occur, the files can be committed to the repository as a new revision.

In the event that conflicts occur, a **merge** is run on the files, and the conflicting lines are marked in the new version of the working file. (The original c working file is saved in the directory as *.#filename.revnumber*.) You can edit the merge file to resolve the conflicts, then **update** and **commit** your changes to the repository.

In environments where multiple developers are working with source code simultaneously, you may wish to use higher level CVS functionality to coordinate file edits. This can be done by using the **watch** and **edit** features.

The **watch** command allows a user to be notified when work is being done on specified files. It forces other users to use **cvs edit** to check out the files as read–write and places a lock on them. How a user is notified is defined in the $CVSROOT/CVSROOT/notify administrative file.

Administrative Files

The CVSROOT directory of the repository contains the files that CVS uses for administrative features. As mentioned earlier, the *modules* file is perhaps the most necessary of these files. Other files can cause a program to run every time someone commits a new file, to format the logging information, or to describe how to notify users when **watch**ed files change.

You can edit administrative files the same way you edit any other source file since they are contained in the repository. Simply check a file out, and commit the changes when finished:

```
%cvs checkout CVSROOT/modules
...edit file...
%cvs commit CVSROOT/modules
```

The following list describes the administrative files that can be used by CVS.

The modules file

This file defines symbolic names for collections of files in your source repository. Each line of the file defines a module, with the name of the module first, options, and the directory names, files, or other module names that comprise the module. When you **checkout** a module, a directory with the name of the module is created as a working directory and populated with the files of the module.

A simple module is created with the following line:

> modname –a *aliases*

This defines the module *modname*. The **–a** option indicates a simple module definition, and *aliases* is either directory names (relative to CVSROOT) or other defined modules. A more generic syntax is:

> modname *[options] dir [files] [&modules]*

In this syntax, a directory *dir* is required in the definition. You can specify that only certain *files* from that directory are to be included. Other modules can be included by preceding their names with an ampersand (&). The following options can be used in module definitions:

−e *program*

Specifies the *program* to run when files in the module are exported.

−i *program*

Specifies the *program* to run when files in the module are commited.

−o *program*

Specifies the *program* to run when files in the module are checked out with
checkout.

−s *status*

Attaches a status to the module. Files in the module will be sorted by this
status tag upon **cvs checkout −s**.

−t *program*

Specifies the *program* to run when a tag is applied to a module file with
rtag.

−u *program*

Specifies the *program* to run when the checked-out module is updated (that
is, when **update** is run from the top−level directory of the working directory).

The cvswrappers file

This file defines scripts that should be run on source files when they are checked
either in or out of the repository. Each line begins with an expression (which can
use wildcards) indicating the files or directory to apply the wrapper to. The following options define the wrapper actions:

−f *'script %s'*

Run *script* on the file when it is checked out. The **%s** will be replaced with
the name of the file.

−t *'script %s %s'*

Run **script** on the file when it is checked in (with **commit**) to the repository.
The first argument to the script is the file to filter; the second argument will
be the path to the directory where the filtered file should go.

−m *'[COPY|MERGE]'*

Specifies how filtered files will be incorporated into the working directory
upon **update**. COPY will simply copy the filtered file into the directory, while
MERGE merges the different changes submitted by multiple users.

−k *'mode'*

Sets the **−k** flag for RCS keyword expansion.

The commitinfo, editinfo, and loginfo files

These three administrative files specify programs that are run whenever files are
committed to the repository. All three files use the same syntax. They provide an
alternative to specifying commit programs with the **−i** flag in the *modules* file.

Lines in these files begin with a regular expression that will be matched against a file name when it is checked in. The words ALL and DEFAULT can be used here to apply the program to all checked-in files, and only to files that do not match a specified line in the administrative file.

The regular expression is followed by whitespace and then a file name or command-line template for the program to be executed.

The *commitinfo* file specifies verification programs that check a file before they are actually committed to the repository. If the program exits with a non-zero status, the commit will be aborted. An ALL designation will be used in addition to the first matching regular expression line or the DEFAULT program.

The *editinfo* file specifies programs to edit or verify the log message of a checked-in file. The ALL keyword is not supported in this file.

The *loginfo* file designates a program to receive the log information after a **commit** is complete. You can add the information to a file, mail the information to an administrator, etc. The program will receive log information on the standard input. If a %s variable is included in the command, it will be replaced with the file's name when passed to the program. An ALL line will be used in addition to the first matching expression line or the DEFAULT program.

The rcsinfo file

The *rcsinfo* file uses syntax similar to the other info administrative files, except that it designates a file containing a log message template to use when a file is checked in. The second entry per line should be a full pathname to the file containing the information.

The cvsignore file

This file contains a list of filename patterns that should be ignored when an **update**, **import**, or **release** is performed. These will be files in your working directory that you will not want under CVS control, such as object, backup, or archive files. CVS has a default list that it already ignores. You can add patterns in the *cvsignore* file (which is per-repository), in the ˜/.cvsignore files in user directories (per user), or in the $CVSIGNORE variable.

The history file

This file stores history information for the source repository. It is automatically created by the **init** command when the repository is created. Information from this file is retrieved by the **history** command.

Environment Variables

The following environment variables are used by CVS:

$CVSIGNORE
> A list of filename patterns, separated by whitespace, that CVS ignores in working directories.

$CVSWRAPPERS
> A list of filename patterns, separated by whitespace, that CVS uses as wrapper programs.

$CVSREAD
> If set, causes **checkout** and **update** to create files as read–only in the working directory. Off by default.

$CVSROOT
> The full pathname to the CVS source repository.

$CVSEDITOR
> Sets which program to use for log messages upon **commit**.

Common Command Options

The following options are supported across a number of CVS commands. They may not work with all commands, but they will have the same meaning and effect throughout. One exception is the **history** command, which supports similarly named options with conflicting meanings. The supported common options will be indicated in the command reference section later in this chapter.

-D *date*
> Uses the most recent source revision prior to *date*. This setting will remain in effect throughout changes in your private copy of the file, i.e., CVS will keep the same date on the file, unless you override it in the **update** command. There are a number of valid formats for the date specification, for example:

```
1 month ago
2 hours ago
400000 seconds ago
last year
last Monday
yesterday
a fortnight ago
11/30/98 10:00:02 EST
January 15, 1998 10:0am
22:00 GMT
```

-f
> When requesting a release via a specific date or symbolic tag, include any files in the recent version that were added after the tagging or date.

-H
> Displays the options available for a command.

-k *flag*
> The -k options of the RCS **co** command. The flags for this option alter the default processing of RCS keywords. See the RCS command reference earlier in this chapter for descriptions.

-l
> The local flag; run the command only in the current working directory and not in subdirectories.

-n
> Bypass the running of a program upon **checkout**, **commit**, **tag**, or **update**, if such a program is specified in the modules database to run on these functions.

-P	Remove directories emptied after an **update** or **checkout**. Without this option, empty directories will be left alone.
-p	Pipe the files retrieved from the source repository (via **checkout** or **update**) to standard output, instead of writing them to the working directory.
-r *tag*	Use the revision specified by *tag*. By default, commands will use the most recent version in the source repository. Two special tags may be used here: HEAD refers to the most recent version in the source depository; BASE refers to the last version you checked out. If you specify a tag on **checkout** or **update**, CVS remembers and continues to use the tag on further updates until you specify otherwise.

CVS Commands

add	**cvs add** [*options*] *files*
	
	Add *files* to your working directory and place them under CVS control. When you next use **commit** to check in your changes, the new files will be added to the repository, and you will be asked to supply a log message.
	
	    -m'*message*'
	            Specify the log *message* in the command instead of opening the editor on **commit**.

admin	**cvs admin** *options files* Interface to the RCS administrative functions. This command simply passes its arguments to **rcs**. The options are the same as those to **rcs** described earlier in this chapter; however, not all of the options are useful for CVS administration.
checkout	**cvs checkout** [*options*] *modules* Create a working directory and copy CVS source files to it. You can specify either the names of *modules*, defined by the *modules* administrative file, or directory names relative to CVSROOT. The working directory is created in the directory where the **checkout** command is executed, and any subdirectories are recursively created and populated with source files. The top-level directory will be created with the same name as the module or source directory. Files are created read-write in the working directory by default. The **-r** option to **cvs** overrides this behavior. *Options* The following standard options can be used with **checkout**: **-D**, **-f**, **-k**, **-l**, **-n**, **-P**, **-p**, and **-r**. The following options are specific to the **checkout** command:

−A	Reset "sticky" options such as tags, dates, or flags set with −k.
−c	Print files to standard output instead of copying them to your working directory.
−d *dir*	Create a directory named *dir* for working files instead of using the module name.
−j *tag*	Merge changes between revisions and copies into the working directory. If you use two −j options, changes from the revision specified in the first option are merged with the second specified revision. If one −j option is used, changes from the "ancestor" revision of the working directory and revision specified with −j are merged. The ancestor revision is the common branch revision of the two. *tag* may be either a revision number or a symbolic tag, with an optional date specifier of the form *tag:date*.
−N	When used with −d *dir*, this option causes full module paths to be used in the working directory. The default is to shorten paths for a specific target directory.
−s	Copy files to standard output (like −c) including the status of all modules. The output is sorted by status string.

---

cvs commit [*options*] [*files*]

Incorporate the changes made in the files of your working directory to the source repository. The files must have incorporated the changes from the latest revision in the source repository, or **commit** will notify you that your working files are not up-to-date and then will exit. To make your working files current with the source, use **update**. By default, **commit** will look for changes to all files in your current working directory, including subdirectories. When changes have been committed, an editor is invoked for you to enter the log message for the changes, unless you have specified a message with the −**m** option.

Options

This command can use the standard options −l, −n, −R, and −r. The following options are also supported by **commit**:

−F *file*	Use the log message contained in *file* when committing.
−f	Force a new revision to be created, even if there are no changes from the current source revision.
−m *mesg*	Use *mesg* as the log message for the committed revision.

cvs	cvs *options*
	cvs *[cvs-options] command [command-options] [args]*

Invoke the CVS program. Can use specific options for general CVS behavior, which must immediately follow **cvs**. Following these options, you may invoke a CVS command with its own options and parameters. The general options for **cvs** are:

–b *bindir*

Use *bindir* as the directory for RCS programs. This option overrides the setting of the $RCSBIN variable. *bindir* should be the full pathname.

–d *rootdir*

Use *rootdir* as the CVS root directory. This option overrides the $CVSROOT variable, and should be specified as a full pathname.

–e *editor*

Use *editor* as the path to the editor CVS uses to enter log information. Overrides the $CVSEDITOR and $EDITOR variables.

–f Ignore settings in user's ˜/.cvsrc file.

–H, ––help

Display usage information about the **cvs** command. Do not use additional commands with this option.

–l Do not log the command to the CVS command history.

–n Retrieve status information resulting from a command without actually executing it. No files are changed

–Q Suppress messages produced by the command.

–q Display only informational messages; less quiet than –Q.

–r Check out files into working directory as read–only.

–s *var=value*

Set the user variable *var* to *value*.

–T *tempdir*

Specify the full pathname *tempdir* as the directory where temporary files are located. This option overrides the setting of the $TEMPDIR variable.

–t Perform a trace on the command.

–v ––version

Display the version number of CVS.

–w Check out files into the working directory as read–write. This option overrides the setting of the $CVSREAD variable, if set.

cvs diff [*options*] [*files*]   diff

Compare files from different revisions. By default, all the files of your
working directory are compared with the revision they were based
on. You may specify one or more filenames or directory names to
compare only those. It is useful to use the standard −r option, once
to compare your working files with the specified revision, or twice to
compare the two specified revisions. When two −r options are specified, your working directory is not used. This command is based on
rcsdiff and, therefore, on **diff**. Any options not recognized by CVS are
passed to **rcsdiff** and **diff**. See the description of **rcsdiff** earlier in this
chapter, and the entry for **diff** in Chapter 2. The standard options supported by this command are −D, −k, −l, −R, and −r.

cvs edit [*options*] [*files*]   edit

Declare *files* for editing. This command makes the files read-write and
informs anyone who has a **watch** on the file that you are going to
edit it. To release the file control, use **cvs commit** or **cvs unedit**. A
temporary **watch** on *files* is also set up for the user. If another person
calls **edit**, **unedit**, **commit**, or **release** on the *files*, the user will be notified. The −a option specifies the types of notification you want to
receive.

Options

   −a [edit|unedit|commit|all|none]
        Specify the action for temporary **watch** of the specified
        files. By default, all actions (**edit**, **unedit**, and **commit**)
        cause notification.

   −l   Local directory only. Do not perform action in subdirec-
        tories.

cvs editors [−l] *files*   editors

List the users currently working on *files* after calling them with **cvs
edit**. The −l option performs the action in only the current directory
and not subdirectories.

cvs export *options module*   export

Export a release copy of the source specified by *modules*. This acts
like **checkout**, except that it doesn't include CVS directories or administrative files. You are required to supply a date (−D *date*) or tag (−r
tag) for the release so that the exported set can be reproduced. The
standard options that are useful with this command are −D, −f, −l,
−n, −R, and −r. The **export** command also supports the following
options:

→

export ←	**−d** *dir*	Create and use directory named *dir* for exported files, instead of using the module name.
	−k *mode*	
		Set the keyword expansion mode for the files.
	−N	When used with **−d**, creates the directory and subdirectories without shortening pathnames used in the repository.

history	**cvs history** [*options*] [*files*]

Display the usage statistics of the commands **checkout**, **commit**, **rtag**, **update**, and **release**. This information is stored in the *history* administrative file. The options to this command allow you to display reports in a number of ways; they are not the same as the common command options, even if they are the same name. The options can be combined in a number of ways to find very specific information from the history.

	−a	Report data for all users.
	−b *string*	
		Report data only back to a record that contains *string* in its module name, file name, or repository path.
	−c	Report information for each **commit** command.
	−D *date*	Report all data since the specified *date*.
	−e	Report all history records.
	−l	Report the last modification only.
	−m *module*	
		Report information only for a specified *module*.
	−o	Report information for each **checkout** command.
	−p *repos*	
		Specify a source repository *repos*.
	−r *rev*	Report information since the revision number or tag specified by *rev*.
	−T	Report information for each **rtag** command.
	−t *tag*	Report records back to the first appearance of the specified *tag* in the history.
	−u *user*	Report information only for the specified *user*.
	−w	Report records only from the current working directory (where the **history** is being executed).
	−x *type*	Report a set of records based on specific *type*. The type may indicate a particular command, the results of an update, or the result of a commit. The command types are:

F   release

O   checkout

T   rtag

The types for **update** results are:

C   A merge resulted in conflicts.

G   A merge was successful.

U   A file was updated from the repository.

W   A working file was not found in the repository and was deleted from the working directory.

The types for **commit** results are:

A   A new file was added to the repository.

M   A file was modified.

R   A file was removed.

cvs import [*options*] *repository vendor release*

Incorporate an entire source distribution into the source repository. This command is used for full updates from an outside source or can be used to create a new repository. The *repository* is the pathname of the new repository relative to CVSROOT, and will be created if it doesn't exist. The imported source is created as a first-level branch revision (i.e., 1.1.1). The *vendor* argument will be the tag for the entire branch, and *release* will be the tag for only the imported files.

Options

The standard **−m** *message* option can be used to supply the log message for this command. Other options supported by **import** are:

−b *branch*

Specify a different *branch* revision number for the imported source. Imported source will always be placed at branch 1.1.1 unless you use this tag.

−k *mode*

Set the RCS keyword expansion *mode*.

−I *name*

Specify files to ignore during import. *name* can be a file name or a pattern. If you want to include all files, without ignoring any, use **−I** !.

−W *name*

Specify a file *name* or pattern to be filtered during import.

init	**cvs init**
	Create a repository in the directory specified by CVSROOT, or a directory named by the **−d** option to CVS.
log	**cvs log** *options files*
	Display the log information for the specified *files*, including file information, revision numbers, author, and the log messages. This command uses information based on the RCS command **rlog**. See the **rlog** command earlier in this chapter for display options.
rdiff	**cvs rdiff** [*options*] *modules*
	Perform a **diff** between two revisions and create a patch file that can be used to build the new version from an old revision. This command operates on the source repository and does not require a check-out or working directory. Specify revisions using either of the standard **−D** or **−r** tags. If you specify only one revision, it will be compared to the current revision.
	Options
	This command uses the following common options: **−D**, **−f**, **−l**, and **−r**. It also supports the following options:

    −c   Use context lines in the **diff** format. The default setting.

    −s   Produce a summary of what files have been changed instead of generating a patch file. The information is displayed on the standard output.

    −t   Perform a **diff** on the last two revisions and display to the standard output. This is an easy way to see the most recent changes.

    −u   Produce unified context diffs.

    −V *version*

                Expand RCS keywords in the format of the RCS *version* you specify. (The RCS expansion format changed in version 5.)

release	**cvs release** [**−d**] *modules*
	Release files from a **checkout** if you no longer have changes to commit to the repository. The **−d** option indicates that files should be deleted from your working directory.
remove	**cvs remove** [*options*] [*files*]
	Remove specified *files* from the source repository. This command forces you to delete the file from your working directory first. When

you execute a **commit**, the file will be removed if there are no con-flicts. If you don't specify *files*, this command will apply to your entire working directory.

Options

    −l   Work in the local directory only.

    −R   Apply this command recursively through your working directory. This is the default setting.

---

cvs rtag [*options*] *tag modules*

Add a symbolic *tag* to the current revision (default) or a specified revision of *modules* in the source repository. To apply tags based on the state of your working directory, use **cvs tag**.

Options

The common options supported by **rtag** are: −D, −f, −F, −l, −n, −R, and −r. The following options are also supported:

    −a   Look for the *tag* in removed files (contained in the *Attic* directory) and remove it from those files, enabling reuse.

    −b   Use tag as a branch tag.

    −d   Delete the tag, instead of adding it.

---

cvs status [*options*] [*files*]

Display the status of files in the working directory with respect to the repository. This command will show you the probable results of an update. The common options supported by this command are −l and −R. Additionally, the −v option displays verbose information about the files.

---

cvs tag [*options*] *tag* [*files*]

Assign a symbolic *tag* to *files* in the repository that are nearest to the versions in your working directory. The tag is immediately applied to the repository files, and "sticks" with the files in your working direc-tory.

Options

This command supports the following common options: −F, −l, and −R. The following options are also supported:

    −b   Create the tag as a branch tag.

→

| tag | −c | Check that the current working files are unmodified with respect to the repository. |
| ← | −d | Delete the tag instead of adding it. |

| unedit | **cvs unedit** [−l] *files* |

Reverse the action of the **edit** command on *files*, not saving any changes made, and reverting the files to their repository versions. This is used to abandon work on a file you have declared to edit, and notifies users who have a **watch** on the files. The −l causes the command to operate in the local directory only, and not in subdirectories.

| update | **cvs update** [*options*] *files* |

Incorporate recent changes from the repository into the *files* of your working directory.

Options

This command supports the standard options −D, −f, −k, −l, −P, −p, −R, and −r. Additional options supported by **update** are:

| | −A | Reset sticky tags, dates, or −k flags. |
| | −d | Create any new directories that appear in the repository that do not exist in your working directory. |

−I *name*

Ignore files in your working directory that match *name*. *name* can be a pattern to match against, and you can use multiple −I options. To not ignore any file, use −I !.

−j[*Rev:date*]

Specify a revision *Rev* with optional *date* from which to update changes. If you specify two −j options, changes from the first revision are merged with the second specified revision and into the working directory. Using one −j option, changes from the ancestor revision to the specified revision are merged into the working directory. The ancestor revision is the common root revision of both the working directory and the specified revision.

−W*files* Filter the specified *files* during update. *files* can be a pattern of the type used in the *.cvswrappers* file.

| watch | **cvs watch** *function* [*options*] *files* |

Enable **watch** features and notifications about *files* that are being worked on. The *function* argument allows you to turn a **watch** on or off, or add and remove users to **watch** notification. The functions are described as follows:

on   Watch files. When a file or directory is checked out, the working copy will be created read-only. Users must use **cvs edit** to work on the files.

off   Remove a watch from files.

add   Add current user to the notification list for watched files. The −a option specifies which types of events the user will be notified of; it is described below.

remove   Remove current user from notification list for watched files. −a options can be used to specify which types of notifications are removed (instead of all).

Options

−a *action*

     Specify the *action* to cause notification. This option is used with the **add** and **remove** functions of **cvs watch**. *action* can be the following: **edit**, **unedit**, or **commit**, which specify when the corresponding commands are issued for the watched files; **all**, which specifies all of the previous actions; and **none**, which specifies none of the actions.

−l   Work only in the specified directory, ignoring subdirectories.

---

cvs watchers [*options*] *files*

List all users who have a **watch** set on *files*. The name of the user, the names of the watched files, and the user's email address are displayed. The only option supported, −l, is the same as for the **watch** command.

CHAPTER 14

Perl 5
Quick Reference

Introduction

The current chapter serves as a quick reference guide to Larry Wall's Perl program. It contains a concise description of all statements, functions, and variables, and lots of other useful information. It is based on Perl Version 5.005.

The purpose of the quick reference is to aid users of Perl in finding the syntax of specific functions and statements, and the meaning of built-in variables. It is *not* a self-contained user guide; basic knowledge of the Perl language is required. It is also *not* complete; some of the more obscure variants of Perl constructs have been left out. But all functions and variables are mentioned in at least one way they can be used.

For more information on Perl, visit the Perl web site at *http://www.perl.com*.

Conventions

this	denotes text that you enter literally.
this	means variable text, i.e., things you must fill in.
this†	means that *this* will default to $_ if omitted.
word	is a keyword, i.e., a word with a special meaning.
	denotes pressing a keyboard key.
[]	denotes an optional part.

Command-Line Options

−a	Turns on autosplit mode when used with **−n** or **−p**. Splits to **@F**.
−c	Checks syntax but does not execute. It does run **BEGIN** and **END** blocks.
−d[:*module*]	Runs the script under the indicated module. Default module is the debugger. Use **−de 0** to start the debugger without a script.
−D*flags*	Sets debugging flags.
−e *commandline*	May be used to enter a single line of script. Multiple **−e** commands may be given to build up a multiline script.
−F*regex*	Specifies a regular expression to split on if **−a** is in effect.
−h	Prints the Perl usage summary. Does not execute.
−i*ext*	Files processed by the **< >** construct are to be edited in place.
−I*dir*	The directory is prepended to the search path for Perl modules, **@INC**. With **−P**, also tells the C preprocessor where to look for include files.
−l[*octnum*]	(That's the letter ell.) Enables automatic line-end processing, e.g., **−l013**.
−m*module*	Imports the *module* before executing the script. *module* may be followed by an equals sign and a comma-separated list of items.
−M*module*	Same as **−m**, but with more trickery.
−n	Assumes an input loop around the script. Lines are not printed.
−p	Assumes an input loop around the script. Lines are printed.
−P	Runs the C preprocessor on the script before compilation by Perl.
−s	Interprets **−xxx** on the command line as a switch and sets the corresponding variable **$xxx** in the script.
−S	Uses the **PATH** environment variable to search for the script.
−T	Turns on taint checking.
−u	Dumps core after compiling the script. To be used with the *undump*(1) program (where available). Obsoleted.
−U	Allows Perl to perform unsafe operations.
−v	Prints the version and patch level of your Perl executable.
−V[:*var*]	Prints Perl configuration information, like **−V:man.dir**.
−w	Prints warnings about possible spelling errors and other error-prone constructs in the script.
−x[*dir*]	Extracts the script from the input stream. If *dir* is specified, Perl switches to this directory before running the script.

−0[*val*]   (That's the number zero.) Designates an initial value for the record separator **$/**. See also −l.

Syntax

Perl is a free-format programming language. This means that in general, it does not matter how a Perl program is written with regard to indentation and lines.

An exception to this rule is when the Perl compiler encounters a sharp or pound symbol (#) in the input: it then discards this symbol and everything following it up to the end of the current input line. This can be used to put comments in Perl programs. Real programmers put lots of useful comments in their programs.

There are places where whitespace does matter: within literal texts, patterns, and formats.

If the Perl compiler encounters the special token __END__, it discards this symbol and stops reading input. Anything following this token is ignored by the Perl compiler, but can be read by the program when it is run.

When Perl is expecting a new statement and encounters a line that starts with =, it skips all input up to and including a line that starts with =cut. This is used to embed program documentation.

Embedded Documentation

Tools exist to extract embedded documentation and generate input suitable for several formatters like troff, LATEX, and HTML. The following commands can be used to control embedded documentation:

=back   See =over.

=begin *FMT*
            Subsequent text up to a matching =end is only included when processed for formatter *FMT.*

=cut   Ends a document section.

=end *FMT*   See =begin.

=for *FMT*   The next paragraph is only included when processed for formatter *FMT.*

=head1 *heading*
            Produces a first-level heading.

=head2 *heading*
            Produces a second-level heading.

=item *text*   See =over.

=over *N*   Starts an enumeration with indent *N*. Items are specified using =item. The enumeration is ended with =back.

=pod   Introduces a document section. Any of the =-commands can be used to introduce a document section.

These commands apply to the paragraph of text that follows them; paragraphs are terminated by at least one empty line.

An indented paragraph is considered to be verbatim text and will be rendered as such.

Within normal paragraphs, markup sequences can be inserted:

B<*text*>	Make text bold (for switches and programs).
C<*code*>	Literal code.
E<*escape*>	A named character, e.g., E<lt> means a < and E<gt> means a >.
F<*file*>	Filename.
I<*text*>	Italicize text (for emphasis and variables).
L<*name*>	A cross reference.
S<*text*>	Do not break on spaces in *text*.
X<*index*>	An index entry.
Z<>	A zero-width character.

Data Types

Array	Indexable list of scalar values
Hash	Associative list of scalar values
Scalar	Strings, numbers, and references

Literal Values

Array (1, 2, 3) is a list of three elements.
(1, 2, 3)[0] is the first element from this list,
(1, 2, 3)[−1] the last element.
( ) is an empty list.
(1..4) is the same as (1,2,3,4),
likewise ('a'..'z').
('a'..'z')[4,7,9] is a slice of a list literal.
qw/foo bar / is the same as ('foo','bar',).

Array reference
  [1,2,3]

Array reference with named indices (pseudo-hash)
  [{*field1* => 1, *field2* => 2, ... }]

Boolean Perl has no boolean data type. Anything that is undefined or evaluates to the null string, the number zero, or the string "0" is considered false, everything else is true (including strings like "00"!).

Code reference
  sub { *statements* }

Filehandles **STDIN, STDOUT, STDERR, ARGV, DATA.**
User-specified: *handle*, $*var*.

Globs   <*pattern*> evaluates to all filenames according to the pattern. Use <${*var*}> or **glob** $*var* to glob from a variable.

Hash (associative list)
(*key1, val1, key2, val2,*)
Also (*key1* => *val1, key2* => *val2,*)

Hash reference
{*key1, val1, key2, val2,* }

Here-Is   <<*identifier*
Shell-style "here document." See the Perl documentation for details.

Numeric   **123 1_234 123.4 5E–10 0xff** (hex) **0377** (octal)

Regular Expression
qr/*string*/*modifiers*
See the section "Regular Expressions" for details.

Special tokens
__FILE__: filename; **__LINE__**: line number; **__PACKAGE__**: current package;
__END__: end of program; remaining lines can be read using the filehandle **DATA**.

String

'abc'
Literal string, no variable interpolation or escape characters, except \' and \\. Also: **q**/**abc**/. Almost any pair of delimiters can be used instead of //.

"abc"
Variables are interpolated and escape sequences are processed. Also: **qq**/**abc**/. Escape sequences: \t (Tab), \n (Newline), \r (Return), \f (Formfeed), \b (Backspace), \a (Alarm), \e (Escape), \033 (octal), \x1b (hex), \c[(control). \l and \u lowercase/uppercase the following character. \L and \U lowercase/uppercase until a \E is encountered. \Q quotes non-word characters until a \E is encountered.

`command`
Evaluates to the output of the *command*. Also: **qx**/*command*/.

Variables

$var   A simple scalar variable.

$var[27] 28th element of array @var.

$p = \@var Now $p is a reference to array @var.

$$p[27]	28th element of array referenced by **$p**. Also, **$p–>[27]**.
$var[-1]	Last element of array **@var**.
$var[$i][$j]	$j-th element of $i-th element of array **@var**.
$var{'Feb'}	A value from hash **%var**.
$p = \%var	Now **$p** is a reference to hash **%var**.
$$p{'Feb'}	A value from hash referenced by **$p**. Also, **$p–>{'Feb'}**.
$#var	Last index of array **@var**.
@var	The entire array; in scalar context, the number of elements in the array.
@var[3,4,5]	A slice of array **@var**.
@var{'a','b'}	A slice of **%var**; same as (**$var{'a'}**,**$var{'b'}**).
%var	The entire hash; in scalar context, true if the hash has elements.
$var{'a',1,}	Emulates a multidimensional list (deprecated).
$c = \&mysub	Now **$c** is a reference to subroutine **mysub**.
$c–>(*args*)	Calls the subroutine via the reference.
pkg::var	A variable from a package, e.g., **$pkg::var**, **@pkg::ary**.
\thingie	Reference to a thingie, e.g., **\$var**, **\%hash**.
*name	Refers to all thingies represented by *name*. ***n1 = *n2** makes all **n1** aliases for **n2**. ***n1 = \$n2** makes the package variable **$n1** an alias for **$n2**.

You can always use a *block* (see the section "Statements") returning the right type of reference instead of the variable identifier, e.g., **${}**, **&{}**. **$$p** is just a shorthand for **${$p}**.

Context

Boolean	A special form of scalar context in which it only matters if the result is true or false.
List	A list value or an array is expected.
Scalar	A single scalar value is expected.
Void	No value is expected. If a value is provided, it is discarded.

The following functions relate to context:

scalar *expr*   Forces scalar context for the expression.

wantarray   Returns true if the current context expects a list value, undef in void context.

Operators and Precedence

Perl operators have the following associativity and precedence, listed from highest precedence to lowest.

Assoc.	Operators	Description
left	terms and list operators	See below.
left	->	Infix dereference operator.
	++ --	Auto-increment (magical on strings). Auto-decrement.
right	**	Exponentiation.
right right right	\ ! ~ + -	Reference to an object (unary). Unary negation, bitwise complement. Unary plus, minus.
left left	=~ !~	Binds a scalar expression to a pattern match. Same, but negates the result.
left	* / % x	Multiplication, division, modulo, repetition.
left	+ - .	Addition, subtraction, concatenation.
left	>> <<	Bitwise shift right, bitwise shift left.
	named unary operators	e.g., sin, chdir, -f, -M.
	< > <= >= lt gt le ge	Numerical relational operators. String relational operators.
	== != <=> eq ne cmp	Numerical equal, not equal, compare. Stringwise equal, not equal, compare. Compare operators return -1 (less), 0 (equal), or 1 (greater).
left	&	Bitwise AND.
left	| ^	Bitwise OR, exclusive OR.
left	&&	Logical AND.
left	||	Logical OR.
	\s+2..\s-2 \s+2\s-2 ...	In scalar context, range operator. In list context, enumeration. Alternative range operator.

Assoc.	Operators	Description
right	?:	Conditional (if ? then : else) operator.
right	= += -= etc.	Assignment operators.
left	,	Comma operator, also list element separator.
left	=>	Same, enforces the left operand to be a string.
	list operators (rightward)	See below.
right	**not**	Low precedence logical NOT.
left	**and**	Low precedence logical AND.
left	**or xor**	Low precedence logical OR, exclusive OR.

Parentheses can be used to group an expression into a term.

A list consists of expressions, variables, or lists, separated by commas. An array variable or an array slice may always be used instead of (or as part of) a list.

Perl functions that can be used as list operators have either very high or very low precedence, depending on whether you look at the left side of the operator or at the right side of the operator. Parentheses can be added around the parameter lists to avoid precedence problems.

The logical operators do not evaluate the right operand if the result is already known after evaluation of the left operand.

Statements

A statement is an expression, optionally followed by a modifier, and terminated with a semicolon. Statements can be combined to form a *block* when enclosed in {}. The semi-colon may be omitted after the last statement of the *block*.

Execution of expressions can depend on other expressions using one of the modifiers if, unless, for, foreach, while, or until, e.g.:

```
expr1 if expr2 ;
expr1 foreach list ;
expr1 until expr2 ;
```

The logical operators | |, &&, or ?: also allow conditional execution:

```
expr1 | | expr2 ;
expr1 ? expr2 : expr3 ;
```

*block*s may be used to control flow:

```
if ( expr ) block [ [ elsif ( expr ) block ] else block ]

unless ( expr ) block [ else block ]
```

[*label*:] while (*expr*) *block* [continue *block*]

[*label*:] until (*expr*) *block* [continue *block*]

[*label*:] for ([*expr*] ; [*expr*] ; [*expr*]) *block*

[*label*:] foreach *var* (*list*) *block*

[*label*:] *block* [continue *block*]

for and foreach can be used interchangeably.

Program flow can be controlled with:

goto *label* Finds the statement labeled with *label* and resumes execution there. *label* may be an expression that evaluates to the name of a label.

last [*label*]

 Immediately exits the loop in question. Skips the continue block.

next [*label*]

 Executes the continue block and starts the next iteration of the loop.

redo [*label*]

 Restarts the loop block without evaluating the conditional again. Skips the continue block.

Special forms are:

do *block* while *expr* ;
do *block* until *expr* ;

which are guaranteed to perform *block* once before testing *expr*, and:

do *block*

which effectively turns *block* into an expression.

Subroutines, Packages, and Modules

&*subroutine* *list*

 Executes a *subroutine* declared by a sub declaration, and returns the value of the last expression evaluated in *subroutine*. *subroutine* can be an expression yielding a reference to a code object. The & may be omitted if the subroutine has been declared before being used, or the *list* is parenthesized.

bless *ref* [, *classname*]

 Turns the object *ref* into an object in *classname*. Returns the reference.

caller [*expr*]

 Returns a list ($package, $file, $line, ...) for a specific subroutine call. **caller** returns this information for the current subroutine, **caller(1)** for the caller of this subroutine, etc. Returns false if no caller.

do *subroutine list*
> Deprecated form of &*subroutine*.

goto &*subroutine*
> Substitutes a call to *subroutine* for the current subroutine.

import *module* [[*version*] *list*]
> Imports the named items from *module*.

no *module* [*list*]
> Cancels imported semantics. See use.

package [*namespace*]
> Designates the remainder of the current block as a package with a namespace, or without one if *namespace* is omitted.

prototype *function*
> Returns the prototype of the function as a string, or undef if the function has no prototype.

require *expr*†
> If *expr* is numeric, requires Perl to be at least that version. Otherwise *expr* must be the name of a file that is included from the Perl library. Does not include more than once, and yields a fatal error if the file does not evaluate to a true value. If *expr* is a bare word, assumes extension .**pm** for the name of the file. This form of module loading does not risk altering your namespace.

return [*expr*]
> Returns from a subroutine with the value specified; if no value, returns undef in scalar context and an empty list in list context.

sub [*name*] [(*proto*)] *block*
> Designates *name* as a subroutine. Parameters are passed by reference as array @_. Returns the value of the last expression evaluated. *proto* can be used to define the required parameters. Without a *block* it is just a forward declaration, without the *name* it is an anonymous subroutine.

[sub] **BEGIN** *block*
> Defines a setup *block* to be called before execution.

[sub] **END** *block*
> Defines a cleanup *block* to be called upon termination.

[sub] **INIT** *block*
> Defines an initialization *block* to be called after compilation, just before execution.

use *module* [[*version*] *list*]
> Loads the named module into the current package at compile time.

Object-Oriented Programming

Perl rules of object-oriented programming are as follows:

- An object is simply a reference that happens to know which class it belongs to. Objects are blessed, references are not.

- A class is simply a package that happens to provide methods to deal with object references. If a package fails to provide a method, the base classes as listed in @ISA are searched.

- A method is simply a subroutine that expects an object reference (or a package name, for static methods) as the first argument. Methods can be called with:

  objref -> method parameters   or
  method objref parameters

Standard Methods

The package **UNIVERSAL** contains methods that are automatically inherited by all other classes:

can *method* Returns a reference to the method if its object has it, undef otherwise.

isa *class*   Returns true if its object is blessed into a subclass of *class.*

VERSION [*need*]
Returns the version of the class. Checks the version if *need* is supplied.

Pragmatic Modules

Pragmatic modules affect the compilation of your program. Pragmatic modules can be activated (imported) with use and deactivated with no. These are usually block scoped.

attrs *attributes*
Sets/gets attributes of a subroutine.
use attrs "method" indicates that the invoking subroutine is a method.
use attrs "locked" protects the invoking subroutine against concurrent access.

autouse *mods*
Each of the named modules will not be loaded until one of its functions is called.

base *classes*
Establishes an IS-A relationship with the base classes at compile time.

blib [*dir*] Uses MakeMaker's uninstalled version of a package. *dir* defaults to the current directory.

constant *name* => *value*
Pragma to declare constants.

diagnostics [−verbose]
Forces verbose warning diagnostics and suppress duplicate warnings.

fields *names*
Implements compile-time class fields using pseudo-hashes.

integer Computes arithmetic in integer instead of double precision.

less *what* Requests less of something from the compiler (unimplemented).

lib *names* Adds libraries to @INC, or remove them.

locale Uses and avoids POSIX locales for built-in operations.

ops *operations*
Restricts unsafe operations when compiling.

overload *operator* => *subref*
Packages for overloading Perl operators. *operator* is the operator (as a string), *subref* a reference to the subroutine handling the overloaded operator.
Example: **use overload "+" => \&my_add;**

re *behaviors*
Alters regular expression behavior.
use re "eval" allows zero-width code evaluation assertions (see the section "Regular Expressions").
use re "taint" propagates tainting.

sigtrap *info* Enables simple signal handling.
Example: **use sigtrap qw(SEGV TRAP);**

strict [*constructs*]
Restricts unsafe constructs.
use strict "refs" restricts the use of symbolic references.
use strict "vars" requires all variables to be either my or fully qualified.
use strict "subs" restricts the use of bareword identifiers that are not subroutines.
Without *constructs*, affects all of them.

subs *names*
Predeclares subroutine names, allowing you to use them without parentheses even before they are declared.
Example: **use subs qw(ding dong);**

vars *names* Predeclares variable names, allowing you to use them under the strict pragma.
Example: **use vars qw($foo @bar);**

vmsish [*features*]

Controls VMS-specific language features. VMS only.

use vmsish "exit" enables VMS-style exit codes.

use vmsish "status" allows system commands to deliver VMS-style exit codes to the calling program.

use vmsish "time" makes all times relative to the local time zone. Without *features*, affects all of them.

Arithmetic Functions

abs *expr*†   Returns the absolute value of its operand.

atan2 *y, x*   Returns the arctangent of *y/x* in the range $-\pi$ to π.

cos *expr*†   Returns the cosine of *expr* (expressed in radians).

exp *expr*†   Returns *e* to the power of *expr*.

int *expr*†   Returns the integer portion of *expr*.

log *expr*†   Returns the natural logarithm (base *e*) of *expr*.

rand [*expr*]

Returns a random fractional number between 0 (inclusive) and the value of *expr* (exclusive). If *expr* is omitted, defaults to 1.

sin *expr*†   Returns the sine of *expr* (expressed in radians).

sqrt *expr*†   Returns the square root of *expr*.

srand [*expr*]

Sets the random number seed for the rand operator.

time   Returns the number of non-leap seconds since whatever time the system considers to be the epoch. Suitable for feeding to gmtime and localtime.

Conversion Functions

chr *expr*†

Returns the character represented by the decimal value *expr*.

gmtime [*expr*]

In list context, converts a time as returned by the time function to a 9-element list (0:$sec, 1:$min, 2:$hour, 3:$mday, 4:$mon, 5:$year, 6:$wday, 7:$yday, 8:$isdst) with the time localized for the standard Greenwich time zone.

In scalar context, converts it to print format.

$mon has the range 0 (January) .. 11 (December) and $wday has the range 0 (Sunday) .. 6 (Saturday).

expr defaults to the current time.

hex *expr*†

Returns the decimal value of *expr* interpreted as a hex string.

localtime [*expr*]
> Like gmtime, but with the time localized for the local time zone.

oct *expr*†
> Returns the decimal value of *expr* interpreted as an octal string. If *expr* starts off with 0x, interprets it as a hex string instead.

ord *expr*†
> Returns the ASCII value of the first character of *expr*.

vec *expr, offset, bits*
> Treats string *expr* as a vector of unsigned integers of *bits* bits each, and yields the decimal value of the element at *offset*. *bits* must be a power of 2 between 1 and 32. May be assigned to.

Structure Conversion

pack *template, list*
> Packs the values in *list* into a binary structure using *template*. Returns a string containing the structure.

unpack *template, expr*
> Unpacks the structure *expr* into a list, using *template*.

template is a sequence of characters as follows:

a	/	A	ASCII string, null- / space-padded
b	/	B	Bit string in ascending / descending order
c	/	C	Signed / unsigned char value
f	/	d	Single / double float in native format
h	/	H	Hex string, low / high nybble first
i	/	I	Signed / unsigned integer value
l	/	L	Signed / unsigned long value
n	/	N	Short / long in network (big endian) byte order
s	/	S	Signed / unsigned short value
u	/	p	Uuencoded string / pointer to a string
P			Pointer to a structure (fixed-length string)
v	/	V	Short / long in VAX (little endian) byte order
w			A BER compressed integer
x	/	@	Null byte / null fill until position
X			Back up a byte

Each character may be followed by a decimal number that will be used as a repeat count; an asterisk (*) specifies all remaining arguments. If the format is preceded with %*n*, unpack returns an *n*-bit checksum instead. *n* defaults to 16. Whitespace may be included in the template for readability.

String Functions

chomp *list*†
> Removes line endings from all elements of the list; returns the (total) number of characters removed.

chop *list*†

Chops off the last character on all elements of the list; returns the last chopped character.

crypt *plaintext, salt*

Encrypts a string (irreversibly).

eval *expr*†

expr is parsed and executed as if it were a Perl program. The value returned is the value of the last expression evaluated. If there is a syntax error or runtime error, **undef** is returned by **eval**, and **$@** is set to the error message. See also **eval** in the section "Miscellaneous."

index *str, substr* [, *offset* [, *replacement*]]

Returns the position of *substr* in *str* at or after *offset*. Replaces the found substring by the replacement text if specified. If the substring is not found, returns **-1**.

lc *expr*†   Returns a lowercase version of *expr*.

lcfirst *expr*†

Returns *expr* with its first character in lowercase.

length *expr*†

Returns the length in bytes of *expr*.

quotemeta *expr*†

Returns *expr* with all regular expression metacharacters quoted.

rindex *str, substr* [, *offset*]

Returns the position of the last *substr* in *str* at or before *offset*.

substr *expr, offset* [, *len*]

Extracts a substring of length *len* starting at *offset* out of *expr* and returns it. If *offset* is negative, counts from the end of the string. If *len* is negative, leaves that many characters off the end of the string. May be assigned to.

uc *expr*†

Returns an uppercase version of *expr*.

ucfirst *expr*†

Returns *expr* with its first character in uppercase.

Array and Hash Functions

delete $*hash*{*key*}

delete @*hash*{*key1, key2,* }

Deletes the specified value(s) from the specified hash. Returns the deleted value(s) (unless *hash* is tied to a package that does not support this).

each %*hash*

Returns a 2-element list consisting of the key and value for the next value of the hash. Entries are returned in an apparently random order. After all values of the hash have been returned, an empty list is returned. The next call to **each** after that will start iterating again. A call to **keys** or **values** will reset the iteration.

exists *expr*

> Checks if the specified hash key exists in this hash.

grep *expr, list*

grep *block list*

> Evaluates *expr* or *block* for each element of the *list*, locally setting $_ to refer to the element. Modifying $_ will modify the corresponding element from *list*. In list context, returns the list of elements from *list* for which *expr* returned **true**. In scalar context, returns the number of such elements.

join *expr, list*

> Joins the separate strings of *list* into a single string with fields separated by the value of *expr*, and returns the string.

keys *%hash*

> In list context, returns a list of all the keys of the named hash. In scalar context, returns the number of elements of the hash.

map *expr, list*

map *block list*

> Evaluates *expr* or *block* for each element of the *list*, locally setting $_ to refer to the element. Modifying $_ will modify the corresponding element from *list*. Returns the list of results.

pop [*@array*]

> Pops off and returns the last value of the array. If *@array* is omitted, pops **@ARGV** or **@_** depending on the current lexical scope.

push *@array, list*

> Pushes the values of the *list* onto the end of the array. Returns the new length of the array.

reverse *list*

> In list context, returns the *list* in reverse order. In scalar context, concatenates the list elements and returns the reverse of the resulting string.

scalar *@array*

> Returns the number of elements in the array.

scalar *%hash*

> Returns a **true** value if the hash has elements defined.

shift [*@array*]

> Shifts the first value of the array off and returns it, shortening the array by 1 and moving everything down. If *@array* is omitted, shifts **@ARGV** or **@_** depending on the current lexical scope.

sort [*subroutine*] *list*

> Sorts the *list* and returns the sorted list value. *subroutine*, if specified, must return less than zero, zero, or greater than zero, depending on how the elements of the list (available to the routine as

package global variables **$a** and **$b**) are to be ordered. *subroutine* may be (a variable containing) the name of a user-defined routine, or a *block*.

splice @*array*, *offset* [, *length* [, *list*]]
Removes the elements of @*array* designated by *offset* and *length*, and replaces them with *list* (if specified). Returns the elements removed. If *offset* is negative, counts from the end of the array.

split [*pattern* [, *expr*† [, *limit*]]]
Splits *expr* (a string) into a list of strings, and returns it. If *limit* is specified, splits into at most that number of fields. If *pattern* is omitted, splits at the whitespace (after skipping any leading whitespace). If not in list context, returns the number of fields and splits to @_. See also the section "Search and Replace Functions."

unshift @*array*, *list*
Prepends *list* to the front of the array, and returns the number of elements in the new array.

values %*hash*
Returns a list consisting of all the values of the named hash.

Regular Expressions

Each character matches itself, unless it is one of the special characters + ? . * ^ $ ( ) [ ] { } | \. The special meaning of these characters can be escaped using a \.

.   Matches an arbitrary character, but not a newline unless the s modifier is used (see m//s in section "Search and Replace Functions").

()   Groups a series of pattern elements to a single element.

^   Matches the beginning of the target. In multiline mode (see m//m in section "Search and Replace Functions") also matches after every newline character.

$ Matches the end of the line, or before a final newline character. In multiline mode also matches before every newline character.

         Denotes a class of characters to match. [^] negates the class.

(|)   Matches one of the alternatives.

(?# *text*)
         Comment.

(?: *regex*)
         Like (*regex*) but does not make back-references. Modifiers may be placed between the ? and : (see ? *modifier*, later in this list).

(?= *regex*)
         Zero-width positive look-ahead assertion.

(?! *regex*)
         Zero-width negative look-ahead assertion.

(?< regex)
>	Zero-width positive look-behind assertion.

(?<! regex)
>	Zero-width negative look-behind assertion.

(?{ code })
>	Executes Perl code while matching. Always succeeds with zero width. Requires the **re** "**eval**" pragma.

(?> regex)
>	Anchored subpattern.

(?(cond)ptrue [| *pfalse*])
>	Selects a pattern depending on the condition. *cond* should be the number of a parenthesised subpattern, or one of the zero-width look-ahead, look-behind and evaluate assertions.

(? modifier)
>	Embedded pattern-match modifier. *modifier* can be one or more of i, m, s, or x. Modifiers can be switched off by preceding the letter(s) with a minus sign.

Quantified subpatterns match as many times as possible. When followed with a ? they match the minimum number of times. These are the quantifiers:

+	Matches the preceding pattern element one or more times.

?	Matches zero or one times.

*	Matches zero or more times.

{n,m}	Denotes the minimum *n* and maximum *m* match count. {*n*} means exactly *n* times; {*n*,} means at least *n* times.

A \ escapes any special meaning of the following character if non-alphanumeric, but it turns most alphanumeric characters into something special:

\w	Matches alphanumeric, including _, \W matches non-alphanumeric.

\s	Matches whitespace, \S matches non-whitespace.

\d	Matches digits, \D matches non-digits.

\A	Matches the beginning of the string.

\Z	Matches the end of the string, or before a newline at the end.

\z	Matches the end of the string.

\b	Matches word boundaries, \B matches non-boundaries.

\G	Matches where the previous m//g search left off.

\t, \n, \r, \f, \a, \e, \0*XX*, \x*XX*, \c*X*, \l, \u, \L, \U, \E and \Q
>	have their usual meaning, see "String" in the section "Literal Values."

\w, \W, \s, \S, \d, and \D
>	These may be used within character classes, but \b denotes a backspace in this context.

Back-references:

\1\9   Refer to matched subexpressions, grouped with ( ), inside the match.

\10 and up
        Can also be used if the pattern matches that many subexpressions.

See also $1$9, $+, $&, $`, and $' in the section "Special Variables."

With modifier x, whitespace and comments can be used in the patterns for read-ability purposes.

Search and Replace Functions

If the right hand side of the =~ or !~ is an expression rather than a search pattern, substitution, or transliteration, it is interpreted as a search pattern at runtime.

[*expr* =~] [m] /*pattern*/ [g [c]] [i] [m] [o] [s] [x]
        Searches *expr* (default: $_) for a pattern.
        If you prepend an m you can use almost any pair of delimiters instead of the slashes.
        For =~, its negation !~ may be used, which is true when =~ would return a false result.
        If used in list context, a list is returned consisting of the subexpressions matched by the parentheses in the pattern, i.e., ($1, $2, $3,).
        Optional modifiers: c prepares for continuation; g matches as many times as possible; i searches in a case-insensitive manner; o interpolates variables only once. m treats the string as multiple lines; s treats the string as a single line; x allows for regular expression extensions.
        If *pattern* is empty, the most recent pattern from a previous success-ful match or replacement is used. With g, the match can be used as an iterator in scalar context.

?*pattern*?
        This is just like the /*pattern*/ search, except that it matches only once between calls to the reset operator.

[$*var* =~] s/*pattern*/*newtext*/ [e] [g] [i] [m] [o] [s] [x]
        Searches the string *var* (default $_) for a pattern, and if found, replaces that part with the replacement text. It returns the number of substitutions made, if any; if no substitutions are made, it returns false. Optional modifiers: g replaces all occurrences of the pattern; e evaluates the replacement string as a Perl expression; for the other modifiers, see /*pattern*/ matching. Almost any delimiter may replace the slashes; if single quotes are used, no interpolation is done on strings between the delimiters. Otherwise, strings are interpolated as if in double quotes. If bracketing delimiters are used, *pattern* and *newtext* may have their own delimiters, e.g., s(foo)[bar].
        If *pattern* is empty, the most recent pattern from a previous success-ful match or replacement is used.

[$*var* =~] tr/*searchlist*/*replacementlist*/ [c] [d] [s]
        Transliterates all occurrences of the characters found in the search list into the corresponding character in the replacement list. It

returns the number of characters replaced. y may be used instead of tr. Optional modifiers: c complements the *searchlist*; d deletes all characters found in *searchlist* that do not have a corresponding character in *replacementlist*; s squeezes all sequences of characters that are translated into the same target character into one occurrence of this character.

pos *scalar†*

Returns the position where the last m//g search left off for *scalar*. May be assigned to.

qr/*string*/*modifiers*

Compiles the string as a pattern and returns the compiled pattern as a scalar value.

study $*var†*

Studies the scalar variable $*var* in anticipation of performing many pattern matches on its contents before the variable is next modified.

File Test Operators

These unary operators take one argument, either a filename or a filehandle, and test the associated file to see if something is true about it. If the argument is omitted, they test $_ (except for −t, which tests **STDIN**). If the special argument _ (underscore) is passed, they use the information from the preceding test or stat call.

−r −w −x

File is readable/writable/executable by effective uid/gid.

−R −W −X

File is readable/writable/executable by real uid/gid.

−o −O File is owned by effective/real uid.

−e −z File exists/has zero size.

−s File exists and has non-zero size. Returns the size.

−f −d File is a plain file/a directory.

−l −S −p

File is a symbolic link/a socket/a named pipe (FIFO).

−b −c File is a block/character special file.

−u −g −k

File has setuid/setgid/sticky bit set.

−t Tests if filehandle (**STDIN** by default) is opened to a tty.

−T −B File is a text/non-text (binary) file. −T and −B return true on a null file, or a file at EOF when testing a filehandle.

−M −A −C

File modification/access/inode-change time. Measured in days. Value returned reflects the file age at the time the script started. See also $^T in the section "Special Variables."

File Operations

Functions operating on a list of files return the number of files successfully operated upon.

chmod *list*
> Changes the permissions of a list of files. The first element of the list must be the numerical mode in octal, e.g., 0644.

chown *list*
> Changes the owner and group of a list of files. The first two elements of the list must be the numerical uid and gid. If gid is −1, the group is not changed.

link *oldfile, newfile*
> Creates a new filename linked to the old filename.

lstat *file*   Like stat, but if the last component of the filename is a symbolic link, stats the link instead of the file it links to.

mkdir *dir, perm*
> Creates a directory with given permissions, e.g., 0755.

readlink *expr*†
> Returns the value of a symbolic link.

rename *oldname, newname*
> Changes the name of a file.

rmdir *filename*†
> Deletes the directory if it is empty.

stat *file*   Returns a 13-element list (0:$dev, 1:$ino, 2:$mode, 3:$nlink, 4:$uid, 5:$gid, 6:$rdev, 7:$size, 8:$atime, 9:$mtime, 10:$ctime, 11:$blksize, 12:$blocks). *file* can be a filehandle, an expression evaluating to a filename, or _ to refer to the last file test operation or **stat** call. Returns an empty list if the **stat** fails. Use the standard module **File::stat** for easy access to this information.

symlink *oldfile, newfile*
> Creates a new filename symbolically linked to the old filename.

truncate *file, size*
> Truncates *file* to *size*. *file* may be a filename or a filehandle.

unlink *list*†
> Deletes a list of files.

utime *list*
> Changes the access and modification times. The first two elements of the list must be the numerical access and modification times. The inode change time will be set to the current time.

Input/Output

In input/output operations, *filehandle* may be a filehandle as opened by the open operator, a predefined filehandle (e.g., **STDOUT**) or a scalar variable that evaluates to a reference to or the name of a filehandle to be used.

<filehandle>
> In scalar context, reads a single line from the file opened on *filehandle*. In list context, reads the rest of the file.

< >
> Reads from the input stream formed by the files specified in **@ARGV**, or standard input if no arguments were supplied.

binmode *filehandle*
> Arranges for the file opened on *filehandle* to be read or written in binary mode as opposed to text mode (null operation on Unix or Mac).

close [*filehandle*]
> Closes the file or pipe associated with the filehandle. Resets $.. If *filehandle* is omitted, closes the currently selected filehandle.

dbmclose %*hash*
> Deprecated, use untie instead.

dbmopen %*hash, dbmname, mode*
> Deprecated, use tie instead.

eof *filehandle*
> Returns true if the next read will return end of file, or if the file is not open.

eof
> Returns the EOF status for the last file read.

eof( )
> ·Indicates EOF on the pseudo-file formed of the files listed on the command line.

fcntl *filehandle, function, $var*
> Implements the *fcntl*(2) function. This function has nonstandard return values.

fileno *filehandle*
> Returns the file descriptor for a given (open) filehandle.

flock *filehandle, operation*
> Calls a system-dependent locking routine on the file. *operation* formed by adding 1 (shared), 2 (exclusive), 4 (non-blocking) or 8 (unlock).

getc [*filehandle*]
> Yields the next character from the file, or an empty string on end of file. If *filehandle* is omitted, reads from **STDIN**.

ioctl *filehandle, function, $var*
> Performs *ioctl*(2) on the file. This function has nonstandard return values.

open *filehandle* [, *filename*]

> Opens a file and associates it with *filehandle*. If *filename* is omitted, the scalar variable of the same name as the *filehandle* must contain the filename. The following filename conventions apply when opening a file:

`"file"`

Opens *file* for input. Also `"<file"`.

`">file"`

Opens *file* for output, creating it if necessary.

`">>file"`

Opens *file* in append mode.

`"+<file"`

Opens existing *file* with read/write access.

`"+>file"`

Clobbers old or create new *file* with read/write access.

`"+>>file"`

Read/write access in append mode.

`"|cmd"`

Opens a pipe to command *cmd*; forks if *cmd* is −.

`"cmd|"`

Opens a pipe from command *cmd*; forks if *cmd* is −. *file* may be &*filehnd*, in which case the new filehandle is connected to the (previously opened) filehandle *filehnd*. If it is &=*n*, *file* will be connected to the given file descriptor. open returns undef upon failure, true otherwise.

pipe *readhandle, writehandle*

> Returns a pair of connected pipes.

print [*filehandle*] [*list*†]

> Prints the elements of *list*, converting them to strings if needed. If *filehandle* is omitted, prints by default to standard output (or to the last selected output channel; see select).

printf [*filehandle*] [*list*]

> Equivalent to print *filehandle* sprintf *list*.

read *filehandle*, $*var*, *length* [, *offset*]

> Reads *length* binary bytes from the file into the variable at *offset*. Returns number of bytes actually read, 0 on eof, and undef on failure.

readline *expr*

> Internal function that implements the < > operator. *expr* must be a typeglob.

readpipe *expr*

> Internal function that implements the qx// operator. *expr* is executed as a system command.

seek *filehandle, position, whence*

> Arbitrarily positions the file. Returns true if successful.

select [*filehandle*]
> Returns the currently selected filehandle. Sets the current default filehandle for output operations if *filehandle* is supplied.

select *rbits, wbits, nbits, timeout*
> Performs a *select*(2) system call with the same parameters.

sprintf *format, list*
> Returns a string resulting from formatting a (possibly empty) list of values. See the section "Formatted Printing" for a complete list of format conversions. See the section "Formats" for an alternative way to obtain formatted output.

sysopen *filehandle, path, mode* [, *perms*]
> Performs an *open*(2) system call. The possible values and flag bits of *mode* are system-dependent; they are available via the standard module **Fcntl**.

sysread *filehandle, $var, length* [, *offset*]
> Reads *length* bytes into $*var* at *offset*. Returns number of bytes actually read, 0 on **eof**, and **undef** on failure.

sysseek *filehandle, position, whence*
> Arbitrarily positions the file for use with sysread and syswrite. See the Perl documentation for details on the nonstandard return values of this function.

syswrite *filehandle, scalar, length* [, *offset*]
> Writes *length* bytes from *scalar* at *offset*.

tell [*filehandle*]
> Returns the current file position for the file. If *filehandle* is omitted, assumes the file last read.

Formatted Printing

printf and sprintf format a list of values according to a format string that may use the following conversions:

%%
: A percent sign.

%c
: The character corresponding to the ordinal value.

%d
: A signed integer.

%e
: A floating-point number (scientific notation).

%f
: A floating-point number (fixed decimal notation).

%g
: A floating-point number (%e or %f notation).

%i
: A synonym for %d.

%n
: The number of characters formatted so far is *stored* into the corresponding variable in the parameter list.

%o
: An unsigned integer, in octal.

%p	A pointer (address in hexadecimal).
%s	A string.
%u	An unsigned integer (decimal).
%x	An unsigned integer (hexadecimal).
%D	An obsolete synonym for %ld.
%E	Like %e, but using an uppercase "E".
%F	An obsolete synonym for %f.
%G	Like %g, but with an uppercase "E" (if applicable).
%O	An obsolete synonym for %lo.
%U	An obsolete synonym for %lu.
%X	Like %x, but using uppercase letters.

The following flags can be put between the % and the conversion letter:

space	Prefix a positive number with a space.
+	Prefix a positive number with a plus sign.
−	Left-justify within the field.
0	Use zeroes instead of spaces to right-justify.
#	Prefix a non-zero octal number with "0", and a non-zero hex number with "0x".
number	Minimum field width.

.number
    For a floating-point number: the number of digits after the decimal point.
    For a string: the maximum length.
    For an integer: the minimum width.

l	Interpret integer as "long" or "unsigned long" according to the C type.
h	Interpret integer as "short" or "unsigned short" according to the C type.
V	Interpret integer according to Perl's type.

An asterisk (*) may be used instead of a number; the value of the next item in the list will be used.

See the section "Formats" for an alternative way to obtain formatted output.

Formats

formline *picture, list*
    Formats *list* according to *picture* and accumulates the result into $^A.

write [*filehandle*]

> Writes a formatted record to the specified file, using the format associated with that file. If *filehandle* is omitted, the currently selected one is taken.

Formats are defined as follows:

```
format [ name ] =
formlist
    .
```

formlist is a sequence of lines, each of which is either a comment line (# in the first column), a picture line, or an argument line. A picture line contains the arguments which will give values to the fields in the lines. Other text is output as given. Argument lines contain lists of values that are output in the format and order of the preceding picture line. *name* defaults to **STDOUT** if omitted.

Picture fields are:

@<<<	Left-adjusted field. Repeat the < to denote the desired width.
@>>>	Right-adjusted field.
@| | |	Centered field.
@#.##	Numeric format with implied decimal point.
@*	Multiline field.

Use ^ instead of @ for multiline block filling.

Use ~ in a picture line to suppress unwanted empty lines.

Use ~~ in a picture line to have this format line repeated until all fields are exhausted.

Set **$-** to zero to force a page break on the next write.

See also **$^**, **$~**, **$^A**, **$^F**, **$-**, and **$=** in the section "Special Variables."

Tying Variables

tie *var*, *classname*, [*list*]

> Ties a variable to a package class that will handle it. *list* is passed to the class constructor.

tied *var* Returns a reference to the object underlying *var*, or **undef** if *var* is not tied to a package class.

untie *var*

> Breaks the binding between the variable and the package class.

A class implementing a tied scalar should define the methods **TIESCALAR**, **FETCH**, **STORE**, and possibly **DESTROY**.

A class implementing a tied ordinary array should define the methods **TIEARRAY**, **FETCH**, **STORE**, **FETCHSIZE**, **STORESIZE**, and perhaps **DESTROY**.

A class implementing a tied hash should define the methods **TIEHASH**, **FETCH**, **STORE**, **EXISTS**, **DELETE CLEAR**, **FIRSTKEY**, **NEXTKEY**, and optionally **DESTROY**.

A class implementing a tied filehandle should define the methods **TIEHANDLE**, at least one of **PRINT, PRINTF, WRITE, READLINE, GETC, READ**, and possibly **CLOSE** and **DESTROY**.

Several base classes to implement tied variables are available in the standard modules library.

Directory Reading Routines

closedir *dirhandle*
> Closes a directory opened by opendir.

opendir *dirhandle, dirname*
> Opens a directory on the handle specified.

readdir *dirhandle*
> In scalar context, returns the next entry from the directory or undef if none remains. In list context, returns a list of all remaining entries from the directory.

rewinddir *dirhandle*
> Positions the directory to the beginning.

seekdir *dirhandle, pos*
> Sets position for readdir on the directory. *pos* should be a file offset as returned by telldir.

telldir *dirhandle*
> Returns the position in the directory.

System Interaction

alarm *expr*
> Schedules a **SIGALRM** to be delivered after *expr* seconds. If *expr* is 0, cancels a pending timer.

chdir [*expr*]
> Changes the working directory. Uses $ENV{HOME} or $ENV{LOG-NAME} if *expr* is omitted.

chroot *filename*†
> Changes the root directory for the process and its children.

die [*list*]
> Prints the value of *list* to **STDERR** and exits with the current value of $! (errno). If $! is 0, exits with the value of ($? >> 8). If ($? >> 8) is 0, exits with 255. *list* defaults to "Died". Inside an eval, the error message is stuffed into $@, and the eval is terminated and returns undef; this makes die the way to raise an exception.

exec [*program*] *list*
> Executes the system command in *list*; does not return. *program* can be used to designate the program to execute *command*.

exit [*expr*]

Exits immediately with the value of *expr,* which defaults to 0 (zero). Calls **END** routines and object destructors before exiting.

fork   Does a *fork*(2) system call. Returns the process ID of the child to the parent process (or **undef** on failure) and zero to the child process.

getlogin   Returns the current login name as known by the system. If it returns false, use **getpwuid**.

getpgrp [*pid*]

Returns the process group for process *pid* (0, or omitted, means the current process).

getppid   Returns the process ID of the parent process.

getpriority *which, who*

Returns the current priority for a process, process group, or user. Use **getpriority 0,0** to designate the current process.

glob *pat*   Returns a list of filenames that match the shell pattern *pat.*

kill *list*   Sends a signal to a list of processes. The first element of the list must be the signal to send (either numeric, or its name as a string). Negative signals kill process groups instead of processes.

setpgrp *pid, pgrp*

Sets the process group for the *pid* (0 means the current process).

setpriority *which, who, priority*

Sets the current priority for a process, process group, or a user.

sleep [*expr*]

Causes the program to sleep for *expr* seconds, or forever if no *expr.* Returns the number of seconds actually slept.

syscall *list*

Calls the system call specified in the first element of the list, passing the rest of the list as arguments to the call. Returns −1 on error.

system [*program*] *list*

Does exactly the same thing as **exec** *list* except that a fork is performed first, and the parent process waits for the child process to complete. During the wait, the signals **SIGINT** and **SIGQUIT** are passed to the child process. Returns the exit status of the child process. 0 indicates success, not failure. *program* can be used to designate the program to execute *command.*

times   Returns a 4-element list (0:$user, 1:$system, 2:$cuser, 3:$csystem) giving the user and system times, in seconds, for this process and the children of this process.

umask [*expr*]

Sets the umask for the process and returns the old one. If *expr* is omitted, returns current umask value.

wait   Waits for a child process to terminate and returns the process ID of the deceased process (−1 if none). The status is returned in $?.

waitpid *pid, flags*
> Performs the same function as the corresponding system call. Returns 1 when process *pid* is dead, −1 if nonexistent.

warn [*list*]
> Prints *list* on **STDERR** like die, but doesn't exit. *list* defaults to **"Warning: something's wrong"**.

Networking

accept *newsocket, genericsocket*
> Accepts a new socket.

bind *socket, name*
> Binds the *name* to the *socket*.

connect *socket, name*
> Connects the *name* to the *socket*.

getpeername *socket*
> Returns the socket address of the other end of the *socket*.

getsockname *socket*
> Returns the name of the socket.

getsockopt *socket, level, optname*
> Returns the socket options.

listen *socket, queuesize*
> Starts listening on the specified *socket*, allowing *queuesize* connections.

recv *socket, $var, length, flags*
> Receives a message on *socket* of *length* bytes into scalar variable $*var*.

send *socket, msg, flags* [, *to*]
> Sends a message on the *socket*.

setsockopt *socket, level, optname, optval*
> Sets the requested socket option.

shutdown *socket, how*
> Shuts down a *socket*.

socket *socket, domain, type, protocol*
> Creates a *socket* in *domain* with *type* and *protocol*.

socketpair *socket1, socket2, domain, type, protocol*
> Works the same as socket, but creates a pair of bidirectional sockets.

System V IPC

Depending on your system configuration, certain system files need to be required to access the message- and semaphore-specific operation names.

msgctl *id, cmd, args*

> Calls *msgctl*(2). If *cmd* is **&IPC_STAT** then *args* must be a variable. See the Perl documentation for details on the nonstandard return values of this function.

msgget *key, flags*

> Creates a message queue for *key*. Returns the message queue identifier.

msgrcv *id, $var, size, type, flags*

> Receives a message from queue *id* into $*var*.

msgsnd *id, msg, flags*

> Sends *msg* to queue *id*.

semctl *id, semnum, cmd, arg*

> Calls *semctl*(2). If *cmd* is **&IPC_STAT** or **&GETALL** then *arg* must be a variable.

semget *key, nsems, size, flags*

> Creates a set of semaphores for *key*. Returns the message semaphore identifier.

semop *key, ...*

> Performs semaphore operations.

shmctl *id, cmd, arg*

> Calls *shmctl*(2). If *cmd* is **&IPC_STAT** then *arg* must be a scalar variable.

shmget *key, size, flags*

> Creates shared memory. Returns the shared memory segment identifier.

shmread *id, $var, pos, size*

> Reads at most *size* bytes of the contents of shared memory segment *id* starting at offset *pos* into $*var*.

shmwrite *id, string, pos, size*

> Writes at most *size* bytes of *string* into the contents of shared memory segment *id* at offset *pos*.

Miscellaneous

defined *expr*

> Tests whether the *expr* has an actual value.

do *filename*

> Executes *filename* as a Perl script. See also **require** in the section "Subroutines, Packages, and Modules."

dump [*label*]

> Immediate core dump. When reincarnated, starts at *label*. Obsolete.

eval { *expr,* }

> Executes the code between { and }. Traps runtime errors and returns as described with **eval**(*expr*), in the section "String Functions."

local *variable*
> Gives a temporary value to the named package variable, which lasts until the enclosing block, file, or eval exits.

my *variable*
> Creates a scope for the variable lexically local to the enclosing block, file, or eval.

ref *expr†*
> Returns a true value if *expr* is a reference. Returns the package name if *expr* has been blessed into a package.

reset [*expr*]
> *expr* is a string of single letters. All variables beginning with one of those letters are reset to their pristine state. If *expr* is omitted, resets ?? searches so that they work again. Only affects the current package.

undef *lvalue†*
> Undefines the *lvalue*. Always returns the undefined value.

Information from System Databases

Information About Users

In scalar context, each of these routines returns a 10-element list: (0:$name, 1:$passwd, 2:$uid, 3:$gid, 4:$quota, 5:$comment, 6:$gcos, 7:$dir, 8:$shell, 9:$expire). Use the standard module **User::pwent** for easy access to this information.

endpwent
> Ends lookup processing.

getpwent
> Gets next user information. In scalar context, returns the username.

getpwnam *name*
> Gets information by name. In scalar context, returns the user ID.

getpwuid *uid*
> Gets information by user ID. In scalar context, returns the username.

setpwent
> Resets lookup processing.

Information About Groups

In list context, each of these routines returns a 4-element list: (0:$name, 1:$passwd, 2:$gid, 3:$members). $members contains a space-separated list of the login names of the group members. Use the standard module **User::grent** for easy access to this information.

endgrent Ends lookup processing.

getgrent Gets next group information. In scalar context, returns the group
name.

getgrgid *gid*
Gets information by group ID. In scalar context, returns the group
name.

getgrnam *name*
Gets information by name. In scalar context, returns the group ID.

setgrent Resets lookup processing.

Information About Networks

In list context, each of these routines returns a 4-element list: (0:$name, 1:$aliases,
2:$addrtype, 3:$net). Use the standard module **Net::netent** for easy access to this
information.

endnetent
Ends lookup processing.

getnetbyaddr *addr, type*
Gets information by address and type. In scalar context, returns the
network name.

getnetbyname *name*
Gets information by network name. In scalar context, returns the
network number.

getnetent
Gets next network information. In scalar context, returns the network name.

setnetent *stayopen*
Resets lookup processing.

Information About Network Hosts

In list context, each of these routines returns a list of at least 5 elements: (0:$name,
1:$aliases, 2:$addrtype, 3:$length, 4:$addr [, more addresses]). Use the standard
module **Net::hostent** for easy access to this information.

endhostent
Ends lookup processing.

gethostbyaddr *addr, addrtype*
Gets information by IP address. In scalar context, returns the hostname.

gethostbyname *name*
Gets information by hostname. In scalar context, returns the host
address.

gethostent
Gets next host information. In scalar context, returns the hostname.

sethostent *stayopen*
> Resets lookup processing.

Information About Network Services

In list context, each of these routines returns a 4-element list: (0:$name, 1:$aliases, 2:$port, 3:$proto). Use the standard module **Net::servent** for easy access to this information.

endservent
> Ends lookup processing.

getservbyname *name, proto*
> Gets information by service name. In scalar context, returns the port number.

getservbyport *port, proto*
> Gets information by service port. In scalar context, returns the service name.

getservent
> Gets next service information. In scalar context, returns the service name.

setservent *stayopen*
> Resets lookup processing.

Information About Network Protocols

In list context, each of these routines returns a 3-element list: (0:$name, 1:$aliases, 2:$proto). Use the standard module **Net::protoent** for easy access to this information.

endprotoent
> Ends lookup processing.

getprotobyname *name*
> Gets information by protocol name. In scalar context, returns the protocol number.

getprotobynumber *number*
> Gets information by protocol number. In scalar context, returns the protocol name.

getprotoent
> Gets next protocol information. In scalar context, returns the protocol name.

setprotoent *stayopen*
> Resets lookup processing.

Special Variables

The alternative names are provided by the standard module **English**.

The following variables are global and should be localized in subroutines:

$_	The default input, output, and pattern-searching space.
$.	The current input line number of the last filehandle read.
$/	The input record separator, newline by default. May be multicharacter.
$,	The output field separator for the print function.
$ "	The separator that joins elements of arrays interpolated in strings.
$\	The output record separator for the print function.
$#	The output format for printed numbers. Deprecated. Use printf instead.
$*	Set to 1 to do multiline matching within strings. Deprecated; see the m and s modifiers in the section "Search and Replace Functions."
$?	The status returned by the last ` ` command, pipe close, wait, waitpid, or system function.
$]	The Perl version number, e.g., 5.005.
$[	The index of the first element in an array or list, and of the first character in a substring. Default is 0. Deprecated. Do not use.
$;	The subscript separator for multidimensional list emulation. Default is "\034".
$!	Used in a numeric context, yields the current value of **errno**. Used in a string context, yields the corresponding error string.
$@	The Perl error message from the last **eval** or do *expr* command.
$:	The set of characters after which a string may be broken to fill continuation fields (starting with ^) in a format.
$0	The name of the file containing the Perl script being executed. May be assigned to.
$$	The process ID of the Perl interpreter running this script. Altered (in the child process) by fork.
$<	The real user ID of this process.
$>	The effective user ID of this process.
$(	The real group ID, or space-separated list of group IDs, of this process.
$)	The effective group ID, or space-separated list of group IDs, of this process.
$^A	The accumulator for formline and write operations.
$^D	The debug flags as passed to Perl using −D.

$^E	Operating system dependent error information.
$^F	The highest system file descriptor, ordinarily 2.
$^H	The current state of syntax checks.
$^I	In-place edit extension as passed to Perl using −i.
$^L	Formfeed character used in formats.
$^M	Emergency memory pool.
$^O	Operating system name.
$^P	Internal debugging flag.
$^S	Current state of the Perl interpreter.
$^T	The time (as delivered by time) when the program started. This value is used by the file test operators −M, −A, and −C.
$^W	The value of the −w option as passed to Perl.
$^X	The name by which this Perl interpreter was invoked.

The following variables are context dependent and need not be localized:

$%	The current page number of the currently selected output channel.
$=	The page length of the current output channel. Default is 60 lines.
$-	The number of lines remaining on the page.
$~	The name of the current report format.
$^	The name of the current top-of-page format.
$|	If set to nonzero, forces a flush after every write or print on the currently selected output channel. Default is 0.
$ARGV	The name of the current file when reading from < >.

The following variables are always local to the current block:

$&	The string matched by the last successful pattern match.
$`	The string preceding what was matched by the last successful match.
$'	The string following what was matched by the last successful match.
$+	The last bracket matched by the last search pattern.
$1$9	Contain the subpatterns from the corresponding sets of parentheses in the last pattern successfully matched. $10 and up are only available if the match contained that many subpatterns.

Special Arrays

The alternative names are provided by the standard module **English**.

@ARGV	Contains the command-line arguments for the script (not including the command name, which is in $0).
@EXPORT	
	Names the methods and other symbols a package exports by default.

@EXPORT_OK
> Names the methods and other symbols a package can export upon explicit request.

@F
> When command-line option −a is used, contains the split of the input lines.

@INC
> Contains the list of places to look for Perl scripts to be evaluated by the do *filename*, use and require commands. Do not modify directly, but use the **use lib** pragma or −I command-line option instead.

@ISA
> List of base classes of the current package.

@_
> Parameter array for subroutines. Also used by split if not in list context.

Special Hashes

%ENV
> Contains the current environment. The key is the name of an environment variable; the value is its current setting.

%EXPORT_TAGS
> Defines names for sets of symbols.

%INC
> List of files that have been included with use, require, or do. The key is the filename as specified; the value the location of the file.

%SIG
> Used to set signal handlers for various signals. The key is the name of the signal (without the **SIG** prefix); the value a subroutine that is executed when the signal occurs. __WARN__ and __DIE__ are pseudo-signals to attach handlers to Perl warnings and exceptions.

Standard Modules

AnyDBM_File
> Provides a framework for multiple dbm files.

AutoLoader
> Loads functions only on demand.

AutoSplit
> Splits a package for autoloading.

B
> Experimental package that implements byte compilation, a Perl to C translator, and other interesting things.

Benchmark
> Benchmarks running times of code.

Bundle::CPAN
> A bundle to play with all the other modules on CPAN.

Carp
> Warns of errors.

CGI
> Simple Common Gateway Interface Class.

CGI::Apache
>CGI addition for Apache's Perl API.

CGI::Cookie
>Interface to Netscape Cookies.

CGI:Fast
>CGI interface for FastCGI.

CGI:Push
>Simple interface to Server Push.

Class::Struct
>Declares struct-like datatypes as Perl classes.

Config   Accesses Perl configuration information.

CPAN   Maintenance of Perl modules from CPAN sites.

Cwd   Gets the pathname of the current working directory.

Data::Dumper
>Reveals Perl data structures as strings.

DB_File   Access to Berkeley DB files.

Devel::SelfStubber
>Generates stubs for a SelfLoading module.

Dirhandle
>Supplies object methods for directory handles.

DynaLoader
>Dynamically loads C libraries into Perl code.

English   Uses nice English names for ugly punctuation variables.

Env   Imports environment variables.

Exporter
>Implements default import method for modules.

ExtUtils::Command
>Replacements for common Unix commands (for Makefiles).

ExtUtils::Embed
>Utilities for embedding Perl in C/C++ applications.

ExtUtils::Install
>Installs files from here to there.

ExtUtils::Installed
>Inventory management of installed modules.

ExtUtils::Liblist
>Determines libraries to use and how to use them.

ExtUtils::MakeMaker
>Creates an extension Makefile.

ExtUtils::Manifest
>Utilities to write and check a MANIFEST file.

ExtUtils::Miniperl
> Writes the C code for **perlmain.c**.

ExtUtils::Mkbootstrap
> Makes a bootstrap file for use by DynaLoader.

ExtUtils::Mksymlists
> Writes linker options files for dynamic extension.

ExtUtils::MM_OS2
> Methods to override Unix behavior in ExtUtils::MakeMaker.

ExtUtils::MM_Unix
> Methods used by ExtUtils::MakeMaker.

ExtUtils::MM_VMS
> Methods to override Unix behavior in ExtUtils::MakeMaker.

ExtUtils::MM_Win32
> Methods to override Unix behavior in ExtUtils::MakeMaker.

ExtUtils::Packlist
> Manages *.packlist* files.

ExtUtils::testlib
> Adds **blib** directories to @INC.

Fatal Replaces functions with equivalents that succeed or die.

Fcntl Loads the C **fcntl.h** defines.

File::Basename
> Parses file specifications.

File::CheckTree
> Runs many filetest checks on a tree.

File::Copy
> Copies files or filehandles.

File::DosGlob
> DOS-like globbing (with extensions).

File::Find
> Traverses a file tree.

File::Path
> Creates or remove a series of directories.

File::Spec
> Portably performs operations on filenames.

File::Spec::Mac
> Methods for MacOS file specs.

File::Spec::OS2
> Methods for OS/2 file specs.

File::Spec::Unix
> Methods used by File::Spec for Unix.

File::Spec::VMS

  Methods for VMS file specs.

File::Spec::Win32

  Methods for Win32 file specs.

File::stat

  By name interface to Perl's built-in stat functions.

FileCache

  Keeps more files open than the system permits.

FileHandle

  Supplies object methods for filehandles.

FindBin Locates directory of original Perl script.

GDBM_File

  Access to the gdbm library.

Getopt::Long

  Extended handling of command-line options. Suits all needs.

Getopt::Std

  Processes single-character switches with switch clustering.

I18N::Collate

  Compares 8-bit scalar data according to the current locale.

IO Loads various I/O modules.

IO::File Supplies object methods for filehandles.

IO::Handle

  Supplies object methods for I/O handles.

IO::Pipe Supplies object methods for pipes.

IO::Seekable

  Supplies seek-based methods for I/O objects.

IO::Select

  Object interface to the select system call.

IO::Socket

  Object interface to socket communications.

IPC::Msg

  Interface to System V Message IPC.

IPC::Open2

  Open a pipe to a process for both reading and writing.

IPC::Open3

  Open a pipe to a process for reading, writing, and error handling.

IPC::Semaphore

  Interface to System V semaphores.

IPC::SysV

  System V IPC object class.

Math::BigFloat
> Arbitrary length float math package.

Math::BigInt
> Arbitrary size integer math package.

Math::Complex
> Complex numbers and associated mathematical functions.

NDBM_File
> tied access to ndbm files.

Net::hostent
> Access by name to gethostent and friends.

Net::netent
> Access by name to getnetent and friends.

Net::Ping
> Checks whether a host is up.

Net::protoent
> Access by name to getprotoent and friends.

Net::servent
> Access by name to getservent and friends.

O   Experimental compiler backend.

Opcode Disables named opcodes when compiling Perl code.

OS2::ExtAttr
> Perl access to extended attributes. OS/2 only.

OS2::PrfDB
> Perl extension to access the OS/2 setting database. OS/2 only.

OS2::Process
> Constants for system() call on OS/2. OS/2 only.

OS2::REXX
> Access to DLLs with REXX calling convention and REXX runtime. OS/2 only.

Pod::Html
> Module to convert POD files to HTML.

Pod::Text
> Converts POD data to formatted ASCII text.

POSIX   Interface to IEEE Std 1003.1.

Safe   Compiles and executes code in restricted compartments.

SDBM_File
> tied access to sdbm files.

Search::Dict
> Searches for key in dictionary file.

SelectSaver
> Saves and restores a selected filehandle.

SelfLoader

Loads functions only on demand.

Shell Runs shell commands transparently within Perl.

Socket Loads the C **socket.h** defines and structure manipulators.

Symbol Manipulates Perl symbols and their names.

Sys::Hostname

Tries every conceivable way to get the name of this system.

Sys::Syslog

Interface to the Unix *syslog*(3) calls.

Term::Cap

Perl interface to Unix *termcap*(3).

Term::Complete

Word completion module.

Term::ReadLine

Interface to various readline packages.

Test::Harness

Runs Perl standard test scripts with statistics.

Text::Abbrev

Creates an abbreviation table from a list.

Text::ParseWords

Parses text into a list of tokens.

Text::Soundex

Implementation of the Soundex Algorithm as described by Donald Knuth.

Text::Tabs

Expands and unexpands tabs.

Text::Wrap

Line wrapping to form simple paragraphs.

Thread Implementation of Perl Threads.

Thread::Queue

Implementation of Thread-safe queues.

Thread::Semaphore

Implementation of Thread-safe semaphores.

Thread::Signal

Implementation of reliable signals using Threads.

Thread::Specific

Thread-specific keys.

Tie::Arrays

Base class definitions for tied arrays.

Tie::Handle

Base class definitions for tied filehandles.

Tie::Hash

Base class definitions for tied hashes.

Tie::RefHash

Use references as hash keys.

Tie::Scalar

Base class definitions for tied scalars.

Tie::StdHash

Basic methods for tied hashes.

Tie::StdScalar

Basic methods for tied scalars.

Tie::SubstrHash

Fixed table-size, fixed key-length hashing.

Time::Local

Efficiently computes time from local and GMT time.

UNIVERSAL

Base class for all classes (blessed references).

User::grent

Access by name to getgrent and friends.

User::pwent

Access by name to getpwent and friends.

VMS::DCLsym

Perl extension to manipulate DCL symbols. VMS only.

VMS::Filespec

Converts between VMS and Unix file specification syntax. VMS only.

VMS::Stdio

Standard I/O functions via VMS extensions. VMS only.

VMS::XSSymSet

Keeps sets of symbol names palatable to the VMS linker.

Environment Variables

Perl uses the following environment variables:

HOME   Used if chdir has no argument.

LOGDIR

Used if chdir has no argument and **HOME** is not set.

PATH   Used in executing subprocesses, and in finding the Perl script if −S is used.

PERL5LIB

A colon-separated list of directories to look in for Perl library files before looking in the standard library and the current directory.

PERL5DB

> The command to get the debugger code. Defaults to **BEGIN { require 'perl5db.pl' }**.

PERLLIB

> Used instead of **PERL5LIB** if the latter is not defined.

Multithreading

Multithreading is an experimental feature in this release. Support for Multithreading needs to be built into the Perl executable.

Multithreading requires the standard module **Thread**. This module implements the join, detach, and yield methods discussed here:

$*thr* -> detach

> Detach a thread so it runs independently.

[$*result* =] $*thr* -> join

> Wait for the thread to complete. The value returned is the return value from the thread's subroutine.

lock *variable*

> Lock a resource against concurrent access.

$*tHR* = new **thread** *sub* [*args*]

> Creates a new thread that starts executing in the referenced subroutine. The *args* are passed to this subroutine. The return value of this subroutine is delivered by the join method.

yield   Explicitly give up the CPU to some other Thread.

The Perl Compiler

The Perl Compiler is an experimental feature in this release.

To compile a Perl program **foo.pl** with the C backend:

> **perl −MO=C,−ofoo.c foo.pl**

To compile **foo.pl** with the CC backend:

> **perl −MO=CC,−ofoo.c foo.pl**

Walk the opcode tree in execution order, printing terse information about each opcode:

> **perl −MO=Terse,exec foo.pl**

Walk the opcode tree in syntax order, printing lengthier debug information about each opcode:

> **perl −MO=Debug foo.pl**

You can also append ",**exec**" to walk in execution order.

Produce a cross-reference report of the line numbers at which all variables, subroutines, and formats are defined and used:

> **perl −MO=Xref foo.pl**

The Perl Debugger

The Perl symbolic debugger is invoked with **perl −d**.

a [*line*] *command*
> Sets an action for *line*.

A   Deletes all line actions.

b [*line* [*condition*]]
> Sets breakpoint at *line*; default is the current line.

b *sub* [*condition*]
> Sets breakpoint at the named subroutine.

b compile *subname*
> Stop after the subroutine is compiled.

b load *file*
> Sets breakpoint at requireing the given file.

b postpone *subname* [*condition*]
> Sets breakpoint at the first line of the subroutine after it is compiled.

c [*line*]
> Continues (until *line*, or another breakpoint, or exit).

d [*line*]
> Deletes breakpoint at the given *line*; default is the current line.

D   Deletes all breakpoints.

f *file*   Switches to *file* and starts listing it.

h   Prints out a long help message.

h *cmd*   Prints out help for the command *cmd*.

h h   Prints out a concise help message.

H [−*number*]
> Displays the last −*number* commands.

l [*range*]
> Lists a range of lines. *range* may be a number, start−end, start+amount, or a subroutine name. If *range* is omitted, lists next window.

l *sub*   Lists the named subroutine.

L   Lists lines that have breakpoints or actions.

m *class* Prints the methods callable via the given *class*.

m *expr*   Evaluates the expression in list context, prints the methods callable on the first element of the result.

n [*expr*]
> Single steps around the subroutine call.

O [*opt* [= *val*]]
> Sets or queries values of debugger options.

p *expr*   Prints *expr*.

q   Quits. You may also use your character.

r   Returns from the current subroutine.

R   Restarts the debugger.

s [*expr*]
> Single steps.

S [!] *pattern*
> Lists the names of all subroutines [not] matching the pattern.

t   Toggles trace mode.

t *expr*   Traces through execution of *expr*.

T   Prints a stack trace.

V [*package* [*pattern*]]
> Lists variables matching *pattern* in a *package*. Default package is **main**.

w [*line*]
> Lists window around the specified line.

W   Deletes all watch-expressions.

W *expr* Adds a global watch-expression.

x *expr* Evaluates *expr* in list context, dumps the result.

X [*pattern*]
> Like **V**, but assumes current package.

command
> Executes *command* as a Perl statement.

.
> Returns to the executed line.

−
> Lists previous window.

= [*alias value*]
> Sets alias, or lists current aliases.

/pattern/
> Searches forward for *pattern*.

?pattern?
> Searches backward for *pattern*.

< *command*
> Sets an action to be executed before every debugger prompt.

<< *command*
> Adds an action to the list of actions to be executed before every debugger prompt.

> *command*
> Sets an action to be executed after every debugger prompt.

>> *command*
> Adds an action to the list of actions to be executed after every debugger prompt.

{ *cmd*   Defines a debugger command to run before each prompt.

{{ *cmd*   Adds a debugger command to the list of debugger commands to run before each prompt.

! [[-] *number* **]**
    Re-executes a command. Default is the previous command.

! [*pattern* **]**
    Re-executes the last command that started with *pattern*.

!! [*command* **]**
    Runs *command* in a subprocess.

| *cmd*   Run debugger command *cmd* through the current pager.

|| *cmd*   Same, temporarily selects **DB::OUT** as well.

    Repeats last **s** or **n**.

CHAPTER 15

System and
Network Administration Overview

Common Commands

Following are tables of commonly used system administration commands.

Archiving

cpio   Create and unpack file archives.
tar   Copy files to or restore files from an archive medium.

Clocks

hwclock   Manage hardware clock.
netdate   Set clock according to *host*'s clock.
rdate   Manage time server.
zdump   Print list of time zones.
zic   Create time conversion information files.

Daemons

bootpd   Internet Boot Protocol daemon.
fingerd   Finger daemon.
ftpd   File Transfer Protocol daemon.
identd   Identify user running TCP/IP process.
imapd   IMAP protocol mailbox server daemon.
inetd   Internet services daemon.
kerneld   Provides automatic kernel module loading.

438

klogd	Manage syslogd.
lpd	Printer daemon.
mountd	NFS mount request server.
named	Internet domain name server.
nfsd	NFS daemon.
pop2d	POP server.
pop3d	POP server.
powerd	Monitor UPS connection.
pppd	Maintain point-to-point protocol (PPP) network connections.
rdistd	Remote file distribution server.
rexecd	Remote execution server.
rlogind	rlogin server.
routed	Routing daemon.
rwhod	Remote who server.
syslogd	System logging daemon.
tcpd	TCP network daemon.
tftpd	Trivial file transfer protocol daemon.
update	Buffer flush daemon.
ypbind	NIS binder process.
yppasswdd	NIS password modification server.
ypserv	NIS server process.

Hardware

arp	Manage the ARP cache.
cfdisk	Maintain disk partitions.
fdisk	Maintain disk partitions.
kbdrate	Manage the keyboard's repeat rate.
ramsize	Print information about RAM disk.
setserial	Set serial port information.
slattach	Attach serial lines as network interfaces.

Host Information

dnsdomainname	Print DNS domain name.
domainname	Print NIS domain name.
host	Print host and zone information.
nslookup	Query Internet domain name servers.

Installation

cpio	Copy file archives.
install	Copy files into locations that provide user access to them.
rdist	Distribute files to remote systems.
tar	Copy files to or restore files from an archive medium.

Mail

makemap	Update **sendmail**'s database maps.
fetchmail	Retrieve mail from remote servers.
rmail	Handle **uucp** mail.
sendmail	Send and receive mail.

Managing the Kernel

insmod	Install new kernel module.
lsmod	List kernel modules.
modprobe	Load new module and its dependent modules.
rmmod	Remove module.

Managing Filesystems

To Unix systems, a *filesystem* is some device (such as a hard drive, floppy, or CD-ROM) that is formatted to store files. Filesystems can be found on hard drives, floppies, CD-ROMs, or other storage media that permit random access.

The exact format and means by which the files are stored are not important; the system provides a common interface for all *filesystem types* that it recognizes. Under Linux, filesystem types include the Second Extended Filesystem, or *ext2fs*, which you probably use to store Linux files. The second extended filesystem was developed primarily for Linux and supports 256-character filenames, 4-terabyte maximum filesystem size, and other useful features. (It is "second" because it is the successor to the extended filesystem type.) Other common filesystem types include the MS-DOS filesystem, which allows files on MS-DOS partitions and floppies to be accessed under Linux, and the ISO 9660 filesystem used by CD-ROMs.

debugfs	Debug **extfs** filesystem.
dumpe2fs	Print super block/blocks group information.
e2fsck	Check and repair a second extended filesystem.
fsck	Check and repair filesystem.
fsck.minix	Check and repair a MINIX filesystem.
fuser	List processes using a filesystem.
mkfs	Make new filesystem.
mkfs.ext2	Make new second extended filesystem.
mkfs.minix	Make new MINIX filesystem.
mklost+found	Make *lost+found* directory.
mkswap	Designate swap space.
mount	Mount a filesystem.
rdev	Describe or change values for root filesystem.
rootflags	List or set flags to use in mounting root filesystem.
showmount	List exported directories.
swapdev	Display or set swap device information.
swapon	Begin using device for swapping.
swapoff	Cease using device for swapping.

sync	Write filesystem buffers to disk.
tune2fs	Manage second extended filesystem.
umount	Unmount a filesystem.

Miscellaneous

cron	Schedule commands for specific times.
dmesg	Print bootup messages after the system is up.
install	Copy files and set their permissions.
ldconfig	Update library links and do caching.
logger	Send messages to the system logger.
login	Sign onto system.
logrotate	Compress and rotate system logs.
rdist	Transfer files between machines.
rstat	Display *host*'s system status.
run-parts	Run all scripts in *directory*.
script	Create typescript of terminal session.

Networking

dip	Establish dial-up IP connections.
gated	Manage routing tables between networks.
ifconfig	Manage network interfaces.
ipfwadm	Administrate accounting/firewall facilities.
named	Translate between domain names and IP addresses.
netstat	Print network status.
portmap	Map daemons to ports.
rarp	Manage RARP table.
route	Manage routing tables.
routed	Dynamically keep routing tables up to date.
rpcinfo	Report RPC information.
traceroute	Trace network route to remote host.

NIS Administration

domainname	Set or display name of current NIS domain.
makedbm	Rebuild NIS databases.
ypbind	Connect to NIS server.
ypcat	Print values in NIS database.
ypinit	Build new NIS databases.
ypmatch	Print value of one or more NIS *keys*.
yppasswd	Change user passwd in NIS database.
yppasswdd	Update NIS database in response to **yppasswd**.
yppoll	Determine version of NIS map at NIS server.
yppush	Propagate NIS map.
ypserv	NIS server daemon.

ypset	Point **ypbind** at a specific server.
ypwhich	Display name of NIS server or map master.
ypxfr	Transfer NIS database from server to local host.

Printing

tunelp	Tune the printer parameters.
lpc	Control line printer.

Security and System Integrity

badblocks	Search for bad blocks.
chroot	Change root directory.

Starting and Stopping the System

bootpd	Internet Boot Protocol daemon.
bootpgw	Internet Boot Protocol gateway.
bootptest	Test **bootpd**.
halt	Stop or shutdown system.
reboot	Shut down, then reboot system.
runlevel	Print system runlevel.
shutdown	Shut down system.
telinit	Change the current runlevel.
uptime	Display uptimes of local machines.

System Activity and Process Management

A number of commands in Chapter 2, *Linux User Commands*, are particularly useful in controlling processes, including **kill**, **killall**, **killall5**, **pidof**, **ps**, and **who**.

fuser	Identify processes using file or filesystem.
netstat	Show network status.
psupdate	Update */boot/psupdate*.
renice	Change the priority of running processes.

Users

chpasswd	Change multiple passwords.
groupmod	Modify groups.
grpck	Check the integrity of group system files.
pwck	Check the integrety of password system files.
rusers	Print **who**-style information on remote machines.
rwall	Print a message to remote users.
useradd	Add a new user.

userdel	Delete a user and his or her home directory.
usermod	Modify a user's information.
w	List logged-in users.
wall	Write to all users.

Networking Overview

Networks connect computers so that the different systems can share information. For users and system administrators, Unix systems have traditionally provided a set of simple but valuable network services, which let you check whether systems are running, refer to files residing on remote systems, communicate via electronic mail, and so on.

For most commands to work over a network, each system must be continuously running a server process in the background, silently waiting to handle the user's request. This kind of process is called a *daemon*; common examples, on which you rely for the most basic functions of your Linux system, are **named** (which translates numeric IP addresses into the alphanumeric names that humans are so fond of), **lpd** (which sends documents to a printer, possibly over a network), and **ftpd** (which allows you to connect to another machine via **ftp**).

Most Unix networking commands are based on Internet Protocols. These are standardized ways of communicating across a network on hierarchical layers. The protocols range from addressing and packet routing at a relatively low layer to finding users and executing user commands at a higher layer.

The basic user commands that most systems support over Internet Protocols are generally called TCP/IP commands, named after the two most common protocols. You can use all of these commands to communicate with other Unix systems besides Linux systems. Many can also be used to communicate with non-Unix systems, because a wide variety of systems support TCP/IP.

This section also covers NFS and NIS, which allow for transparent file and information sharing across networks, and **sendmail**.

TCP/IP Administration Commands

ftpd	Server for file transfers.
gated	Manage routing tables between networks.
host	Print host and zone information.
ifconfig	Configure network interface parameters.
named	Translate between domain names and IP addresses.
netstat	Print network status.
nslookup	Query domain name servers.
ping	Check that a remote host is online and responding.
pppd	Create PPP serial connection.
rdate	Notify time server that date has changed.
route	Manage routing tables.
routed	Dynamically keep routing tables up to date.

slattach	Attach serial lines as network interfaces.
telnetd	Server for TELNET sessions from remote hosts.
tftpd	Server for restricted set of file transfers.

NFS and NIS Administration Commands

portmap	DARPA port to RPC program number mapper.
rpcinfo	Report RPC information.
domainname	Set or display name of current NIS domain.
makedbm	Rebuild NIS databases.
ypbind	Connect to NIS server.
ypcat	Print values in NIS database.
ypinit	Build new NIS databases.
ypmatch	Print value of one or more NIS *keys*.
yppasswd	Change user password in NIS database.
yppasswdd	Update NIS database in response to **yppasswd**.
yppoll	Determine version of NIS map at NIS server.
yppush	Propagate NIS map.
ypserv	NIS server daemon.
ypset	Point **ypbind** at a specific server.
ypwhich	Display name of NIS server or map master.
ypxfr	Transfer NIS database from server to local host.

Overview of TCP/IP

TCP/IP is a set of communications protocols that define how different types of computers talk to each other. It's named for its two most common protocols, the Transmission Control Protocol and the Internet Protocol. The Internet Protocol moves data between hosts: it splits data into packets, which are then forwarded to machines via the network. The Transmission Control Protocol ensures that the packets in a message are reassembled in the correct order at their final destination, and that any missing datagrams are resent until they are correctly received. Other protocols provided as part of TCP/IP include:

Address Resolution Protocol (ARP)
> Translates between Internet and local hardware addresses (Ethernet et al.).

Internet Control Message Protocol (ICMP)
> Error-message and control protocol.

Point-to-Point Protocol (PPP)
> Enables TCP/IP (and other protocols) to be carried across both synchronous and asynchronous point-to-point serial links.

Reverse Address Resolution Protocol (RARP)
> Translates between local hardware and Internet addresses (opposite of ARP).

Serial Line Internet Protocol (SLIP)
>Carries IP over serial lines.

Simple Mail Transport Protocol (SMTP)
>Used by **sendmail** to send mail via TCP/IP.

Simple Network Management Protocol (SNMP)
>Performs distributed network management functions via TCP/IP.

User Datagram Protocol (UDP)
>Provides data transfer, without the reliable delivery capabilities of TCP.

Background about TCP/IP is described in the three-volume set *Internetworking with TCP/IP*, by Douglas R. Comer, published by Prentice-Hall. The commands in this chapter and the next are described in more detail in *TCP/IP Network Administration, Second Edition*, by Craig Hunt, and *Linux Network Administrator's Guide*, by Olaf Kirch, both published by O'Reilly & Associates.

In the architecture of TCP/IP protocols, data is passed down the stack (toward the Network Access Layer) when it is being sent to the network, and up the stack when it is being received from the network (see Figure 15–1).

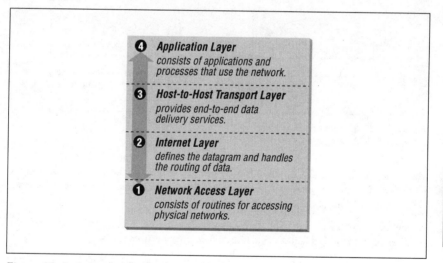

Figure 15–1: Layers in the TCP/IP protocol architecture

IP Addresses

The IP (Internet) address is a 32-bit binary number that differentiates your machine from all others on the network. Each machine must have a unique IP address. An IP address contains two parts: a network part and a host part. The number of address bits used to identify the network and host differ according to the class of the address. There are three main address classes: A, B, and C (see Figure 15–2). The left-most bits indicate what class each address is.

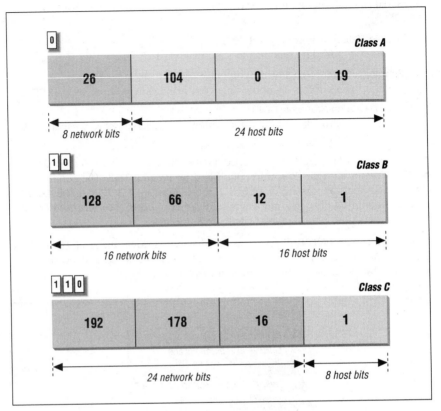

Figure 15–2: IP address structure

A more recent standard called Classless Inter-Domain Routing (CIDR) extends the class system's idea of using initial bits to identify where packets should be routed. Under CIDR, a new domain can be created with any number of fixed left-most bits (not just a multiple of 8).

A new standard called IPv6 changes the method of addressing and increases the number of fields, but it will be a while before anyone uses it.

If you wish to connect to the Internet, contact the Network Information Center and have them assign you a network address. If you are not connecting to an outside network, you can choose your own network address, as long as it conforms to the IP address syntax. You should use special reserved addresses provided for in RFC 1597, which lists IP network numbers for private networks that don't have to be registered with the IANA (Internet Assigned Numbers Authority). An IP address is different from an Ethernet address, which is assigned by the manufacturer of the physical Ethernet card.

Gateways and Routing

Gateways are hosts responsible for exchanging routing information and forwarding data from one network to another. Each portion of a network that is under a separate local administration is called an autonomous system (AS). Autonomous systems connect to each other via exterior gateways. An AS may also contain its own system of networks, linked via interior gateways.

Gateway protocols

Gateway protocols include:

EGP (Exterior Gateway Protocol)

BGP (Border Gateway Protocol)
> Protocols for exterior gateways to exchange information.

RIP (Routing Information Protocol)
> Interior gateway protocol; most popular for LANs.

Hello protocol

OSPF (Open Shortest Path First)
> Interior gateway protocols.

Routing daemons

gated and **routed**, the routing daemons, can be run on a host to make it function as a gateway. Only one of them can run on a host at any given time. **gated** is the gateway routing daemon, and allows a host to function as both an exterior and interior gateway. It simplifies the routing configuration by combining the protocols RIP, Hello, BGP, EGP, and OSPF into a single package.

routed, a network routing daemon that uses RIP, allows a host to function as an interior gateway only. **routed** manages the Internet Routing tables. For more details on **gated** and **routed**, see the TCP/IP commands in Chapter 16, *System and Network Administration Commands*.

Routing tables

Routing tables provide information needed to route packets to their destinations. This information includes destination network, gateway to use, route status, and number of packets transmitted. Routing tables can be displayed with the **netstat** command.

Name Service

Each host on a network has a name that points to information about the host. Hostnames can be assigned to any device that has an IP address. Name service translates the hostnames (easy for people to remember) to IP addresses (the numbers the computer deals with).

DNS and BIND

The Domain Name Service (DNS) is a distributed database of information about hosts on a network. Its structure is similar to that of the Unix filesystem—an inverted tree, with the root at the top. The branches of the tree are called domains (or subdomains), and correspond to IP addresses. The most popular implementation of DNS is the BIND (Berkeley Internet Name Domain) software.

DNS works as a client-server model. The *resolver* is the client, the software that asks questions about host information. The *name server* is the process that answers the questions. The server side of BIND is the **named** daemon. You can interactively query name servers for host information with the **nslookup** command. For more details on **named** and **nslookup**, see the TCP/IP commands in Chapter 16.

As the name server of its domain, your machine would be responsible for keeping (and providing on request) the names of the machines in its domain. Other name servers on the network would forward requests for these machines to it.

Domain names

The full domain name is the sequence of names, starting from the current domain and going back to the root, with a period separating the names. For instance, *oreilly.com* indicates the domain *oreilly* (for O'Reilly & Associates) which is under the domain *com* (for commercial). One machine under this domain is *www.oreilly.com*. Top-level domains include:

com	Commercial organizations
edu	Educational organizations
gov	Government organizations
mil	Military departments
net	Commercial Internet organizations, usually Internet Service Providers
org	Miscellaneous organizations

Countries also have top-level domains.

Configuring TCP/IP

ifconfig

The network interface represents the way that the networking software uses the hardware—the driver, the IP address, and so forth. To configure a network interface, use the **ifconfig** command. With **ifconfig**, you can assign an address to a network interface, setting the netmask, broadcast address, and IP address at boot time. You can also set network interface parameters, including the use of ARP, the use of driver-dependent debugging code, the use of one-packet mode, and the address of the correspondent on the other end of a point-to-point link. For more information on **ifconfig**, see the TCP/IP commands in Chapter 16.

Serial-line communication

There are two protocols for serial line communication: Serial Line IP (SLIP) and Point-to-Point Protocol (PPP). These protocols let computers transfer information using the serial port instead of a network card and a serial cable in place of an Ethernet cable.

Under Linux, the SLIP driver is installed in the kernel. To convert a serial line to SLIP mode, use the **slattach** program (details on **slattach** are available in Chapter 16). Don't forget that, after putting the line in SLIP mode, you still have to run **ifconfig** to configure the network interface. For example, if your machine is named *tanuki* and you have dialed in to *ruby*:

```
# ifconfig sl0 tanuki pointopoint ruby
# route add ruby
# route add default gw ruby
```

This configures the interface as a point-to-point link to **ruby**, adds the route to **ruby**, and makes it a default route, specifying **ruby** as the gateway.

PPP was intended to remedy some of SLIP's failings; it can hold packets from non-Internet protocols, it implements client authorization and error detection/correction, and it dynamically configures each network protocol that passes through it. Under Linux, PPP exists as a driver in the kernel and as the daemon **pppd**. For more information on **pppd**, see Chapter 16.

Troubleshooting TCP/IP

The following commands can be used to troubleshoot TCP/IP. For more details on these commands, see the TCP/IP commands in Chapter 16.

ifconfig	Provide information about the basic configuration of the network interface.
netstat	Display network status.
ping	Indicate whether a remote host can be reached.
nslookup	Query the DNS name service.
traceroute	Trace route taken by packets to reach network host.

Overview of Firewalls and Masquerading

A firewall computer is a secure system that sits between an internal network and an external network (i.e., the Internet). It is configured with a set of rules that it uses to determine what traffic is allowed to pass and what traffic is barred. While a firewall is generally intended to protect the network from malicious or even accidentally harmful traffic from the outside, it can also be configured to monitor traffic leaving the network. As the sole entry point into the system, the firewall makes it easier to construct defenses and monitor activity.

The firewall can also be set up to present a single IP address to the outside world, even though it may use multiple IP addresses internally. This is known as *masquerading*. Masquerading offers several advantages, including that it can act as additional protection in that it hides the very existence of a network; it also saves the trouble and expense of obtaining multiple IP addresses.

Both IP firewalling and masquerading are implemented in Linux version 2.0 with the **ipfwadm** utility. Version 2.2 introduces a new *ipchains* firewalling feature, but it was introduced too late for this edition.

This discussion of **ipfwadm** applies to Version 2 Linux kernels prior to Version 2.1.102. As this book is being written, the new version is about to be released; it includes a major reimplementation of firewalling and masquerading, and the **ipfwadm** utility is being replaced with the **ipchain** utility. See the "IPCHAINS-HOWTO" for more information.

To set up a Linux system as a firewall, you need to compile firewall support into the kernel by running **make config** and selecting all of the following networking options:

- Network firewalls

- TCP/IP networking

- IP: firewalling

- IP: firewall packet logging

If you want your firewall to support masquerading, select the following three options as well:

- IP: masquerading

- IP: ipautofw masq support

- IP: ICMP masquerading

The firewalling facility provides the following four categories of rule sets, maintained in the kernel as four lists:

Accounting
A set of rules against which all packets sent or received are compared. For every packet that matches, a packet counter and a byte counter associated with that rule are incremented.

Input firewall
Rules that determine whether an incoming IP packet is accepted. All incoming packets are matched against these rules; the first rule that matches determines the policy to use. Input rules are applied to all incoming traffic, whether it is intended for this host or for a remote host.

Output firewall
Rules that determine whether an outgoing IP packet is allowed to be sent. All outgoing IP packets are matched against these rules; the first rule that matches

determines the policy to use. Output rules are applied to all outgoing traffic, whether it was initiated at the firewall host or at a remote host.

Forwarding firewall

Rules that determine the permissions for forwarding IP packets that were sent from a remote host with an intended destination of another remote host. All forwarding IP packets are matched against these rules; the first rule that matches determines the policy to use. Forwarding rules affect only traffic traveling across the firewall.

For input, output, and forwarding firewall rules, all matches increment the rule's packet and byte counters. If no rule matches, the default policy for that category of rules is used. Each rule implements one of three policies:

accept

Allow matching packets to be received, sent, or forwarded.

deny

Block matching packets from being received, sent, or forwarded.

reject

Block matching packets from being received, sent, or forwarded, and also return an ICMP error message to the sending host.

Use **ipfwadm** to define the rules. Normally you'll create a file that contains the rule definitions, calling **ipfwadm** once for each rule. For more information on the kinds of decisions you need to make and the considerations that go into defining the rules, see a general book on firewalls such as the O'Reilly book *Building Internet Firewalls* by D. Brent Chapman and Elizabeth D. Zwicky; there are also relevant HOW-TOs, such as the "Firewalling and Proxy Server HOWTO" and the "Linux IP Masquerade mini HOWTO." Chapter 16 has the details of **ipfwadm**.

Overview of NFS

NFS is a distributed filesystem that allows users to mount remote filesystems as if they were local. NFS uses a client-server model, where a server exports directories to be shared, and clients mount the directories to access the files in them. NFS eliminates the need to keep copies of files on several machines by letting the clients all share a single copy of a file on the server. NFS is an RPC-based application-level protocol. For more information on the architecture of network protocols, see the section "Overview of TCP/IP."

Administering NFS

Setting up NFS clients and servers involves starting the NFS daemons, exporting filesystems from the NFS servers, and mounting them on the clients. The */etc/exports* file is the NFS server configuration file; it controls which files and directories are exported and what kinds of access are allowed. Names and addresses for clients receiving services are kept in the */etc/hosts* file.

Daemons

NFS server daemons, called **nfsd** daemons, run on the server and accept RPC calls from clients. NFS servers also run the **mountd** daemon to handle mount requests. On the client, caching and buffering are handled by **biod**, the block I/O daemon. The **portmap** daemon maps RPC program numbers to the appropriate TCP/IP port numbers.

Exporting filesystems

To set up an NFS server, first check that all the hosts that will mount your filesystem can reach your host. Next, edit the */etc/exports* file to include the mount-point pathname of the filesystem to be exported. If you are running **mountd**, the files will be exported as the permissions in */etc/exports* allow.

Mounting filesystems

To enable an NFS client, mount a remote filesystem after NFS is started, either by using the **mount** command or by specifying default remote filesystems in */etc/fstab*. A **mount** request calls the server's **mountd** daemon, which checks the access permissions of the client and returns a pointer to a filesystem. Once a directory is mounted, it remains attached to the local filesystem until it is dismounted with the **umount** command, or until the local system is rebooted.

Usually, only a privileged user can mount filesystems with NFS. However, you can enable users to mount and unmount selected filesystems using the **mount** and **umount** commands if the "user" option is set in */etc/fstab*. This can reduce traffic by having filesystems mounted only when needed. To enable user mounting, create an entry in */etc/fstab* for each filesystem to be mounted.

Overview of NIS

NIS refers to the service formerly know as Sun Yellow Pages (YP). It is used to make configuration information consistent on all machines in a network. It does this by designating a single host as the master of all the system administration files and databases, and distributing this information to all other hosts on the network. The information is compiled into databases called maps. NIS is built on the RPC protocol. There are currently two NIS servers freely available for Linux, **yps** and **ypserv**.

Servers

In NIS, there are two types of servers—master and slave servers. Master servers are responsible for maintaining the maps and distributing them to the slave servers. The files are then available locally to requesting processes.

Domains

An NIS domain is a group of hosts that use the same set of maps. The maps are contained in a subdirectory of */var/yp* having the same name as the domain. The machines in a domain share password, hosts, and group file information. NIS domain names are set with the **domainname** command.

NIS maps

NIS stores information in database files called maps. Each map consists of a pair of **dbm** database files, one containing a directory of keys (a bitmap of indices), and the other containing data values. The non-ASCII structure of **dbm** files neccessitates using NIS tools such as **yppush** to move maps between machines.

The file */var/yp/YP_MAP_X_LATE* contains a complete listing of active NIS maps as well as NIS aliases for NIS maps. All maps must be listed here in order for NIS to serve them.

Map manipulation utilities

The following utilities are used to administer NIS maps:

makedbm   Make **dbm** files. Modify only *ypservers* map and any nondefault maps.

ypinit   Build and install NIS databases. Manipulate maps when NIS is being initialized. Should not be used when NIS is already running.

yppush   Transfer updated maps from the master server.

Administering NIS

NIS is enabled by setting up NIS servers and NIS clients. The descriptions given here describe NIS setup using **ypserv**, which does not support a master/slave server configuration. All NIS command depend on the RPC portmap program, so make sure it is installed and running before setting up NIS.

Setting up an NIS server

Setting up an NIS server involves:

1. Setting a domain name for NIS using **domainname**

2. Editing the *ypMakefile*, which identifies which databases to build and what sources to use in building them

3. Copying the *ypMakefile* to */var/yp/Makefile*

4. Running **make** from the */var/yp* directory, which builds the databases and initializes the server

5. Starting **ypserv**, the NIS server daemon.

Setting up an NIS client

Setting up an NIS client involves: Setting the domain name for NIS using **domainname**, which should be the same name used by the NIS server; and running **ypbind**.

NIS user accounts

NIS networks have two kinds of user accounts: distributed and local. Distributed accounts must be administered from the master machine; they provide information that is uniform on each machine in an NIS domain. Changes made to distributed accounts are distributed via NIS maps. Local accounts are administered from the local computer; they provide account information unique to a specific machine. They are not affected by NIS maps, and changes made to local accounts do not affect NIS. When NIS is installed, preexisting accounts default to local accounts.

RPC and XDR

RPC (Remote Procedure Call) is the session protocol used by both NFS and NIS. It allows a host to make a procedure call that appears to be local, but is really executed remotely, on another machine on the network. RPC is implemented as a library of procedures, plus a network standard for ordering bytes and data structures called XDR (eXternal Data Representation).

CHAPTER 16

System and Network Administration Commands

This chapter presents Linux system administration commands. See Chapter 15 for a description of their relationships to protocols and layers of network software. Other O'Reilly books cover related topics. *Essential System Administration*, Second Edition, by Æleen Frisch, describes how to use the local administration commands, while *TCP/IP Network Administration*, by Craig Hunt, and the *Linux Network Administrator's Guide*, by Olaf Kirch, explain the TCP/IP commands. Finally, NFS and NIS commands are covered in *Managing NFS and NIS* by Hal Stern.

Alphabetical Summary of Commands

agetty [*options*] *port baudrate* [*term*]	**agetty**

The Linux version of **getty**. Set terminal type, modes, speed, and line discipline. **agetty** is invoked by **init**. It is the second process in the series **init-getty-login-shell**, which ultimately connects a user with the Linux system. **agetty** reads the user's login name and invokes the **login** command with the user's name as an argument. While reading the name, **agetty** attempts to adapt the system to the speed and type of device being used.

You must specify a port, which **agetty** will search for in the /*dev* directory. You may use -, in which case **agetty** reads from standard input. You must also specify *baudrate*, which may be a comma-separated list of rates, through which **agetty** will step. Optionally, you may specify the *term*, which is used to override the TERM environment variable.

→

agetty
←
	Options
	
	-h Specify hardware, not software, flow control.
	
	-i Suppress printing of /etc/issue before printing the login prompt.
	
	-l program
	  Specify the use of program instead of /bin/login.
	
	-m Attempt to guess the appropriate baud rate.
	
	-t timeout
	  Specifies that **agetty** should exit if the **open** on the line succeeds and there is no response to the login prompt in timeout seconds.
	
	-L Do not require carrier detect: operate locally only. Use this when connecting terminals.

arp	**arp** [options]
	
	TCP/IP command. Clear, add to, or dump the kernel's ARP cache (/proc/net/arp).
	
	Options
	
	-v Verbose mode.
	
	-t type Search for type entries when examining the ARP cache. type must be **ether** (IEEE 802.3 10Mbps Ethernet) or **ax25** (AX.25 packet radio); **ether** is the default.
	
	-a [hosts]
	  Display hosts' entries, or, if none are specified, all entries.
	
	-d host Remove host's entry.
	
	-s host hardware-address
	  Add the entry host hardware-address, where **ether** class addresses are 6 hexadecimal bytes, colon-separated.
	
	-f file Read entries from file and add them.

badblocks	**badblocks** [options] device block-count Search device for bad blocks. You must specify the number of blocks on the device (block-count).

badblocks

-b *blocksize*   Expect *blocksize*-byte blocks.

-o *file*   Direct output to *file*.

-v   Verbose mode.

-w   Test by writing to each block and then reading back from it.

---

bootpd [*options*] [*configfile* [*dumpfile*]]

bootpd

TCP/IP command. Internet Boot Protocol server. **bootpd** is normally run by */etc/inetd* by including the following line in the file */etc/inetd.conf*:

```
bootps dgram udp wait root /etc/bootpd bootpd
```

This causes **bootpd** to be started only when a boot request arrives. It may also be started in stand-alone mode, from the command line. Upon startup, **bootpd** first reads its configuration file, */etc/bootptab* (or the *configfile* listed on the command line), then begins listening for BOOTREQUEST packets.

bootpd looks in */etc/services* to find the port numbers it should use. Two entries are extracted: **bootps**—the bootp server listening port—and **bootpc**—the destination port used to reply to clients.

If **bootpd** is compiled with the −DDEBUG option, receipt of a SIGUSR1 signal causes it to dump its memory-resident database to the file */etc/bootpd.dump* or the command-line specified *dumpfile*.

Options

-c *directory* Force **bootpd** to work in *directory*.

-d *level*   Specify the debugging level. Omitting *level* will increment the level by 1.

-t *timeout*   Specify a timeout value in minutes. A timeout value of zero means forever.

Configuration file

The **bootpd** configuration file has a format in which two-character, case-sensitive tag symbols are used to represent host parameters. These parameter declarations are separated by colons. The general format is:

```
hostname:tg=value:tg=value:tg=value
```

where *hostname* is the actual name of a bootp client and *tg*

→

bootpd ←	is a tag symbol. The currently recognized tags are listed below. ***Tags*** **bf** Bootfile **bs** Bootfile size in 512-octet blocks **cs** Cookie server address list **ds** Domain name server address list **gw** Gateway address list **ha** Host hardware address **hd** Bootfile home directory **hn** Send hostname **ht** Host hardware type (see Assigned Numbers RFC) **im** Impress server address list **ip** Host IP address **lg** Log server address list **lp** **lpr** server address list **ns** IEN-116 name server address list **rl** Resource location protocol server address list **sm** Host subnet mask **tc** Table continuation **to** Time offset in seconds from UTC **ts** Time server addresss list **vm** Vendor magic cookie selector There is also a generic tag, **T***n*, where *n* is an RFC 1048 vendor field tag number. Generic data may be represented as either a stream of hexadecimal numbers or as a quoted string of ASCII characters.
bootpgw	**bootpgw** [*options*] *server* Internet Boot Protocol Gateway. Maintain a gateway that forwards **bootpd** requests to *server*. In addition to dealing with BOOTREPLY packets, also deal with BOOTREQUEST packets. **bootpgw** is normally run by */etc/inetd* by including the following line in the file */etc/inetd.conf*: `bootps dgram udp wait root /etc/bootpgw bootpgw` This causes **bootpgw** to be started only when a boot request arrives. **bootpgw** takes all the same options as **bootpd**, except **-c**.
bootptest	**bootptest** [*options*] *server* [*template*] TCP/IP command. Test *server*'s **bootpd** daemon by sending requests every second for ten seconds or until the server responds. Read options from the *template* file, if provided.

Options

-f *file*   Read the boot filename from *file*.

-h   Identify client by hardware, not IP, address.

-m *magic -number*

             Provide *magic-number* as the first word of the vendor options field.

---

cfdisk [*options*] [*device*]

Partition a hard disk. *device* may be */dev/hda* (default), */dev/hdb*, */dev/sda*, */dev/sdb*, */dev/sdc*, or */dev/sdd*. See also **fdisk**.

Options

-a   Highlight the current partition with a cursor, not reverse video.

-c *cylinders* Specify the number of cylinders.

-h *heads*   Specify the number of heads.

-s *sectors*   Specify the number of sectors per track.

-z   Do not read the partition table; partition from scratch.

-P *format*   Display the partition table in *format*, which must be **r** (raw data), **s** (sector order), or **t** (raw format).

Commands

up arrow, down arrow

             Move among partitions.

b   Toggle partition's bootable flag.

d   Delete partition (allow other partitions to use its space).

g   Alter the disk's geometry. Prompt for what to change: cylinders, heads, or sectors (**c**, **h**, or **s**, respectively).

h   Help.

m   Attempt to ensure maximum usage of disk space in the partition.

n   Create a new partition. Prompt for more information.

Sys Admin Commands

→

cfdisk	p	Display the partition table.
←	q	Quit without saving information.
	t	Prompt for a new filesystem type, and change to that type.
	u	Change the partition size units, rotating from megabytes to sectors to cylinders and back.
	W	Save information. Note that this letter must be uppercase.

chpasswd

chpasswd [*option*]

Change user passwords in a batch. **chpasswd** accepts input in the form of one *username:password* pair per line. If the −**e** option is not specified, *password* will be encrypted before being stored.

Option

    −**e**   Passwords given are already encrypted.

chroot

chroot *newroot* [*command*]

Change root directory for *command*, or, if none is specified, for a new copy of the user's shell. This command or shell is executed relative to the new root. The meaning of any initial / in pathnames is changed to *newroot* for a command and any of its children. In addition, the initial working directory is *newroot*. This command is restricted to privileged users.

cron

cron

Normally started in a system startup file. Execute commands at scheduled times, as specified in users' files in */var/cron/tabs*. Each file shares its name with the user who owns it. The files are controlled via the command **crontab**.

debugfs

debugfs [[*option*] *device*]

Debug an **ext2** file system. *device* is the special file corresponding to the device containing the **ext2** file system (e.g., */dev/hda3*).

Option

    −**w**   Open the filesystem read-write.

cat *file*   Dump the contents of an inode to standard output.

cd *directory*   Change the current working directory to *directory*.

chroot *directory*

Change the root directory to be the specified inode.

close   Close the currently open file system.

clri *file*   Clear the contents of the inode corresponding to *file*.

dump *file out_file*

Dump the contents of an inode to *out_file*.

expand_dir *directory*

Expand *directory*.

find_free_block [*goal*]

Find the first free block starting from *goal* and allocate it.

find_free_inode [*dir* [*mode*]]

Find a free inode and allocate it.

freeb *block*   Mark *block* as not allocated.

freei *file*   Free the inode corresponding to *file*.

help   Print a list of commands understood by **debugfs**.

icheck *block*   Do block-to-inode translation.

initialize *device blocksize*

Create an **ext2** file system on *device*.

kill_file *file*   Remove *file* and deallocate its blocks.

ln *source_file dest_file*

Create a link.

ls [*pathname*]   Emulate the **ls** command.

modify_inode *file*

Modify the contents of the inode corresponding to *file*.

mkdir *directory*

Make *directory*.

mknod *file* [p|[[c|b] *major minor*]]

Create a special device file.

Sys Admin
Commands

→

debugfs	**ncheck** *inode*	Do inode-to-name translation.
←	**open** [-w] *device*	
		Open a file system.
	pwd	Print the current working directory.
	quit	Quit **debugfs**.
	rm *file*	Remove *file*.
	rmdir *directory*	
		Remove *directory*.
	setb *block*	Mark *block* as allocated.
	seti *file*	Mark in use the inode corresponding to *file*.
	show_super_stats	
		List the contents of the super block.
	stat *file*	Dump the contents of the inode corresponding to *file*.
	testb *block*	Test whether *block* is marked as allocated.
	testi *file*	Test whether the inode correponding to *file* is marked as allocated.
	unlink *file*	Remove a link.
	write *source_file file*	
		Create a file in the filesystem named *file*, and copy the contents of *source_file* into the destination file.

---

depmod

depmod [*options*] *modules*

Create a dependency file for the modules given on the command line. This dependency file can be used by **modprobe** to automatically load the relevant *modules*. The normal use of **depmod** is to include the line **/sbin/depmod -a** in one of the files in */etc/rc.d* so the correct module dependancies will be available after booting the system.

Options

    −a   Create dependencies for all modules listed in */etc/conf.modules*.

    −d   Debug mode. Show all commands being issued.

| -e | Print a list of all unresoved symbols. |
| -v | Print a list of all processed modules. |

Files

/etc/conf.modules

Information about modules: which ones depend on others, and which directories correspond to particular types of modules.

/sbin/insmod, /sbin/rmmod

Programs which **depmod** relies on.

---

dip [*options*] [*chat scriptfile*]

Set up or initiate dialup Internet connections. **dip** can be used to establish connections for users dialing out or dialing in. Commands can be used in interactive mode, or placed in a scriptfile for use in dial-out connections. To establish dial-in connections, **dip** is often used as a shell, and may be executed using the commands **diplogin** or **diplogini**.

Options

-a	In dial-in mode, prompt for username and password. Same as the **dplogini** command.
-i	Initiate a login shell for a dial-in connection. Same as the **diplogin** command.
-k	Kill the most recent **dip** process or the process running on the device specified by the -l option.
-l *device*	Used with the -k command. Specifies a tty *device*.
-m *mtu*	Maximum Transfer Unit. The default is 296.
-p *protocol*	The *protocol* to use: SLIP, CSLIP, PPP, or TERM.
-t	Command mode. This is usually done for testing.
-v	Verbose mode.

Commands

Most of these commands can be used either in interactive mode or in a script file.

beep *times*

Beep the terminal the specified number of *times*.

→

bootp Retrieve local and remote IP addresses using the BOOTP protocol.

break Send a BREAK.

chatkey *keyword code*
Map a modem response keyword to a numeric code.

config [interface|routing] [pre|up|down|post] *arguments*
Modify **interface** characteristics or the **routing** table, before the link comes up, when it is up, when it goes down, or after it is down. The syntax for *arguments* is the same as arguments for the **ifconfig** or **route** commands.

databits 7|8
Set the number of data bits.

dec *$variable* [*value*]
Decrement *$variable* by *value*. The default is 1.

default Set default route to the IP address of the host connected to.

dial *phonenumber* [*timeout*]
Dial *phonenumber*. Abort if remote modem doesn't answer within *timeout* seconds. Set **$errlvl** according to the modem response.

echo on|off
Enable or disable the display of modem commands.

exit [*n*] Exit the script. Optionally return the number *n* as the exit status.

flush Clear the input buffer.

get *$variable* [ask|remote [*timeout*]] *value*
Set *$variable* to *value*. If **ask** is specified, prompt the user for a value. If **remote** is specified, retrieve the value from the remote system. Abort after *timeout* seconds.

goto *label* Jump to the section identified by *label*.

help List available commands.

if *expr* goto *label*
Jump to the section identified by *label* if the expression evaluates to true. An expression compares a variable to a constant using one of these operators: =, !=, <, >, <=, or >=.

inc *$variable* [*value*]
> Increment *$variable* by *value*. The default is
> 1.

init *string* Set the *string* used to initialize the modem.
> The default is ATE0 Q0 V1 X1.

mode *protocol*
> Set the connection *protocol*. Valid values are
> SLIP, CSLIP, PPP, and TERM. The default is
> SLIP.

netmask *mask*
> Set the subnet mask.

parity E|O|N
> Set the line parity to even, odd, or none.

password Prompt user for password.

proxyarp Install a proxy ARP entry in the local ARP
> table.

print *$variable*
> Display the content of *$variable*

psend *command*
> Execute *command* in a shell, and send out-
> put to the serial device. Commands are exe-
> cuted using the user's real UID.

port *device*
> Specify the serial device the modem is
> attached to.

quit Exit with a nonzero exit status. Abort the
> connection.

reset Reset the modem.

securid Prompt user for the variable part of an ACE
> System SecureID password and send it
> together with the stored prefix to the
> remote system.

securidf *prefix*
> Store the fixed part of an ACE System
> SecureID password.

send *string*
> Send *string* to the serial device.

shell *command*
> Execute command in a shell using the
> user's real UID.

Sys Admin Commands

dip ←	**skey** [*timeout*]
	Wait for an S/Key challenge, then prompt user for the secret key. Generate and send the response. Abort if challenge is not received within *timeout* seconds. S/Key support must be compiled into **dip**.
	sleep *time* Wait *time* seconds.
	speed *bits-per-second*
	Set the port speed. Default is 38400.
	stopbits 1│2
	Set the number of stop bits.
	term Enable terminal mode. Pass keyboard input directly to the serial device.
	timeout *time*
	Set the number of seconds the line can be inactive before the link is closed.
	wait *text* [*timeout*]
	Wait *timeout* seconds for *text* to arrive from the remote system. If *timeout* is not specified, wait forever.
dmesg	**dmesg** [*options*]
	Display the system control messages from the kernel ring buffer. This buffer stores all messages since the last system boot or the most recent ones, if the buffer has been filled.
	Options
	−c Clear buffer after printing messages.
	−n *level* Set the level of system message that will display on console.
dnsdomainname	**dnsdomainname**
	TCP/IP command. Print the system's DNS domain name. See also **hostname**.
domainname	**domainname** [*name*]
	NFS/NIS command. Set or display name of current NIS domain. With no argument, **domainname** dislays the name of the current NIS domain. Only a privileged user can set the domain name by giving an argument; this is usually done in a startup script.

dumpe2fs *device*

Print information about *device*'s superblock and blocks group.

e2fsck [*options*] *device*
fsck.ext2 *[options] device*

Similar to **fsck**, but specifically intended for Linux second extended filesystems. When checking a second extended filesystem, **fsck** calls this command.

Options

    -b *superblock*

        Use *superblock* instead of default superblock.

    -d   Debugging mode.

    -f   Force checking, even if kernel has already marked the filesystem as valid. **e2fsck** will normally exit without checking if the system appears to be clean.

    -l *file*   Consult *file* for a list of bad blocks, in addition to checking for others.

    -n   Ensure that no changes are made to the filesystem. When queried, answer "no."

    -p   "Preen." Repair all bad blocks noninteractively.

    -t   Display timing statistics.

    -v   Verbose.

    -y   When queried, answer "yes."

    -B *size*   Expect to find the superblock at *size*; if it's not there, exit.

    -F   Flush buffer caches before checking.

    -L *file*   Consult *file* for list of bad blocks instead of checking filesystem for them.

fdisk [*options*] [*device*]

Maintain disk partitions via a menu. **fdisk** displays information about disk partitions, creates and deletes disk partitions, and changes the active partition. It is possible to assign a different operating system to each of the four partitions, though only one partition is active at any given time. You can also divide a physical partition into several logical partitions. The minimum recommended size for a Linux

→

fdisk ←	system partition is 40 megabytes. Normally, *device* will be */dev/hda, /dev/hdb, /dev/sda, /dev/sdb, /dev/hdc, /dev/hdd,* etc. See also **cfdisk**.

Options

–l   List partition tables and exit.

–s*partition*
Display the size of *partition*, unless it is a DOS partition.

Commands

a	Toggle a bootable flag on current partition.
d	Delete current partition.
l	List all partition types.
m	Main menu.
n	Create a new partition; prompt for more information.
p	Print a list of all partitions, and information about each.
q	Quit; do not save.
t	Replace the type of the current partition.
u	Modify the display/entry units, which must be cylinders or sectors.
v	Verify: check for errors; display a summary of the amount of unallocated sectors.
w	Save changes; exit.

---

fingerd

in.fingerd [*option*]

TCP/IP command. Remote user information server. **fingerd** provides a network interface to the **finger** program. It listens for TCP connections on the **finger** port, and, for each connection, reads a single input line, passes the line to **finger**, and copies the output of **finger** to the user on the client machine. **fingerd** is started by **inetd**, and must have an entry in **inetd**'s configuration file, */etc/inetd.conf.*

Option

–w   Include additional information, such as uptime and the name of the operating system.

fsck [*options*] [*filesystem*] ...

Call the filesystem checker for the appropriate system type, to check and repair filesystems. If a filesystem is consistent, the number of files, number of blocks used, and number of blocks free are reported. If a filesystem is inconsistent, **fsck** prompts before each correction is attempted. **fsck**'s exit code can be interpreted as the sum of all of those conditions that apply:

1	Errors were found and corrected.
2	Reboot suggested.
4	Errors were found, but not corrected.
8	**fsck** encountered an operational error.
16	**fsck** was called incorrectly.
128	A shared library error was detected.

Options

--	Pass all subsequent options to filesystem-specific checker. All options that **fsck** doesn't recognize will also be passed.
−r	Interactive mode: prompt before making any repairs.
−s	Serial mode.
−t *fstype*	Specify the filesystem type. Do not check filesystems of any other type.
−A	Check all filesystems listed in */etc/fstab*.
−N	Suppress normal execution; just display what would be done.
−R	Meaningful only with −A: check all filesystems listed in */etc/fstab* except the root filesystem.
−T	Suppress printing of title.
−V	Verbose mode.

fetchmail [*options*] [*servers...*]

Retrieve mail from mail servers and forward it to the local mail-delivery system. **fetchmail** retrieves mail from servers that support the common mail protocols POP2, POP3, IMAP2bis, and IMAP4. Messages are delivered via SMTP through port 25 on the local host, and through your system's mail delivery agent (such as *sendmail*), where they can be read through the user's mail client. **fetchmail** settings

fetchmail

←

are stored in the `~/.fetchmailrc` file. Parameters and servers can also be set on the command line, which will override settings in the *.fetchmailrc* file. **fetchmail** is compatible with the **popclient** program, and users can use both without having to adjust file settings.

Options

    −a, −−all

        Retrieve all messages from server, even ones that have already been seen, but left on the server. The default is to only retrieve new messages.

    −A *type*, **−−auth** *type*

        Specify the type of authentication. *type* may be: `password`, `kerberos_v5`, or `kerberos`. Authentication type is usually established by **fetchmail** by default, so this option isn't very useful.

    −B *n*, **−−fetchlimit** *n*

        Set the maximum number of messages (*n*) accepted from a server per query.

    −b *n*, **−−batchlimit** *n*

        Set the maximum number of messages sent to an SMTP listener per connection. When this limit is reached, the connection will be broken and reestablished. The default of 0 means no limit.

    −c, −−check

        Check for mail on a single server without retrieving or deleting messages. Works with IMAP, but not well with other protocols, if at all.

    −D [*domain*], **−−smtpaddress** [*domain*]

        Specify the *domain* named placed in RCPT TO lines sent to SMTP. The default is the localhost.

    −E *header*, **−−envelope** *header*

        Change the header assumed to contain the mail's envelope address (usually "X-Envelope-to:") to *header*.

    −e *n*, **−−expunge** *n*

        Tell an IMAP server to EXPUNGE, i.e., purge messages marked for deletion, after *n* deletes. A setting of 0 indicates expunging only at the end of the session. Normally, an **expunge** occurs afer each delete.

−F, −−flush

For POP3 and IMAP servers, remove previously retrieved messages from the server before retrieving new ones.

−f *file,* **−−fetchmailrc** *file*

Specify a non-default name for the **fetchmail** configuration file.

−I *specification,* **−−interface** *specification*

Require that the mail server machine is up and running at a specified IP address (or range) before polling. The *specification* is given as *interface/ipaddress/mask.* The first part indicates the type of TCP connection expected (*sl0, ppp0,* etc.), the second is the IP address, and the third is te bitmask for the IP, assumed to be 255.255.255.255.

−K, −−nokeep

Delete all retrieved messages from the mailserver.

−k, −−keep

Keep copies of all retrieved messages on the mailserver.

−l *size,* **−−limit** *size*

Set the maximum message size that will be retrieved from a server. Messages larger than this size will be left on the server and marked unread.

−M *interface,* **−−monitor** *interface*

In daemon mode, monitor the specified TCP/IP *interface* for any activity besides itself, and skip the poll if there is no other activity. Useful for PPP connections that automatically timeout with no activity.

−m *command,* **−−mda** *command*

Pass mail directly to mail-delivery agent, rather than sending to port 25. The *command* is the path and options for the mailer, such as `/usr/lib/sendmail -oem`. A `%T` in the command will be replaced with the local delivery address, and an `%F` will be replaced with the message's From address.

−n, −−norewrite

Do not expand local mail IDs to full addresses. This option will disable expected

Sys Admin Commands

→

addressing, and should only be used to find problems.

−P *n*, **−−port** *n*

Specify a port to connect to on the mail server. The default port numbers for supported protocols are usually sufficient.

−p *proto*, **−−protocol** *proto*

Specify the protocol to use when polling a mail server. *proto* can be:

POP2

Post Office Protocol 2

POP3

Post Office Protocol 3

APOP

POP3 with MD5 authentication

RPOP

POP3 with RPOP authentication

KPOP

POP3 with Kerberos V4 authentication on port 1109

IMAP

Either IMAP2bis, IMAP4, or IMAP4rev1. **fetchmail** autodetects their capabilities.

IMAP-K4

IMAP4 or IMAP4rev1 with Kerberos v4 authentication

IMAP-GSS

IMAP4 or IMAP4rev1 with GSSAPI authentication

ETRN
ESMTP

−Q *string*, **−−qvirtual** *string*

Remove the prefix *string*, which is the local user's hostid, from the address in the envelope header (such as "Delivered-To:").

−r *folder*, **−−folder** *folder*

Retrieve the specified mail *folder* from the mail server.

−s, **−−silent**

Suppress status messages during a fetch.

−U, **−−uidl**

For POP3, track the age of kept messages via unique ID listing.

−u *name,* **−−username** *name*
> Specify the user *name* to use when logging into the mail server.

−V, −−version
> Print the version information for **fetchmail** and display the options set for each mail server. Performs no fetch.

−v, −−verbose
> Display all status messages during a fetch. Overrides −q.

−Z *nnn,* **−−antispam** *nnn*
> Specify the SMTP error *nnn* to signal a spam-block from the client. If *nnn* is -1, this option is disabled.

fsck.minix [*options*] *device*

Similar to **fsck**, but specifically intended for Linux MINIX filesystems.

Options

−a   Automatic mode: repair without prompting.

−f   Force checking, even if kernel has already marked the file system. **fsck.minix** will normally exit without checking if the system appears to be clean.

−l   List filesystems.

−m   Enable MINIX-like "mode not cleared" warnings.

−r   Interactive mode: prompt before making any repairs.

−s   Display information about superblocks.

−v   Verbose mode.

in.ftpd [*options*]

TCP/IP command. Internet File Transfer Protocol server. The server uses the TCP protocol and listens at the port specified in the **ftp** service specification. **ftpd** is started by **inetd**, and must have an entry in **inetd**'s configuration file, */etc/inetd.conf.*

→

ftpd
←
	Options
	
	    −d Write debugging information to the syslog.
	
	    −l Log each FTP session in the syslog.
	
	    −T*maxtimeout*
	             Set maximum timeout period in seconds.
	             Default limit is 2 hours.
	
	    −t*timeout*
	             Set timeout period to *timeout* seconds.

fuser	**fuser** [*options*] [*files*	*filesystems*]
		
		Identify processes that are using a file or filesystem. **fuser** outputs the process IDs of the processes that are using the *files* or local *filesystems*. Each process ID is followed by a letter code: **c** if process is using file as current directory, **e** if executable, **f** if an open file, **m** if a shared library, and **r** if the root directory. Any user with permission to read */dev/kmem* and */dev/mem* can use **fuser**, but only a privileged user can terminate another user's process. **fuser** does not work on remote (NFS) files.
		
		If more than one group of files is specified, the options may be respecified for each additional group of files. A lone dash (−) cancels the options currently in force, and the new set of options applies to the next group of files.
		
		Options
		
		    − Return all options to defaults.
		
		    −*signal* Send *signal* instead of SIGKILL.
		
		    −a Display information on all specified files, even if they are not being accessed by any processes.
		
		    −k Send SIGKILL signal to each process.
		
		    −l List signal names.
		
		    −m Expect *files* to exist on a mounted filesystem; include all files accessing that filesystem.
		
		    −s Silent.
		
		    −u User login name, in parentheses, also follows process ID.
		
		    −v Verbose.

gated [*options*]

TCP/IP command. Gateway routing daemon. **gated** handles multiple routing protocols and replaces **routed** and any routing daemons that speak the Hello, EGP, or BGP routing protocols. **gated** currently handles the RIP, BGP, EGP, Hello, and OSPF routing protocols, and can be configured to perform all or any combination of the five.

Options

    −c   Parse configuration file for syntax errors, then exit **gated**, leaving a dump file in */usr/tmp/gated_dump*.

  −f *config_file*
                     Use alternate configuration file, *config_file*. Default is */etc/gated.conf*.

    −n   Do not modify kernel's routing table.

  −t [*trace_options*]
                     Start **gated** with the specified tracing options enabled. If no flags are specified, assume **general**. The trace flags are:

                    adv Management of policy blocks

                    all Includes **normal**, **policy**, **route**, **state**, **task**, and **timer**

                    general
                       Includes **normal** and **route**

                    iflist
                       The kernel interface list

                    normal
                       Normal protocols instances

                    parse
                       Lexical analyzer and parser

                    policy
                       Instances in which policy is applied to imported and exported routes

                    route
                       Any changes to routing table

                    state
                       State machine transitions

                    symbols
                       Symbols read from kernel—note that they are read before the configuration file is parsed, so this option must be specified on the command line

→

gated ←		task
		System tasks and interfaces
		timer
		Timer usage
	−C	Parse configuration file for errors and set exit code to indicate if there were any (1) or not (0); then exit.
	−N	Do not daemonize.

gdc

gdc [*options*] *command*

TCP/IP command. Administer **gated**. Various commands start and stop the daemon, send signals to it, maintain the configuration files, and manage state and core dumps.

Options

−c *size*	Specify maximum core dump size.
−f *size*	Specify maximum file dump size.
−m *size*	Specify maximum data segment size.
−n	Suppress editing of the kernel forwarding table.
−q	Quiet mode: suppress warnings and log errors to **syslogd** instead of standard error.
−s *size*	Specify maximum stack size.
−t *seconds*	Wait *seconds* seconds (default 10) for **gated** to complete specified operations at start and stop time.

Commands

BACKOUT	Restore */etc/gated.conf* from */etc/gated.conf-*, whether or not the latter exists.
backout	Restore */etc/gated.conf* from */etc/gated.conf-*, assuming the latter exists.
checkconf	Report any syntax errors in */etc/gated.conf*.
checknew	Report any syntax errors in */etc/gated.conf+*.
COREDUMP	Force **gated** to core dump and exit.

createconf	Create an empty */etc/gated.conf+* if one does not already exist, and set it to mode 664, owner **root**, group **gdmaint**.
dump	Force **gated** to dump to */usr/tmp/gated_dump* and then continue normal operation.
interface	Reload interface configuration.
KILL	Terminate immediately (ungracefully).
modeconf	Set all configuration files to mode 664, owner **root**, group **gdmaint**.
newconf	Make sure that */etc/gated.conf+* exists and move it to */etc/gated.conf.* Save the old */etc/gated.conf* as */etc/gated.conf–*.
reconfig	Reload configuration file.
restart	Stop and restart **gated**.
rmcore	Remove any **gated** core files.
rmdmp	Remove any **gated** state dump files.
rmparse	Remove any **gated** files that report on parse errors. These are generated by the **gcd checkconf** and **gcd checknew** commands.
running	Exit with zero status if **gated** is running and non-zero if it is not.
start	Start **gated**, unless it is already running, in which case return an error.
stop	Stop **gated** as gracefully as possible.
term	Terminate gracefully.
toggletrace	Toggle tracing.

Files

/etc/gcd.conf+
> The test configuration file. Once you're satisfied that it works, you should run *gated newconf* to install it as */etc/gated.conf.*

/etc/gated.conf–
> A backup of the old configuration file.

/etc/gated.conf– –
> A backup of the backup of the old configuration file.

Sys Admin Commands

→

gdc
←
	/etc/gated.conf
	    The actual configuration file.
	
	/etc/gated.pid
	    gated's process ID.
	
	/usr/tmp/gated_dump
	    The state dump file.
	
	/usr/tmp/gated_parse
	    A list of the parse errors generated by reading the configuration file.

getty	**getty** [*options*] *port* [*speed* [*term* [*lined*]]] Set terminal type, modes, speed, and line discipline. Linux systems may use **agetty** instead, which uses a different syntax. **getty** is invoked by **init**. It is the second process in the series **init-getty-login-shell** which ultimately connects a user with the Linux system. **getty** reads the user's login name and invokes the **login** command with the user's name as an argument. While reading the name, **getty** attempts to adapt the system to the speed and type of device being used. You must specify a *port* argument, which **getty** will use to attach itself to the device */dev/port*. **getty** will then scan the defaults file, usually */etc/default/getty*, for runtime values and parameters. These may also be specified, for the most part, on the command line, but the values in the defaults file take precedence. The *speed* argument is used to point to an entry in the file */etc/gettydefs*, which contains the initial baudrate, tty settings, and login prompt, and final speed and settings for the connection. The first entry in */etc/gettydefs* is the default. *term* specifies the type of terminal, with *lined* the optional line discipline to use.

Options

−c *file*	Check the *gettydefs* file. *file* is the name of the *gettydefs* file. Produces the files' values and reports parsing errors to standard output.
−d *file*	Use a different default file.
−h	Do not force a hangup on the port when initializing.
−r *delay*	Wait for single character from port, then wait *delay* seconds before proceeding.
−t *timeout*	If no user name is accepted within *timeout* seconds, close connection.

−w *string*	Wait for *string* characters from port before proceeding.	**getty**

groupmod [*options*] *group*   **groupmod**

Modify group information for *group*.

Options

−g *gid*	Change the numerical value of the group ID. Any files that have the old *gid* will have to be changed manually. The new *gid* must be unique unless the −o option is used.
−n *name*	Change the group name to *name*.
−o	Override. Accept a non-unique *gid*.

grpck [*option*] [*files*]   **grpck**

Remove corrupt or duplicate entries in the */etc/group* and */etc/gshadow* files. Generate warnings for other errors found. **grpck** will prompt for a yes or no before deleting entries. If the user replies no, the program will exit. If run in a non-interractive mode, the reply to all prompts is no. Alternate group and gshadow *files* can be checked. If other errors are found, the user will be encouraged to run the **groupmod** command.

Option

−n	Non-interactive mode.

Exit Codes

0	Success.
1	Syntax error.
2	One or more bad group entries found.
3	Could not open group files.
4	Could not lock group files.
5	Could not write group files.

halt [*options*]   **halt**

Insert a note in */var/log/wtmp*; if the system is in runlevel 0 or 6, stop all processes; otherwise, call **shutdown −nf**.

Sys Admin Commands

→

halt ←	**Options** −d Suppress writing to */var/log/wtmp*. −f Call **halt** even when **shutdown −nf** would normally be called (i.e., force a call to **halt**, even when not in runlevel 0 or 6). −n Suppress normal call to **sync**. −w Suppress normal execution; simply write to */var/log/wtmp*.

---

host

host [*options*] *host* [*server*]
host [*options*] *zone* [*server*]

Print information about specified hosts or zones in DNS. Hosts may be IP addresses or hostnames; **host** converts IP addresses to hostnames by default, and appends the local domain to hosts without a trailing dot. Default servers are determined in */etc/resolv.conf.* For more information about hosts and zones, try Chapters 1 and 2 of *DNS and BIND*, by Paul Albitz and Cricket Liu, published by O'Reilly & Associates.

Options

−a   Same as −t ANY.

−c *class*
     Search for specified resource record class (IN, INTERNET, CS, CSNET, CH, CHAOS, HS, HESIOD, ANY, or *). Default is IN.

−d   Debugging mode. −dd is a more verbose version.

−e   Do not print information about domains outside of specified zone. For hostname queries, do not print "additional information" or "authoritative nameserver".

−f *file*   Output to *file* as well as standard out.

−i   Given an IP address, return the corresponding *in-addr.arpa* address, class (always PTR), and hostname.

−l *zone*
     List all machines in *zone*.

−m   Print only MR, MG, and MB records; recursively expand MR (renamed mail box) and MG (mail group) records to MB (mail box) records.

−o	Do not print output to standard out.
−p [*server*]	For use with −l. Query only the zone's primary nameserver (or *server*) for zone transfers, instead of those authoritative servers that respond. Useful for testing unregistered zones.
−q	Quiet. Suppress warning, but not error, messages.
−r	Do not ask contacted server to query other servers, but require only the information that it has cached.
−t *type*	Look for *type* entries in the resource record. *type* may be A, NS, PTR, ANY, or * (all).
−u	Use TCP, not UDP.
−v	Verbose. Include all fields from resource record, even time-to-live and class, as well as "additional information" and "authoritative nameservers" (provided by the remote nameserver).
−vv	Very verbose. Include information about *host*'s defaults.
−w	Never give up on queried server.
−x	Allow multiple hosts or zones to be specified. If a server is also specified, the argument must be preceeded by −X.
−A	For hostnames, look up the associated IP address, and then reverse look up the hostname, to see if a match occurs. For IP addresses, look up the associated hostname, and determine whether the host recognizes that address as its own. For zones, check IP addresses for all hosts. Exit silently if no incongruities are discovered.
−C	Similar to −l, but also checks to see if the zone's nameservers are really authoritative. The zone's SOA (start of authority) records specify authoritative nameservers (in NS fields). Those servers are queried; if they do not have SOA records, host reports a lame delegation. Other checks are made as well.
−D	Similar to −H, but includes the names of hosts with more than one address per defined name.

→

-E   Similar to -H, but does not treat extra-zone hosts as errors. Extra-zone hosts are hosts in an undefined subdomain.

-H *zone*
Print the number of unique hosts within *zone*. Do not include aliases. Also list all errors found (extra-zone names, duplicate hosts).

-F *file*   Redirect standard out to *file*, and print extra resource record output only on standard out.

-G *zone*
Similar to -H, but includes the names of gateway hosts.

-I *chars*
Do not print warnings about domain names containing illegal characters *chars*, such as _.

-L *level*
For use with -l. List all delegated zones within this zone, up to *level* deep, recursively.

-P *servers*
For use with -l. *servers* should be a comma-separated list. Specify preferred hosts for secondary servers to use when copying over zone data. Highest priority is given to those servers that match the most domain components in a given part of *servers*.

-R   Treat non-fully-qualified host names as BIND does, searching each component of the local domain.

-S   For use with -l. Print all hosts within the zone to standard out. Do not print hosts within sub-zones. Include class and IP address. Print warning messages (illegal names, lame delegations, missing records, etc.) to standard error.

-T   Print time-to-live values (how long information about each host will remain cached before the nameserver refreshes it).

-X   Specify a server to query, and allow multiple hosts or zones to be specified.

-Z   When printing recource records, include trailing dot in domain names, and print time-to-live value and class name.

hwclock [*options*]

Read or set the hardware clock. **hwclock** maintains change information in */etc/adjtime*, which can be used to adjust the clock based on how much it drifts over time. **hwclock** replaces the **clock** command. The single letter options are included for compatibility with the older command.

Options

You may specify only one of the following options:

-a   Adjust the hardware clock based on information in */etc/adjtime* and set the system clock to the new time.

--adjust
       Adjust the hardware clock based on information in */etc/adjtime*.

--date *date*
       Only meaningful with the --set option. *date* is a string appropriate for use with the **date** command.

--debug
       Print information about what **hwclock** is doing.

-r, --show
       Print the current time stored in the hardware clock.

-s, --hctosys
       Set the system time in accordance with the hardware clock.

--set Set the hardware clock according to the time given in the --date parameter.

--test Do not actually change anything. This is good for checking syntax.

-u, --utc
       The hardware clock is stored in Universal Coordinated Time.

--version
       Print version and exit.

-w, --systohc
       Set the hardware clock in accordance with the system time.

icmpinfo [*options*]

TCP/IP command. Intercept and interpret ICMP packets. Print the address and name of the message's sender, the

→

Sys Admin
Commands

icmpinfo ←	source port, the destination port, the sequence, and the packet size. By default, provide information only about packets that are behaving oddly.
	
	Options
	
	    -k Kill the **syslogd** process begun by -l.
	    -l Record via **syslogd**. Only a privileged user may use this option.
	    -n Use IP addresses instead of hostnames.
	    -p Suppress decoding of port number: do not attempt to guess the name of the service that is listening at that port.
	    -s Include IP address of interface that received the packet, in case there are several interfaces on the host machine.
	    -v Verbose. Include information about normal ICMP packets. You may also specify **-vv** and **-vvv** for extra verbosity.

identd	**in.identd** [*options*] [*kernelfile* [*kmemfile*]]
	
	TCP/IP command. Provide the name of the user whose process is running a specified TCP/IP connection. You may specify the kernel and its memory space.
	
	Options
	
	    -a *ip_address*
	        Bind to *ip_address*. Useful only with **-b**. By default, bind to the INADDR_ANY address.
	    -b Run standalone; not for use with **inetd**.
	    -d Allow debugging requests.
	    -g*gid* Attempt to run in the group *gid*. Useful only with **-b**.
	    -i Run as a daemon, one process per request.
	    -l Log via **syslogd**.
	    -m Allow multiple requests per session.
	    -n Return user IDs instead of user names.
	    -N Do not provide a user's name or user ID if the file *.noident* exists in the user's home directory.
	    -o When queried for the type of operating system, always return OTHER.

−p*port* Listen at *port* instead of the default, port 113.

−t*seconds*

> Exit if no new requests have been received before *seconds* seconds have passed. Note that, with −i or −w, the next new request will result in **identd** being restarted. Default is infinity (never exit).

−u*uid* Attempt to run as *uid*. Useful only with −b.

−V Print version and exit.

−w Run as a daemon, one process for all requests.

---

ifconfig [*interface*]
ifconfig [*interface address_family parameters addresses*]

TCP/IP command. Assign an address to a network interface and/or configure network interface parameters. **ifconfig** is typically used at boot time to define the network address of each interface on a machine. It may be used at a later time to redefine an interface's address or other parameters. Without arguments, **ifconfig** displays the current configuration for a network interface. Used with a single *interface* argument, **ifconfig** displays that interface's current configuration.

Arguments

interface

> String of the form *name unit*, for example *en0*.

address_family

> Since an interface may receive transmissions in differing protocols, each of which may require separate naming schemes, you can specify the *address_family* to change the interpretation of the remaining parameters. You may specify **inet** (the default; for TCP/IP), **ax25** (AX.25 Packet Radio), **ddp** (Appletalk Phase 2), or **ipx** (Novell).

Parameters

> The following parameters may be set with **ifconfig**:

> allmulti/−allmulti

>> Enable/disable sending of incoming frames to the kernel's network layer.

→

ifconfig
←

arp/–arp
> Enable/disable use of the Address Resolution Protocol in mapping between network-level addresses and link-level addresses.

broadcast
> (**inet** only) Specify address to use to represent broadcasts to the network. Default is the address with a host part of all 1's, i.e., x.y.z.255 for a class C network.

debug/–debug
> Enable/disable driver-dependent debugging code.

dest_address
> Specify the address of the correspondent on the other end of a point-to-point link.

down
> Mark an interface "down" (unresponsive).

hw *class address*
> Set the interface's hardware class and address. *class* may be **ether** (Ethernet), **ax25** (AX.25 Packet Radio), or **ARCnet**.

irq *addr*
> Set the device's interrupt line.

metric *n*
> Set routing metric of the interface to *n*. Default is 0.

mtu *num*
> Set the interface's Maximum Transfer Unit (MTU).

multicast
> Set the multicast flag.

netmask *mask*
> (**inet** only) Specify how much of the address to reserve for subdividing networks into subnetworks. *mask* can be specified as a single hexadecimal number with a leading 0x, with a dot notation Internet address, or with a pseudo-network name listed in the network table */etc/networks*.

pointopoint/–pointopoint [*address*]
> Enable/disable point-to-point interfacing, so that the connection between the two

machines is dedicated.

up Mark an interface "up" (ready to send and receive).

trailers/–trailers
　　Request/disable use of a "trailer" link-level encapsulation when sending.

address Either a hostname present in the hostname database (*/etc/hosts*), or an Internet address expressed in the Internet standard dot notation.

imapd

TCP/IP command. The Interactive Mail Access Protocol (IMAP) server daemon. **imapd** is invoked by **inetd** and listens on port 143 for requests from IMAP clients. IMAP allows mail programs to access remote mailboxes as if they were local. IMAP is a richer protocol than POP because it allows a client to retrieve message-level information from a server mailbox instead of the entire mailbox. IMAP can be used for online and offline reading. The popular Pine mail client contains support for IMAP.

inetd [*option*] [*configuration_file*]

TCP/IP command. Internet services daemon. **inetd** listens on multiple ports for incoming connection requests. When it receives one, it spawns the appropriate server. When started, **inetd** reads its configuration information from either *configuration_file*, or from the default configuration file */etc/inetd.conf*. It then issues a call to **getservbyname**, creates a socket for each server, and binds each socket to the port for that server. It does a **listen** on all connection-based sockets, then waits, using **select** for a connection or datagram.

When a connection request is received on a listening socket, **inetd** does an **accept**, creating a new socket. It then forks, dups, and execs the appropriate server. The invoked server has I/O to **stdin**, **stdout**, and **stderr** done to the new socket, connecting the server to the client process.

When there is data waiting on a datagram socket, **inetd** forks, dups, and execs the appropriate server, passing it any server program arguments. A datagram server has I/O to **stdin**, **stdout**, and **stderr** done to the original socket. If the datagram socket is marked as **wait**, the invoked server must process the message before **inetd** considers the socket

→

inetd
←
	available for new connections. If the socket is marked **nowait**, **inetd** continues to process incoming messages on that port.
	
	The following servers may be started by **inetd**: **bootpd**, **bootpgw**, **fingerd**, **ftpd**, **imapd**, **popd**, **rexecd**, **rlogind**, **rshd**, **talkd**, **telnetd**, and **tftpd**. Do not arrange for **inetd** to start **named**, **routed**, **rwhod**, **sendmail**, **listen**, or any NFS server.
	
	inetd rereads its configuration file when it receives a hangup signal, **SIGHUP**. Services may be added, deleted, or modified when the configuration file is reread.
	
	Option
	
	   −d Turn on socket-level debugging and print debugging information to **stdout**.
	
	Files
	
	   /etc/inetd.conf
	      Default configuration file.
	
	   /var/run/inetd.pid
	      inetd's process ID.

init	init [*option*] [*runlevel*]
	
	Option
	
	   −t *seconds*
	      When changing run levels, send SIGKILL *seconds* after SIGTERM. Default is 20.
	
	Files
	
	init is the first process run by any Unix machine at boot time. It verifies the integrity of all filesystems and then creates other processes, using fork-and-exec, as specified by */etc/inittab*. Which processes may be run are controlled by *runlevel*. All process terminations are recorded in */var/run/utmp* and */var/log/wtmp*. When the run level changes, **init** sends SIGTERM and then, after 20 seconds, SIGKILL to all processes that cannot be run in the new run level.
	
	Run levels
	
	The current run level may be changed by **telinit**, which is often just a link to **init**. The default run levels vary from distribution to distribution, but these are standard:

0	Halt the system.	**init**
1, s, S	Single user mode.	
6	Reboot the system.	
q, Q	Reread */etc/inittab.*	

Check the */etc/inittab* file for run levels on your system.

---

insmod [*options*] *file* [*symbol=value* ...]   **insmod**

Load the module *file* into the kernel, changing any symbols that are defined on the command line. If the module file is named *file.o* or *file.mod*, the module will be named *file.*

Options

    −f   Force loading of module, even if some problems are encountered.

    −m   Output a load map.

    −o *name*   Name module *name* instead of attempting to name it from the object file's name.

    −x   Do not export: do not add any external symbols from the module to the kernel's symbol table.

---

install [*options*] [*file*] *directories*   **install**

Used primarily in makefiles to update files. **install** copies files into user-specified directories. It will not overwrite a file. Similar to **cp**, but attempts to set permission modes, owner, and group.

Options

    −d, −−directory
           Create any missing directories.

    −g *group,* **−−group** *group*
           Set group ID of new file to *group* (privileged users only).

    −m *mode,* **−−mode** *mode*
           Set permissions of new file to *mode* (octal or symbolic). By default, the mode is **0755**.

    −o [*owner*], **−−owner** [*owner*]
           Set ownership to *owner,* or, if unspecified, to root (privileged users only).

    −s, −−strip
           Strip symbol tables.

*Sys Admin
Commands*

ipfwadm

ipfwadm *category command parameters* [*options*]
ipfwadm −M [−l | −s] [*options*]

Administer a firewall and its rules, firewall accounting, and IP masquerading. There are four categories of rules: IP packet accounting, IP input firewall, IP output firewall, and IP forwarding firewall. The rules are maintained in lists, with a separate list for each category. See the manpage for **ipfw**(4) for a more detailed description of how the lists work.

Each **ipfwadm** command specifies only one category and one rule. To create a secure firewall, you issue multiple **ipfwadm** commands; the combination of their rules work together to ensure that your firewall operates as you intend it to. The second form of the command is for masquerading. The commands −l and −s described below are the only ones that can be used with the masquerading category, −M.

Categories

One of the following flags is required to indicate the category of rules to which the command that follows the category applies.

−A [*direction*]

> IP accounting rules. Optionally, a direction can be specified:

> in Count only incoming packets.

> out Count only outgoing packets.

> both
>> Count both incoming and outgoing packets; this is the default.

−F IP forwarding firewall rules.

−I IP input firewall rules.

−M IP masquerading administration. Can be used only with the −l or −s command.

−O IP output firewall rules.

Commands

The category is followed by a command indicating the specific action to be taken. Unless otherwise specified, only one action can be given on a command line. For the commands that can include a policy, the valid policies are:

accept Allow matching packets to be received, sent, or forwarded.

deny   Block matching packets from being received, sent, or forwarded.

reject   Block matching packets from being received, sent, or forwarded and also return an ICMP error message to the sending host.

The commands are:

−a [*policy*]

Append one or more rules to the end of the rules for the category. No policy is specified for accounting rules. For firewall rules, a policy is required. When the source and/or destination names resolve to more than one address, a rule is added for each possible address combination.

−c

Check whether this IP packet would be accepted, denied, or rejected by the type of firewall represented by this category. Valid only when the category is **−I**, **−O**, or **−F**. Requires the **−V** parameter to be specified (see "Parameters," below).

−d [*policy*]

Delete one or more entries from the list of rules for the category. No policy is specified for accounting rules. The parameters specified with this command must exactly match the parameters from an append or insert command, or no match will be found and the rule will not be removed. Only the first matching rule in the list of rules is deleted.

−f

Remove (flush) all rules for the category.

−h

Display a help message with a brief description of the command syntax. Specified with no category:

        `% ipfwadm -h`

−i [*policy*]

Insert a new rule at the beginning of the selected list for the category. No policy is specified for accounting rules. For firewall rules, a policy is required. When the source and/or destination names resolve to more than one address, a rule is added for each possible address combination.

→

| ipfwadm | −l | List all rules for the category. This command may be combined with the −z command to reset the packet and byte counters after listing their current values. Unless the −x option is also specified, the packet and byte counters are shown as *number*K or *number*M, rounded to the nearest integer. See also the −e and −x options described under "Options" below. |
| ← | | |

−p *policy* Change the default policy for the selected type of firewall to *policy*. The default policy is used when no matching rule is found. Valid only with −I, −O, or −F.

−s *tcp tcpfin udp*
> Set the masquerading timeout values; valid only with −M. The three parameters are required and represent the timeout value in seconds for TCP sessions, TCP sessions after receiving a FIN packet, and UDP packets, respectively. A timeout value of 0 preserves the current timeout value of the corresponding entry.

−z   Reset the packet and byte counters for all rules in the category. This command may be combined with the −l command.

Parameters

The following parameters can be specified with the −a, −i, −d, or −c commands, except as noted. Multiple parameters can be specified on a single **ipfwadm** command line.

−D *address*[/*mask*] [*port* ...]
> The destination specification (optional). See the description of −S for the syntax, default values, and other requirements. ICMP types cannot be specified with −D.

−P *protocol*
> The protocol of the rule or packet; possible values are **tcp**, **udp**, **icmp**, or **all**. Defaults to **all**, which matches all protocols. −P cannot be specified with the −c command.

−S **address**[/*mask*] [*port* ...]
> The source IP address, specified as a hostname, a network name, or an IP address. The source address and mask default to 0.0.0.0/0. If −S is specified, −P must also be specified. The optional mask is specified as

a network mask or as the number of 1's on the left of the network mask (e.g., a mask of 24 is equivalent to 255.255.255.0). The mask defaults to 32. One or more values of *port* may optionally be specified, indicating what ports or ICMP types the rule applies to. The default is **all**. Ports may be specified by their */etc/services* entry. The syntax for indicating a range of ports is:

```
lowport:highport
```

For example:

```
-S 172.29.16.1/24 ftp:ftp-data
```

−V *address*

The address of the network interface the packet is received from (if category is **−I**) or is being sent to (if category is **−O**). *address* can be a hostname or an IP address, and defaults to 0.0.0.0, which matches any interface address. **−V** is required with the **−c** command:

```
-V 172.29.16.1
```

−W *name* Identical to **−V**, but takes a device name instead of its address:

```
-W ppp0
```

Options

−b Bidirectional mode. The rule matches IP packets in both directions. This option is valid only with the **−a**, **−i**, and **−d** commands.

−e Extended output. Used with the **−l** command to also show the interface address and any rule options. When listing firewall rules, also shows the packet and byte counters and the TOS (type of service) masks. When used with **−M**, also shows information related to delta sequence numbers.

−k Match TCP acknowledgment packets, i.e., only TCP packets with the ACK bit set. This option is ignored for all other protocols and is valid only with the **−a**, **−i**, and **−d** commands.

ipfwadm
←

−m   Accept masquerade packets for forwarding, making them appear to have originated from the local host. Recognizes reverse packets and automatically demasquerades them, bypassing the forwarding firewall. This option is valid only in forwarding firewall rules with policy `accept`. The kernel must have been compiled with CONFIG_IP_MASQUERADE defined.

−n   Numeric output. Prints IP addresses and port numbers in numeric format.

−o   Log packets that match this rule to the kernel log. This option is valid only with the −a, −i, and −d commands. The kernel must have been compiled with CONFIG_IP_FIREWALL_VERBOSE defined.

−r [*port*]   Redirect packets to a local socket, even if they were sent to a remote host. If *port* is 0 (the default), the packet's destination port is used. This option is valid only in input firewall rules with policy `accept`. The kernel must have been compiled with CONFIG_IP_TRANSPARENT_ PROXY defined.

−t *andmask xormask*
     Specify masks used for modifying the TOS field in the IP header. When a packet is accepted (with or without masquerading) by a firewall rule, its TOS field is bitwise and'ed with *andmask* and the result is bitwise xor'ed with *xormask*. The masks are specified as 8-bit hexadecimal values. This option is valid only with the −a, −i, and −d commands and has no effect when used with accounting rules or with firewall rules for rejecting or denying a packet.

−v   Verbose output. Prints detailed information about the rule or packet to be added, deleted, or checked. This option is valid only with the −a, −i, −d, and −c commands.

−x   Expand numbers. Displays the exact value of the packet and byte counters, instead of a rounded value. This option is valid only when the counters are being listed anyway (see also the −e option).

−y	Match TCP packets with the SYN bit set and the ACK bit cleared. This option is ignored for packets of other protocols and is valid only with the −a, −i, and −d commands.	ipfwadm

kbdrate [*options*]

Control the rate at which the keyboard repeats characters, as well as its delay time. Using this command without options sets a repeat rate of 10.9 characters per second; the default delay is 250 milliseconds. When Linux boots, however, it sets the keyboard rate to 30 characters per second.

Options

−s   Suppress printing of messages.

−r *rate*   Specify the repeat rate, which must be one of the following numbers (all in characters per second): 2.0, 2.1, 2.3, 2.5, 2.7, 3.0, 3.3, 3.7, 4.0, 4.3, 4.6, 5.0, 5.5, 6.0, 6.7, 7.5, 8.0, 8.6, 9.2, 10.0, 10.9, 12.0, 13.3, 15.0, 16.0, 17.1, 18.5, 20.0, 21.8, 24.0, 26.7, or 30.0.

−d *delay*   Specify the delay, which must be one of the following (in milliseconds): 250mS, 500mS, 750mS, or 1000mS.

kerneld

kerneld automatically loads kernel modules when they are needed, thereby reducing kernel memory usage from unused loaded modules and replacing manual loading of modules with **modprobe** or **insmod**. If a module has not been used for more than one minute, **kerneld** automatically removes it.

kerneld comes with the modules-utilities package and is set up during kernel configuration; its functionality is provided by interactions between that package and the kernel. **kerneld** is aware of most common types of modules. When more than one possible module can be used for a device (such as a network driver), **kerneld** uses the configuration file */etc/conf.modules*, which contains path information and aliases for all loadable modules, to determine the correct module choice.

kerneld can also be used to implement dial-on-demand networking, such as SLIP or PPP connections. The network

→

kerneld ←	connection request can be processed by **kerneld** to load the proper modules and set up the connection to the server.
klogd	**klogd** [*options*] Control which kernel messages are displayed on the console; prioritize all messages, and log them through **syslogd**. On many operating systems, **syslogd** performs all the work of **klogd**, but on Linux the features are separated. Kernel messages are gleaned from the */proc* filesystem and from system calls to **syslogd**. By default no messages appear on the console. Messages are sorted into 8 levels, 0–7, and the level number is prepended to each message.

Priority levels

0	Emergency situation (**KERN_EMERG**).
1	A crucial error has occurred (**KERN_ALERT**).
2	A serious error has occurred (**KERN_CRIT**).
3	An error has occurred (**KERN_ERR**).
4	A warning message (**KERN_WARNING**).
5	The situation is normal, but should be checked (**KERN_NOTICE**).
6	Information only (**KERN_INFO**).
7	Debugging messages (**KERN_DEBUG**).

Options

−c *level*	Print all messages of a higher priority (lower number) than *level* to the console.
−d	Debugging mode.
−f *file*	Print all messages to *file*; suppress normal logging.
−k *file*	Use *file* as source of kernel symbols.
−n	Avoid auto backgrounding. This is needed when **klogd** is started from **init**.
−o	One-shot mode. Prioritize and log all current messages, then immediately exit.
−s	Suppress reading of messages from the */proc* filesystem.

Files

/usr/include/linux/kernel.h, */usr/include/sys/syslog.h*
Sources for definitions of each logging level.

/proc/kmsg
> A file examined by **klogd** for messages.

/var/run/klogd.pid
> **klogd**'s process ID.

---

ksysms [*options*]

Print a list of all exported kernel symbols (name, address, and defining module, if applicable).

Options

−a	Include symbols from unloaded modules.
−h	Suppress header message.
−m	Include starting address and size. Useful only for symbols in loaded modules.

Files

/proc/ksyms
> Another source of the same information.

---

ldconfig [*options*] *directories*

Examine the libraries in *directory*, */etc/ld.so.conf*, */usr/lib*, and */lib*; update links and cache where necessary. Usually run in startup files or after the installation of new shared libraries.

Options

−D	Debug. Suppress all normal operations.
−l	Library mode. Expect libraries as arguments, not directories. Manually link specified libraries.
−n	Suppress examination of */usr/lib* and */lib* and reading of */etc/ld.so.conf*; do not cache.
−N	Do not cache; only link.
−p	Print all directories and candidate libraries in the cache. Expects no arguments.
−v	Verbose. Include version number, and announce each directory as it is scanned and links as they are created.
−X	Do not link; only rebuild cache.

→

ldconfig
←
	Files
	
	/lib/ld.so Linker and loader.
	
	/etc/ld.so.conf
	        List of directories that contain libraries.
	
	/etc/ld.so.cache
	        List of the libraries found in those libraries
	        mentioned in */etc/ld.so.conf.*

logger	**logger** [*options*] [*message...*]
	
	TCP/IP command. Add entries to the system log (via **syslogd**). A message can be given on the command line, or standard input is logged.
	
	Options
	
	    −f *file* Read *message* from *file*.
	
	    −i Include the process ID of the **logger** process.
	
	    −p *pri* Enter message with the specified priority *pri*. Default is "user.notice".
	
	    −t *tag* Mark every line in the log with the specifed *tag*.

login	**login** [*name* ǀ *option*] Log in to the system. **login** asks for a username (*name* can be supplied on the command line), and password (if appropriate). If successful, **login** updates accounting files, sets various environment variables, notifies users if they have mail, and executes startup shell files. No user except **root** is able to log in when */etc/nologin* exists. That file will be displayed before the connection is terminated. **Root** may connect only on a tty that is included in */etc/securetty*. If ˜*/.hushlogin* exists, execute a quiet login. If */var/adm/lastlog* exists, print the time of the last login. **Options** −f Suppress second login authentication.

−h *host*	Specify name of remote host. Normally used by servers, not humans; may be used only by **root**.	**login**
−p	Preserve previous environment.	

---

logrotate [*options*] *config_files*

Manipulate log files according to commands given in *config_files*.

Options

−d
: Debug mode. No changes will be made to log files.

−s, −−state *file*
: Save state information in *file*. The default is */var/lib/logrotate.status*.

−−usage
: Usage version and copyright information.

Commands

compress
: Compress old versions of log files with **gzip**.

copytruncate
: Copy log file, then truncate it in place. For use with programs whose logging cannot be temporarily halted.

create [*permissions*] [*owner*] [*group*]
: After rotation, recreate log file with the specified *permissions, owner,* and *group. permissions* must be given in octal. If any of these parameters is missing, the log file's original attributes will be used.

daily
: Rotate log files every day.

delaycompress
: Don't compress log file until the next rotation.

errors *address*
: Mail any errors to the given *address.*

endscript
: End a **postrotate** or **prerotate** script.

ifempty
: Rotate log file even if it is empty. Overrides the default **notifempty** option.

include *file*
: Read the *file* into current file. If *file* is a directory, read all files in that directory into the current file except those specified in the **tabooext** command.

Sys Admin Commands

→

logrotate ←	**mail** *address* Mail any deleted logs to *address*.

monthly   Rotate log files only the first time **logrotate** is run in a month.

nocompress
        Override **compress**.

nocopytruncate
        Override **copytruncate**.

nocreate   Override **create**.

nodelaycompress
        Override **delaycompress**.

noolddir   Override **olddir**.

notifempty
        Override **ifempty**.

olddir *directory*.
        Move logs into *directory* for rotation. *directory* must be on the same physical device as the original log files.

postrotate Begin a script of directives to apply after the log file is rotated. The script ends when the **endscript** directive is read.

prerotate Begin a script of directives to apply before a log file is rotated. The script ends when the **endscript** directive is read.

rotate *number*
        The *number* of times to rotate a log file before removing it.

size *n*[k|M]
        Rotate log file when it is greater than *n* bytes. *n* can optionally be followed by **k** for kilobytes or **M** for megabytes.

lpc	**lpc** [*command*]

Control line printer. If executed without a command, **lpc** will accept commands from standard input.

Commands

?, help [*commands*]
        Get a list of commands or help on specific commands.

abort all|*printer*

> Terminate current printer daemon and disable printing for the specified *printer*.

clean all|*printer*

> Remove files that cannot be printed from the specified printer queues.

disable all|*printer*

> Disable specified printer queues.

down all|*printer message*

> Disable specified printer queues and put *message* in the printer status file.

enable all|*printer*

> Enable the specified printer queues.

exit, quit   Exit **lpc**.

restart all|*printer*

> Try to restart printer daemons for the specified printers.

start all|*printer*

> Enable the printer queues and start printing daemons for the specified printers.

status all|*printer*

> Return the status of the specified printers.

stop all|*printer*

> Disable the specified printer daemons after any current jobs are completed.

topq printer [*jobnumbers*] [*users*]

> Put the specifed jobs at the top of the printer's queue in the order the jobs are listed.

up all|*printer*

> Enable print queues and restart daemons for the specified printers.

---

lpd [*option*] [*port*]

TCP/IP command. Line printer daemon. **lpd** is usually invoked at boot time from the *rc2* file. It makes a single pass through the printer configuration file (traditionally */etc/printcap*) to find out about the existing printers, and prints any files left after a crash. It then accepts requests to print files in a queue, transfer files to a spooling area, display a queue's status, or remove jobs from a queue. In each case, it forks a child process for each request, then continues to listen for subsequent requests. If *port* is specified, **lpd**

$\rightarrow$

listens on that port; otherwise, it uses **getservbyname** to ascertain the correct port.

The file *lock* in each spool directory prevents multiple daemons from becoming active simultaneously. After the daemon has set the lock, it scans the directory for files beginning wth **cf**. Lines in each **cf** file specify files to be printed, or nonprinting actions to be performed. Each line begins with a key character, which specifies informatin about the print job, or what to do with the remainder of the line. Key characters are:

C	classification—string to be used for the classification line on the burst page
c	**cifplot** file
f	formatted file—name of a file to print that is already formatted
g	graph file
H	hostname—name of machine where **lpd** was invoked
J	jobname—string to be used for the jobname on the burst page
L	literal—this line contains identification information from the password file, and causes the banner page to be printed
l	formatted file, but suppress pagebreaks and printing of control characters
M	mail—send mail to the specified user when the current print job completes
n	**ditroff** file
P	person—login name of person who invoked **lpd**
r	DVI file
T	Title—string to be used as the title for **pr**
t	**troff** file
U	unlink—name of file to remove upon completion of printing

Option

−l	Enable logging of all valid requests.

Files

> | | |
> |---|---|
> | */etc/printcap* | Printer description file |
> | */var/spool/** | Spool directories |
> | */var/spool/*/minfree* | |
> | | Minimum free space to leave |
> | */dev/lp** | Printer devices |
> | */etc/hosts.equiv* | Machine names allowed printer access |
> | */etc/hosts.lpd* | Machine names allowed printer access, but not under same administrative control |

---

lsmod

List all loaded modules: their name, size (in 4k units), and, if appropriate, a list of referring modules.

Files

>   */proc/modules*
>   > Source of the same information.

---

makedbm [*options*] *infile outfile*

NFS/NIS command. Make NIS **dbm** file. **makedbm** takes *infile* and converts it to a pair of files in **ndbm** format, namely *outfile.pag* and *outfile.dir*. Each line of the input file is converted to a single **dbm** record. All characters up to the first TAB or SPACE form the key, and the rest of the line is the data. If line ends with \&, the data for that record is continued on to the next line. It is left for the NIS clients to interpret #; **makedbm** does not treat it as a comment character. *infile* can be –, in which case the standard input is read.

makedbm generates a special entry with the key yp_*last_modified*, which is the date of infile (or the current time, if infile is –).

Options

> | | |
> |---|---|
> | –b | Interdomain. Propagate a map to all servers using the interdomain name server **named**. |

>   –d yp_*domain_name*
>   > Create a special entry with the key yp_*domain_name*.

>   –i yp_*input_file*
>   > Create a special entry with the key yp_*input_file*.

→

makedbm ←	−l Convert keys of the given map to lower-case.

−l   Convert keys of the given map to lower-case.

−m yp_*master_name*
            Create a special entry with the key yp_*master_name*. If no master hostname is specified, yp_*master_name* is set to the local hostname.

−o yp_*output_file*
            Create a special entry with the key yp_*output_name*.

−s   Secure map. Accept connections from secure NIS networks only.

−u dbm *filename*
            Undo a **dbm** file—print out a **dbm** file, one entry per line, with a single space separating keys from values.

Example

It is easy to write shell scripts to convert standard files such as */etc/passwd* to the key value form used by **makedbm**. For example, the **awk** program:

```
BEGIN { FS =":";OFS = "\t";}
{ print $1, $0}
```

takes the */etc/passwd* file and converts it to a form that can be read by **makdbm** to make the NIS file *passwd.byname*. That is, the key is a username and the value is the remaining line in the */etc/passwd* file.

---

makemap	**makemap** [*options*] *type name*

makemap [*options*] *type name*

Transfer from standard input to **sendmail**'s database maps. Input should be formatted as:

               key value

You may comment lines with #, may substitute parameters with %n, and must escape literal % by entering it as %%. The *type* must be one of **dbm**, **btree**, or **hash**. The *name* is a filename to which **makemap** appends standard suffixes.

Options

−f   Suppress conversion of uppercase to lower-case.

−N   Append a zero byte to each key.

−o	Append to existing file instead of replacing it.	**makemap**
−r	If some keys already exist, replace them. (By default, **makemap** will exit when encountering a duplicated key.)	
−v	Verbose mode.	

---

mke2fs [*options*] *device* [*blocks*]
mkfs.ext2 *[options] device [blocks]*

mke2fs

Format *device* as a Linux second extended filesystem. You may specfy the number of blocks on the device, or allow **mke2fs** to guess.

Options

−b *block-size*
Specify block size in bytes.

−c
Scan *device* for bad blocks before execution.

−f *fragment-size*
Specify fragment size in bytes.

−i *bytes-per-inode*
Create an inode for each *bytes-per-inode* of space. *bytes-per-inode* must be 1024 or greater; it is 4096 by default.

−l *filename*
Consult *filename* for a list of bad blocks.

−m *percentage*
Reserve *percentage* percent of the blocks for use by privileged users.

−q
Quiet mode.

−v
Verbose mode.

−S
Write only superblock and group descriptors; suppress writing of inode table and block and inode bitmaps. Useful only when attempting to salvage damaged systems.

---

mkfs [*options*] [*fs−options*] *filesys* [*blocks*]

mkfs

Construct a filesystem on a device (such as a hard disk partition). *filesys* is either the name of the device or the mount point. **mkfs** is actually a frontend that invokes the appropriate version of **mkfs** according to a filesystem type specified by the −t option. For example, a Linux second extended

→

mkfs
←
	filesystem uses **mkfs.ext2** (which is the same as **mke2fs**); MS-DOS filesystems use **mkfs.msdos**. *fs-options* are options specific to the filesystem type. *blocks* is the size of the filesystem in 1024-byte blocks.
	
	Options
	
	    –V Produce verbose output, including all commands executed to create the specific filesystem.
	
	    –t *fs-type* Tells **mkfs** what type of filesystem to construct.
	
	    filesystem-specific options
	    These options must follow generic options and not be combined with them. Most filesystem builders support these three options:
	
	    –c Check for bad blocks on the device before building the filesystem.
	
	    –l *file*
	    Read the file *file* for the list of bad blocks on the device.
	
	    –v Produce verbose ouput.

mkfs.minix	**mkfs.minix** [*options*] *device size* Creates a MINIX filesystem. See **mkfs**.
mklost+found	**mklost+found** Create a *lost+found* directory in the current working directory. Intended for Linux second extended filesystems.
mkswap	**mkswap** [*option*] *device* [*size*] Create swap space on *device*. You may specify its *size* in blocks; each block is a page of about 4K. *Option* –c Check for bad blocks before creating the swap space.
modprobe	**modprobe** [*options*] [*modules*] With no options, attempt to load the specified module, as well as all modules on which it depends. If more than one

module is specified, attempt to load further modules only if the previous module failed to load.

Options

 −a   Load all listed modules, not just the first one.

 −l [*pattern*]

      List all existing modules. This option may be combined with -t to specify a type of module, or you may include a *pattern* to search for.

 −r   Remove the specified modules, as well as the modules on which they depend.

 −t *type*   Load only a specific type of module. Consult */etc/conf.modules* for the directories in which all modules of that type reside.

Files

 /etc/conf.modules

      Information about modules: which ones depend on others, which directories correspond to particular types of modules.

 /sbin/insmod, /sbin/rmmod, /sbin/depmod

      Programs that **modprobe** relies on.

---

mount [*options*] [*special–device*] [*directory*]

Mount a file structure. **mount** announces to the system that a removable file structure is present on *special-device*. The file structure is mounted on *directory*, which must already exist and should be empty; it then becomes the name of the root of the newly mounted file structure. If **mount** is invoked with no arguments, it displays the name of each mounted device, the directory on which it is mounted, whether the file structure is read-only, and the date it was mounted. Only a privileged user can use the **mount** command.

Options

 −a   Mount all filesystems listed in */etc/fstab*. Note: this is the only option that cannot take a *special-device* or *node* argument.

 −f   Fake mount. Go through the motions of checking the device and directory, but do not actually mount the filesystem.

Sys Admin Commands

→

mount ←	−n	Do not record the mount in */etc/mtab*.
	−o *option*	Note: this is the only option to **mount** that requires a *special-device* or *node* argument. Qualify the mount with one of the specified *options*:

async
> Read input and output to the device asynchronously.

auto
> Allow mounting with the −a option.

defaults
> Use all options' default values (**async, auto, dev, exec, nouser, rw, suid**).

dev
> Interpret any special devices that exist on the filesystem.

exec
> Allow binaries to be executed.

noauto
> Do not allow mounting via the −a option.

nodev
> Do not interpret any special devices which exist on the filesystem.

noexec
> Do not allow the execution of binaries on the filesystem.

nosuid
> Do not acknowledge any **suid** or **sgid** bits.

nouser
> Only privileged users will have access to the filesystem.

remount
> Expect the filesystem to have already been mounted, and remount it.

ro Allow read-only access to the filesystem.

rw Allow read/write access to the filesystem.

suid
> Acknowledge **suid** and **sgid** bits.

sync
> Read input and output to the device synchronously.

user
> Allow unprivileged users to mount the filesystem. Note that the defaults on such a system will be **nodev, noexec,** and **nosuid,** unless otherwise specified.

check=relaxed|normal|strict
> Specify how strictly to regulate the integration of an MS-DOS filesystem when mounting it.

conv=binary|text|auto
> Specify method by which to convert files on MS-DOS and ISO-9660 filesystems.

debug
> Turn debugging on for MS-DOS and **ext2fs** filesystems.

errors=continue|remount|ro|panic
> Specify action to take when encountering an error. **ext2fs** filesystems only.

-r
    Mount filesystem read-only.

-t *type*
    Specify the filesystem type. Possible values are: **minix, ext, ext2, xiafs, hpfs, msdos, umsdos, vfat, proc, nfs, iso9660, smbfs, ncpfs, affs, ufs, romfs, sysv, xenix,** and **coherent.** Note that **ext** and **xiafs** are valid only for kernels older than 2.1.21 and that **sysv** should be used instead of **xenix** and **coherent.**

-v
    Display mount information verbosely.

-w
    Mount filesystem read/write. This is the default.

Files

/etc/fstab
    List of filesystems to be mounted and options to use when mounting them.

/etc/mtab
    List of filesystems that are currently mounted, and the options with which they were mounted.

mountd	**rpc.mountd** [*options*]

NFS/NIS command. NFS mount request server. **mountd** reads the file */etc/exports* to determine which filesystems are available for mounting by which machines. It also provides information as to what filesystems are mounted by which clients. See also **nfsd**.

Options

    -d, --debug
        Debug mode. Output all debugging information via **syslogd**.

    -f *file*, **--exports-file** *file*
        Read the export permissions from *file* instead of */etc/exports*.

    -n, --allow-non-root
        Accept even those mount requests that enter via a non-reserved port.

    -p, --promiscuous
        Accept requests from any host that sends them.

    -r, --re-export
        Allow re-exportation of imported filesystems.

    -v, --version
        Print the version number.

Files

    /etc/exports
        Information about mount permissions. |
| **named** | **named** [*options*]

TCP/IP command. Internet domain name server. **named** is used by resolver libraries to provide access to the Internet distributed naming database. With no arguments, **named** reads */etc/named.boot* for any initial data and listens for queries on a privileged port. See RFC 1034 and RFC 1035 for more details.

There are several different **named** binaries available at different Linux archives, displaying various behaviors. If your version doesn't behave like the one described here, never fear—it should have come with documentation. |

Options

 −d *debuglevel*

    Print debugging information. *debuglevel* is a number indicating the level of messages printed.

 −p *port* Use *port* as the port number. Default is 42.

 [−b] *bootfile* File to use instead of *named.boot*. The **−b** is optional and allows you to specify a filename that begins with a leading dash.

Files

 /etc/named.boot

    Read when **named** starts up.

---

netdate [*options*] [*protocol*] *hostname...*

TCP/IP command. Set the system time according to the time provided by one of the hosts in the list *hostname*. **netdate** tries to ascertain which host is the most reliable source. When run by an unprivileged user, **netdate** reports the current time, without attempting to set the system clock. You may specify the *protocol*—**udp** (the default) or **tcp**—once, or several times for various hosts.

Options

 −l *time* The most reliable host is chosen from the list by sorting the hosts into groups based on the times they return when questioned. The first host from the largest group is then polled a second time. The differences between its time and the local host's time on each poll are recorded. These two differences are then compared. If the gap between them is greater than *time* (the default is five seconds), the host is rejected as inaccurate.

 −v   Display the groups into which hosts are sorted.

---

netstat [*options*]

TCP/IP command. Show network status. For all active sockets, print the protocol, the number of bytes waiting to be

→

Sys Admin Commands

netstat
←
	received, the number of bytes to be sent, the port number, the remote address and port, and the state of the socket.
	
	Options
	
	    −a Show the state of all sockets, not just active ones.
	
	    −c Display information continuously, refreshing once every second.
	
	    −i Include statistics for network devices.
	
	    −n Show network addresses as numbers.
	
	    −o Include additional information such as user name.
	
	    −r Show routing tables.
	
	    −t List only TCP sockets.
	
	    −u List only UDP sockets.
	
	    −v Print the version number and exit.
	
	    −w List only raw sockets.
	
	    −x List only Unix domain sockets.

nfsd	**rpc.nfsd** [*options*] Daemon that starts the NFS server daemons that handle client filesystem requests. These daemons are user-level processes. The options are exactly the same as in **mountd**.
nslookup	**nslookup** [−*option...*] [*host_to_find*	− [*server*]] TCP/IP command. Query Internet domain name servers. **nslookup** has two modes: interactive and noninteractive. Interactive mode allows the user to query name servers for information about various hosts and domains or to print a list of hosts in a domain. It is entered either when no arguments are given (default name server will be used), or when the first argument is a hyphen and the second argument is the hostname or Internet address of a name server. Noninteractive mode is used to print just the name and requested information for a host or domain. It is used when the name of the host to be looked up is given as the first argument. Any of the *keyword=value* pairs listed under the interactive **set** command can be used as an option on the command line by prefacing the keyword with a '−'. The optional second argument specifies a name server.

Options

All of the options under the **set** interactive command can be entered on the command line, with the syntax −*keyword*[=*value*].

Interactive commands

exit   Exit **nslookup**.

finger [*name*] [>|>>*filename*]
> Connect with finger server on current host, optionally creating or appending to *filename*.

help, ? Print a brief summary of commands.

host [*server*]
> Look up information for *host* using the current default server or using *server* if specified.

ls −[ahd] *domain* [>|>>*filename*]
> List information available for *domain*, optionally creating or appending to *filename*. The −**a** option lists aliases of hosts in the domain. −**h** lists CPU and operating system information for the domain. −**d** lists all contents of a zone transfer.

lserver *domain*
> Change the default server to *domain*. Use the initial server to look up information about *domain*.

root   Change default server to the server for the root of the domain name space.

server *domain*
> Change the default server to *domain*. Use the current default server to look up information about *domain*.

set *keyword*[=*value*]
> Change state information affecting the lookups. Valid keywords are:
>
> **all** Print the current values of the frequently used options to **set**.
>
> class=*name*
> > Set query class to IN (Internet), CHAOS, HESIOD, or ANY. Default is IN.
>
> domain=*name*
> > Change default domain name to *name*.

→

nslookup
←

[no]debug
> Turn debugging mode on or off.

[no]d2
> Turn exhaustive debugging mode on or off.

[no]defname
> Append default domain name to every lookup.

[no]ignoretc
> Ignore truncate error.

[no]recurse
> Tell name server to query or not query other servers if it does not have the information.

[no]search
> With *defname*, search for each name in parent domains of current domain.

[no]vc
> Always use a virtual circuit when sending requests to the server.

port=*port*
> Connect to name server using *port*.

querytype=*value*
> See **type**=*value*.

retry=*number*
> Set number of retries to *number*.

root=*host*
> Change name of root server to *host*.

srchlist=*domain*
> Set search list to *domain*.

timeout=*number*
> Change time-out interval for waiting for a reply to *number* seconds.

type=*value*
> Change type of information returned from a query to one of:

A	Host's Internet address
ANY	Any available information
CNAME	Canonical name for an alias
HINFO	Host CPU and operating system type
MD	Mail destination

MG	Mail group member
MINFO	Mailbox or mail list information
MR	Mail rename domain name
MX	Mail exchanger
NS	Nameserver for the named zone
PTR	Host name or pointer to other information
SOA	Domain start-of-authority
TXT	Text information
UINFO	User information
WKS	Supported well-known services

view *filename*

Sort and list output of previous **ls** command(s) with **more**.

/usr/sbin/rpc.pcnfsd

NFS/NIS command. NFS authentication and print request server. **pcnfsd** is an RPC server that supports ONC clients on PC systems. **pcnfsd** reads the configuration file */etc/pcnfsd.conf*, if present, then services RPC requests directed to program number 150001. This current release of the **pcnfsd** daemon (as of this printing) supports both version 1 and version 2 of the **pcnfsd** protocol. Requests serviced by **pcnfsd** fall into three categories: authentication, printing, and other. Only the authentication and printing services have administrative significance.

Authentication

When **pcnfsd** receives a PCNFSD_AUTH or PCNFSD2_AUTH request, it will log in the user by validating the username and password, returning the corresponding user ID, group IDs, home directory, and umask. At this time, **pcnfsd** will also append a record to the *wtmp* database. If you do not want to record PC logins in this way, add the line:

```
wtmp off
```

to the */etc/pcnfsd.conf* file.

Printing

pcnfsd supports a printing model based on the use of NFS to transfer the actual print data from the client to the server. The client system issues a PCNFSD_PR_INIT or PCNFSD2_PR_INIT request, and the server returns the path to a spool directory that the client may use and that is exported

$\rightarrow$

pcnfsd ←	by NFS. **pcnfsd** creates a subdirectory for each of its clients; the parent directory is normally */usr/spool/pcnfs* and the subdirectory is the hostname of the client system. If you want to use a different parent directory, add the line:

> **spooldir** *path*

to the */etc/pcnfsd.conf* file. Once a client has mounted the spool directory and has transferred print data to a file in this directory, **pcnfsd** will issue a PCNFSD_PR_START or PCN-FSD2_PR_START request. **pcnfsd** constructs a command based on the printing services of the server operating system and executes the command using the identity of the PC user. Every print request includes the name of the printer to be used. **pcnfsd** interprets a printer as either a destination serviced by the system print spooler or as a virtual printer. Virtual printers are defined by the following line in the */etc/pcnfsd.conf* file:

> **printer** *name alias-for command*

where *name* is the name of the printer you want to define, *alias-for* is the name of a real printer that corresponds to this printer, and *command* is a command that will be executed whenever a file is printed on *name*.

pop2d	**in.pop2d**

Allow users to connect to port 109 and request the contents of their mailbox in */var/spool/mail*. **pop2d** requires a username and password before providing mail, and can serve individual messages. See also **pop3d**.

Commands

Each command must be entered on a separate line.

HELO	Prompt for username and password.
FOLD	Open */var/spool/mail/$USER*.
HOST	Open */var/spool/pop/$USER*.
READ	Read a message.
RETR	Retrieve a message.
ACKS	Save the last message retrieved and move to next message.
ACKD	Delete the last message retrieved and move to next message.

| NACK | Save the last message retrieved and expect to resend it. | pop2d |
| QUIT | Exit. | |

---

in.pop3d

pop3d

pop3d is a more recent version of **pop2d**. It behaves similarly, but accepts a slightly different list of commands.

Commands

USER	Prompt for name.
PASS	Prompt for password.
STAT	Display the number of messages in the mailbox and its total size.
LIST	Display individual messages' sizes.
DELE	Delete a message.
NOOP	Perform a null operation.
LAST	Print the number of the most recently received message that has been read.
RSET	Reset: clear all deletion marks.
TOP	Print the first part of a message.
QUIT	Exit.

---

rpc.portmap [*option*]

portmap

NFS/NIS command. RPC program number to IP port mapper. **portmap** is a server that converts RPC program numbers to IP port numbers. It must be running in order to make RPC calls. When an RPC server is started, it tells **portmap** what port number it is listening to and what RPC program numbers it is prepared to serve. When a client wishes to make an RPC call to a given program number, it first contacts **portmap** on the server machine to determine the port number where RPC packets should be sent. **portmap** must be the first RPC server started.

Option

| -d | Run **portmap** in debugging mode. Does not allow **portmap** to run as a daemon. |

---

ping [*options*] *host*

ping

Confirm that a remote host is online and responding. **ping** is intended for use in network testing, measurement, and

$\rightarrow$

management. Because of the load it can impose on the network, it is unwise to use **ping** during normal operations or from automated scripts.

Options

−c *count*

Stop after sending (and receiving) *count* ECHO_RESPONSE packets.

−d Set SO_DEBUG option on socket being used.

−f Flood **ping**-output packets as fast as they come back, or 100 times per second, whichever is more. This can be very hard on a network and should be used with caution; only a privileged user may use this option.

−i *wait*

Wait *wait* seconds between sending each packet. Default is to wait one second between each packet. This option is incompatible with the −f option.

−l *preload*

Send *preload* number of packets as fast as possible before falling into normal mode of behavior.

−n Numeric output only. No attempt will be made to look up symbolic names for host addresses.

−p *digits*

Specify up to 16 pad bytes to fill out packet sent. This is useful for diagnosing data-dependent problems in a network. *digits* are in hex. For example, −p ff will cause the sent packet to be filled with all ones.

−q Quiet output—nothing is displayed except the summary lines at startup time and when finished.

−r Bypass the normal routing tables and send directly to a host on an attached network.

−s *packetsize*

Specify number of data bytes to be sent. Default is 56, which translates into 64 ICMP data bytes when combined with the eight bytes of ICMP header data.

−v Verbose—list ICMP packets received other than ECHO_RESPONSE.

−R	Set the IP record route option, which will store the route of the packet inside the IP header. The contents of the record route will be printed if the **−v** option is given, and will be set on return packets if the target host preserves the record route option across echoes, or the **−l** option is given.	**ping**

powerd *device*

Monitor the connection to an uninterruptible power supply, which the user must specify via *device*. When power goes low, signal **init** to run its **powerwait** and **powerfail** entries; when full power is restored, signal **init** to run its **powerokwait** entries.

pppd [*options*] [*tty*] [*speed*]

PPP stands for the Point-to-Point Protocol; it allows datagram transmission over a serial connection. **pppd** attempts to configure *tty* for PPP (searching in */dev*), or, by default, the controlling terminal. You can also specify a baud rate of *speed*.

Options

asyncmap *map*
> Specify which control characters cannot pass over the line. *map* should be a 32-bit hex number, where each bit represents a character to escape. For example, bit 00000001 represents the character 0x00; bit 80000000 represents the character 0x1f or _. You may specify multiple characters.

auth
> Require self-authentication by peers before allowing packets to move.

connect *command*
> Connect as specified by *command*, which may be a binary or shell command.

debug, −d Increment the debugging level.

defaultroute
> Add a new default route in which the peer is the gateway. When the connection shuts down, remove the route.

−detach Operate in the foreground. By default, **pppd** forks and operates in the background.

→

disconnect *command*
> Close the connection as specified by *command*, which may be a binary or shell command.

domain *d*   Specify a domain name of *d*.

escape *character-list*
> Escape all characters in *character-list*, which should be a comma-separated list of hex numbers. You cannot escape 0x20–0x3f or 0x5e.

file *file*   Consult *file* for options.

lock   Allow only **pppd** to access the device.

mru *bytes*   Refuse packets of more than *bytes* bytes.

name *name*
> Specify a machine name for the local system.

netmask *mask*
> Specify netmask (for example, 255.255.255.0).

passive, −p
> Do not exit if peer does not respond to attempts to initiate a connection. Instead, wait for a valid packet from the peer.

silent   Send no packets until after receiving one.

[*local_IP_address*]:[*remote_IP_address*]
> Specify the local and/or remote interface IP addresses, as hostnames or numeric addresses.

Files

/var/run/pppn.pid
> **pppd**'s process ID. The *n* in *pppn.pid* is the number of the PPP interface unit corresponding to this **pppd** process.

/etc/ppp/ip-up
> Binary or script to be executed when the PPP link becomes active.

/etc/ppp/ip-down
> Binary or script to be executed when the PPP link goes down.

/etc/ppp/pap-secrets
> Contains usernames, passwords, and IP addresses for use in PAP authentication.

/etc/ppp/options
> System defaults. Options in this file are set
> *before* the command-line options.

~/.ppprc   The user's default options. These are read
> before command-line options, but after the
> system defaults.

/etc/ppp/options.ttyname
> Name of the default serial port.

---

psupdate [*mapfile*]

Update the **psupdate** database (on some systems */boot/psupdate*, on others, */etc/psdatabase*), which contains information about the kernel image system map file. If no *mapfile* is specified, **psupdate** uses the default (which is either */usr/src/linux/vmlinux* or */usr/src/linux/tools/zSystem*, depending on the distribution).

---

pwck [*option*] [*files*]

Remove corrupt or duplicate entries in the */etc/passwd* and */etc/shadow* files. **pwck** will prompt for a **yes** or **no** before deleting entries. If the user replies **no**, the program will exit. Alternate passwd and shadow *files* can be checked. If correctable errors are found, the user will be encouraged to run the **usermod** command.

Option

−n
> Non-interactive mode. Don't prompt for input, and delete no entries. Return appropriate exit status.

Exit Status

0   Success.

1   Syntax error.

2   One or more bad password entries found.

3   Could not open password files.

4   Could not lock password files.

5   Could not write password files.

---

ramsize [*option*] [*image* [*size* [*offset*]]]

If no options are specified, print usage information for the RAM disk. The pair of bytes at offset 504 in the kernel image normally specify the RAM size; with a kernel *image*

→

ramsize ←	argument, print the information found at that offset. To change that information, specify a new *size* (in kilobytes). You may also specify a different *offset*. Note that **rdev −r** is the same as **ramsize**. *Option* −o *offset* Same as specifying an *offset* as an argument.

rarp	**rarp** [*options*]
	
	 Administer the Reverse Address Resolution Protocol (RARP) table (usually */proc/net/rarp*).
	
	 Options
	
	     −a [*hostname*]
	         Show all entries. If *hostname* is specified, show only the entries relevant to *hostname*, which may be a list.
	
	     −d *hostname*
	         Remove the entries relevant to *hostname*, which may be a list.
	
	     −s *hostname hw_addr*
	         Add a new entry for *hostname*, with the hardware address *hw_addr*.
	
	     −t *type* Check only for *type* entries when consulting or changing the table. *type* my be **ether** (the default) or **ax25**.
	
	     −v Verbose mode.

rdate	**rdate** [*option*] TCP/IP command. Notify the time server that date has changed. If the local time server is a master, it will notify all of the slaves that the time has been changed. If the local time server is a slave, it will request that the master update the time. *Option* −p Print the date; do not attempt to set it.
rdev	**rdev** [*options*] [*image* [*value* [*offset*]]] If no arguments are specified, display a line, in */etc/mtab* syntax, that describes the root filesystem. Otherwise, change the values of the bytes in the kernel image that describe the

RAM disk size (by default located at byte offset 504 in the kernel), VGA mode (default 506), and root device (default 508). You must specify the kernel *image* to change, and may specify a new *value* and a different *offset*.

Options

−o *offset*	Same as specifying an *offset* as an argument.
−r	Behave like **ramsize**.
−s	Behave like **swapdev**.
−v	Behave like **vidmode**.
−R	Behave like **rootflags**.

rdist [*options*] [*names*]

rdist

Remote file distribution client program. **rdist** maintains identical copies of files over multiple hosts. It reads commands from a file named *distfile* to direct the updating of files and/or directories. An alternative *distfile* can be specified with the −**f** option or the −**c** option.

Options

−a *num*
  Do not update filesystems with fewer than *num* bytes free.

−c *name* [*login@*]*host*[:*dest*]
  Interpret the arguments as a small *distfile*, where *login* is the user to log in as, *host* is the destination host, *name* is the local file to transfer, and *dest* is the remote name where the file should be installed.

−d *var=value*
  Define *var* to have *value*. This option defines or overrides variable definitions in the *distfile*. Set the variable *var* to *value*.

−f *file*
  Read input from *file* (by default, *distfile*). If *file* is −, read from standard input.

−l *options*
  Specify logging options on the local machine.

−m *machine*
  Update only *machine*. May be specified multiple times for multiple machines.

Sys Admin
Commands

→

Alphabetical Summary of Commands — *rdist*   523

rdist	−n	Suppress normal execution. Instead, print the commands that would have been executed.
←	−o*options*	Specify one or more *options*, which must be comma-separated.

chknfs
Suppress operations on files that reside on NFS filesystems.

chkreadonly
Check filesystem to be sure it is not read-only before attempting to perform updates.

chksym
Do not update files that exist on the local host but are symbolic links on the remote host.

compare
Compare files; use this comparison as the criteria for determining which files should be updated, rather than using age.

follow
Interpret symbolic links, copying the file to which the link points instead of creating a link on the remote machine.

ignlnks
Ignore links that appear to be unresolvable.

nochkgroup
Do not update a file's group ownership unless the entire file needs updating.

nochkmode
Do not update file mode unless the entire file needs updating.

nochkowner
Do not update file ownership unless the entire file needs updating.

nodescend
Suppress recursive descent into directories.

noexec
> Suppress **rdist** of executables that are in *a.out* format.

numchkgroup
> Check group ownership by group ID instead of by name.

numchkowner
> Check file ownership by user ID instead of by name.

quiet
> Quiet mode; does not print commands as they execute.

remove
> Remove files that exist on the remote host but not the local host.

savetargets
> Save updated files in *name.old.*

verify
> Print a list of all files on the remote machine that are out of date, but do not update them.

whole
> Preserve directory structure by creating subdirectories on the remote machine. For example, if you **rdist** the file */foo/bar* into the directory */baz*, it would produce the file */baz/foo/bar*, instead of the default, */baz/bar*.

younger
> Do not update files that are younger than the master files.

−p *path*   Specify the path to search for **rdistd** on the remote machine.

−t *seconds*   Specify the timeout period (default 900 seconds) after which **rdist** will sever the connection if the remote server has not yet responded.

−A *num*   Specify the minumum number of inodes that **rdist** requires.

−D   Debugging mode.

−F   Execute all commands sequentially, without forking.

Sys Admin Commands

→

rdist ←	−L *options*	Specify logging options on the remote machine.
	−M *num*	Do not allow more than *num* child rdist processes to run simultaneously. Default is 4.
	−P *path*	Specify path to *rsh* on the local machine.

rdistd

rdistd *options*

Start the **rdist** server. Note that you *must* specify the −S option, unless you are simply querying for version information with −V.

Options

−D	Debugging mode.
−S	Start the server.
−V	Display the version number and exit immediately.

reboot

reboot [*options*]

Close out filesystems, shut down the system, then reboot the system. Because this command immediately stops all processes, it should be run only in single-user mode. If the system is not in run level 0 or 6, **reboot** calls **shutdown −nf**.

Options

−d	Suppress writing to */var/log/wtmp*.
−f	Call **reboot** even when **shutdown** would normally be called.
−n	Suppress normal call to **sync**.
−w	Suppress normal execution; simply write to */var/log/wtmp*.

rexecd

rexecd *command−line*

TCP/IP command. Server for the **rexec** routine, providing remote execution facilities with authentication based on usernames and passwords. **rexecd** is started by **inetd** and must have an entry in **inetd**'s configuration file, */etc/inetd.conf*. When **rexecd** receives a service request, the following protocol is initiated:

1. The server reads characters from the socket up to a null byte. The resulting string is interpreted as an ASCII number, base 10.

2. If the number received in step 1 is nonzero, it is interpreted as the port number of a secondary stream to be used for **stderr**. A second connection is then created to the specified port on the client's machine.

3. A null-terminated username of at most 16 characters is retrieved on the initial socket.

4. A null-terminated, unencrypted password of at most 16 characters is retrieved on the initial socket.

5. A null-terminated command to be passed to a shell is retrieved on the initial socket. The length of the command is limited by the upper bound on the size of the system's argument list.

6. **rexecd** then validates the user, as is done at login time, and, if the authentication was successful, changes to the user's home directory and establishes the user and group protections of the user.

7. A null byte is returned on the connection associated with **stderr** and the command line is passed to the normal login shell of the user. The shell inherits the network connections established by **rexecd**.

Diagnostics

`username too long`
> Name is longer than 16 characters.

`password too long`
> Password is longer than 16 characters.

`command too long`
> Command passed exceeds the size of the argument list.

`Login incorrect`
> No password file entry for the username exists.

`Password incorrect`
> Wrong password was supplied.

`No remote directory`
> **chdir** to home directory failed.

`Try again`
> **fork** by server failed.

`<shellname>:...`
> **fork** by server failed. User's login shell could not be started.

Sys Admin
Commands

rlogind	**rlogind** [*options*]
	TCP/IP command. Server for the **rlogin** program, providing a remote login facility, with authentication based on privileged port numbers from trusted hosts. **rlogind** is invoked by **inetd** when a remote login connection is requested, and executes the following protocol:
	• The server checks the client's source port. If the port is not in the range 0-1023, the server aborts the connection.
	• The server checks the client's source address and requests the corresponding hostname. If the hostname cannot be determined, the dot-notation representation of the host address is used.
	The login process propagates the client terminal's baud rate and terminal type, as found in the environment variable, TERM.
	Options
	−a Verify hostname.
	−l Do not authenticate hosts via a nonroot .*rhosts* file.
	−n Suppress keep-alive messages.
rmail	**rmail** *user...*
	TCP/IP command. Handle remote mail received via **uucp**, collapsing From lines in the form generated by **mail** into a single line of the form return-path!sender and passing the processed mail onto **sendmail**. **rmail** is explicitly designed for use with **uucp** and **sendmail**.
rmmod	**rmmod** [*option*] *modules*
	Unload a module or list of modules from the kernel. This command is successful only if the specified modules are not in use and no other modules are dependent on them.
	Option
	−r Recursively remove stacked modules (all modules that use the specified module).
rootflags	**rootflags** [*option*] *image* [*flags* [*offset*]]
	Sets *flags* for a kernel *image*. If no arguments are specified, print *flags* for the kernel image. *flags* is a two byte integer

located at offset 498 in a kernel *image*. Currently the only
effect of *flags* is to mount the root filesystem in read-only
mode if *flags* is non-zero. You may change *flags* by specifying the kernel *image* to change, the new *flags*, and the
byte-offset at which to place the new information (the
default is 498). Note that **rdev -R** is a synonym for **rootflags**.
If **LILO** is used, **rootflags** is not needed. *flags* can be set
from the **LILO** prompt during a boot.

Option

    −o *offset*   Same as specifying an *offset* as an argument.

---

route [*option*] [*command*]

TCP/IP command. Manually manipulate the routing tables
normally maintained by **routed**. **route** accepts two commands: **add**, to add a route, and **del**, to delete a route. The
two commands have the following syntax:

    add [**-net** | **-host**] *address* [**gw** *gateway*]
        [**netmask** *mask*] [**mss** *tcp-mss*] [**dev** *device*]
    del *address*

address is treated as a plain route unless **−net** is specified
or *address* is found in */etc/networks*. **−host** can be used to
specify that *address* is a plain route whether or not it is
found in */etc/networks*. The keyword *default* means to use
this route for all requests if no other route is known. You
can specify the *gateway* through which to route packets
headed for that address, its *netmask*, TCP *mss*, and the
device with which to associate the route. Only a privileged
user may modify the routing tables.

If no command is specified, **route** prints the routing tables.

Option

    −n   Prevent attempts to print host and network
                names symbolically when reporting actions.

---

routed [*options*] [*logfile*]

TCP/IP command. Network routing daemon. **routed** is
invoked by a privileged user at boot time to manage the
Internet Routing Tables. The routing daemon uses a variant
of the Xerox NS Routing Information Protocol in maintaining up-to-date kernel routing-table entries. When **routed** is
started, it uses the SIOCGIFCONF ioctl to find those directly
connected interfaces configured into the system and marked
up. **routed** transmits a REQUEST packet on each interface,

→

routed ←	then enters a loop, listening for REQUEST and RESPONSE packets from other hosts. When a REQUEST packet is received, **routed** formulates a reply based on the information maintained in its internal tables. The generated RESPONSE packet contains a list of known routes. Any RESPONSE packets received are used to update the Routing Tables as appropriate.
	When an update is applied, **routed** records the change in its internal tables, updates the kernal Routing Table, and generates a RESPONSE packet reflecting these changes to all directly connected hosts and networks.

Options

-d   Debugging mode. Log additional information to the *logfile*.

-g   Offer a route to the default destination.

-q   Opposite of -s option.

-s   Force **routed** to supply routing information, whether it is acting as an internetwork router or not.

-t   Stop **routed** from going into background and releasing itself from the controlling terminal, so that interrupts from the keyboard will kill the process.

---

rpcinfo

rpcinfo [*options*] [*host*] [*program*] [*version*]

NFS/NIS command. Report RPC information. *program* can be either a name or a number. If a *version* is specified, **rpcinfo** attempts to call that version of the specified *program*. Otherwise, it attempts to find all the registered version numbers for the specified *program* by calling version 0, and it attempts to call each registered version.

Options

-b *program version*
          Make an RPC broadcast to the specified *program* and *version*, using UDP, and report all hosts that respond.

-d *program version*
          Delete the specified *version* of *program*'s registration. Can be executed only by the user who added the registration or a privileged user.

−n *portnum*

> Use *portnum* as the port number for the −t and −u options, instead of the port number given by the portmapper.

−p [*host*] Probe the portmapper on host and print a list of all registered RPC programs. If *host* is not specified, it defaults to the value returned by **hostname**.

−t *host program* [*version*]

> Make an RPC call to *program* on the specified *host*, using TCP, and report whether a response was received.

−u *host program* [*version*]

> Make an RPC call to *program* on the specified *host*, using UDP, and report whether a response was received.

Examples

To show all of the RPC services registered on the local machine, use:

```
$ rpcinfo -p
```

To show all of the RPC services registered on the machine named **klaxon**, use:

```
$ rpcinfo -p klaxon
```

To show all machines on the local net that are running the Network Information Service (NIS), use:

```
$ rpcinfo -b ypserv version | uniq
```

where *version* is the current NIS version obtained from the results of the −p switch above.

rpm [*options*]

The Red Hat Package Manager. A freely available packaging system for software distribution and installation. RPM packages are built, installed, and queried with the **rpm** command. RPM package names usually end with a *.rpm* extension. **rpm** has ten modes, each with its own options. The user modes for installing, uninstalling, and querying packages are described here. See the **rpm** manpage and the RPM HOW-TO for information on some advanced options and the modes for building an RPM package. RPM provides a configuration file for specifying frequently used options. The system configuration file is usually */etc/rpmrc*, and users can set up their own *$HOME/.rpmrc* file. You can use

→

the **−−showrc** option to show the values RPM will use for all the options that may be set in an *rpmrc* file:

```
rpm --showrc
```

The **rpm** command includes an FTP client, so you can specify an *ftp://* URL to install or query a package across the Internet. You can use an FTP-style URL wherever *package-file* is specified in the commands presented here.

General options

The following options can be used with all modes:

−−dbpath *path*
> Use *path* as the path to the RPM database.

−−ftpport *port*
> Use *port* as the FTP port.

−−ftpproxy *host*
> Use *host* as a proxy server for all transfers. Specified if you are ftping through a firewall system that uses a proxy.

−−help Print a long usage message (running **rpm** with no options gives a shorter usage message).

−−keep-temps
> Do not remove temporary files (*/tmp/rpm-**) on completion. Used for debugging **rpm**.

−−quiet Display only error messages.

−−rcfile *filename*
> Use *filename* as the configuration file instead of the system configuration file */etc/rpmrc* or *$HOME/.rpmrc*.

−−root *dir*
> Use *dir* as the root directory for all operations.

−−version Print the version number of **rpm**.

−vv Print debugging information.

Install mode

Install or upgrade an RPM package. The syntax of the **install** command is:

```
rpm -i [install-options] package_file ...
rpm --install [install-options] package_file ...
```

To install a new version of a package and remove an existing version at the same time, use the upgrade command instead:

```
rpm -U [install-options] package_file ...
rpm --upgrade [install-options] package_file ...
```

Installation and upgrade options are:

--allfiles   Install or upgrade all files.

--excludedocs
>   Don't install any documentation files.

--force   Force the installation. Equivalent to using **--replacepkgs**, **--replacefiles**, and **--oldpackage**.

-h, --hash
>   Print 50 hash marks as the package archive is unpacked. Use with **-v** for a nicer display.

--includedocs
>   Install documentation files. This is needed only if **excludedocs: 1** is specified in an *rpmrc* file.

--nodeps   Don't check whether this package depends on the presence of other packages.

--noscripts
>   Don't execute any preinstall or postinstall scripts.

--oldpackage
>   Allow an upgrade to replace a newer package with an older one.

--percent
>   Print percent-completion messages as files are unpacked.

--prefix *path*
>   Set the installation prefix to *path* for relocatable packages.

--replacefiles
>   Install the packages even if they replace files from other installed packages.

--replacepkgs
>   Install the packages even if some of them are already installed.

--test   Go through the installation to see what it would do, but don't actually install the package.

→

rpm

←

Query mode

The syntax for the **query** command is:

```
rpm -q [information-options] [package-options]
rpm --query [information-options] [package-options]
```

There are two subsets of query options: *package selection* options that determine what packages to query and *information selection* options that determine what information to provide. The package selection options are:

package_name
> Query the installed package *package_name*.

−a   Query all installed packages.

−f *file*   Find out what package owns *file*.

−p *package_file*
> Query the uninstalled package *package_file*.

The information selection options are:

−c   List configuration files in the package.

−−**changelog**
> Display the log of change information for the package.

−d   List documentation files in the package.

−−**dump** Dump information for each file in the package. This option must be used with at least one of −l, −c, or −d. The output includes the following information in this order: **path size mtime md5sum mode owner group isconfig isdoc rdev symlink**.

−i   Display package information, including the name, version, and description.

−l   List all files in the package.

−−**provides**
> List the capabilities this package provides.

−R, −−**requires**
> List any packages this package depends on.

−s   List each file in the package and its state. The possible states are **normal, not installed,** or **replaced**.

−−**scripts** List any package-specific shell scripts used during installation and uninstallation of the package.

The syntax for the **uninstall** command is:

```
rpm -e package_name...
rpm --erase package_name...
```

--allmatches

Remove all versions of the package. Only one package should be specified, otherwise an error results.

--nodeps Don't check dependencies before uninstalling any packages.

--noscripts

Don't execute any preuninstall or postuninstall scripts.

--test Don't really uninstall anything, just go through the motions.

Verify mode

The syntax for the **verify** command is:

```
rpm -V|-y|--verify [package-selection-options]
```

Verify mode compares information about the installed files in a package with information about the files that came in the original package and displays any discrepencies. The information compared includes the size, MD5 sum, permissions, type, owner, and group of each file. Uninstalled files are ignored.

The package selection options are the same as for query mode.

The output is formatted as an 8-character string, possibly followed by a "c" to indicate a configuration file, and then the filename. Each of the eight characters in the string represents the result of comparing one file attribute to the value of that attribute from the RPM database. A period (.) indicates that the file passed that test. The following characters indicate failure of the corresponding test:

5 MD5 sum
S File size
L Symlink
T Mtime
D Device
U User
G Group
M Mode (includes permissions and file type)

→

rpm ←	***Rebuild mode***
	The syntax of the command to rebuild the RPM database is:
	rpm --rebuilddb [*options*]
	The options available with rebuild mode are the **--dbpath** and **--root** options described earlier under "General options".
	Signature-check mode
	RPM packages may have a PGP signature built into them. PGP configuration information is read from */etc/rpmrc*. The syntax of the signature-check mode is:
	rpm --checksig *package_file*...
	PGP has to be available on your system to check the signature.
rshd	**rshd** [*options*]
	TCP/IP command. Remote shell server for programs such as **rcmd** and **rcp**, which need to execute a noninteractive shell on remote machines. **rshd** is started by **inetd**, and must have an entry in **inetd**'s configuration file, */etc/inetd.conf*.
	All options are exactly the same as those in **rlogind**, except for -L, which is unique to **rshd**.
	Option
	–L Log all successful connections and failed attempts via **syslogd**.
rstat	**rstat** *host*
	TCP/IP command. Summarize *host*'s system status: the current time, uptime, and load averages, the average number of jobs in the run queue. Queries the remote host's **rstat_svc** daemon.
run–parts	**run–parts** [*options*] [*directory*]
	Run, in lexical order, all scripts found in *directory*. Exclude scripts whose filename include nonalphanumeric characters (besides underscores and hyphens).
	Options
	-- Interpret all subsequent arguments as filenames, not options.

‑‑test	Print information listing which scripts would be run, but suppress actual execution of them.	**run‑parts**
‑‑umask=_umask_	Specify _umask_. The default is 022.	

runlevel

Display the previous and current system runlevels.

runlevel

ruptime [_options_]

ruptime

TCP/IP command. Provide information on how long each machine on the local network has been up, and which users are logged in to each. If a machine has not reported in for 11 minutes, assume it is down. The listing is sorted by hostname.

Options

‑a	Include users who have been idle for more than one hour.
‑l	Sort machines by load average.
‑r	Reverse the normal sort order.
‑t	Sort machines by uptime.
‑u	Sort machines by the number of users logged in.

rusers [_options_] [_host_]

rusers

TCP/IP command. List the users logged on to _host_, or to all local machines, in **who** format (hostname, user names).

Options

‑a	Include machines with no users logged in.
‑l	Include more information: tty, date, time, idle time, remote host.

rwall _host_ [_file_]

rwall

TCP/IP command. Print a message to all users logged on to _host_. If _file_ is specified, read the message from it; otherwise, read from standard input.

rwhod	**rwhod**
	TCP/IP command. System status server that maintains the database used by the **rwho** and **ruptime** programs. Its operation is predicated on the ability to broadcast messages on a network. As a producer of information, **rwhod** periodically queries the state of the system and constructs status messages, which are broadcast on a network. As a consumer of information, it listens for other **rwhod** servers' status messages, validates them, then records them in a collection of files located in the directory */var/spool/rwho*. Messages received by the **rwhod** server are discarded unless they originated at an **rwhod** server's port. Status messages are generated approximately once every three minutes.
script	**script** [*option*] [*file*]
	Fork the current shell and make a typescript of a terminal session. The typescript is written to *file*. If no *file* is given, the typescript is saved in the file *typescript*. The script ends when the forked shell exits.
	Option
	–a Append to *file* or *typescript* instead of overwriting the previous contents.
sendmail	**sendmail** [*flags*] [*address...*]
	sendmail is a mail router. It accepts mail from a user's mail program, interprets the mail address, rewrites the address into the proper form for the delivery program, and routes the mail to the correct delivery program.
	Command-line flags
	–b*x* Set operation mode to *x*. Operation modes are:
	a Run in ARPAnet mode.
	d Run as a daemon.
	i Initialize the alias database.
	m Deliver mail (default).
	p Print the mail queue.
	s Speak SMTP on input side.
	t Run in test mode.
	v Verify addresses, do not collect or deliver.

−C*file*	Use configuration file *file*.
−d*level*	Set debugging level.
−F*name*	Set full name of user to *name*.
−f*name*	Sender's name is *name*.
−h*cnt*	Set hop count (number of times message has been processed by **sendmail**) to *cnt*.
−n	Do not alias or forward.
−o*x value*	Set option *x* to value *value*. Options are described below.
−p*protocol*	

        Receive messages via the *protocol* protocol.

−q[*time*]	Process queued messages immediately, or at intervals indicated by *time* (for example, −q30m for every half hour).
−r*name*	Obsolete form of −f.
−t	Read head for To:, Cc:, and Bcc: lines, and send to everyone on those lists.
−v	Verbose.
−X *file*	Log all traffic to *file*. Not to be used for normal logging.

Configuration options

The following options can be set with the −o flag on the command line, or the O line in the configuration file:

7	Format all incoming messages in seven bits.
a*min*	If the D option is set, wait *min* minutes for the *aliases* file to be rebuilt before returning an alias database out-of-date warning.
A*file*	Use alternate alias file.
b*minblocks/maxsize*	

        Require at least *minblocks* to be free, and optionally, set the maximum message size to *maxsize*. If *maxsize* is omitted, the slash is optional.

B*char*	Set unquoted space replacement character.
c	On mailers that are considered "expensive" to connect to, don't initiate immediate connection.
C*num*	Checkpoint the queue when mailing to multiple recipients. **sendmail** will rewrite the

Sys Admin Commands

→

		list of recipients after each group of *num* recipients have been processed.
d*x*		Set the delivery mode to *x*. Delivery modes are **d** for deferred delivery, **i** for interactive (synchronous) delivery, **b** for background (asynchronous) delivery, and **q** for queue only—i.e., deliver the next time the queue is run.
D		Try to automatically rebuild the alias database if necessary.
e*x*		Set error processing to mode *x*. Valid modes are **m** to mail back the error message, **w** to write back the error message, **p** to print the errors on the terminal (default), **q** to throw away error messages, and **e** to do special processing for the BerkNet.
E*text*		Set error message header. *text* is either text to add to an error message or the name of a file. A file name must include its full path and begin with a "/".
f		Save Unix-style `From:` lines at the front of messages.
F*mode*		Set default file permissions for temporary files. If this option is missing, default permissions are 0644.
G		Compare local mail names to the GECOS section in the password file.
g *n*		Default group ID to use when calling mailers.
H*file*		SMTP help file.
h *num*		Allow a maximum of *num* hops per message.
i		Do not take dots on a line by themselves as a message terminator.
I *arg*		Use DNS lookups and tune them. Queue messages on connection refused. The *arg* arguments are identical to **resolver** flags without the RES_ prefix. Each flag can be preceded by a plus or minus to enable or disable the corresponding name server option. There must be a white space between the **I** and the first flag.

j	Use MIME format for error messages.
J*path*	Set an alternative *.forward* search path.
k*num*	Specify size of the connection cache.
K*time*	Timeout connections after *time*.
l	Do not ignore **Errors-To:** header.
L*n*	Specify log level.
m	Send to "me" (the sender) also if I am in an alias expansion.
M*Xvalue*	Define a macro's value in command line. Assign *value* to macro *X*.
n	When running **newaliases**, validate the right side of aliases.
o	If set, this message may have old-style headers. If not set, this message is guaranteed to have new-style headers (i.e., commas instead of spaces between addresses).
p*what,what,...*	Tune how private you want the SMTP daemon. The *what* arguments should be separated from one another by commas. The *what* arguments may be any of the following:

public
Make SMTP fully public (default).

needmailhelo
Require site to send HELO or ELHO to before sending mail.

needexpnhelo
Require site to send HELO or ELHO before answering an address expansion request.

needvrfyhelo
As above but for verification requests.

noexpn
Deny all expansion requests.

novrfy
Deny all verification requests.

authwarnings
Insert special headers in mail messages advising recipients that the message may not be authentic.

→

goaway
> Set all of the above (except **public**).

restrictmailq
> Allow only users of the same group as the owner of the queue directory to examine the mail queue.

restrictqrun
> Limit queue processing to root and the owner of the queue directory.

P*user*   Send copies of all failed mail to *user* (usually postmaster).

q*fact*   Multiplier (factor) for high-load queueing.

Q*queuedir*
> Select the directory in which to queue messages.

R   Don't prune route addresses.

S*file*   Save statistics in the named file.

s   Always instantiate the queue file, even under circumstances where it is not strictly necessary.

T*time*   Set the timeout on undelivered messages in the queue to the specified time.

t*stz, dtz* Set name of the time zone.

U*database*
> Consult the user database *database* for forwarding information.

u*N*   Set default user ID for mailers.

v   Run in verbose mode.

V*host*   Fall-back MX host. *host* should be the fully qualified domain name of the fallback host.

w   Use a record for an ambiguous MX.

x*load*   Queues messages when load level is higher than *load*.

X*load*   Refuse SMTP connections when load is higher than *load*.

y*factor*   Penalize large recipient lists by *factor*.

Y   Deliver each job that is run from the queue in a separate process. This helps limit the size of running processes on systems with very low amounts of memory.

zfactor Multiplier for priority increments. This determines how much weight to give to a messages's precedence header. **sendmail**'s default is 1800.

Z*inc* Increment priority of items remaining in queue by *inc* after each job is processed. **sendmail** uses 90000 by default.

sendmail support files

/usr/lib/sendmail
> Binary of **sendmail**.

/usr/bin/newaliases
> Link to */usr/lib/sendmail*; causes the alias database to be rebuilt.

/usr/bin/mailq
> Prints a listing of the mail queue.

/etc/sendmail.cf
> Configuration file, in text form.

/etc/sendmail.hf
> SMTP help file.

/usr/lib/sendmail.st
> Statistics file. Doesn't need to be present.

/etc/aliases
> Alias file, in text form.

/etc/aliases.{pag,dir}
> Alias file in **dbm** format.

/var/spool/mqueue
> Directory in which the mail queue and temporary files reside.

/var/spool/mqueue/qf
> Control (queue) files for messages.

/var/spool/mqueue/df
> Data files.

/var/spool/mqueue/lf
> Lock files.

/var/spool/mqueue/tf
> Temporary versions of *qf* files, used during queue-file rebuild.

/var/spool/mqueue/nf
> Used when creating a unique ID.

/var/spool/mqueue/xf
> Transcript of current session.

showmount	**showmount** [*options*] [*host*]
	
	NFS/NIS command. Show information about an NFS server. This information is maintained by the **mountd** server on *host*. The default value for *host* is the value returned by **hostname**. With no options, show the clients that have mounted directories from the host. **showmount** is usually found in */usr/sbin*, which is not in the default search path.
	
	Options
	
	    -a, --all Print all remote mounts in the format:
	
	        hostname:directory
	
	            where *hostname* is the name of the client and *directory* is the root of the filesystem that has been mounted.
	
	    -d, --directories
	        List directories that have been remotely mounted by clients.
	
	    -e, --exports
	        Print the list of exported filesystems.
	
	    -h, --help
	        Provide a short help summary.
	
	    --no-headers
	        Do not print headers.
	
	    -v, --version
	        Report the current version number of the program.

shutdown	**shutdown** [*options*] *when* [*message*] Terminate all processing. *when* may be a specific time (in *hh:mm* format), a number of minutes to wait (in **+***m* format), or **now**. A broadcast *message* notifies all users to log off the system. Processes are signalled with SIGTERM, to allow them to exit gracefully. */etc/init* is called to perform the actual shutdown, which consists of placing the system in runlevel 1. Only privileged users can execute the **shutdown** command. Broadcast messages, default or defined, are displayed at regular intervals during the grace period; the closer the shutdown time, the more frequent the message.

-c	Cancel a shutdown that is in progress.
-f	Reboot fast, by suppressing the normal call to **fsck** when rebooting.
-h	Halt the system when shutdown is complete.
-k	Print the warning message, but suppress actual shutdown.
-n	Perform shutdown without a call to **init**.
-r	Reboot the system when shutdown is complete.
-t *sec*	Ensure a *sec*-second delay between killing processes and changing the runlevel.

slattach [*options*] [*tty*]

TCP/IP command. Attach serial lines as network interfaces, thereby preparing them for use as point-to-point connections. Only a privileged user may attach or detach a network interface.

Options

-c *command*
: Run *command* when the connection is severed.

-d	Debugging mode.
-e	Exit immediately after initializing the line.
-h	Exit when the connection is severed.
-l	Create UUCP style lockfile in */var/spool/uucp*.
-L	Enable 3-wire operation.
-m	Suppress initialization of the line to 8 bits raw mode.
-n	Similar to **mesg n**.

-p *protocol*
: Specify *protocol*, which may be **slip**, **adaptive**, **ppp**, or **kiss**.

-q	Quiet mode, supress messages.
-s *speed*	Specify line speed.

swapdev	**swapdev** [*option*] [*image* [*swapdevice* [*offset*]]]
	If no arguments are given, display usage information about the swap device. If just the location of the kernel *image* is specified, print the information found there. To change that information, specify the new *swapdevice*. You may also specify the *offset* in the kernel image to change. Note that **rdev -s** is a synonym for **swapdev**.
	Option
	-o *offset* Synonymous to specifying an *offset* as an argument.
swapon	**swapon** [*options*] *device*
	Make *device* (which may be a space-separated list) available for swapping and paging.
	Options
	-a Consult */etc/fstab* for devices marked **sw**. Use those in place of the *device* argument.
	-p *priority*
	Specifies a *priority* for the swap area. Higher priority areas will be used up before lower priority areas are used.
swapoff	**swapoff -a** | *device*
	Stop making *device* (which may be a space-separated list) availible for swapping and paging.
	Option
	-a Consult */etc/fstab* for devices marked **sw**. Use those in place of the *device* argument.
sync	**sync**
	Write filesystem buffers to disk. **sync** executes the **sync()** system call. If the system is to be stopped, **sync** must be called to ensure filesystem integrity. Note that **shutdown** automatically calls **sync** before shutting down the system. **sync** may take several seconds to complete, so the system should be told to **sleep** briefly if you are about to manually call **halt** or **reboot**. Note that **shutdown** is the preferred way to halt or reboot your system, since it takes care of **sync**-ing and other housekeeping for you.

sysklogd

sysklogd, the Linux program that provides **syslogd** functionality, behaves exactly like the BSD version of **syslogd**. The difference should be completely transparent to the user. However, **sysklogd** is coded very differently and supports a slightly extended syntax. It is invoked as **syslogd**. See also **klogd**.

Options

−d　　　　Turn on debugging.

−f *configfile*
　　　　Specify alternate configuration file.

−h　　　　Forward messages from remote hosts to forwarding hosts.

−l *hostlist*　Specify hostnames that should be logged with just their hostname, not their fully qualified domain name. Multiple hosts should be separated with a colon (:).

−m *markinterval*
　　　　Select number of minutes between mark messages.

−n　　　　Avoid auto-backgrounding. This is needed when starting syslogd from **init**.

−p *socket*　Send log to *socket* instead of */dev/log*.

−r　　　　Receive messages from the network using an internet domain socket with the **syslog** service.

−s *domainlist*
　　　　Strip off domainnames specified in *domainlist* before logging. Multiple domain names should be separated by a colon (:).

syslogd

TCP/IP command. Log system messages into a set of files described by the configuration file */etc/syslog.conf*. Each message is one line. A message can contain a priority code, marked by a number in angle braces at the beginning of the line. Priorities are defined in *<sys/syslog.h>*. **syslogd** reads from an Internet domain socket specified in */etc/services*. To bring **syslogd** down, send it a terminate signal.

systat	**systat** [*options*] *host*
	Get information about the network or system status of a remote host by querying its **netstat**, **systat**, or **daytime** service.
	Options
	−n, −−netstat
	Specifically query the host's **netstat** service.
	−p *port*, **−−port** *port*
	Specify port to query.
	−s, −−systat
	Specifically query the host's **systat** service.
	−t, −−time
	Specifically query the host's **daytime** service.
talkd	**talkd** [*option*]
	TCP/IP command. Remote user communication server. **talkd** notifies a user that somebody else wants to initiate a conversation. A **talk** client initiates a rendezvous by sending a CTL_MSG of type LOOK_UP to the server. This causes the server to search its invitation tables for an existing invitation for the client. If the lookup fails, the caller sends an ANNOUNCE message causing the server to broadcast an announcement on the callee's login ports requesting contact. When the callee responds, the local server responds with the rendezvous address, and a stream connection is established through which the conversation takes place.
	Option
	−d Write debugging information to the **syslogd** log file.
tar	**tar** [*options*] [*tarfile*] [*other-files*]
	Copy *files* to or restore *files* from an archive medium. If any *files* are directories, **tar** acts on the entire subtree. Options need not be preceded by − (though they may be). The exception to this rule is when you are using a long-style option (such as --**modification-time**). In that case, the exact syntax is:
	tar −−*long-option* −*function-options files*
	For example:
	`tar --modification-time -xvf tarfile.tar`

You must use exactly one of these, and it must come before any other options.

−c, −−create
> Create a new archive.

−d, −−compare
> Compare the files stored in *tarfile* with *other-files*. Report any differences: missing files, different sizes, different file attributes (such as permissions or modification time).

−r, −−append
> Append *other-files* to the end of an existing archive.

−t, −−list   Print the names of *other-files* if they are stored on the archive (if *other-files* are not specified, print names of all files).

−u, −−update
> Add files if not in the archive or if modified.

−x, −−extract, −−get
> Extract *other-files* from an archive (if *other-files* are not specified, extract all files).

−A, −−catenate, −−concatenate
> Concatenate a second tar file on to the end of the first.

Options

   n   Select device *n*, where *n* is 0, . . . ,9999. The default is found in */etc/default/tar*.

[*drive*][*density*]
> Set drive (0–7) and storage density (**l**, **m**, or **h**, corresponding to low, medium, or high).

−−atime-preserve
> Preserve original access-time on extracted files.

−b, −−block-size=*n*
> Set block size to *n* × 512 bytes.

−−checkpoint
> List directory names encountered.

−−exclude=*file*
> Remove *file* from any list of files.

→

-f *arch*, **--file=***filename*
> Store files in or extract files from archive *arch*. Note that *filename* may take the form *hostname:filename*.

--force-local
> Interpret filenames in the form *hostname:filename* as local files.

-g, --listed-incremental
> Create new-style incremental backup.

-h, --dereference
> Dereference symbolic links.

-i, --ignore-zeros
> Ignore zero-sized blocks (i.e., *EOFs*).

--ignore-failed-read
> Ignore unreadable files to be archived. Default behavior is to exit when encountering these.

-k, --keep-old-files
> When extracting files, do not overwrite files with similar names. Instead, print an error message.

-l, --one-file-system
> Do not archive files from other file systems.

-m, --modification-time
> Do not restore file modification times; update them to the time of extraction.

--null Allow filenames to be null-terminated with -T. Override -C.

--old, --portability, --preserve
> Equivalent to invoking both the -p and -s options.

-p, --same-permissions, --preserve-permissions
> Keep ownership of extracted files same as that of original permissions.

--remove-files
> Remove originals after inclusion in archive.

--rsh-command=*command*
> Do not connect to remote host with **rsh**; instead, use *command*.

-s, --same-order, --preserve-order
> When extracting, sort filenames to correspond to the order in the archive.

--totals   Print byte totals.

--use-compress-program=*program*
>   Compress archived files with *program*, or uncompress extracted files with *program*.

-v, --verbose
>   Verbose. Print filenames as they are added or extracted.

-w, --interactive
>   Wait for user confirmation (**y**) before taking any actions.

-z, --gzip, --ungzip
>   Compress files with **gzip** before archiving them, or uncompress them with **gunzip** before extracting them.

-C, --directory=*directory*
>   **cd** to *directory* before beginning **tar** operation.

-F, --info-script, --new-volume-script=*script*
>   Implies -M (multiple archive files). Run *script* at the end of each file.

-G, --incremental
>   Create old-style incremental backup.

-K *file*, **--starting-file** *file*
>   Begin **tar** operation at file *file* in archive.

-L, --tape-lgenth=*length*
>   Write a maximum of *length* × 1024 bytes to each tape.

-M, --multi-volume
>   Expect archive to multi-volume. With -c, create such an archive.

-N *date*, **--after-date** *date*
>   Ignore files older than *date*.

-O, --to-stdout
>   Print extracted files on standard out.

-P, --absolute-paths
>   Do not remove initial slashes (/) from input filenames.

-R, --record-number
>   Display archive's record number.

-S, --sparse
>   Treat short file specially and more efficiently.

$\rightarrow$

tar
←
	-T *filename*, --**files-from** *filename*
	　　Consult *filename* for files to extract or create.
	
	-V *name*, --**label**=*name*
	　　Name this volume *name*.
	
	-W, --**verify**
	　　Check archive for corruption after creation.
	
	-X *file*, --**exclude** *file*
	　　Consult *file* for list of files to exclude.
	
	-Z, --**compress**, --**uncompress**
	　　Compress files with **compress** before archiving them, or uncompress them with **uncompress** before extracting them.
	
	Examples
	
	Create an archive of */bin* and */usr/bin* (**c**), show the command working (**v**), and store on the tape in */dev/rmt0*:
	
	　　`tar cvf /dev/rmt0 /bin /usr/bin`
	
	List the tape's contents in a format like **ls** −**l**:
	
	　　`tar tvf /dev/rmt0`
	
	Extract the */bin* directory:
	
	　　`tar xvf /dev/rmt0 /bin`
	
	Create an archive of the current directory and store it in a file *backup.tar*:
	
	　　`tar cvf - `find . -print` > backup.tar`
	
	(The − tells **tar** to store the archive on standard output, which is then redirected.)

tcpd	**tcpd** TCP/IP command. Monitor incoming TCP/IP requests (such as those for **telnet**, **ftp**, **finger**, **exec**, **rlogin**). Provide checking and logging services; then pass the request to the appropriate daemon.
tcpdchk	**tcpdchk** [*options*] TCP/IP command. Consult the TCP wrapper configuration (in */etc/hosts.allow* and */etc/hosts.deny*); display a list of all possible problems with it; attempt to suggest possible fixes.

-a   Include a list of rules; do not require an
        ALLOW keyword before allowing sites to
        access the local host.

-d   Consult *./hosts.allow* and *./hosts.deny*
        instead of *etc/hosts.allow* and
        /etc/hosts.deny.

-i *conf-file*

        Specify location of *inetd.conf* or *tlid.conf*
        file. These are files that **tcpdchk** automati-
        cally uses in its evaluation of TCP wrapper
        files.

-v   Verbose mode.

tcpdmatch [*options*] *daemon client*

TCP/IP command. Predict the TCP wrapper's response to a
specific request. You must specify which *daemon* the
request is made to (the syntax may be *daemon@host* for
requests to remote machines) and the *client* from which the
request originates (the syntax may be *user@client* for a specific user, or a wildcard). Consult */etc/hosts.allow* and
/etc/hosts.deny to determine the TCP wrapper's actions.

Options

-d   Consult *./hosts.allow* and *./hosts.deny*
        instead of *etc/hosts.allow* and
        /etc/hosts.deny.

-i *conf-file*

        Specify location of *inetd.conf* or *tlid.conf*
        file. These are files that **tcpdmatch** automat-
        ically uses in its evaluation of TCP wrapper
        files.

telinit [*option*] [*runlevel*]

Signal **init** to change the system's runlevel. **telinit** is actually
just a link to **init**, the grandparent of all processes.

Option

-t *seconds*

        Send SIGKILL *seconds* after SIGTERM.
        Default is 20.

→

telinit
←
	Runlevels
	
	The default runlevels vary from distribution to distribution, but these are standard:
	
	    0 Halt the system.
	
	    1, s, S Single user.
	
	    6 Reboot the system.
	
	    a, b, c Process only entries in */etc/inittab* that are marked with run level **a**, **b**, or **c**.
	
	    q, Q Reread */etc/inittab*.
	
	Check the */etc/inittab* file for runlevels on your system.

telnetd	**telnetd** [*options*]
	
	TCP/IP command. TELNET protocol server. **telnetd** is invoked by the Internet server for requests to connect to the TELNET port (port 23 by default). **telnetd** allocates a pseudo-terminal device for a client, thereby creating a login process that has the slave side of the pseudo-terminal serving as **stdin**, **stdout**, and **stderr**. **telnetd** manipulates the master side of the pseudo-terminal by implementing the TELNET protocol and by passing characters between the remote client and the login process.
	
	Options
	
	  –debug [*port*]
	          Start **telnetd** manually instead of through **inetd**. *port* may be specified as an alternate TCP port number on which to run **telnetd**.
	
	  –D *modifier*(s)
	          Debugging mode. This allows **telnet** to print out debugging information to the connection, enabling the user to see what **telnet** is doing. Several modifiers are available for the debugging mode:
	
	      exercise
	          Has not been implemented yet.
	
	      netdata
	          Display data stream received by **telnetd**.
	
	      options
	          Print information about the negotiation of the TELNET options.

ptydata
> Display data written to the pseudo-ter-
> minal device.

report
> Print **options** information, as well as
> some additional information about what
> processing is going on.

tftpd [*homedir*]

TCP/IP command. Trivial File Transfer Protocol server. **tftpd**
is normally started by **inetd** and operates at the port indicated in the **tftp** Internet service description in the
/etc/inetd.conf file. By default, the entry for **tftpd** in
/etc/inetd.conf is commented out; the comment character
must be deleted to make **tfptd** operational. Before responding to a request, the server attempts to change its current
directory to *homedir*; the default value is **tftpboot**.

traceroute [*options*] *host* [*packetsize*]

TCP/IP command. Trace route taken by packets to reach
network host. **traceroute** attempts tracing by launching UDP
probe packets with a small TTL (time to live), then listening
for an ICMP "time exceeded" reply from a gateway. *host* is
the destination hostname or the IP number of host to reach.
packetsize is the packet size in bytes of the probe datagram.
Default is 38 bytes.

Options

-d
> Turn on socket-level debugging.

-g *addr*
> Enable the IP LSRR (Loose Source Record
> Route) option in addition to the TTL tests,
> to ask how someone at IP address *addr* can
> reach a particular target.

-l
> Include the time-to-live value for each
> packet received.

-m *max_ttl*
> Set maximum time-to-live used in outgoing
> probe packets to *max-ttl* hops. Default is 30
> hops.

-n
> Print hop addresses numerically rather than
> symbolically.

-p *port*
> Set base UDP port number used for probe
> packets to *port*. Default is (decimal) 33434.

Sys Admin Commands

$\rightarrow$

traceroute ←	−q *n*	Set number of probe packets for each time-to-live setting to the value *n*. Default is three.
	−r	Bypass normal routing tables and send directly to a host on an attached network.
	−s *src_addr*	Use *src_addr* as the IP address that will serve as the source address in outgoing probe packets.
	−t *tos*	Set the type-of-service in probe packets to *tos* (default zero). The value must be a decimal integer in the range 0 to 255.
	−v	Verbose—received ICMP packets (other than TIME_EXCEEDED and PORT_UNREACHABLE) will be listed.
	−w *wait*	Set time to wait for a response to an outgoing probe packet to *wait* seconds (default is 3 seconds).

tune2fs	**tune2fs** [*options*] *device*

Tune the parameters of a Linux second extended filesystem by adjusting various parameters. You must specify the *device* on which the filesystem resides; it must not be mounted read/write when you change its parameters.

Options

−c *mount-counts*
: Specify the maximum number of mount counts between two checks on the filesystem.

−e *behavior*
: Specify the kernel's behavior when encountering errors. *behavior* must be one of:

continue
: Continue as usual.

remount-ro
: Remount the offending filesystem in read-only mode.

panic
: Cause a kernel panic.

−g *group*
: Allow *group* (a group ID or name) to use reserved blocks.

−i *interval*[d|w|m]

        Specify the maximum interval between filesystem checks. Units may be in days (**d**), weeks (**w**), or months (**m**). If *interval* is 0, checking will not be time-dependent.

−l   Display a list of the superblock's contents.

−m *percentage*

        Specify the percentage of blocks that will be reserved for use by privileged users.

−r *num*   Specify the number of blocks that will be reserved for use by privileged users.

−u *user*   Allow *user* (a user ID or name) to use reserved blocks.

---

tunelp *device* [*options*]

Control a line printer's device parameters. Without options, print information about device(s).

Options

−a [on|off]

        Specify whether or not to abort if the printer encounters an error. By default, do not abort.

−c *n*   Retry device *n* times if it refuses a character. (Default is 250.) After exhausting *n*, sleep before retrying.

−i *irq*   Use *irq* for specified parallel port. Ignore **−t** and **−c**. If 0, restore noninterrupt driven (polling) action.

−o [on|off]

        Specify whether to abort if device is not online or is out of paper.

−q [on|off]

        Specify whether to print current IRQ setting.

−r   Reset port.

−s   Display printer's current status.

−t *time*   Specify a delay of *time* in jiffies to sleep before resending a refused character to the device. A jiffy is defined as either one tick of the system clock or one AC cycle time; it should be approximately 1/100 of a second.

→

tunelp ←	−w *time* Specify a delay of *time* in jiffies to sleep before resending a strobe signal. −C [on|off] Specify whether to be extremely careful in checking for printer error.

umount	**umount** [*options*] [*special-device/directory*]
	
	Unmount a filesystem. **umount** announces to the system that the removable file structure previously mounted on device *special-device* is to be removed. **umount** also works by specifying the directory. Any pending I/O for the filesystem is completed, and the file structure is flagged as clean.
	
	Options
	
	    −a Unmount all filesystems that are listed in */etc/mtab*.
	
	    −n Unmount, but do not record changes in */etc/mtab*.
	
	    −t *type* Unmount only filesystems of type *type*.

update	**update** [*options*]
	
	update is a daemon that controls how often the kernel's disk buffers are flushed to disk. **update** is also known as **bdflush**. The daemon forks a couple of processes to call system functions *flush()* and *sync()*. When called by an unprivileged user, no daemon is created. Instead, **update** calls *sync()* and then exits. By default, update will wake up every five seconds and *flush()* some dirty buffers. If that doesn't work, it will try waking up every thirty seconds to *sync()* the buffers to disk. Not all of the listed options are available in every verision of **update**.
	
	Options
	
	    −d Display the kernel parameters. This does not start the update daemon.
	
	    −f *seconds*
	        Call *flush()* at this interval. Default is 5.
	
	    −h Help. Print a command summary.
	
	    −s *seconds*
	        Call *sync()* at this interval. Default is 30.
	
	    −S Always use *sync()* instead of flush.

−0 *percent*

   Flush buffers when the specified *percent* of the buffer cache is dirty.

−1 *blocks* The maximum number of dirty blocks to write out per wake-cycle.

−2 *buffers* The number of clean buffers to try to obtain each time the free buffers are refilled.

−3 *blocks* Flush buffers if dirty blocks exceed *blocks* when trying to refill the buffers.

−4 *percent*

   Percent of buffer cache to scan when looking for free clusters.

−5 *seconds*

   Time for a data buffer to age before being flushed.

−6 *seconds*

   Time for a non-data buffer to age before being flushed.

−7 *constant*

   The time constant to use for load average.

−8 *ratio* How low the load average can be before trimming back the number of buffers.

---

useradd [*options*] [*user*]

Create new user accounts or update default account information. Unless invoked with the −D option, *user* must be given. **useradd** will create new entries in system files. Home directories and initial files may also be created as needed.

Options

−c *comment*

   Comment field.

−d *dir* Home directory. The default is to use *user* as the directory name under the *home* directory specified with the −D option.

−e *date* Account expiration *date*. *date* is in the format MM/DD/YYYY. Two digit year fields are also accepted. The value is stored as the number of days since January 1, 1970. This option requires the use of shadow passwords.

Sys Admin Commands

→

useradd ←	−f *days*	Permanently disable account this many *days* after the password has expired. A value of -1 disables this feature. This option requires the use of shadow passwords.
	−g *group*	Initial *group* name or ID number. If a different default group has not been specified using the −D option, the default group is 1.
	−G *groups*	Supplementary *groups* given by name or number in a comma-separated list with no white space.
	−k [*dir*]	Copy default files to user's home directory. Only meaningful when used with the −m option. Default files are copied from */etc/skel/* unless an alternate *dir* is specified.
	−m	Make user's home directory if it does not exist. The default is not to make the home directory.
	−o	Override. Accept a non-unique *uid* with the −u option.
	−s *shell*	Login *shell*.
	−u *uid*	Numerical user ID. The value must be unique unless the −o option is used. The default value is the smallest ID value greater than 99 and greater than every other *uid*.
	−D [*options*]	Set or display defaults. If *options* are specified, set them. If no options are specified, display current defaults.

−D *Options*

	−b *dir*	Home directory prefix to be used in creating home directories. If the -d option is not used when creating an account, the *user* name will be appended to *dir*.
	−e *date*	Expire *date*. Requires the use of shadow passwords.
	−f *days*	Number of *days* after a password expires to disable an account. Requires the use of shadow passwords.
	−g *group*	Initial *group* name or ID number.
	−s *shell*	Login *shell*.

userdel [*option*] *user*

Delete all entries for *user* in system account files.

Option

> −r   Remove the home directory of *user* and any files contained in it.

---

usermod [*options*] *user*

Modify *user* account information.

Options

> −c *comment*
> > Comment field.
>
> −d *dir*   Home directory.
>
> −e *date*   Account expiration *date*. *date* is in the format MM/DD/YYYY. Two digit year fields are also accepted, but the value is stored as the number of days since January 1, 1970. This option requires the use of shadow passwords.
>
> −f *days*   Permanently disable account this many *days* after the password has expired. A value of -1 disables this feature. This option requires the use of shadow passwords.
>
> −g *group*   Initial *group* name or number.
>
> −G *groups*
> > Supplementary *groups* given by name or number in a comma-separated list with no white space. *user* will be removed from any groups to which they currently belong that are not included in *groups*.
>
> −l *name*   Login *name*. This cannot be changed while the user is logged in.
>
> −o   Override. Accept a non-unique *uid* with the −u option.
>
> −s *shell*   Login *shell*.
>
> −u *uid*   Numerical user ID. The value must be unique unless the −o option is used. Any files owned by *user* in the user's home directory will have their user ID changed automatically. Files outside of the home directory will not be changed. *user* should

Sys Admin Commands

→

usermod ←	not be executing any processes while this is changed.
vidmode	**vidmode** [*option*] *image* [*mode* [*offset*]] Sets the video mode for a kernel *image*. If no arguments are specified, print current *mode* value. *mode* is a one-byte value located at offset 506 in a kernel image. You may change the *mode* by specifying the kernel *image* to change, the new *mode*, and the byte-offset at which to place the new information (the default is 506). Note that **rdev -v** is a synonym for **vidmode**. If **LILO** is used, **vidmode** is not needed. The video mode can be set from the **LILO** prompt during a boot. *Modes* -3 Prompt -2 Extended VGA -1 Normal VGA 0 Same as entering 0 at the prompt 1 Same as entering 1 at the prompt 2 Same as entering 2 at the prompt 3 Same as entering 3 at the prompt n Same as entering n at the prompt *Option* -o *offset* Same as specifying an *offset* as an argument.
w	**w** [*options*] [*users*] Print summaries of system usage, currently logged-in users, and what they are doing. **w** is essentially a combination of **uptime**, **who**, and **ps -a**. Display output for one user by specifying *user*. *Options* -h Suppress headings and **uptime** information. -i Sort by idle time. -n Suppress translation of IP addresses to names.

Files

  /var/run/utmp
      List of users currently logged on.

wall [*file*]

Write to all users. **wall** reads a message from the standard input until an end-of-file. It then sends this message to all users currently logged in, preceded by `Broadcast Message from . . . .` If *file* is specified, read input from that, rather from standard input.

ypbind [*options*]

NFS/NIS command. NIS binder process. **ypbind** is a daemon process typically activated at system startup time. Its function is to remember information that lets client processes on a single node communicate with some **ypserv** process. The information **ypbind** remembers is called a *binding*—the association of a domain name with the Internet address of the NIS server and the port on that host at which the **ypserv** process is listening for service requests. This information is cached in the file */var/yp/bindings/domainname.version*.

Options

  –ypset   May be used to change the binding. This option is very dangerous and should only be used for debugging the network from a remote machine.

  –ypsetme **ypset** requests may be issued from this machine only. Security is based on IP address checking, which can be defeated on networks where untrusted individuals may inject packets. This option is not recommended.

ypcat [*options*] *mname*

NFS/NIS command. Print values in an NIS database specified by *mname*, which may be either a mapname or a map nickname.

Options

  –d *domain*
      Specify *domain* other than default domain.

$\rightarrow$

ypcat	–k	Display keys for maps in which values are null or key is not part of value.
←	–t	Do not translate *mname* to mapname.
	–x	Display map nickname table listing the nicknames (*mnames*) known, and mapname associated with each nickname. Do not require a *mname* argument.

ypinit

ypinit [*options*]

NFS/NIS command. Build and install an NIS database on an NIS server. **ypinit** can be used to set up a master or a slave server or slave copier. Only a privileged user can run **ypinit**.

Options

–c *master_name*
> Set up a slave copier database. *master_name* should be the hostname of an NIS server, either the master server for all the maps or a server on which the database is up-to-date and stable.

–m
> Indicates that the local host is to be the NIS server.

–s *master_name*
> Set up a slave server database. *master_name* should be the hostname of an NIS server, either the master server for all the maps or a server on which the database is up-to-date and stable.

ypmatch

ypmatch [*options*] *key...mname*

NFS/NIS command. Print value of one or more *keys* from an NIS map specified by *mname*. *mname* may be either a mapname or a map nickname.

Options

–d *domain*
> Specify *domain* other than default domain.

–k
> Before printing value of a key, print key itself, followed by a colon (:).

–t
> Do not translate nickname to mapname.

–x
> Display map nickname table listing the nicknames (*mnames*) known, and mapname associ-

ated with each nickname. Do not require an *mname* argument.	**ypmatch**
yppasswd [*name*] NFS/NIS command. Change login password in network information service. See **yppasswd** in Chapter 2, *Linux User Commands*.	**yppasswd**
rpc.yppasswdd [*option*] NFS/NIS command. Server for modifying the NIS password file. **yppasswdd** handles password change requests from **yppasswd**. It changes a password entry only if the password represented by **yppasswd** matches the encrypted password of that entry, and if the user ID and group ID match those in the server's */etc/passwd* file. Then it updates */etc/passwd* and the password maps on the local server. *Option* −s Support shadow password functions.	**yppasswdd**

yppoll [*options*] *mapname*
 	
NFS/NIS command. Determine version of NIS map at NIS server. **yppoll** asks a **ypserv** process for the order number and the hostname of the master NIS server for the named map.
 	
Options
 	
    −h *host*
            Ask the **ypserv** process at *host* about the map parameters. If *host* is not specified, the hostname of the NIS server for the local host (the one returned by **ypwhich**) is used.
 	
    −d *domain*
            Use *domain* instead of the default domain.
	yppoll

yppush [*options*] *mapnames* NFS/NIS command. Force propagation of changed NIS map. **yppush** copies a new version of a NIS map, *mapname*, from the master NIS server to the slave NIS servers. It first constructs a list of NIS server hosts by reading the NIS map **ypservers** with the −d option's *domain* argument. Keys within this map are the ASCII names of the machines on which the NIS servers run. A "transfer map" request is sent to the NIS server at each host, along with the information	**yppush**

→

yppush
←
	needed by the transfer agent to call back the **yppush**. When the attempt has been completed and the transfer agent has sent **yppush** a status message, the results may be printed to **stdout**. Normally invoked by */var/yp/Makefile*.
	
	Options
	
	    −d *domain*
	        Specify a *domain*.
	
	    −v Verbose—print message when each server is called and for each response.

ypserv	**ypserv** [*options*]
	
	NFS/NIS command. NIS server process. **ypserv** is a daemon process typically activated at system startup time. It runs only on NIS server machines with a complete NIS database. Its primary function is to look up information in its local database of NIS maps. The operations performed by **ypserv** are defined for the implementor by the NIS protocol specification, and for the programmer by the header file *<rpcvc/yp_prot.h>*. Communication to and from **ypserv** is by means of RPC calls.
	
	Options
	
	    −d NIS service should go to the DNS for more host information.
	
	    −localonly
	        Indicates **ypserv** should not respond to outside requests.
	
	Files and directories
	
	    /var/yp/[domainname]/
	        Location of NIS databases.
	
	    /var/yp/Makefile
	        Makefile that is responsible for creating yp databases.

ypset	**ypset** [*options*] *server* NFS/NIS command. Point **ypbind** at a particular server. **ypset** tells **ypbind** to get NIS services for the specified domain from the **ypserv** process running on *server*. *server* indicates the NIS server to bind to and can be specified as a name or an IP address.

−d *domain*

Use *domain* instead of the default domain.

−h *host*

Set **ypbind**'s binding on *host*, instead of locally. *host* can be specified as a name or an IP address.

ypwhich [*options*] [*host*]

NFS/NIS command. Return hostname of NIS server or map master. Without arguments, **ypwhich** cites the NIS server for the local machine. If *host* is specified, that machine is queried to find out which NIS master it is using.

Options

−d *domain*

Use *domain* instead of the default domain.

−m *map*

Find master NIS server for a map. No host can be specified with **−m**. *map* may be a mapname or a nickname for a map.

−t *mapname*

Inhibit nickname translation.

−x   Display map nickname table. Do not allow any other options.

ypxfr [*options*] *mapname*

NFS/NIS command. Transfer an NIS map from the server to the local host by making use of normal NIS services. **ypxfr** creates a temporary map in the directory */etc/yp/domain* (where *domain* is the default domain for the local host), fills it by enumerating the map's entries, and fetches the map parameters and loads them. If run interactively, **ypxfr** writes its output to the terminal. However, if it is invoked without a controlling terminal, and if the log file */usr/admin/nislog* exists, it appends all its output to that file.

Options

−b   Preserve the resolver flag in the map during the transfer.

−C *tid prog ipadd port*

This option is only for use by **ypserv**. When **ypserv** invokes **ypxfr**, it specifies that **ypxfr** should call back a **yppush** process at the host

→

ypxfr ←	with IP address *ipaddr*, registered as program number *prog*, listening on port *port*, and waiting for a response to transaction *tid*.
	−c Do not send a "Clear current map" request to the local **ypserv** process.
	−d *domain* Specify a domain other than the default domain.
	−f Force the transfer to occur even if the version at the master is older than the local version.
	−h *host* Get the map from *host*, regardless of what the map says the master is. If host is not specified, **ypxfr** asks the NIS service for the name of the master, and tries to get the map from there. *host* may be a name or an internet address in the form *h.h.h.h*.
	−S Only use NIS servers running as **root** and using a reserved port.
	−s *domain* Specify a source *domain* from which to transfer a map that should be the same across domains (such as the *services.byname* map).

zdump	**zdump** [*options*] [*zones*]
	
	Dump a list of all known time zones, or, if an argument is provided, a specific zone or list of zones. Include each zone's current time with its name.
	
	Options
	
	  −c *year*
	      Specify a cutoff year to limit verbose output. Meaningful only with **−v**.
	
	  −v Verbose mode. Include additional information about each zone.

zic	**zic** [*options*] [*files*] Create time conversion information files from the file or files specified. If the specified file is −, read information from standard input.

Options

−d *directory*

    Place the newly created files in *directory*. Default is */usr/local/etc/zoneinfo.*

−l *timezone*

    Specify a *timezone* to use for local time. **zic** links the zone information for *timezone* with the zone **localtime**.

−p *timezone*

    Set the default rules for handling POSIX-format environment variables to the zone name specified by *timezone*.

−s

    Store time values only if they are the same when signed as when unsigned.

−v

    Verbose mode. Include extra error checking and warnings.

−y *command*

    Check year types with *command*. Default is **yearistype**.

−L *file*   Consult *file* for information about leap seconds.

The source file(s) for **zic** should be formatted as a sequence of rule lines, zone lines, and link lines. An optional file containing leap second rules can be specified on the command line. Rule lines describe how time should be calculated. They describe changes in time, daylight savings time, war time, and any other changes that might affect a particular time zone. Zone lines specify which rules apply to a given zone. Link lines link similar zones together. Leap lines describe the exact time when leap seconds should be added or subtracted. Each of these lines are made up of fields. Fields are separated from one another by any number of white space characters. Comment lines are preceded by a #. The fields used in each line are listed below.

Rule line fields

`Rule NAME FROM TO TYPE IN ON AT SAVE LETTERS`

  NAME   Name this set of rules.

  FROM   Specify the first year to which this rule applies. Gregorian calendar dates are assumed. Instead of specifying an actual year, you may specify *minimum* or *maximum* for the minimum or maximum year representable as an integer.

TO Specify the last year to which this rule applies. Syntax is the same as for the FROM field.

TYPE Specify the type of year to which this rule should be applied. The wildcard – instructs that all years be included. Any given year's type will be checked with the command given with the –y option, or the default **yearistype** *year type*. An exit status of 0 is taken to mean the year is of the given type, an exit status of 1 means that it is not of the given type (see –y option).

IN Specify month in which this rule should be applied.

ON Specify day in which this rule should be applied. Whitespace is not allowed. For example:

1   The 1st

firstSun
The first Sunday

Sun>=3
The first Sunday to occur before or on the 3rd

AT Specify the time after which the rule is in effect. For example, you may use **13**, **13**:00, or **13**:00:00 for one o'clock pm. You may include one of several suffixes (without whitespace between):

s   Local standard time.

u, g, z
Universal time.

w   Wall clock time (default).

SAVE Add this amount of time to the local standard time. Formatted like AT, without suffixes.

LETTERS
Specify letter or letters to be used in time zone abbreviations (for example, S for EST). For no abbreviation, enter –.

Zone line fields

Zone *NAME GMTOFF RULES/SAVE FORMAT* [*UNTIL*]

NAME Time zone name.

GMTOFF

> The amount of hours by which this time zone differs from GMT. Formatted like AT. Negative times are subtracted from GMT; by default, times are added to it.

RULES/SAVE

> Either the name of the rule to apply to this zone, or the amount of time to add to local standard time. To make the zone the same as local standard time, specify -.

FORMAT

> How to format time zone abbreviations. Specify the variable part with %s.

UNTIL Change the rule for the zone at this date. The next line must specify the new zone information, and therefore must omit the string "Zone" and the NAME field.

Link line fields

```
Link LINK-FROM LINK-TO
```

LINK-FROM

> The name of the zone that is being linked.

LINK-TO

> An alternate name for the zone which was specified as LINK-FROM.

Leap line fields

```
Leap YEAR MONTH DAY HH:MM:SS CORR R/S
```

YEAR MONTH DAY HH:MM:SS

> Specify when the leap second happened.

CORR Uses a "+" or a "–" to show whether the second was added or skipped.

R/S An abbreviation of Rolling or Stationary to describe whether the leap second should be applied to local wall clock time, or to GMT.

Sys Admin Commands

CHAPTER 17

Boot Methods

This chapter describes some techniques for booting your Linux system. Depending on your hardware and whether you want to run any other operating systems, you can configure the system to boot Linux automatically or to provide a choice between several operating systems. Choosing between operating systems is generally referred to as *dual-booting*, but you can boot more than two—e.g., Linux, Windows 95/98, and Windows NT. This chapter covers the following topics:

- The boot process

- LILO: The Linux loader

- Loadlin: Booting from MS-DOS

- Dual-booting Linux and Windows NT

- Boot-time kernel options

- **initrd**: Using a RAM disk

The Boot Process

Once your Linux system is up and running, booting the system is generally pretty straightforward. But with the wide variety of hardware and software in use, there are many possibilities for configuring your boot process. The three most common choices are:

- Boot Linux from a floppy, leaving any other operating system to boot from the hard drive.

- Use the Linux Loader, LILO.* This is probably the most common method of booting and lets you boot both Linux and other operating systems.

- Run Loadlin, which is an MS-DOS program that boots Linux from within DOS.

Other boot managers are available that can load Linux, but we don't discuss them in this chapter. We also won't talk further about booting from a floppy except to say that whatever method you choose for booting, you should be sure to have a working boot floppy available for emergency use. In particular, don't experiment with the files and options in this chapter unless you have a boot floppy, because any error could leave you unable to boot from the hard disk.

On an Intel-based PC, the first sector of every hard disk is known as the boot sector and contains the partition table for that disk and possibly also code for booting an operating system. The boot sector of the first hard disk is known as the master boot record (MBR) because when you boot the system, the BIOS transfers control to a program that lives on that sector along with the partition table. That code is the *boot loader*, the code that initiates an operating system. When you add Linux to the system, you need to modify the boot loader, replace it, or boot from a floppy disk to start Linux.

In Linux, each disk and each partition on the disk is treated as a device. So, for example, the entire first hard disk is known as */dev/hda* and the entire second hard disk, if there is one, is */dev/hdb*. The first partition of the first hard drive is */dev/hda1* and the second partition is */dev/hda2*; the first partition of the second hard drive is */dev/hdb1*, etc. If your drives are SCSI instead of IDE, the naming works the same way except that the devices are */dev/sda*, */dev/sda1*, etc. Thus, if you want to specify that the Linux partition is the second partition of the first hard drive (as in the examples in this chapter), you refer to it as */dev/hda2*.

The rest of the chapter describes the various techniques for booting Linux, and the options that you can specify to configure both the boot loader that you use and the Linux kernel. Both LILO and Loadlin let you pass options to the loader and they also let you specify options for the kernel.

LILO: The Linux Loader

Once you've made the decision to install LILO, you still need to decide how it should be configured. If you want your system to dual-boot Linux and Windows 95/98, you can install LILO on the master boot record (MBR) and set it up to let you select the system to boot. Dual-booting Linux and Windows NT is not quite as straightforward, because Windows NT has its own loader on the MBR, and it expects to be the one in charge. Therefore, you need to make Linux an option in the NT loader and install LILO in the Linux partition as a secondary boot loader. The result is that the Windows NT loader transfers control to LILO, which then boots Linux. See the section "Dual-Booting Linux and Windows NT" later in this chapter for more information.

---

* LILO is the standard boot program for i386-architecture machines. On the Alpha, the equivalent boot program is called MILO (Mini Loader) and on the Sparc, it is SILO.

In addition to booting Linux, LILO can boot other operating systems, such as MS-DOS, Windows 95/98, or OS/2. During installation, the major Linux distributions provide the opportunity to install LILO; it can also be installed later if necessary. LILO can be installed on the master boot record (MBR) of your hard drive or as a secondary boot loader on the Linux partition. LILO consists of several pieces, including the boot loader itself, a configuration file (*/etc/lilo.conf*), a map file (*/boot/map*) containing the location of the kernel, and the **lilo** command (*/sbin/lilo*), which reads the configuration file and uses the information to create or update the map file and to install the files LILO needs.

If LILO is installed on the MBR, it replaces the MS-DOS boot loader. If you have problems with your installation or you simply want to uninstall LILO and restore the original boot loader, you can do one of the following:

- Boot Linux from a floppy disk and restore the backed-up boot sector:

  ```
  % /sbin/lilo -u
  ```

- Boot to DOS and run a special version of the **fdisk** command that rebuilds the MBR:

  ```
  C:> fdisk /mbr
  ```

One thing to remember about LILO is that it has two aspects: the boot loader and the **lilo** command. The **lilo** command configures and installs the boot loader, and updates it as necessary. The boot loader is the code that executes at system boot time and boots Linux or another operating system.

The LILO Configuration File

The **lilo** command reads the LILO configuration file, */etc/lilo.conf*, to get the information it needs to install LILO. Among other things, it builds a map file containing the locations of all disk sectors needed for booting.

Note that any time you change */etc/lilo.conf*, or rebuild or move a kernel image, you need to rerun **lilo** to rebuild the map file and update LILO.

The configuration file starts with a section of global options, described in the next section. Global options are those that apply to every system boot, regardless of what operating system you are booting. Here is an example of a global section (a hash sign, #, begins a comment):

```
boot = /dev/hda          # The boot device is /dev/hda
map = /boot/map          # Save the map file as /boot/map
install = /boot/boot.b   # The file to install as the new boot sector
prompt                   # Always display the boot prompt
timeout = 30             # Set a 3-second (30 tenths of a second) timeout
```

Following the global section, there is one section of options for each Linux kernel and for each non-Linux operating system that you want LILO to be able to boot. Each of those sections is referred to as an "image" section, because each boots a different kernel image (shorthand for a binary file containing a kernel) or another operating system. Each Linux image section begins with an **image=** line. For example, a Linux section might look like this:

```
image = /boot/vmlinuz        # Linux image file
   label = linux             # Label that appears at the boot prompt
   root = /dev/hda2          # Location of the root filesystem
   vga = ask                 # Always prompt the user for VGA mode
   read-only                 # Mount read-only to run fsck for a filesystem check
```

The equivalent section for a non-Linux operating system begins with **other=** instead of **image=**. For example:

```
other = /dev/hda1           # Location of the partition
   label = dos
   table = /dev/hda         # Location of the partition table
```

Put LILO configuration options that apply to all images into the global section of */etc/lilo.conf* and options that apply to a particular image into the section for that image. If an option is specified in both the global section and an image section, the setting in the image section overrides the global setting for that image.

Here is an example of a complete */etc/lilo.conf* file for a system that has the Linux partition on */dev/hda2*:

```
## Global section
boot=/dev/hda2
map=/boot/map
delay=30
timeout=50
prompt
vga=ask

## Image section: For regular Linux
image=/boot/vmlinuz
  label=linux
  root=/dev/hda2
  install=/boot/boot.b
  map=/boot/map
  read-only

## Image section: For testing a new Linux kernel
image=/testvmlinuz
  label=testlinux
  root=/dev/hda2
  install=/boot/boot.b
  map=/boot/map
  read-only
  optional                  # Omit image if not available when map is built

## Image section: For booting DOS
other=/dev/hda1
  label=dos
  loader=/boot/chain.b
  table=/dev/hda            # the current partition table

## Image section: For booting Windows 95
other=/dev/hda1
  label=win95
  loader=/boot/chain.b
  table=/dev/hda
```

Global options

In addition to the options listed here, the kernel options **append**, **read-only**, **read-write**, **root**, and **vga** (described in the section "Kernel options" below) can also be set as global options.

backup=*backup-file*
> Copies the original boot sector to *backup-file* instead of to the file */boot/boot.nnnn*, where *nnnn* is a number that depends on the disk device type.

boot=*boot-device*
> Sets the name of the device that contains the boot sector. **boot** defaults to the device currently mounted as root, such as */dev/hda2*. Specifying a device such as */dev/hda* (without a number) indicates that LILO should be installed in the master boot record; the alternative is to set it up on a particular partition such as */dev/hda2*.

compact
> Merges read requests for adjacent disk sectors to speed up booting. Use of **compact** is particularly recommended when booting from a floppy disk. Use of **compact** may conflict with **linear**.

default=*name*
> Uses the image *name* as the default boot image. If **default** is omitted, the first image specified in the configuration file is used.

delay=*tsecs*
> Specifies, in tenths of a second, how long the boot loader should wait before booting the default image. If **serial** is set, **delay** is set to 20 at a minimum. The default is not to wait.

disk=*device-name*
> Defines parameters for the disk specified by *device-name* if LILO can't figure them out. Normally, LILO can determine the disk parameters itself and this option isn't needed. When **disk** is specified, it is followed by one or more parameter lines, such as:
>
> ```
> disk=/dev/sda
>   bios = 0x80     # First disk is usually 0x80, second is usually 0x81
>   sectors= ...
>   heads= ...
> ```

Note that this option is not the same as the disk geometry parameters you can specify with the **hd** boot command-line option. With **disk**, the information is being given to LILO; with **hd**, it is being passed to the kernel. The parameters that can be specified with **disk** are briefly listed here. They are described in detail in the "LILO User's Guide," which comes with the LILO distribution.

bios=*bios-device-code*
> The number the BIOS uses to refer to the device. See the example above.

cylinders=*cylinders*
> The number of cylinders on the disk.

heads=*heads*
> The number of heads on the disk.

inaccessible
> Tells LILO that the BIOS can't read the disk; used to prevent the system from becoming unbootable if LILO thinks the BIOS can read it.

partition=*partition-device*
> Starts a new section for a partition. The section contains one variable, **start=***partition-offset* that specifies the zero-based number of the first sector of the partition:

```
partition=/dev/sda1
    start=2048
```

sectors=*sectors*
> The number of sectors per track.

disktab=*disktab-file*
> This option has been superceded by the **disk=** option.

fix-table
> If set, allows **lilo** to adjust 3D addresses (addresses specified as sector/head/cylinder) in partition tables. This is sometimes necessary if a partition isn't track-aligned and another operating system such as MS-DOS is on the same disk. See the *lilo.conf* manpage for details.

force-backup=*backup-file*
> Like **backup**, but overwrites an old backup copy if one exists.

ignore-table
> Tells **lilo** to ignore corrupt partition tables.

install=*boot-sector*
> Installs the specified file as the new boot sector. If **install** is omitted, the boot sector defaults to */boot/boot.b*.

linear
> Generates linear sector addresses, which do not depend on disk geometry, instead of 3D (sector/head/cylinder) addresses. If LILO can't determine your disk's geometry itself, you can try using **linear**; if that doesn't work, then you need to specify the geometry with **disk=**. Note, however, that **linear** sometimes doesn't work with floppy disks, and it may conflict with **compact**.

map=*map-file*
> Specifies the location of the map file. Defaults to */boot/map*.

message=*message-file*
> Specifies a file containing a message to be displayed before the boot prompt. The message can include a formfeed character (CTRL-L) to clear the screen. The map file must be rebuilt by rerunning the **lilo** command if the message file is changed or moved. The maximum length of the file is 65,535 bytes.

nowarn
> Disables warning messages.

Booting

optional

Specifies that any image that is not available when the map is created should be omitted and not offered as an option at the boot prompt. Like the per-image option **optional**, but applies to all images.

password=*password*

Specifies a password that the user is prompted to enter when trying to load an image. The password is not encrypted in the configuration file, so if passwords are used, permissions should be set so that only the superuser is able to read the file. This option is like the per-image version, except that all images are password-protected and they all have the same password.

prompt

Automatically displays the boot prompt without waiting for the user to press the Shift, Alt, or Scroll Lock key. Note that setting **prompt** without also setting **timeout** prevents unattended reboots.

restricted

Can be used with **password** to indicate that a password needs to be entered only if the user specifies parameters on the command line. Like the per-image **restricted** option, but applies to all images.

serial=*parameters*

Allows the boot loader to accept input from a serial line as well as from the keyboard. Sending a break on the serial line corresponds to pressing a shift key on the console to get the boot loader's attention. All boot images should be password-protected if serial access is insecure (e.g., if the line is connected to a modem). Setting **serial** automatically raises the value of **delay** to 20 (i.e., two seconds) if it is less than that. The parameter string *parameters* has the following syntax:

```
port[,bps[parity[bits]]]
```

For example, to initialize COM1 with the default parameters:

```
serial=0,2400n8
```

The parameters are:

port

The port number of the serial port. The default is 0, which corresponds to COM1 (*/dev/ttys0*). The value can be one of 0 through 3, for the four possible COM ports.

bps The baud rate of the serial port. Possible values of *bps* are 110, 300, 1200, 2400, 4800, 9600, 19200, and 38400. The default is 2400 bps.

parity

The parity used on the serial line. Parity is specified as: *n* or *N* for no parity, *e* or *E* for even parity, and *o* or *O* for odd parity. However, the boot loader ignores input parity and strips the eighth bit.

bits Specifies whether a character contains 7 or 8 bits. Default is 8 with no parity, and 7 otherwise.

timeout=*tsecs*

Sets a timeout (specified in tenths of a second) for keyboard input. If no key has been pressed after the specified time, the default image is automatically booted. **timeout** is also used to determine when to stop waiting for password input. The default timeout is infinite.

verbose=*level*

Turns on verbose output, where higher values of *level* produce more output. If −v is also specified on the **lilo** command line, the level is incremented by one for each occurrence of −v. The maximum verbosity level is 5.

Image options

The following options are specified for a particular image.

alias=*name*

Provides an alternate name for the image that can be used instead of the name specified with the **label** option.

image=*pathname*

Specifies the file or device containing the boot image of a bootable Linux kernel. Each per-image section that specifies a bootable Linux kernel starts with an **image** option. See also the **range** option.

label=*name*

Specifies the name that is used for the image at the boot prompt. Defaults to the filename of the image file (without the path).

loader=*chain-loader*

For a non-Linux operating system, specifies the chain loader to which LILO should pass control for booting that operating system. The default is */boot/chain.b*. If the system will be booted from a drive that is not either the first hard disk or a floppy, the chain loader must be specified.

lock

Tells LILO to record the boot command line and use it as the default for future boots until it is overridden by a new boot command line. **lock** is useful if there is a set of options that you need to enter on the boot command line every time you boot the system.

optional

Specifies that the image should be omitted if it is not available when the map is created by the **lilo** command. Useful for specifying test kernels that are not always present.

password=*password*

Specifies that the image is password-protected and provides the password that the user is prompted for when booting. The password is not encrypted in the configuration file, so if passwords are used, only the superuser should be able to read the file.

range=*sectors*

Used with the **image** option, when the image is specified as a device (e.g., **image=**/dev/fd0), to indicate the range of sectors to be mapped into the map file. *sectors* can be given as the range *start–end* or as *start+number,* where *start* and *end* are zero-based sector numbers and *number* is the increment beyond *start* to include. If only *start* is specified, only that one sector is mapped. For example:

```
image = /dev/fd0
   range = 1+512   # take 512 sectors, starting with sector 1
```

restricted

Specifies that a password is required for booting the image only if boot parameters are specified on the command line.

table=*device*

Specifies, for a non-Linux operating system, the device that contains the partition table. If **table** is omitted, the boot loader does not pass partition information to the operating system being booted. Note that */sbin/lilo* must be re-run if the partition table is modified. This option cannot be used with **unsafe.**

unsafe

Can be used in the per-image section for a non-Linux operating system to indicate that the boot sector should not be accessed when the map is created. If **unsafe** is specified, there is some checking that isn't done, but it can be useful for running the **lilo** command without having to insert a floppy disk when the boot sector is on a fixed-format floppy disk device. This option cannot be used with **table.**

Kernel options

The following kernel options can be specified in */etc/lilo.conf* as well as on the boot command line.

append=*string*

Appends the options specified in *string* to the parameter line passed to the kernel. This is typically used to specify certain hardware parameters. For example, if your system has more than 64M of memory (i.e., more than your BIOS can recognize), you can use **append:**

```
append = "mem=128M"
```

initrd=*filename*

Specifies the file to load into */dev/initrd* when booting with a RAM disk. See also the options **load_ramdisk, prompt_ramdisk, ramdisk_size,** and **ramdisk_start** and the section "initrd: Using a RAM Disk."

literal=*string*

like **append,** but replaces all other kernel boot options.

noinitrd

Preserve the contents of */dev/initrd* so they can be read once after the kernel is booted.

prompt_ramdisk=n

Specifies whether the kernel should prompt you to insert the floppy disk that contains the RAM disk image, for use during Linux installation. Values of n are:

0   Don't prompt. Usually used for an installation where the kernel and the RAM disk image both fit on one floppy.

1   Prompt. This is the default.

ramdisk=$size$

Obsolete; should now be used only with kernels older than version 1.3.48. For newer kernels, see the options **load_ramdisk**, **prompt_ramdisk**, **ramdisk_size**, and **ramdisk_start**.

ramdisk_size=n

Specifies the amount of memory, in kilobytes, to be allocated for the RAM disk. The default is 4096, which allocates four megabytes.

ramdisk_start=$offset$

Used for a Linux installation where both the kernel and the RAM disk image are on the same floppy. $offset$ indicates the offset on the floppy where the RAM disk image begins; it is specified in kilobytes.

root=$root\text{-}device$

Specifies the device that should be mounted as root. If the special name **current** is used, the root device is set to the device on which the root filesystem is currently mounted. Defaults to the root-device setting contained in the kernel image.

vga=$mode$

Specifies the VGA text mode that should be selected when booting. $mode$ defaults to the VGA mode setting in the kernel image. The values are case-insensitive. They are:

ask Prompt the user for the text mode. Pressing Enter in response to the prompt displays a list of the available modes.

extended (or **ext**)
Select 80x50 text mode.

normal
Select normal 80x25 text mode.

$number$
Use the text mode that corresponds to $number$. A list of available modes for your video card can be obtained by booting with **vga=ask** and pressing Enter.

The lilo Command

You need to run the **lilo** command to install the LILO boot loader and to update it whenever the kernel changes or to reflect changes to */etc/lilo.conf.*

The path to the **lilo** command is usually */sbin/lilo*. The syntax of the command is:

```
lilo [options]
```

Some of the options correspond to */etc/lilo.conf* keywords:

Configuration Keyword	Command Option
boot=*bootdev*	−b *bootdev*
compact	−c
delay=*tsecs*	−d *tsecs*
default=*label*	−D *label*
disktab=*file*	−f *file*
install=*bootsector*	−i *bootsector*
linear	−l
map=*mapfile*	−m *mapfile*
fix-table	−P fix
ignore-table	−P ignore
backup=*file*	−s *file*
force-backup=*file*	−S *file*
verbose=*level*	−v

These options should be put in the configuration file whenever possible; putting them on the **lilo** command line instead of in */etc/lilo.conf* is now deprecated. The next section describes those options that can be given only on the **lilo** command line; the others are described in the previous section.

lilo Command Options

The following list describes the **lilo** command options. Multiple options are given separately:

```
% lilo -q -v
```

−C *config-file*

Specifies an alternative to the default configuration file (*/etc/lilo.conf*). **lilo** uses the configuration file to determine what files to map when it installs LILO.

−I *label*

Prints the path to the kernel specified by *label* to standard output or an error message if no matching label is found. For example:

```
% lilo -I linux
/boot/vmlinuz-2.0.34-0.6
```

−q Lists the currently mapped files. **lilo** maintains a file, by default */boot/map*, containing the name and location of the kernel(s) to boot. Running **lilo** with this option prints the names of the files in the map file to standard output. For example:

```
% lilo -q
linux          *
test
```

The asterisk in the example indicates that linux is the default.

−r *root-directory*

Specifies that before doing anything else, *lilo* should **chroot** to the indicated directory. Used for repairing a setup from a boot floppy—you can boot from a floppy but have **lilo** use the boot files from the hard drive. For example, if you issue the following commands:

```
% mount /dev/hda2 /mnt
% lilo -r /mnt
```

lilo will get the files it needs from the hard drive.

−R *command-line*

Sets the default command for the boot loader the next time it executes. The command executes once and then is removed by the boot loader. This option is typically used in reboot scripts, just before calling **shutdown −r**.

−t   Indicates that this is a test. Does not really write a new boot sector or map file. Can be used with **−v** to find out what **lilo** would do during a normal run.

−u *device-name*

Uninstalls **lilo** by restoring the saved boot sector from */boot/boot.nnnn*, after validating it against a timestamp. *device-name* is the name of the device on which LILO is installed, such as */dev/hda2*.

−U *device-name*

Like **−u**, but does not check the timestamp.

−v   Specifies verbose output.

−V   Prints the **lilo** version number.

Loadlin: Booting from MS-DOS

Loadlin is a Linux boot loader that you run from within a bootable MS-DOS partition; the system must be in real DOS mode, not in an MS-DOS window running under Windows 95/98/NT. No installation is required; you just need to copy the executable file *loadlin.exe* from the Loadlin distribution to your MS-DOS partition.* You also need a compressed Linux kernel (e.g., *vmlinuz*), which you can load from a floppy, from the DOS partition, or from a RAM disk. For example:

```
C:> loadlin c:\vmlinuz root=/dev/hda2
```

This example loads the Linux kernel image *vmlinuz*, passing it the boot parameter **root=/dev/hda2** telling the kernel that the Linux root partition is */dev/hda2*. For more about using a RAM disk, see the section "initr: Using a RAM disk" later in this chapter.

---

* If Loadlin didn't come with your Linux distribution, you can download it from any of the major Linux sites, such as the Linux Documentation Project site at *http://metalab.unc.edu/LDP/*.

If you want to use Loadlin with Windows 95/98, see the "Loadlin User Guide" and the "Loadlin+Win95 mini-HOWTO" for how to do that. Note that if your disk uses the FAT32 filesystem, the standard techniques for using Loadlin and Windows 95 won't work; if this is the case, or if you aren't sure if you have FAT16 or FAT32, it's important to read the mini-HOWTO before you proceed.

Loadlin can be run directly from the DOS prompt, as in the example, or it can be invoked from CONFIG.SYS or AUTOEXEC.BAT. Like LILO, Loadlin takes both options that direct its operation and options (also referred to as parameters) that it passes to the kernel.

There are two forms of the Loadlin syntax:

```
LOADLIN @params
LOADLIN [zimage_file] [options] [boot_params]
```

Using a parameter file

In the first form of the syntax above, *params* is a DOS file that contains the options you want Loadlin to run with. The Loadlin distribution comes with a sample parameter file, *test.par*, that you can use as a basis for creating your own. Each line in a parameter file contains one parameter. If you want to specify the name of the Linux kernel to use (the **image=** parameter), it must be the first entry in the file. Comments start with a hash sign (#). The entries in the parameter file can be overridden or appended on the command line. For example, to override the value of **vga** set in the parameter file:

```
C:> LOADLIN @myparam vga=normal
```

Putting parameters on the command line

In the second form of the Loadlin syntax above, *zimage_file* is the name of a Linux kernel to run, followed by a list of Loadlin options and/or boot options. Specifying **LOADLIN** with no parameters gives a help message listing the Loadlin options and some of the possible kernel boot options. The message is long enough that you probably want to pipe the output through **more**:

```
C:> LOADLIN | more
```

The Loadlin options are:

−clone
> Bypasses certain checks—read the "LOADLIN User Guide" that comes with the Loadlin distribution before using.

−d *file*
> Debug mode. Like −t but sends output to *file* as well as to standard output.

−dskreset
> Causes disks to be reset after loading but before booting Linux.

−noheap
> For use by serious Linux hackers only; disables use of the setup heap.

−t   Test mode. Goes through the loading process, but doesn't actually start Linux. Also sets −v.

−txmode
Sets the screen to text mode (80x25) on startup.

−v   Verbose. Prints parameter and configuration information to standard output.

−wait=_nn_
After loading, waits _nn_ (DOS) ticks before booting Linux.

In addition to these Loadlin options, the help message prints a number of kernel boot options that you can specify. The boot options that it prints are only a few of the many available boot options. See also the "BootPrompt-HOWTO" for a more complete list.

Dual-Booting Linux and Windows NT

As we said earlier, when you run Windows NT, its boot loader expects to be the one in charge; therefore, the normal way to dual-boot Windows NT and Linux is to add Linux as an option on the NT boot menu.

To accomplish this, you need to provide the NT loader with a copy of the Linux boot sector. Here's how you do that on a computer running Windows NT with an NTFS filesystem (note that Windows NT should be installed on your system already). See the "NT OS Loader + Linux mini-HOWTO" for more information and other alternatives.

You should have a Linux boot floppy available so that, if necessary, you can boot Linux before the NT boot loader has been modified. You also should have a DOS-formatted floppy to transfer the boot sector to the Windows NT partition. If LILO is already installed, you may need to modify _/etc/lilo.conf_ as described below. Otherwise, you'll either install it as part of the Linux installation or you can install it with the _QuickInst_ script that comes with LILO. Once LILO is installed, and you have a configuration file, you can set up the system for dual-booting.

Note that the following instructions assume your Linux partition is on _/dev/hda2_. If Linux is on another partition, be sure to replace _/dev/hda2_ in the following examples with the correct partition.

1. Specify the Linux root partition as your boot device. If you are editing _/etc/lilo.conf_ manually, your entry will look like this:

   ```
   boot=/dev/hda2
   ```

   and will be the same as the **root=** entry.

2. Run the **lilo** command to install LILO on the Linux root partition.

3. At this point, if you need to reboot Linux, you'll have to use the boot floppy, because the NT loader hasn't been set up yet to boot Linux.

Booting

4. From Linux, run the **dd** command to make a copy of the Linux boot sector:

```
% dd if=/dev/hda2 of=/bootsect.lnx bs=512 count=1
```

This command copies one block, with a blocksize of 512 bytes, from the input file */dev/hda2* to the output file */bootsect.lnx.* (The output filename can be whatever makes sense to you; it doesn't have to be *bootsect.lnx.*)

5. Copy *bootsect.lnx* to a DOS-formatted floppy disk:

```
% mount -t msdos /dev/fd0 /mnt
% cp /bootsect.lnx /mnt
% umount /mnt
```

6. Reboot the system to Windows NT and copy the boot sector from the floppy disk to the hard disk. For example, using the command line to copy the file:

```
C:> copy a:\bootsect.lnx c:\bootsect.lnx
```

It doesn't matter where on the hard drive you put the file because you'll tell the NT loader where to find it in step 8.

7. Modify the attributes of the file *boot.ini** to remove the system and read-only attributes so you can edit it:

```
C:> attrib -s -r c:\boot.ini
```

8. Edit *boot.ini* with a text editor to add the line:

```
C:\bootsect.lnx="Linux"
```

This line adds Linux to the boot menu and tells the Windows NT boot loader where to find the Linux boot sector. You can insert the line anywhere in the [operating systems] section of the file. Its position in the file determines where it will show up on the boot menu when you reboot your computer. Adding it at the end, for example, results in a *boot.ini* file that looks something like this (the second multi(0) entry is wrapped to fit in the margins of this page):

```
[boot loader]
timeout=30
default=multi(0)disk(0)rdisk(0)partition(1)\WINNT
[operating systems]
multi(0)disk(0)rdisk(0)partition(1)\WINNT="Windows NT Server Version 4.00"
multi(0)disk(0)rdisk(0)partition(1)\WINNT="Windows NT Server Version 4.00
  [VGA mode]" /basevideo /sos
C:\bootsect.lnx="Linux"
```

9. Rerun **attrib** to restore the system and read-only attributes:

```
C:> attrib +s +r c:\boot.ini
```

Now you can shut down Windows NT and reboot; NT will prompt you with a menu that looks something like this:

---

* *boot.ini* is the Windows NT counterpart to */etc/lilo.conf.* It defines what operating systems the NT loader can boot.

```
OS Loader V4.00

Please select the operating system to start:

Windows NT Workstation Version 4.00
Windows NT Workstation Version 4.00 [VGA mode]
Linux
```

Select Linux, and the NT loader reads the Linux boot sector and transfers control to LILO, on the Linux partition.

If you later modify */etc/lilo.conf* or rebuild the kernel, you need to rerun the **lilo** command, create a new *bootsect.lnx* file, and replace the version of *bootsect.lnx* on the Windows NT partition with the new version. That is, you need to rerun steps 2–6.

 If you have any problems or you simply want to remove LILO later, you can reverse the installation procedure: boot to Windows NT, change the system and read-only attributes on *boot.ini*, re-edit *boot.ini* to remove the Linux entry, save the file, restore the system and read-only attributes, and remove the Linux boot sector from the NT partition.

Boot-Time Kernel Options

The Loadlin and LILO sections of this chapter described some of the options you can specify when you boot Linux. There are many more options that can be specified. This section touches on the ways to pass options to the kernel and then describes some of the kinds of parameters you might want to use. The parameters in this section affect the kernel and therefore apply regardless of which boot loader you use.

As always with Unix systems, there are a number of choices for the boot process itself. If you are using Loadlin, you can pass parameters to the kernel on the command line or in a file.

If LILO is your boot loader, you can add to or override the parameters specified in */etc/lilo.conf* during the boot process as follows:

- If **prompt** is set in */etc/lilo.conf*, LILO always presents the boot prompt and waits for input. At the prompt, you can choose the operating system to be booted. If you choose Linux, you can also specify parameters.

- If **prompt** isn't set, when the word LILO appears, press Control, Shift, or Alt, and the boot prompt appears. You can also press the Scroll Lock key before LILO is printed and not have to wait poised over the keyboard for the right moment.

- At the boot prompt, specify the system you want to boot or press Tab to get a list of the available choices. You can then enter the name of the image to boot. For example:

```
LILO boot: <press Tab>
linux   test   dos
boot: linux
```

You can also add boot command options:

```
boot: linux single
```

- If you don't provide any input, LILO waits the amount of time specified in the **delay** parameter and then boots the default operating system with the default parameters as set in */etc/lilo.conf*.

Some of the boot parameters have been mentioned earlier. Many of the others are hardware-specific and are too numerous to mention here. For a complete list of parameters and a discussion of the booting process, see the "BootPrompt-HOWTO." Some of the parameters not shown earlier that you might find useful are listed below; many more are covered in the HOWTO. Most of the following parameters are used to provide information or instructions for the kernel, rather than to LILO.

debug
Prints all kernel messages to the console.

hd=*cylinders,heads,sectors*
Specifies the hard drive geometry to the kernel. Useful if Linux has trouble recognizing the geometry of your drive, especially if it's an IDE drive with more than 1024 cylinders.

load_ramdisk=*n*
Tells the kernel whether to load a ramdisk image for use during Linux installation. Values of *n* are:

0   Don't try to load the image. This is the default.

1   Load the image from a floppy disk to the RAM disk.

mem=*size*
Specifies the amount of system memory installed. Useful if your BIOS reports memory only up to 64M and your system has more memory installed. Specify as a number with **M** or **k** (case-insensitive) appended:

```
mem=128M
```

Because **mem** would have to be included on the command line for every boot, it is often specified on a command line saved with **lock** or with **append** to be added to the parameters passed to the kernel.

number
Starts Linux at the runlevel specified by *number*. A runlevel is an operating state that the system can be booted to, such as a multi-user system or a system configuration running the X Windows System. A runlevel is generally one of the numbers from 1 to 6; the default is usually 3. The runlevels and their corresponding states are defined in the file */etc/inittab*. See the manpage for */etc/inittab* for more information.

noinitrd

When set, disables the two-stage boot and preserves the contents of */dev/ini-trd* so the data is available after the kernel has booted. */dev/initrd* can be read only once and then its contents are returned to the system.

ro Mounts the root filesystem read-only. Used for doing system maintenance, such as checking the filesystem integrity, when you don't want anything written to the filesystem.

rw Mounts the root filesystem read-write. If neither **ro** or **rw** is specified, the default value (usually **rw**) stored in the kernel image is used.

single

Starts Linux in single-user mode. This option is used for system administration and recovery. It gives you a root prompt as soon as the system boots, with minimal initialization. No other logins are allowed.

initrd: Using a RAM Disk

Modern Linux distributions use a modular kernel, which allows modules to be added without requiring that the kernel be rebuilt. If your root filesystem is on a device whose driver is a module, as is frequently true of SCSI disks, you can use the **initrd** facility, which provides a two-stage boot process, to first set up a temporary root filesystem in a RAM disk containing the modules you need to add (e.g., the SCSI driver), and then load the modules and mount the real root filesystem. The RAM disk containing the temporary filesystem is the special device file */dev/initrd*.

Before you can use **initrd**, both RAM disk support (CONFIG_BLK_DEV_RAM=y) and initial RAM disk support (CONFIG_BLK_DEV_INITRD=y) must be compiled into the Linux kernel. Then you need to prepare the normal root filesystem and create the RAM disk image. Your Linux distribution may have utilities to do some of the setup for you; for example, the Red Hat distribution comes with the **mkini-trd** command, which builds the **initrd** image. For detailed information, see the **ini-trd** manpage and the file *initrd.txt* (the path may vary but is usually something like */usr/src/linux/Distribution/initrd.txt*).

Once your Linux system has been set up for **initrd**, you can do one of the following, depending on which boot loader you are using.

- If LILO is your boot loader, add the **initrd** option to the appropriate image section:

```
image = /vmlinuz
    initrd = /boot/initrd  # the file to load as the contents of /dev/initrd
    ...
```

Run the **/sbin/lilo** command, and you can reboot with **initrd**.

- If you are using Loadlin, add the **initrd** option to the command line:

```
loadlin c:\linux\vmlinuz initrd=c:\linux\initrd
```

Booting

Index

A

a command (sed), 299
abbrev command (ex), 286
abbreviation commands, Emacs, 258
abs function (Perl), 404
accept function (Perl), 420
access mode (see permissions, file)
accounting rules (firewalls), 450
add command (CVS), 377, 382
addresses
    email, verifying, 154
    IP, 445
    line, ex editor, 285
    pattern, sed editor, 296–297
addsuffix variable (csh/tcsh), 211
admin command (CVS), 382
agetty command (Linux), 455
alarm function (Perl), 418
alias command, 183, 227
aliases, special tcsh, 245
alignment, Emacs commands for, 259
alloc command (csh/tcsh), 228
angle brackets <> for Perl I/O, 413
AnyDBM_File module, 427
append command (ex), 286
ar command (Linux), 321
arch command (Linux), 7
architecture type, 7
archive files, 26–29, 321, 438, 548
args command (ex), 286
argv variable (csh/tcsh), 211
arithmetic
    bash arithmetic expressions, 180
    bc language, 11–15
    Perl arithmetic functions, 404
arp command (TCP/IP), 456
arrays
    gawk and, 312
    Perl, 395
    Perl functions for, 406
    Perl special arrays, 426
as command (Linux), 322
asterisk (*)
    bash
        shell metacharacter, 169
    regular expression character, 408
at command (Linux), 7
atan function (Perl), 404

atan2 command (gawk), 313
atq commands, 9
atrm command (Linux), 9
attributes, file, 18, 95
attrs module (Perl), 402
$Author keyword, 363
autocorrect variable (csh/tcsh), 211
autoexpand variable (csh/tcsh), 211
autolist variable (csh/tcsh), 211
AutoLoader module, 427
autologout variable (csh/tcsh), 211
AutoSplit module, 427
autouse module (Perl), 402
awk program, 248, 250
    (see also gawk scripting language)

B

b command (sed), 299
B module, 427
background jobs, 183, 246
back-references, 410
backslash_quote variable (csh/tcsh),
    211
backslash (\)
    character escapes, 249
    regular expression escapes, 409
Backspace key, Emacs and, 253
backups (see archive files)
badblocks command (Linux), 456
bang (see !)
banner command (Linux), 10
base module (Perl), 402
bash command (Linux), 11
bash shell, 167–202
    built-in commands, 182–201
    (see also shells)
batch command (Linux), 10
batch execution at specified date/time,
    30
bc language, 11–15
bdflush command (Linux), 558
Benchmark module, 427
Berkeley Software Distribution (BSD),
    3, 6
bg command, 183, 228
biff command (Linux), 15
/bin/echo command (see echo com-
    mand)

overload module (Perl), 403
owd variable (csh/tcsh), 211
ownership, file, 21
    (see also permissions, file)

P

p command (sed), 302
P command (sed), 303
pack function (Perl), 405
packages, Perl, 400
paragraphs, Emacs and, 256, 259
partitioning disks, 459, 467
password, expiry, 17
passwords, 160, 460, 521, 565
paste command (Linux), 108
patch command (Linux), 356
path
    current working directory, 114
    man page, 101
PATH environment variable, 433
pathchk command (Linux), 109
pattern addressing (sed), 296–297
pattern-matching, 247–252
    bash operators for, 178
    gawk language and, 309–311
    (see also regular expressions)
pending jobs (see jobs)
performance
    CPU load, 146
    graphing system load average, 145
    setting keyboard repeat speed, 495
Perl
    embedded documentation, 394
Perl Compiler, 434
Perl Debugger, 435–437
Perl language, 109, 392–437
    command-line options, 393–394
    environment variables, 433
    file test operators, 411
    functions, 404–424
        arithmetic, 404
        array- and hash-related, 406
        conversion, 404
        directory reading, 418
        file operations, 412
        formats, 416
        formatted printing, 415
        input/output, 413
        networking, 420, 423–424

        search and replace, 410
        string-related, 405
        system interaction, 418
    literals values, 395–396
    Multithreading module, 434
    operators, 398
    pragmatic modules, 402
    regular expressions, 408–410
    special variables, arrays, hashes, 425–427
    standard modules, 427–433
    statements, 399
    subroutines, packages, modules, 400
    syntax, 394
    System V IPC, 420
    tying variables, 417
    variables, 396–397
PERL5DB environment variable, 434
PERL5LIB environment variable, 433
PERLLIB environment variable, 434
permissions, file
    changing, 19
    file ownership, 21
    groups, 19, 107
    octal numbers for, 20
pidof command (Linux), 109
PIDs (process identifiers), 66, 109
    (see also processes)
ping command (Linux), 517
pinging hosts, 517
pipe function (Perl), 414
.plan file, 56
plus sign (+)
    pattern-matching metacharacter, 249
    regular expression character, 408
Pod modules, 431
pod (Perl documentation), 394
policies, firewall, 451
pop function (Perl), 407
popd command (csh/tcsh), 239
pos command (Perl), 411
POSIX module, 431
powerd daemon, 519
PPP (Point-to-Point Protocol), 449, 519
pppd daemon, 519
pr command (Linux), 110
pragmatic modules, Perl, 402
precedence of Perl operators, 398

Z

z command (ex), 293
zcat command (Linux), 73–75, 160
zcmp command (Linux), 161
zdiff command (Linux), 161
zdump command (Linux), 568

zforce command (Linux), 161
zgrep command (Linux), 161
zic command (Linux), 568
zmore command (Linux), 161
znew command (Linux), 162

About the Author

Ellen Siever is a writer at O'Reilly & Associates. In addition to this edition of *Linux in a Nutshell*, she was a co-author of *Perl in a Nutshell* and co-compiler and co-editor of the *Perl Modules Reference* for the Unix edition of the *Perl Resource Kit*. Before coming to O'Reilly, she was a programmer for many years, doing mainframe assembler language and database programming. In addition to computers, her interests include her family, travel, and photography, and she's now trying to learn to draw.

Colophon

Our look is the result of reader comments, our own experimentation, and feedback from distribution channels. Distinctive covers complement our distinctive approach to technical topics, breathing personality and life into potentially dry subjects.

The animal featured on the cover of *Linux in a Nutshell* is an Arabian horse. Known for its grace and intelligence, the Arabian is one of the oldest breeds of horse, with evidence of its existence dating back 5000 years. The Arabian was very instrumental as an ancestor to other popular breeds, most notably the Thoroughbred in the 17th and 18th centuries. Possibly one of the more characteristic horse breeds, the typical Arabian has large expressive eyes and nostrils, small ears, and a short, sturdy back. Its stamina suits it particularly well for endurance riding, where the breed dominates the sport. Its wonderful temperament makes the Arabian an all-around favorite riding horse in North America, though it also can be found in more specialized competitions such as dressage, jumping, and reining.

Edie Freedman designed the cover of this book, using a 19th-century engraving from the Dover Pictorial Archive. The cover layout was produced by Kathleen Wilson, using QuarkXPress 3.32 with ITC Garamond font from Adobe.

Nicole Gipson Arigo was the production editor and project manager. Claire Cloutier LeBlanc and Sheryl Avruch provided quality control reviews. Seth Maislin wrote the index, and Robert Romano created the illustrations in Adobe Photoshop 4.0 and Macromedia Freehand 7.0. The inside layout was designed by Edie Freedman and Nancy Priest and was formatted in troff by Len Muellner, using ITC Garamond Light and ITC Garamond Book fonts.

More Titles from O'Reilly

Linux

Linux Multimedia Guide

By Jeff Tranter
1st Edition September 1996
386 pages, ISBN 1-56592-219-0

Linux is increasingly popular among computer enthusiasts of all types, and one of the applications where it is flourishing is multimedia. This book tells you how to program such popular devices as sound cards, CD-ROMs, and joysticks. It also describes the best free software packages that support manipulation of graphics, audio, and video and offers guidance on fitting the pieces together.

Running Linux, 2nd Edition

By Matt Welsh & Lar Kaufman
2nd Edition August 1996
650 pages, ISBN 1-56592-151-8

Linux is the most exciting development today in the UNIX world—and some would say in the world of the PC-compatible. A complete, UNIX-compatible operating system developed by volunteers on the Internet, Linux is distributed freely in electronic form and for low cost from many vendors. This second edition of *Running Linux* covers everything you need to understand, install, and start using your Linux system, including a comprehensive installation tutorial, complete information on system maintenance, tools for document development and programming, and guidelines for network and web site administration.

Using Samba

By Peter Kelly, Perry Donham & David Collier-Brown
1st Edition May 1999 (est.)
300 pages (est.), Includes CD-ROM
ISBN 1-56592-449-5

Samba turns a UNIX or Linux system into a file and print server for Microsoft Windows network clients. This complete guide to Samba administration covers basic 2.0 configuration, security, logging, and troubleshooting. Whether you're playing on one note or a full three-octave range, this book will help you maintain an efficient and secure server. Includes a CD-ROM of sources and ready-to-install binaries.

Linux Network Administrator's Guide

By Olaf Kirch
1st Edition January 1995
370 pages, ISBN 1-56592-087-2

One of the most successful books to come from the Linux Documentation Project is the *Linux Network Administrator's Guide*. It touches on all the essential networking software included with Linux, plus some hardware considerations. Topics include serial connections, UUCP, routing and DNS, mail and News, SLIP and PPP, NFS, and NIS.

Linux Device Drivers

By Alessandro Rubini
1st Edition February 1998
432 pages, ISBN 1-56592-292-1

This practical guide is for anyone who wants to support computer peripherals under the Linux operating system or who wants to develop new hardware and run it under Linux. It shows step-by-step how to write a driver for character devices, block devices, and network interfaces, illustrated with examples you can compile and run. Focuses on portability.

Learning the bash Shell, 2nd Edition

By Cameron Newham & Bill Rosenblatt
2nd Edition January 1998
336 pages, ISBN 1-56592-347-2

This second edition covers all of the features of *bash* Version 2.0, while still applying to *bash* Version 1.x. It includes one-dimensional arrays, parameter expansion, more pattern-matching operations, new commands, security improvements, additions to ReadLine, improved configuration and installation, and an additional programming aid, the *bash* shell debugger.

O'REILLY®

UNIX Basics

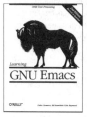

How to stay in touch with O'Reilly

1. Visit Our Award-Winning Site

http://www.oreilly.com/

★ "Top 100 Sites on the Web" —*PC Magazine*
★ "Top 5% Web sites" —*Point Communications*
★ "3-Star site" —*The McKinley Group*

Our web site contains a library of comprehensive product information (including book excerpts and tables of contents), downloadable software, background articles, interviews with technology leaders, links to relevant sites, book cover art, and more. File us in your Bookmarks or Hotlist!

2. Join Our Email Mailing Lists

New Product Releases

To receive automatic email with brief descriptions of all new O'Reilly products as they are released, send email to:
listproc@online.oreilly.com
Put the following information in the first line of your message (*not* in the Subject field):
subscribe oreilly-news

O'Reilly Events

If you'd also like us to send information about trade show events, special promotions, and other O'Reilly events, send email to:
listproc@online.oreilly.com
Put the following information in the first line of your message (*not* in the Subject field):
subscribe oreilly-events

3. Get Examples from Our Books via FTP

There are two ways to access an archive of example files from our books:

Regular FTP

- ftp to:
  ftp.oreilly.com
  (login: anonymous
  password: your email address)
- Point your web browser to:
  ftp://ftp.oreilly.com/

FTPMAIL

- Send an email message to:
  ftpmail@online.oreilly.com
  (Write "help" in the message body)

4. Contact Us via Email

order@oreilly.com
To place a book or software order online. Good for North American and international customers.

subscriptions@oreilly.com
To place an order for any of our newsletters or periodicals.

books@oreilly.com
General questions about any of our books.

software@oreilly.com
For general questions and product information about our software. Check out O'Reilly Software Online at **http://software.oreilly.com/** for software and technical support information. Registered O'Reilly software users send your questions to:
website-support@oreilly.com

cs@oreilly.com
For answers to problems regarding your order or our products.

booktech@oreilly.com
For book content technical questions or corrections.

proposals@oreilly.com
To submit new book or software proposals to our editors and product managers.

international@oreilly.com
For information about our international distributors or translation queries. For a list of our distributors outside of North America check out:
http://www.oreilly.com/www/order/country.html

O'Reilly & Associates, Inc.
101 Morris Street, Sebastopol, CA 95472 USA
TEL   707-829-0515 or 800-998-9938
         (6am to 5pm PST)
FAX   707-829-0104

O'REILLY®

TO ORDER: **800-998-9938** • **order@oreilly.com** • **http://www.oreilly.com/**
OUR PRODUCTS ARE AVAILABLE AT A BOOKSTORE OR SOFTWARE STORE NEAR YOU.
FOR INFORMATION: **800-998-9938** • **707-829-0515** • **info@oreilly.com**

International Distributors

UK, EUROPE, MIDDLE EAST AND AFRICA (EXCEPT FRANCE, GERMANY, AUSTRIA, SWITZERLAND, LUXEMBOURG, LIECHTENSTEIN, AND EASTERN EUROPE)

INQUIRIES
O'Reilly UK Limited
4 Castle Street
Farnham
Surrey, GU9 7HS
United Kingdom
Telephone: 44-1252-711776
Fax: 44-1252-734211
Email: josette@oreilly.com

ORDERS
Wiley Distribution Services Ltd.
1 Oldlands Way
Bognor Regis
West Sussex PO22 9SA
United Kingdom
Telephone: 44-1243-779777
Fax: 44-1243-820250
Email: cs-books@wiley.co.uk

FRANCE

ORDERS
GEODIF
61, Bd Saint-Germain
75240 Paris Cedex 05, France
Tel: 33-1-44-41-46-16 (French books)
Tel: 33-1-44-41-11-87 (English books)
Fax: 33-1-44-41-11-44
Email: distribution@eyrolles.com

INQUIRIES
Éditions O'Reilly
18 rue Séguier
75006 Paris, France
Tel: 33-1-40-51-52-30
Fax: 33-1-40-51-52-31
Email: france@editions-oreilly.fr

GERMANY, SWITZERLAND, AUSTRIA, EASTERN EUROPE, LUXEMBOURG, AND LIECHTENSTEIN

INQUIRIES & ORDERS
O'Reilly Verlag
Balthasarstr. 81
D-50670 Köln
Germany
Telephone: 49-221-973160-91
Fax: 49-221-973160-8
Email: anfragen@oreilly.de (inquiries)
Email: order@oreilly.de (orders)

CANADA (FRENCH LANGUAGE BOOKS)
Les Éditions Flammarion ltée
375, Avenue Laurier Ouest
Montréal (Québec) H2V 2K3
Tel: 00-1-514-277-8807
Fax: 00-1-514-278-2085
Email: info@flammarion.qc.ca

HONG KONG
City Discount Subscription Service, Ltd.
Unit D, 3rd Floor, Yan's Tower
27 Wong Chuk Hang Road
Aberdeen, Hong Kong
Tel: 852-2580-3539
Fax: 852-2580-6463
Email: citydis@ppn.com.hk

KOREA
Hanbit Media, Inc.
Sonyoung Bldg. 202
Yeksam-dong 736-36
Kangnam-ku
Seoul, Korea
Tel: 822-554-9610
Fax: 822-556-0363
Email: hant93@chollian.dacom.co.kr

PHILIPPINES
Mutual Books, Inc.
429-D Shaw Boulevard
Mandaluyong City, Metro
Manila, Philippines
Tel: 632-725-7538
Fax: 632-721-3056
Email: mbikikog@mnl.sequel.net

TAIWAN
O'Reilly Taiwan
No. 3, Lane 131
Hang-Chow South Road
Section 1, Taipei, Taiwan
Tel: 886-2-23968990
Fax: 886-2-23968916
Email: benh@oreilly.com

CHINA
O'Reilly China
Room 2410
160, FuXingMenNeiDaJie
XiCheng District
Beijing
China PR 100031
Email: frederic@oreilly.com

INDIA
Computer Bookshop (India) Pvt. Ltd.
190 Dr. D.N. Road, Fort
Bombay 400 001 India
Tel: 91-22-207-0989
Fax: 91-22-262-3551
Email: cbsbom@giasbm01.vsnl.net.in

JAPAN
O'Reilly Japan, Inc.
Kiyoshige Building 2F
12-Bancho, Sanei-cho
Shinjuku-ku
Tokyo 160-0008 Japan
Tel: 81-3-3356-5227
Fax: 81-3-3356-5261
Email: japan@oreilly.com

ALL OTHER ASIAN COUNTRIES
O'Reilly & Associates, Inc.
101 Morris Street
Sebastopol, CA 95472 USA
Tel: 707-829-0515
Fax: 707-829-0104
Email: order@oreilly.com

AUSTRALIA
WoodsLane Pty., Ltd.
7/5 Vuko Place
Warriewood NSW 2102
Australia
Tel: 61-2-9970-5111
Fax: 61-2-9970-5002
Email: info@woodslane.com.au

NEW ZEALAND
Woodslane New Zealand, Ltd.
21 Cooks Street (P.O. Box 575)
Waganui, New Zealand
Tel: 64-6-347-6543
Fax: 64-6-345-4840
Email: info@woodslane.com.au

LATIN AMERICA
McGraw-Hill Interamericana
Editores, S.A. de C.V.
Cedro No. 512
Col. Atlampa
06450, Mexico, D.F.
Tel: 52-5-547-6777
Fax: 52-5-547-3336
Email: mcgraw-hill@infosel.net.mx